THE LAW OF AQUACULTURE

The law relating to the farming of fish and shellfish in Britain

Also by William Howarth

Freshwater Fishery Law (1987)

Water Pollution Law (1988)

THE LAW OF AQUACULTURE
The law relating to the farming of fish and shellfish in Britain

William Howarth

B.A., LL.M., Lecturer in Law
University College of Wales, Aberystwyth

Fishing News Books

First published 1990

British Library
Cataloguing in Publication Data
Howarth, William
    The law of aquaculture: the law relating
    to the farming of fish and shellfish in
    Britain.
        1. Great Britain. Fish farming. Law
        2. Great Britain. Shellfish. Culture. Law
        I. Title
        344.103'7693

ISBN 0-85238-170-0 /

Fishing News Books
A division of Blackwell Scientific
    Publications Ltd
Editorial Offices:
Osney Mead, Oxford OX2 0EL
    (Orders: Tel. 0865 240201)
8 John Street, London WC1N 2ES
23 Ainslie Place, Edinburgh EH3 6AJ
3 Cambridge Center, Suite 208,
    Cambridge MA 02142, USA
107 Barry Street, Carlton,
    Victoria 3053, Australia

Set by DP Photosetting, Aylesbury, Bucks
Printed and bound in Great Britain by
Mackays of Chatham PLC, Chatham, Kent

Contents

Preface

It seemed like a good idea at the time ... My previous work in writing *Freshwater Fishery Law* (1987) and *Water Pollution Law* (1988) impressed upon me that the flourishing activity of aquaculture in Britain was not satisfactorily covered by any text providing an account of the diverse legal provisions involved. Subsequent research for a number of articles on the law of fish farming convinced me of the range and gravity of the issues warranting discussion. A concise statement of the legal position of aquaculture would, I hoped, provide a useful volume to which fish and shellfish farmers and their legal advisers might refer to gain a general view of the legal status of the activity and an insight into some of the key problems to which it gives rise.

Having agreed to write an account of the law of aquaculture and embarked upon the task of researching the area, the initial objectives of brevity and simplicity were soon frustrated by the nature of the subject matter. I found the area beset by numerous legal complexities spanning a great many traditional legal divisions without previous coverage or obvious ordering. Unavoidably, the absence of a consensus of opinion or authoritative guidance has involved a considerable amount of deliberation as to the bounds and composition of the subject. Whilst the layout which follows seeks to reflect the natural order into which the legal issues fall, the exposition is made as systematic and generally relevant as possible by restricting coverage to legal matters relating to the practices and problems encountered in the main forms of commercial aquaculture presently undertaken in Britain.

The cost of securing comprehensiveness, within limits, is a book which is considerably more detailed and correspondingly longer than originally envisaged. The length, and in some respects intricacy, of what follows is excused only by inherent difficulties in the content. Aquaculture is a rapidly developing industry frequently striving to fall into ill-fitting legal categories formulated, in many instances, long before modern fish farming practices came into being. Despite the intrinsic difficulty of the subject matter, it is hoped that the work meets its original objective to the extent of providing a comprehensive and clear account of the law of aquaculture which will be of assistance to all who are involved in the law or practice of the enterprise.

Acknowledgements

My background in law teaching and research provides me with no first-hand experience in the techniques of aquaculture to impart. Despite ignorance in this respect, however, I have been exceptionally fortunate in enlisting the help of an embarrassingly large number of persons who have contributed information, guidance and the benefit of experience in a broad range of disciplines bordering on the law and practice of aquaculture. To all who have helped I am profoundly grateful.

Most deserving of recognition are those that have generously given up their time to read and comment upon previous drafts of this work. Roy Apsey and Barry Edwards, in the Fisheries IIA Division of the Ministry of Agriculture, Fisheries and Food, have been outstanding in this respect drawing my attention to numerous shortcomings in a previous version of the text, and keeping me up to the moment with legal developments at a time when aquaculture law is changing faster than ever before. Equally in relation to the situation in Scotland, Robert Williamson, the Inspector of Salmon and Freshwater Fisheries for Scotland, has been a willing and generous contributor of his intimate knowledge of the peculiarities of that jurisdiction and has provided a most valuable input in relation to the Scots law on the subject. Likewise my good friend Ron Millichamp, formerly Fisheries Officer with the Welsh Water Authority, has been a constant source of advice and experience and a sounding-board for a range of formative ideas to which he invariably responded tolerantly and constructively.

The diverse collection of organisations involved in the practice, administration and regulation of aquaculture in Britain has required me to solicit information from a wide range of individuals and organisations in order to provide a balanced and informed treatment of a variety of specialized areas. Mr M.J. Gravestock, the Crown Estate Receiver for Scotland, has been diligent in correcting a range of misapprehensions concerning the standing of the Crown Estate in relation to coastal fish farming by commenting extensively upon earlier versions of Chapter 3. Similarly, Mrs Joy Wingfield, of the Royal Pharmaceutical Society of Great Britain, gave me the benefit of her considerable knowledge of the law relating to veterinary medicines in commenting upon Chapter 13. Chapter 15 was read by Mr J.R. Aldous, Clerk and Chief Fishery Officer to North Western and North Wales Sea Fisheries Committee, who contributed the benefit of his extensive knowledge of all matters relating to the law of shellfish. The section in Chapter 16 dealing with the role of the Fishmongers' Company in relation to the marketing of fish was compiled from a fascinating dossier of information supplied by Mr C.P. Leftwich, who also read an earlier draft of this passage. The list of standard consent conditions included in Chapter 11 is reproduced by the kind permission of the Water Authorities Association.

Other sizable gaps in my knowledge were filled by information supplied by Mr D. Robertson, Legal Administrator to the Sea Fish Industry Authority, who provided me with a helpful account of the involvement of the Authority in aquaculture. Likewise, Mr R. Latham, of the Marine Directorate of the Department of Transport, contributed an instructive outline of the participation of the Department in relation to regulation of coastal fish farming on navigational grounds. Mr P.R. Fane, Secretary of the Fish Farmers' Specialist Branch of the National Farmers' Union, provided information about the involvement of the NFU in fish farming. Mr L. Beck, Co-ordinating Manager for River Quality with the Yorkshire Water Authority, supplied valuable information about the practical and regulatory aspects of maintaining water quality in relation to fish farms' discharges.

Helpful suggestions as to sources to pursue in researching the law of aquaculture came from numerous individuals and organisations who were able to point me in useful directions in my search for information. Worthy of special mention amongst these were Mr J. Chandler, Fisheries Officer with the Southern Water Authority; Mr C. Ing, Managing Director of Marine Harvest Ltd; Dr B. Slater, Editor of *Fish*, the Magazine of the Institute of Fisheries Management; Rear Admiral D.J. Mackenzie, Director of the Atlantic Salmon Trust; Dr D.H. Mills of the Department of Forestry and Natural Resources in the University of Edinburgh; Professor Susan A. Shaw of the Institute for Retail Studies in the University of Stirling; Dr R. Clarke of the Institute of Aquaculture in the University of Stirling; Dr E. Edwards, Director of the Shellfish Association of Great Britain; Dr G. Dear and Mr A.L.S. Munro of the Marine Laboratory of the Department of Agriculture and Fisheries for Scotland; Mr J. Rhydderch, Clerk and Chief Fishery Officer to the South Wales Sea Fisheries Committee; Mr D.F. Miller, Depute Director of the Tay River Purification Board; Dr J.E. Thorpe of the Freshwater Fisheries Laboratory of the Department of Agriculture and Fisheries for Scotland; Dr C. Newbold, Chief Scientist, Directorate of the Nature Conservancy Council; Mr A. Miller of the Scottish Development Department; Mr A. Brown of the Department of Planning of the Highland Regional Council; Mr A.D. Wyatt, Senior Legal Assistant to the Winchester City Council; Mr S. Ansell, Mr R.M. Bayliss and Mr J. Atkinson of the Fisheries IIA Division of the Ministry of Agriculture, Fisheries and Food; Dr J.F. Muir and Dr C.E. Nash of the Fisheries Department of the Food and Agriculture Organisation of the United Nations; Dr R.L. Welcomme, Secretary of the European Inland Fisheries Advisory Committee; Mr I.C. Sinclair, Authority Secretary and Solicitor with Severn Trent Water; and Dr J. Domaniewski of the Department of Agriculture in the University of Reading. I think that this list is complete, but if there are others that have been overlooked I extend the same gratitude to them.

Closer to home, I have to thank my colleagues in the Department of Law, University College of Wales, Aberystwyth, for their help on particular legal matters and their general support whilst I have been involved in this project. Likewise, Dr J.D. Fish and Dr P. Wathern of the Department of Biological Sciences have been most helpful in providing much guidance on technical and environmental matters concerning fish farming. The staff and facilities of the Hugh Owen Library and the National Library of Wales have been an invaluable aid in allowing me to trace and obtain a great many diverse and obscure legal and technical materials. My parents have been an unfailing source of encouragement and enthusiasm for this project, as has Dr Ann Cresswell who has read and painstakingly scrutinised every word I have written for error or infelicity whilst managing to keep the rest of my life in proportion throughout my obsession with the law of aquaculture. Finally, were it not for the support of Mr W.E. Redman of Fishing News Books Ltd and Mr R. Miles of Blackwell Scientific Publications Ltd this work would never have been commenced or concluded. Their encouragement for the project has been the most vital of ingredients.

Despite the support of all these persons and organisations, the final work is not intended to represent the views of any of the individuals or bodies from whom information has been drawn, and for that reason any errors that it may contain are the responsibility of the author alone.

The law is stated as at 6 July 1989, the date of the Water Act 1989 gaining royal assent, and assuming that the provisions of the Act are fully operative.

William Howarth,
Department of Law,
University College of Wales,
Aberystwyth.

Table of Cases

References are to section numbers.

Table of Statutes

References are to section numbers.

Table of Statutory Instruments

References are to section numbers.

Chapter 1

The Legal Nature of Aquaculture

1.01 The definition of aquaculture

The development of various kinds of aquacultural operation over the past few years has been such that the meaning of the word 'aquaculture' has been refined in several respects to reflect advancements at different stages in the state of the art and science. Hence, in a broader original sense, 'aquaculture' had served to encompass the cultivation of all natural products of water, and even the growth of non-aquatic plants in nutrient solutions, an activity now usually referred to as 'hydroponics'. A narrowing down of the concept, however, was suggested in the proposal that 'aquaculture' involves three essential ideas:

'First, it indicates that something is "cultured", or deliberately manipulated, to achieve a desired end product. Second, the culturing process is carried out in an aqueous medium: something is grown in water. Third, the 'something' that is cultured is, in the broad context, anything that naturally lives in water, be it from the animal or plant kingdom; only aquatic species are included.' (Wildsmith (1982) p. 1)

An additional refinement which is adopted in this work is a somewhat stipulative narrowing of the definition to reflect the present commercial centres of attention in the farming of fish and shellfish, and the exclusion of aquatic cultivation of plants. 'Aquaculture', therefore, is used in this work as a synonym for 'fish farming' and 'shellfish farming', and by implication the husbandry of all other animals and plants is excluded. Moreover, no over-riding conceptual distinction is drawn between the legal problems involved in fresh water and salt water fish farming and accordingly aquaculture embraces sea fish farming, sometimes distinguished by the title 'mariculture'.

Within the bounds of fish and shellfish farming it is to be emphasised that this is a work on the *law* rather than the practice of aquaculture. (General reading on aquaculture includes: Schwind (1977); Edwards (1978); Milne (1979); Bryant, Jauncy and Atack (1980); Sedgwick (1985); Huet (1986); Stevenson (1987); Beveridge (1987); Laird and Needham (1988); Sedgwick (1988); and Shepherd and Bromage (1988)). For that reason most of the discussion is focussed upon those activities which represent the most significant commercial forms of fish farming activity in Britain, ordered primarily according to the associated legal issues. The law considered is that of England and Wales and Scotland. The law of Northern Ireland is not dealt with in this work.

Whilst legal categorisation tends to over-ride operational distinctions, the legal issues to be discussed arise in the context of three main enterprises: the freshwater farming of trout, and the farming of salmon and shellfish in coastal waters. It is conceded from the outset that this threefold emphasis upon the main centres of commercial aquacultural activity is not fully representative of the breadth and diversity of fish farming activity presently undertaken in Britain. In particular, little consideration is given to the experimental developments in aquaculture which may change the fundamental character of fish farming activities in the near future, particularly in relation to the farming of marine species of fish. Legal comprehensiveness, or near comprehensiveness, is sought, however, by the exclusion of fish farming issues generated outside the three main areas. Nonetheless it is likely that the legal problems of farming trout, salmon and shellfish, as the established commercial species, will be shared by those cultivating less commonly reared species, and will serve to indicate some of the legal difficulties to be encountered by future kinds of aquacultural development.

Implicit in the emphasis which is placed upon legal issues surrounding the farming of trout, salmon and shellfish is the recognition that the primary purpose of aquaculture is the production of fish for food. It is appreciated that apart from food production, fish are also supplied for sporting or scientific purposes or to be kept for display in ponds and aquaria. Nevertheless, for the purpose of laying down parameters for the discussion, the farming of fish for food production is unavoidably a focus of attention. The distinction between farming fish for human consumption and other purposes, is of special importance where the privileged 'agricultural' status of the activity is in contention (discussed in [2.06] below) since for this reason, and others, fish which are reared for purposes other than human consumption are sometimes differently provided for in law.

Another significant point of categorisation is the relationship between fish farming and traditional fishing activities and the appropriateness of applying fishery regulations to fish farming activities. Broadly, the distinction between these two spheres of endeavour lies in the amount of husbandry which is entailed in producing the end product. Some parts of aquaculture lie close to the boundary between farming and fishing; for example, shellfish farming may involve naturally propagated molluscs at a mature stage of development being brought to a particular bed for fattening or cleansing before being dispatched for sale. Other kinds of aquaculture are more clearly distinguished from fishery activities, for example, where they involve the rearing of fish entirely under artificial conditions which do not directly impinge upon the natural aquatic environment. Where this is the case justifiable exemption is given from the conservationally motivated provisions of general fishery laws, since there is no need for conservation of a cultivated species which is required to be harvested at a size and a time dictated by marketing considerations. Clearly, if exemption from general fishery law were not provided for aquaculture, application of conservation legislation would be misconceived and obstructive. Nonetheless the limited availability of exemption of certain forms of aquaculture from fishery conservation legislation makes the distinction between fishing and fish farming an important one in deciding whether a particular exemption is to apply.

Whilst it is possible to suggest a general operational definition of aquaculture as the farming of fish and shellfish in order to provide an indication of the subject matter of this book, it is less easy to provide a comprehensive definition of aquaculture for legal purposes. Indeed, the range of differently formulated definitions of 'fish farming' which are to be found in various enactments presently in operation leads to the conclusion that each definition must be restricted in its application to the context in which it is propounded. The unfortunate but unavoidable conclusion must be that the legal meaning of 'fish farming' depends almost entirely upon the context which is at issue, and caution is to be exercised in extending the use of any particular definition beyond the purpose for which it is intended.

1.02 *The practice and problems of aquaculture*

Although the farming of fish can be traced back to ancient times, (Bowden (1981) p. 1) the most important aquacultural practices currently followed in Britain are, for the most part, of fairly recent origin. Certain rights of shellfishery date from an early period, and the farming of trout for stocking angling waters was undertaken in the second half of last century, but the farming of trout as a commercial activity is a practice which has been developed this century. The farming of salmon is an modern innovation, having commenced on a commercial scale in only the last two decades (Kirk (1987); Association of River Authorities (1978) Ch.1; and Anderson (1973)). Despite their relative novelty, however, these activities have proved their technical feasibility and commercial value. Hence, at present, there are approximately 1000 fish farming businesses in the United Kingdom, with a turnover in 1988 of approximately £110m, an amount expected to increase considerably in the next few years (Ministry of Agriculture, Fisheries and Food (1989)). This production is largely the result of intensive rearing of salmon and trout, and shellfish cultivation principally involving the rearing of oysters, mussels and clams. All the indications, however, are that production of these species will increase dramatically over the next few years, as will the diversity of farmed species (Ministry of Agriculture, Fisheries and Food (1987)). Inevitably the expansion of this new industry will bring with it a range of technical and legal problems, the first indications of which are becoming evident from present activities.

As a matter of theory there are good reasons why the aquaculture industry ought to be environmentally regulated in its own self interest. Farming fish is intimately dependent upon the maintenance of a high standard of aquatic environment, with water quantity and quality as particularly indispensable prerequisites. In the first instance, fish farming is particularly vulnerable to excessive abstraction and water contamination from a range of industrial, agricultural and domestic sources. Beyond received pollution, however, fish farming is susceptible to environmental damage caused by the activity of aquaculture itself. Hence, the general interests of the industry justify a range of measures directed towards the regulation of water abstraction levels, and the prevention of unacceptable levels of pollution and emissions of harmful substances from fish farms, as a means of ensuring continuation of conditions which make aquaculture possible. Likewise the movement of fish between locations is an unavoidable part of aquacultural activity, but carries a significant threat in facilitating the spread of disease between farmed populations, and from farmed populations into the wild and *vice versa*. Once again, restrictions are justified by reference to the needs of the industry itself and the general aquatic environment in which it functions. It follows that many of the legal restrictions which are discussed in the following chapters are referable to the overall commercial interests of the industry itself. Although the form and functioning of the law of aquaculture may appear bureaucratic and obstructive in individual cases, in many respects its higher aim can be seen to be that of safeguarding the longer term needs of the industry as a whole.

Alongside the need for environmental self-regulation, aquaculture is not insulated from the wider environment in which it functions, and in particular it shares many of the adverse features which arise as a general consequence of modern trends towards agricultural intensification (generally, see Royal Commission on Environmental Pollution (1979)). Few would consider functional rectangular hatchery buildings and prominently positioned sea cages attractive visual features, especially when situated in rural areas of high scenic value. Within certain limitations, therefore, fish farming development is made subject to public controls upon land use as a means to preserving the visual environment by containing development within areas in which intrusion is least damaging and conflicts with other land and water users are least difficult to reconcile. Other forms of restriction which seek to accommodate the development of aquaculture alongside existing land and water uses regulate the relationship between fish farming and fishery and navigational interests, and the extent to which fish farming may permissibly interfere with natural flora and fauna in order to control predators and pests. Broadly, the objectives underlying such restrictions are that a reasonable balance should be drawn between the continuation of existing activities and the conservation of existing natural resources and the controlled expansion of an industry which is of enormous commercial potential and capable of providing employment in rural areas in which it is greatly needed. Whether this balance is appropriately drawn in all respects is frequently, and perhaps inevitably, a matter of controversy. Given the novelty of the industry and speed with which it has expanded some would regard such controversy as an inevitable consequence of an industrial innovation being subject to regulatory systems which in many respects considerably predate modern aquacultural practices. In other respects the law of aquaculture is in a state of rapid and, in some respects, unpredictable legal evolution, as is the practice of aquaculture itself.

1.03   Changes under the Water Act 1989

Writing a legal text has been likened to taking a snapshot of a moving object, in that the image which is provided is inevitably little better than a historical record of a target that changes faster than can be recorded. The rapid development of aquacultural enterprise and the laws which regulate it makes this especially true with respect to the subject matter of this book which has been written at a time of dramatic change in the law. Two particular reforms are worthy of special note at this point. The first is the Water Act 1989 which gives effect to the privatisation of water authorities in England and Wales, and also makes innumerable changes to the general structure of water law. The second is the proposal to introduce new measures at European Community level to facilitate the harmonisation of trade laws relating to aquaculture and fishery products prior to the completion of the internal European market in 1992 (considered in the following section).

The Water Act 1989, which received royal assent on 6 July 1989, brings about major changes in the structure and organisation of the water industry in England and Wales. Broadly, the objective of the Act is to establish a new public body, the National Rivers Authority, which will take over the responsibilities of water authorities in England and Wales in relation to water pollution, water resource management, fisheries and other matters. In addition, the Act provides for the establishment of limited companies to take over duties as water supply and sewerage undertakers from water authorities, subject to ultimate regulation of water supply and sewerage services by the Secretary of State and a Director General of Water Services. Hence duties presently exercised by water authorities will be divided between the public regulatory body and the privately owned water utility companies.

Alongside the profound constitutional changes made to the water industry in England and Wales under the Water Act 1989, legislative opportunity has been taken to make a large number of particular changes in many detailed aspects of water law some of which affect the law of Scotland. Two particular matters are likely to be of special concern in relation to fish farming and, though these reforms are considered in greater depth later in the text (see Chapters 9 and 11 below) it is worth noting their general effect at this stage. First, new provision is made for the abstraction of water in England and Wales, involving the introduction of schemes to allow for the imposition of charges for the abstraction of water under an abstraction licence (s.129 Water Act 1989) and a limit of 20 cubic metres per day is imposed upon the amount of water which may be abstracted without the need for a licence for agricultural purposes including certain kinds of fish farming (s.128 and Sch.13 para.6(3)). Second, in England and Wales the provisions of Part II of the Control of Pollution Act 1974, governing the pollution of water, are replaced, with some modifications, by Chapter I of Part III of the Act, and Schedule 12 setting out detailed provisions relating to the granting of discharge consents for operations including fish farms. A significant feature of the new provisions in relation to fish farms is the facility for charges to be imposed in respect of discharge consents (s.113 and Sch.12 para.9). In Scotland, Part II of the Control of Pollution Act 1974 is retained as the principal measure concerning water pollution, but it is substantially amended by Sch.23 to the Water Act 1989 to bring the law of Scotland substantially into line with that in England and Wales.

1.04   Changes in European Community Law

The other major legal change concerning aquaculture is the imminent introduction of trade harmonisation measures being considered at European Community level. These provisions are a means to the completion of the internal market in goods, including aquacultural products, by the removal of technical barriers and obstructions to free movement and trade (Treaty of

Rome 1957, as amended by the Single European Act 1987, Arts.30 to 36; see Shaw (1988), and Howarth (1989D)). Specifically, three measures are presently under consideration by the European Commission: a proposed regulation on the health conditions affecting the production and the placing on the market of live bivalve molluscs, a proposed regulation on the health conditions affecting the production and placing on the market of fishery products (considered in [16.04] below) and a proposed regulation concerning the health conditions governing the intra-Community movement and import from third countries of fishery products (considered in [7.04] below). The first two of these deal primarily with matters of public health, with the former seeking to remove disparities in national laws governing the health requirements for live bivalve molluscs, and the latter to harmonise requirements for the production and marketing of fresh, frozen or processed fishery products within the Member States of the Community. The third measure is potentially of far greater effect on aquacultural practice in seeking to remove certain restrictions upon the movement of live fish and shellfish within the Community, and clearly has fundamental ecological and disease control implications. Although some way from completion at the time of writing, it is evident that these three measures will have major effects upon aquaculture when implemented in the United Kingdom.

1.05   The law of aquaculture in Britain

The objective of this work is to provide an account of the law relating to aquaculture in Britain. This involves coverage of the distinct laws and legal systems operative in England and Wales and in Scotland, which whilst sharing many common features also illustrate important differences. To some extent differences are terminological or referable to separate enactments applying within the different jurisdictions. In other respects, however, differences are substantive, and a complete statement of the law involves discussion of the distinct provisions operative in different parts of Britain. Every effort has been made to achieve comprehensive coverage of the relevant statute and case law of the two legal systems and to indicate the points of legal bifurcation. In those respects in which no jurisdictional distinctions are drawn, however, it is to be understood that the law of Scotland is the same as that of England and Wales. Occasionally reference is made to provisions applicable to the 'United Kingdom', particularly in contexts where a provision of international law or European Community law is under discussion. This is intended to indicate that the provision is applicable to Northern Ireland as well as Britain.

Chapter 2

Fish Farms in Planning Law

2.01 *The extent of planning control*

Although the selection of a suitable site for a fish farm is largely determined by a range of technical, economic and logistic considerations, important legal constraints may also restrict the commencement of a fish farming enterprise in an otherwise suitable location. This chapter, and the two which follow it, are concerned with areas of law which may constrain the initial establishment of fish farms by denial of necessary authorisations or financial support where for planning or other reasons development is proposed in undesirable locations.

Broadly, the legal restrictions upon the siting of a fish farming venture fall under two headings depending upon whether the activity is to take place in inland waters or in coastal waters over the seabed or foreshore. This is not intended as an operational distinction between freshwater and marine fish farming, but rather as a distinction between those developments which fall within the jurisdiction of the planning authorities and those which do not. Hence it may be that a marine fish farmer wishes to construct a hatchery or equipment store at a coastal location to operate in conjunction with sea cages moored some distance into coastal waters. In such circumstances the shore-based part of the operation would fall for consideration under planning law, whilst the siting of the sea cages would be subject to quite separate legal requirements concerning the use of the seabed and the marine waters above it. Although it is recognised that in practice fish farming in coastal waters will often operate in conjunction with land-based hatchery and rearing facilities, the legal features of land-based and freshwater fish farming are best considered separately from those of fish farming taking place in coastal waters. Accordingly, this chapter deals with planning restrictions upon freshwater and land-based fish farming, whilst the constraints upon coastal fish farming are considered in the following chapter.

In the following discussion of the detail of planning law applicable to fish farming some landmarks of the subject are usefully kept in view. First, planning law serves to restrict the 'development' of land by requiring authorisation for changes of the use of the land or buildings, or for operations which change the nature of the land or the buildings upon it. Second, 'agricultural' *uses* of land are generally exempt from the requirement of development consent for changes of use, but this does not encompass the conduct of operations which change the nature of the land or buildings upon it. Third, certain kinds of operational agricultural development are specifically exempted from the requirement of obtaining planning permission, and specific provision is made for the excavation of fish ponds at *established* fish farms in this respect. Finally, as a theme running throughout these issues, the extent to which a fish farm is able to benefit from preferential planning rules is determined by whether the operation which is envisaged comes within the peculiarly formulated definition of 'agriculture' specified for planning control purposes.

2.02   The concept of 'development' in planning law

For a landowner seeking to establish a land-based fish farm, a first consideration must be the constraint upon land use which arises through the operation of planning law. The Town and Country Planning Act 1971, applicable to England and Wales, and the Town and Country Planning (Scotland) Act 1972, in Scotland, provide an intricate network of provisions governing the legitimate 'development' of land. Although the application of planning law to fish farming is circumscribed by a number of detailed exemptions and qualifications relating to agricultural activities, the basic idea of 'development', and the legal requirement of obtaining permission for development from the appropriate local planning authority, remains the key concept around which the bulk of planning law revolves.

'Development' is defined as 'the carrying out of building, engineering or other operations in, on, over or under land, or the making of any material change in the use of any buildings or other land' (s.22(1) Town and Country Planning Act 1971; and s.19(1) Town and Country Planning (Scotland) Act 1972). Notably the wording of this definition anticipates development being brought about in two possible ways, *either* operationally, through the carrying out of 'building, engineering or other operations', *or* through a 'material change of use' of land. It is important to stress the distinct 'operational' and 'change of use' limbs of the definition of development. Hence, as a matter of general principle, a person seeking to embark upon a fish farming venture would be bringing about a development of land either where a new building was to be constructed for use as a fish hatchery, as an operational development, or where an existing building were to be put to a new use as a hatchery, as a development by change of use. Likewise, the excavation of a pond for the containment of farmed fish would be a development, as an 'operation' involving a change in the physical characteristics of the land. Equally, an existing pond converted to fish farming use from some other purpose would be development by change of use. Subject to certain exceptions which might arise because of the nature of the development, the fundamental principle of planning law is that 'planning permission is required for the carrying out of any development of land' brought about by an operation or material change in the use of land or buildings (s.23(1) Town and Country Planning Act 1971; and s.20(1) Town and Country Planning (Scotland) Act 1972).

2.03   Agricultural uses of land excluded from 'development'

A significant relaxation of general planning controls arises in relation to certain activities on agricultural land which are deemed not to constitute development and, therefore, do not require planning consent. For these purposes 'agriculture' is defined to include, amongst other things, 'the breeding and keeping of livestock including any creature kept for the production of food, wool, skins or fur' (s.290 Town and Country Planning Act 1971; and s.275(1) Town and Country Planning (Scotland) Act 1972; and see below). Setting aside discussion of the extent to which aquaculture falls within the esoteric legal definition of 'agriculture' for later consideration (in [2.06] below) it is to be noted that this definition is peculiar in that it places emphasis upon the *purpose* for which creatures are kept, rather than the intrinsic character of the activity of keeping them. That is to say, the manner in which fish are reared is of less importance than the *intention* with which they are reared. It is only where fish are reared for the purpose of producing food that a change in the nature of the enterprise will be deemed not to constitute development. To that effect it is stipulated that the use of any land for the purposes of agriculture, and the use for that purpose of any building occupied together with the land, is taken *not* to involve development for planning purposes (s.22(2)(e) Town and Country Planning Act 1971; and s.19(2)(e) Town and Country Planning (Scotland) Act 1972).

The bare statement of the exemption of certain agricultural activities from the requirement of planning permission is to be read with some caution since its interpretation is likely to be somewhat restrictive. In particular, it is to be stressed that the exception relates only to the material change of *use* of land and buildings. It authorises a change in the use of an existing building or physical state of the land to aquaculture from some other use. This presupposes that the building or feature to be put to aquacultural use is already in existence. Most significantly, the agricultural use exception does not authorise the construction of *new* ponds or buildings. In principle, if not always in practice, such an activity would continue to amount to a development requiring planning permission within the operational limb of the definition of development.

2.04 Agricultural development under the General Development Order

Beyond the exemption for agricultural uses of land, for some kinds of fish farming a more extensive exception from the requirement of planning consent for development may be available. This arises in respect of operations and activities which are the subject of direct authorisation in planning law. The Secretary of State is required to make an order, known as the General Development Order (Town and Country Planning (General Development Order) 1988, SI 1988 No.1813; the Scottish equivalent is the Town and Country Planning (General Development) (Scotland) Order 1981, SI 1981 No.830, as amended by SIs 1983 No.1620, 1984 No.237, 1985 No.1014 and 1985 No.2007, which makes substantially similar provision for Scotland). (For ease of exposition the following discussion is couched in terms of the Order applicable to England and Wales.) This provides for the automatic granting of planning permission for a range of specified developments (s.24 Town and Country Planning Act 1971; and s.21(1) Town and Country Planning (Scotland) Act 1972). Developments within the scope of the Order are authorised without the need for the developer to make any application for planning permission to the local planning authority.

Most pertinently in the aquacultural context, Class A of Part 6 of Schedule

2 to the Town and Country Planning General Development Order 1988, applicable in England and Wales, stipulates that the carrying on on agricultural land of works for the erection or alteration of a building, or any excavation or engineering operation, reasonably necessary for the purposes of agriculture within the unit, will constitute permitted development for which planning permission is directly granted by virtue of the Order.

The permission provided for works and excavations on agricultural land under the 1988 Order is made subject to a range of conditions, and it is specifically stated that this kind of development is *not* permitted in the following circumstances:

(a) the development would be carried out on agricultural land less than 0.4 hectare in area;
(b) it would consist of or include the erection, extension or alteration of a dwelling;
(c) a building, structure or works not designed for the purposes of agriculture would be provided on the land;
(d) the ground to be covered by:
    (i) any works or structure (other than a fence) for the purposes of accommodating livestock or any plant or machinery arising from engineering operations; or
    (ii) any building erected or any building as extended or altered by virtue of this Class,
    which would exceed 465 square metres, calculated according to a specified method.
(e) the height of any part of the building, structure or works within 3 kilometres of the perimeter of an aerodrome would exceed 3 metres;
(f) the height of any part of the building, structure or works not within 3 kilometres of the perimeter of an aerodrome would exceed 12 metres;
(g) any part of the development would be within 25 metres of the metalled portion of a trunk or classified road;
(h) it would consist of engineering operations of a kind which are separately provided for in relation to the construction of fishponds (see [2.05] below); or
(i) it would consist of or include the erection or construction of, or the carrying out of any works to, a building, structure or excavation used or to be used for the accommodation of livestock or for the storage of slurry or sewage sludge, and the building, structure or works is or would be within 400 metres of any protected building (Art.A(1) Class 6 of Schedule to General Development Order 1988). (This condition, however, does not apply in Scotland.)

The 25 metres requirement, under (g), arose as an issue in *Fayrewood Fish Farms Ltd* v. *Secretary of State for the Environment and Hampshire County Council* ([1984] JPL 267) where fish farm excavations were held to fall outside the condition because 10 per cent of the excavations came within 25 metres of the metalled portion of a classified road.

Although the authorisation for agricultural development provided for under the Class A of Part 6 of the 1988 Order looks to be a helpful one for those proposing to conduct operations for the purpose of establishing a fish farm, in situations where this involves pond excavation this exemption may be unavailable because of two additional conditions which are imposed upon excavatory operations. First, it is stated that, where an operation involves the extraction of any mineral from the land, or the removal of any mineral from a mineral-working deposit on the land, the mineral is not to be moved *off the land*, unless planning permission for the winning and working of that mineral has been granted on an appropriate application made under the Act (Art.A2(1)(b)). Second, in the case of development which involves the deposit of waste materials on or under the land, no waste materials are to be brought onto the land from elsewhere, except for excavation or engineering development reasonably necessary for the purposes of agriculture or the creation of a hard surface, where the materials are incorporated into the building or works forthwith (Art.A(2)(1)(c)). Likewise, under Class B of Part 6 of Schedule 2 to the 1988 Order, exemption from development consent for agricultural operations is stated to include the winning and working of any minerals reasonably necessary for agricultural purposes. In relation to this exemption, however, no mineral extracted during the course of the operation may be moved to any place outside the land from which they were extracted, except to other land which is held or occupied with that land and is used for the purpose of agriculture (Art.B(2)).

The practical effect of the provisions relating to mineral extraction and waste deposition is that the general exemption for agricultural development is purposefully limited to prevent certain operations of an agricultural character being used as a pretext to circumvent more rigorous planning controls applicable to mineral extraction and waste disposal operations. Previously the distinction between genuinely agricultural operations and the the use of the agricultural exemption for ulterior purposes was difficult to determine. Hence in *Northavon District Council* v. *Secretary of State For the Environment* ((1980) 40 P&CR 332) the infilling of a gully was found to be for the purpose of improving the agricultural productivity of the land, whilst in *Macpherson* v. *Secretary of State for Scotland* ([1985] SLT 13) the infilling of a glen to a depth of over 60 feet was found to be a tipping operation outside the deemed permission. Another pertinent example of the purported use of this exemption involved a ministerial appeal where it was proposed to construct fish ponds, to contain carp, which were to be 15 to 20 feet deep and involve the excavation of approximately 400,000 tonnes of sand and gravel in their construction. Expert witnesses disputed the need for pools of such depth for carp farming and submitted that the ponds need be only 1 metre to 1.2 metres deep. It was decided that the proposal to excavate to the greater depth was unnecessary, and therefore could not be within the requirement that the operation be 'requisite for the use of that land for the purposes of agriculture', and consequently fell outside the planning exemption for agricultural activities under the General Development Order (Ministerial planning appeal against *Hertfordshire County Council* [1983] JPL 256).

Fortunately, however, special provision has been made for the excavation of fish ponds at certain fish farms. As a consequence, the difficulties surrounding the restrictions upon the agricultural exemption for excavatory and waste disposal operations will only arise in situations where the operation concerned is of major proportions. Most occasions on which an existing fish farmer wishes to expand, for example by excavating to create an additional stock pond, will come within the specific exemption intended to cover such situations.

2.05   Excavation of fishponds

Alongside the authorisation for general agricultural developments provided under the General Development Order 1988, applicable to England and Wales, explicit provision is made for the excavation of fishponds as a part of the business of fish farming as a permitted development. Class C of Part 6 of Schedule 2 to the Order permits the carrying out on agricultural land, used for the purposes of any registered business of fish farming or of shellfish farming, of operations for the construction of fishponds, or other engineering operations for the purposes of that business. This exception is stated to be subject to the conditions that development is *not* permitted in the following cases:

(a) where the area of the site within which the operations would be carried out exceeds 2 hectares;
(b) where any part of the operation would be carried out within 25 metres of the metalled portion of a trunk or classified road;
(c) in a case where the operations would involve the winning or working of minerals –

  (i)   any excavation would exceed a depth of 2.5 metres; or
  (ii) the area of any excavation, taken together with any other excavations carried out on the land within the preceding two years, would exceed 0.2 hectares (Art.C(1)).

For the purposes of this exemption, 'construction of fishponds' includes the excavation of land and the winning and working of minerals for that purpose. 'Fishpond' is stated to mean a pond, tank, reservoir, stew or other structure used for the keeping of live fish or the cultivation or propagation of shellfish (Art.C(2)).

Although the planning exemption for the construction of fish ponds and engineering operations for the purposes of a fish farming business is a valuable planning concession for aquaculture, its limitations must be noted. Significantly, the exemption is limited to 'registered' businesses of fish farming or shellfish farming, which is stated to mean businesses registered in a register kept by the Minister of Agriculture, Fisheries and Food or the Secretary of State, as the case may be, for the purposes of an order made under section 7 of the Diseases of Fish Act 1983. This is a reference to the system of registration of fish farms for disease control purposes discussed below (in [6.02]). 'Fish farming', within the extent of the 1983 Act is defined as the keeping of live fish with a view to their sale or to their transfer to other waters, and 'shellfish farming' as the culture or propagation of shellfish, whether in marine or inland waters or on land, with a view to their sale or to their transfer to other waters or land (s.7(8) Diseases of Fish Act 1983).

A circular issued by the Department of the Environment emphasises that the permission provided for fishpond excavation was added to the Order to ensure that only an *established* fish or shellfish farmer will be able to benefit from the exemption for fishpond construction as an exempted agricultural development (Department of the Environment (1986A) paras.14 and 15, explaining SI 1985 No.1391, which first introduced the exemption for fishpond construction). The test of 'establishment' for these purposes is whether the business is registered under the Diseases of Fish Act 1983 (s.7 Diseases of Fish Act 1983) and in particular under the Registration of Fish Farming and Shellfish Farming Businesses Order 1985 made under that Act (SI 1985 No.1391, discussed in [6.03] below). Hence, registration requirement means that the authorisation will not avail a person wishing to embark upon the creation of a new fish farm.

Another feature arising from the registration requirement is that since the registers of fish farms maintained by the Minister of Agriculture, Fisheries and Food and the respective Secretaries of State for Wales and Scotland are not available for public inspection, access to information upon the registers will require the consent of the person who first provided it before it may be divulged. It follows that a fish farmer proposing pond excavation under the provision will need to give approval for a planning authority to be informed of the pertinent parts of the register to enable the authority to verify the registration of the fish farm concerned (Department of the Environment (1986A) para.15; and s.9(1)(a) Disease of Fish Act 1983, see [6.04] below).

A final point, relating both to the planning exemption for the construction of fishponds and also the other agricultural exemptions discussed in the previous section, is that these exemptions are only available in relation to 'agricultural land'. 'Agricultural land' is defined to mean any land which, before development permitted under Part 6 of the General Development Order is carried out, is land in use for the purposes of a trade or business of *agriculture*, and excludes any dwelling house or garden (Art.D Part 6, Sch.2 Town and Country Planning (General Development Order) 1988, SI 1988 No.1813). This definition raises a general difficulty in relation to the status of aquaculture under planning law which has been set on one side up to this point for ease of exposition but is nonetheless of crucial importance.

2.06 *'Agriculture' and aquaculture under planning law*

Having considered the exclusion of agricultural uses of land from the meaning of 'development', and the general authorisation of agricultural developments and fishpond excavation under the General Development Order, the discussion must turn to confront a general difficulty which arises in each of these contexts. This is the definition of 'agriculture' in respect of which these planning exemptions are available. (Generally, see McAnuff (1979) pp. 189 to 190; Howarth (1987B); and Scrase (1988).) As previously noted, this is stated to include the breeding and keeping of livestock including any creature kept for the production of food (s.290(1) Town and Country Planning Act 1971; and s.275(1) Town and Country Planning (Scotland) Act 1972). It follows that if aquaculture is to come within the definition of 'agriculture' either fish must constitute 'livestock', or the fish concerned must be kept for the production of food. Unfortunately, this definition of 'agriculture' was formulated before modern aquacultural practices were envisaged (under s.109(3) Agriculture Act 1947) and is silent on the matter of whether or not fish constitute 'livestock', and the issue has been left to be resolved by the courts.

A leading case on the meaning of 'agriculture', as it is defined in planning law, is that of *Belmont Farm Ltd.* v. *Minister of Housing and Local Government* ((1962)

13 P&CR 417; see also *Minister of Agriculture* v. *Appleton* [1970] 1 QB 221) where the owners of a farm decided to use part of a farm for the training and breeding of horses for show-jumping, and for that purpose erected a large aircraft hangar. It was maintained by the owners that the training and breeding of show-jumping horses was a use of the land for the purposes of agriculture, and the building work was therefore a permitted development under the General Development Order then operative (Town and Country Planning (General Development Order) 1950, SI 1950 No.728). The horses in question were not 'kept for the production of food, wool, skins or fur', or for the purpose of their use in farming the land, within the provisions of the Order. Therefore, the operation which had taken place could only be for the purposes of agriculture if it could be shown that the animals were within the definition of 'livestock', the keeping of which was specifically stated to come within the meaning of 'agriculture'.

In construing the expression 'livestock' the court held that although the word was capable of being understood in a broad sense to include all live creatures the breeding of which is regulated by man, as a term of contrast to dead stock (see *Peterborough Royal Foxhound Show Society* v. *Commissioners of Inland Revenue* [1936] 2 KB 497, at p. 500) it was a narrower sense of the expression which had been intended by Parliament in the context at issue. In this narrower meaning, horses did not amount to 'livestock' unless kept for the purpose of their use in the farming of land. It followed that the owners of the farm had effected a development in erecting the building for which planning permission was required, and that the development was not exempted from the requirement to obtain consent under the General Development Order. The same reasoning was followed in a ministerial appeal against the determination of *Isle of Anglesey Borough Council* ([1985] JPL 198) where it was held that the use of land for the rearing and breeding of ponies could not be regarded as 'agricultural' for planning purposes. Likewise, in the context of a claim for a rating exemption, the House of Lords has recently approved the *Belmont Farm* decision in holding that thoroughbred horses are not 'livestock' within the definition of 'agriculture' applicable for rating purposes (*Hemens* v. *Whitsbury Farm and Stud Ltd* [1987] 1 All ER 72).

In relation to the predicament of fish farmers in respect of agricultural exemptions from planning law, the interpretation placed upon 'livestock' in the *Belmont Farm case* has some important implications. Most significantly it follows from that decision that fish are unlikely to come within the ordinary meaning of 'livestock'. (In other contexts different conclusions have been reached, see *Cresswell* v. *B.O.C. Ltd* [1979] EG 1195 on the meaning of 'livestock' for rating purposes; see Markson (1976); and [5.02] below.) Consequently aquaculture will only be treated as 'agriculture' for planning purposes where it can be shown that the fish in question are 'creatures kept for the production of food', as an activity specifically stated to come within the breeding and keeping of *livestock* which would not otherwise do so. In the case of those fish farms rearing fish for direct sale to consumers or for processing for consumption this requirement should not present any difficulty. In a range of other aquacultural enterprises, however, the requirement may be problematic.

Because of the requirement that the object of the activity is to produce fish for food, rather than for any other purpose, capricious results ensue in the case of persons who seek to rear fish for sporting or ornamental purposes, as such activities may not be classified as 'agriculture' (*Earl of Normanton* v. *Giles* [1980] 1 All ER 106). Moreover, this anomaly in the law has been compounded by the manner in which the legislation has been interpreted by planning inspectors and the Secretary of State. In one Ministerial planning appeal, concerning the change of use of existing pools left after gravel extraction to use as a fish farm, the prospective fish farmer sought the 'option' of producing carp for sale to fishing clubs and pet shops in order to keep open future business possibilities for the farm. It was decided that since the farmer sought to produce fish other than for food, the proposal fell outside the scope of the exception relating to agriculture and planning permission would be required (Appeal against *South Kesteven District Council* [1980] JPL 480). The implication of this decision is that a fish farm which conducts *any part* of its enterprise other than for the production of food is subject to a more rigorous planning requirement than would apply to a farm producing fish exclusively for food.

Another uncertain feature of the agricultural exemption for permitted aquacultural developments is the relationship between the proposed works and the land on which they are to take place. Previously the agricultural exemption under the General Development Order was available only where it was shown that the operation proposed on land was 'requisite for the purposes of agriculture' (under Class VI(1) Schedule 1 Town and Country Planning (General Development Order) 1977, SI 1977 No.289). Under the new 1988 Order, applicable in England and Wales, the formulation is that the works concerned are 'reasonably necessary' for the purposes of agriculture, but it is not clear that this makes any substantial change to the requirement that some connection must be shown between the land being usable for agriculture and the works proposed.

The precise nature of the connection between the use of land for agricultural purposes and the works in respect of which planning exemption was claimed has been a matter of some difficulty in the past. The phrase 'requisite for the purposes of agriculture' was criticised by a Lord Justice of Appeal as 'anachronistic phraseology ... out of step with the present practical agricultural context' (Purchas L.J. in *Jones* v. *Metropolitan Borough of Stockport* [1984] JPL 274, at p. 277). In a situation in which a fish farmer seeks to erect a building to serve as a hatchery and food store, for example, it is unclear to what extent the building need be connected with the use of the surrounding land for it to be 'requisite' for agricultural use of the land.

The most decisive cases on the meaning of 'requisite for agriculture' were apparently based upon the premise that proposed works were an unavoidable step needing to be taken before any agricultural use could be made of the land at issue. Hence in one decided case the 'requisite for agriculture' condition was satisfied where part of the proposed site for a fish farm was in a neglected condition and 'incapable of normal agricultural use' (Ministerial planning appeal concerning *Dacorum District Council* [1984] JPL 662). In another case the requirement was satisfied where the development of a fish farm was held to be the only practical use for water-logged land (Ministerial planning appeal concerning *Chichester District Council* [1981] JPL 274). On the other hand, it was also suggested that the test is less strict than indicated by these decisions and will be satisfied where it can be shown the building is 'reasonably required' for agricultural use of the land without being *essential* for such use (*Jones* v. *Metropolitan Borough of Stockport* [1984] JPL 274, at p. 277; and Ministerial appeal against *Bridgnorth District Council* [1986] JPL 230 where this test was applied).

In an attempt to clarify the meaning of the 'requisite for agriculture' requirement, the Department of the Environment stated in a consultation paper that the phrase was to be understood to mean that an agricultural building will be permitted only if its intended use is ancillary to an agricultural activity carried out on the open land comprising the agricultural unit as a whole (see Anon. (1984) at p. 220). If this same interpretation is adopted by future courts in dealing with the new formulation of the requirement, as 'reasonably necessary for the purposes of agriculture', it would follow that fish farming buildings would only be permitted where other land is also used for fish farming purposes. Hence it would not be open to a prospective fish farmer to construct a new building as a self-contained indoor hatchery which operated independently of the use of surrounding agricultural land.

2.07   *Directions restricting the General Development Order*

Summarising the preceding sections of this chapter, development consent for a fish farm will be available under the General Development Order 1988 where it falls within the category of permitted development for agriculture, allowing the carrying out on agricultural land of works for the erection of a building or excavation operations which are reasonably necessary for the purposes of agriculture. It has been noted that this authorisation for permitted developments is subject to a number of conditions and qualifications, and that separate provision is made for the excavation of fishponds on existing fish farms. Despite the general availability of permitted development status for certain kinds of fish farm development, an exception may arise in circumstances where a local planning authority, with Ministerial approval, is granted permission to remove the permitted development status granted under the General Development Order. The possibility of a Direction restricting a particular kind of permitted development is available where the Secretary of State, or the appropriate local planning authority, is satisfied that it is expedient that a development should not be carried out unless permission is granted for it on application (Art.4 Town and Country Planning (General Development Order) 1988, SI 1988 No.1813). A direction of this kind by a local planning authority requires the approval of the Secretary of State, who may approve the direction with or without modifications (Art.5).

An instance of a direction restricting permitted development having been made in relation to fish farms is to be found in a Direction issued by the Winchester City Council, and approved by the Secretary of State in 1981 (under Art.4 Town and Country Planning (General Development Order) 1977, SI 1977 No.289). The terms of this Direction are that the carrying out on agricultural land of building or engineering operations requisite for the use of that land for the purpose of fish farming are not to be carried out on specified land unless planning permission is granted on application. The land specified is stated to be along the valley of the River Itchen from near the source at a point north of Cheriton, to a point north of Shawford, all in the

County of Hampshire and more particularly shown on a plan attached to the Direction. Notably this is an area in which a considerable number of fish farms are already located and clearly the purpose of the order is to prevent environmental damage to the River Itchen and numerous Sites of Special Scientific Interest alongside it. The Direction provides an interesting illustration of local variation in the operation of planning law where an excessive number of fish farming developments in a sensitive catchment necessitates subjection of further development to a requirement of development consent from the local planning authority.

Chapter 3

Coastal Fish Farming and the Crown Estate

3.01 Crown ownership of the foreshore and seabed

The legal order confronting a prospective coastal fish farmer is very different from that regulating the land-based or freshwater fish farmer. The provisions of the Town and Country Planning Act 1971 and the Town and Country Planning (Scotland) Act 1972 (discussed in Chapter 2 above) only regulate development in, on, over or under *land*, and have no application to operations and activities below the limit of the foreshore (see Anon (1949) *Argyll and Bute District Council* v. *Secretary of State for Scotland* [1977] SLT 33; and Warham (1974) JPL 705). It is to be noted that the precise definition of the 'foreshore' is formulated differently in England and Wales than in Scotland. In England and Wales the foreshore is that part of the seashore between mean high and mean low water, whilst in Scotland it is defined as the area of seashore between the high and low water marks of ordinary spring tides (*Fisherrow Harbour Commissioners* v. *Mussleborough Real Estate Co.* (1903) 5 F 387; and Marston (1981) at pp. 249 to 250). It follows that fish farming in coastal waters falls outside the ambit of planning law, and that those legal powers which do circumscribe the establishment of marine fish farming enterprises arise for quite different legal reasons from those applicable to freshwater enterprises.

The starting point for any discussion of the legal position of a prospective marine fish farmer lies in the rights of the Crown in respect of the ownership of the foreshore and the seabed. The essential principle is that of Crown ownership of the foreshore and seabed beneath coastal waters and tidal estuaries. Hence it has been stated that

> 'Over the British seas, the King of England claims an absolute dominion and ownership, as Lord Paramount, against all the world. . . . This dominion and ownership over the British seas, vested by our law in the King, is not confined to the mere usufruct [that is, the right of use or enjoyment] of the water, and the maritime jurisdiction, but it includes the very *fundum* or soil at the bottom of the sea [sometimes referred to as the *solum*]. . . . This dominion not only extends over the open seas, but also over all *creeks, arms of the sea, havens, ports*, and *tide-rivers*, as far as the reach of the tide, around the coasts of the kingdom. All waters, in short, which communicate with the sea, and are within the *flux* and *reflux* of its tides, are part and parcel of the sea itself, and subject, in all respects, to like ownership.' (Hall (1875) pp. 2 to 3; and see *Le Strange* v. *Rowe* (1866) 4 F&F 1048.)

The Crown's ownership of the foreshore and seabed extends to the limits of the territorial sea. Traditionally this encompassed the seabed to a distance of three nautical miles measured seaward from the low water mark, but the distance has recently been extended to a distance of 12 nautical miles from baselines established by Order in Council by the Territorial Sea Act 1987 (s.1(1) Territorial Sea Act 1987). The extent of crown ownership may, however, be subject to certain local qualifications in situations where the Crown has at some time in the distant past granted ownership to a private individual (*Luss Estates Co.* v. *B.P. (Grangemouth Refinery) Ltd* |1982| SLT 457) or where mineral rights have been vested in other bodies by statute, such as the right to coal which is vested in the National Coal Board, (s.42(1) Coal Act 1938, and Coal Industry Nationalisation Act 1946) or where local laws have the effect of excluding Crown ownership (Howarth (1988B)). Other than in these exceptional matters, however, the foreshore and seabed below the high water mark is owned by the Crown. It is the Crown's right of ownership of the foreshore and seabed which carries with it the right to alienate the property by selling it, and the right to grant leases of the soil to those who seek to make use of the seabed and column of water above it. Although there are public rights of navigation, fishery and certain other rights in the sea which must be respected by the Crown, beyond these, rights over the seabed can only be lawfully exercised with authorisation from the Crown.

3.02 The Crown Estate Commissioners

Having noted the theoretical stance of the Crown in respect of foreshore and seabed ownership, the practical position in the present day is that the personal exercise of seabed rights by the sovereign has long ceased to operate. The management of the seabed, and a collection of other lands referred to as 'the Crown Estate', has passed to a special body administering the estate on behalf of the Crown. The seabed has ceased to be a part of the private estate of the monarch, and the revenue from the estate has been surrendered for the duration of the monarch's reign and six months thereafter, in return for the provision by Parliament of a fund to meet the expenses of the monarchy known as the 'Civil List' (Civil List Act 1952). In the place of the Sovereign, the estate is administered by a body known as the 'Crown Estate Commissioners', the status and powers of whom are provided for under the Crown Estate Act 1961. Under this enactment the Commissioners are to be persons appointed by the Queen by warrant, at salaries determined by the Minister with responsibility for the Civil Service (s.1 and Sch.1 para.1; and Hailsham (1977) paras.1451 to 1458 and 1470 to 1475). The Commissioners have the power to regulate their own procedure and, with ministerial approval, to appoint officers and servants, with salaries being paid by Parliament and activities subject to the overall scrutiny of the Parliamentary Commissioner for Administration (s.4 Parliamentary Commissioner Act 1967).

Under the statutory powers given to the Crown Estate Commissioners, the properties which, as a matter of legal theory, pass to a sovereign by way of hereditary possessions are managed on behalf of, and in the name of, the Crown. This imposes a duty upon the Commissioners to do all things proper for the effective exercise of their duties to maintain the Estate and, in addition, they are to improve the estate and enhance its value and the financial return obtained from it where this can be done with due regard to the requirements of 'good management' (s.1 Crown Estate Act 1961). The income from the estate, after deduction of overheads, is put at the disposal of Parliament by payment into the Exchequer. In respect of the foreshore and seabed these duties entail a vesting of ownership, along with the assumption of managerial responsibilities, with the Commissioners

The status of the Crown Estate Commissioners, as trustees and administrators of the estate, carries with it the authority to enter into such transactions on behalf of the Crown as follow from the Crown's right of ownership of the estate. In particular this confers upon the Commissioners the power to create leases and to charge rent to persons making certain uses of the foreshore and seabed. An illustrative decision on this power is *Crown Estate Commissioners* v. *Fairlie Yacht Slip Ltd* ((1979) SC 156) where a company had laid down moorings on the seabed for use by yachts and other craft, and an action was brought by the Commissioners for a declaration that they had the sole and exclusive right to permit the laying of such moorings. It was held by the court, without being seriously contested between the parties, that the Crown has a proprietary right in the seabed within the territorial waters of the United Kingdom, subject only to certain public rights over the seabed, most notably the right of navigation and of white fishing. On behalf of the Company, however, it was claimed that the public right of navigation included a right to lay moorings which, it was contended, were for a purpose within the public right of navigation. The court found, however, that the public right of navigation extended only to the free passage of ships and matters incidental to that, and did not include the placing of permanent fixtures on the seabed to permit the mooring of vessels. It followed that the actions of the Company were unlawful since they had been performed without the consent of the Commissioners. In relation to marine fish farming, it may be observed that the same requirement of consent by the Commissioners is a prerequisite to the lawful stationing of sea rearing cages or shellfish rafts on or over the seabed.

The decision in the *Fairlie Yacht Slip case* provides verification of the Crown's right of ownership of the seabed. It also confirms the Commissioners' power, subject to the observance of public rights of navigation and fishery, to lease the use of the seabed for particular purposes, charging appropriate rents for that facility. It has been suggested, however, that the powers granted by virtue of the Crown Estate Act 1961 were of greatest importance in enabling the Commissioners to manage those urban and agricultural property holdings, which constitute the more valuable part of the Crown Estate at the time of its enactment. Significantly the powers provided for under the 1961 Act were not designed to establish a comprehensive system of controls over the foreshore or seabed analogous to those of planning authorities over land-based development, as the Commissioners were neither established nor empowered to act as a regulatory body with an overall responsibility for coastal development (Deans (1986) at p. 178). Hence, until fairly recently, the exercise of their licensing power for seabed use has tended to operate on a rather piecemeal basis, considering individual applications for consent in the light of their particular merits without any attempt to oversee the optimal utilisation of the overall coastal resources at their disposal.

As will be seen in the following discussion, the Commissioners have over recent years become significantly more conscious of the need to consider representations from a range of interested parties in the exercise of their licensing power and particularly when determining applications for fish farm leases. Nonetheless the power to lease the sea bed remains subject to the over-riding administrative obligation set out in the Crown Estate Act 1961. This requires the Commissioners to maintain and enhance the value of the Crown Estate, and to administer the Estate with due regard to the requirements of 'good management' (s.1(3) 1961 Act).

3.03   Consultation procedures and the Crown Estate

The difficulty of co-ordinating the development of the Scottish fish farming industry, and resolving conflicts arising through competing claims upon coastal resources, was noted by the Montgomery Committee of Inquiry into the Islands Councils of Scotland (1984 Cmnd. 9216) who observed that

'Fish farming is an example where there may be conflict between one type of fish farming and another or between fish farming and other industries. Local authorities have no powers to control developments in the sea. The only control over whether a development may take place is that exercised by the Crown Estate Commissioners ... However, this control is limited only to their discretion whether or not to grant a lease to applicants. The procedure does not facilitate consideration of the respective merits of different developments or longer term planning for the use of areas along a local authority's coast line.' (para.7.11)

Specifically, the Montgomery Committee recommended that, 'the present study into possible control of offshore activities would be carried through as a matter of urgency with the object of introducing a form of control which should at the very least involve consultation with the local authorities concerned' (Recommendation 19, para.7.14). As a response to this suggestion the Secretary of State for Scotland entered into discussions with the Crown Estate Commissioners which have resulted in new procedures for consultation with interested parties being introduced. The consultative procedures apply to all Scottish coastal waters other than Shetland, where authorisation is provided by licences issued by the Islands Council (under Zetland County Council Act 1974) from 1986.

Broadly, the new consultative procedures involve the submission of applications for leases on a standard application form requesting, amongst other matters, indications as to on-shore developments proposed, and advising applicants to seek any necessary planning permission. Submission of an application form requires applicants to pay a standard fee, presently £50, to cover the cost of advertisement in a newspaper in the locality of the proposed development. The advertisement will invite representations to be submitted to the Crown Estate Receiver or, where an objection related to the hindrance or obstruction of navigation, directly to the Department of Transport (see [3.07] below). The advertisement will indicate where a copy of the application and associated plans may be inspected, and that representations may be made within 28 days of the publication of the advertisement.

Along with making arrangements for the publication of the advertisement, the Crown Estate Receiver will inform a number of specified interested organisations of the application and invite them to comment within the consultation period. The consultees, comprising approximately 30 bodies and agencies include the holders of any leases already granted by the Commissioners for developments in the same area, port or harbour authorities in relation to applications within their areas of jurisdiction, the Department of Agriculture and Fisheries for Scotland, the Nature Conservancy Council, the Countryside Commission for Scotland, the Department of Transport, the Highlands and Islands Development Board, the Scottish Landowners' Federation, the National Trust for Scotland where the Trust is owner of land adjacent to the proposed development or where the land is subject to a conservation agreement, and the River Purification Board. In addition, direct consultation will also take place with the Islands Councils, the Regional Councils in Highland, Border and Dumfries/Galloway and district planning authorities elsewhere.

In the event of a site being available for leasing, the Crown Estate Commissioners will consider all the representations made in relation to an application and have regard to both local and national matters including environmental and amenity features of the proposed development. The outcome of this process will be either that the application is granted, or refused, or granted subject to variation of the proposal to take account of representations. In any instance where representations have been submitted the Commissioners will give reasons for their decision to the applicant and to all interested parties. In the event of the Commissioners being minded to refuse an application they may discuss the matter with the applicant and objectors and allow a further period of 14 days for the submission and consideration of further representations, after which a final decision will be taken. Normally it would be anticipated that the consultation procedure would enable the Commissioners to make a determination as to whether to grant a lease within a three month period from the date of submission of the application (Crown Estate (1986)).

3.04   *The Crown Estate Guidelines*

As a result of experience gained in operating the consultation procedures arising out of the Montgomery Committee recommendations, the Crown Estate Commissioners published *Fish Farming – Guidelines on Siting and Design of Marine Fish Farms in Scotland* in December 1987 (Crown Estate (1987); see also, Cobham Resource Consultants (1987), which was a principal source in devising the *Guidelines*). The Crown Estate *Guidelines* are stated to be an offer of guidance to marine fish farmers in Scotland on the siting and design of their installations which, because of the need for innovation and flexibility in a new industry, recognise the impracticability of imposing rigid rules and standards on the industry. Nonetheless the *Guidelines* are intended to be a helpful indication as to how the careful choice of site and equipment, and attention to operating methods, can reduce conflicts with other fish farmers and with fishing, recreation and conservation interests (para.2). The hope of the Commissioners is that it may be possible to modify certain fish farming development proposals to achieve compatibility between potentially conflicting interests. It is to be stressed from the outset that the *Guidelines* possess no authoritative status in law but will, in practice, serve as a valuable indication as to the manner in which the Commissioners' discretion is likely to be exercised in determining applications for seabed leases.

A. Three objectives

In respect of the selection of fish farming sites the Crown Estate's *Guidelines* identify three 'objectives'. First, the developer must either find a site which is appropriate to the aquacultural technology available, or alternatively match the technology to the sites which are available. That is to say, the selection of sites according to water condition, depth, shelter and access, which are the usual primary considerations in a fish farming development, is likely to lead to conventional sites in sheltered sea lochs where the potential for further development is likely to be controversial and constrained. As an alternative the use of more advanced fish cage construction, for example, may enable the developer to consider more exposed sites where the scope for expansion is greater. A second objective in the selection of a site is the need to agree with other operators as to the desirable separation distance between sites, or to negotiate joint arrangements which permit closer siting. It is recognised that a degree of spacing between fish farms is necessary to avoid the threat of disease spreading from one farm to its neighbours, but in each case the precise distance of separation which is required will depend upon peculiar features of topography, hydrography, ecology and the size of the operations concerned. The third objective is the need for discussion with the appropriate planning authority as to the development of a suitable land base or, alternatively, to devise a means of servicing the farm without the need for onshore development. In the future, however, it is recognised that, with the greater use of sites in more remote areas, using more durable cages and remote control systems for feeding and maintenance, new servicing methods may be adopted which make farms less dependent upon a nearby land base.

B. Three constraints

In addition to the objectives which need to be satisfied in a lease application the *Guidelines* specify three 'constraints' which should be met in respect of the application. First, the size of the site should be limited to the minimum necessary, or an explanation should be provided as to why a larger area is sought. The problem which has arisen in past applications is that developers have submitted applications in respect of large areas of seabed giving the impression that the area was to be fully occupied by cages and fish farming structures. If a larger area than that to be occupied at any one time is applied for in order to permit cages to be moved from time to time to allow the seabed to lie fallow for periods, then that purpose should be clearly explained in the application. A second constraint is the need to avoid important fishing grounds, anchorages, scenic and wildlife areas, or to take steps to ensure that the effects upon these areas will be insignificant. The difficulty in this respect is that many sites which are otherwise suitable for fish farming will raise controversy because they will impinge upon important conservation, navigation or fishery areas. In such instances the *Guidelines* invite applicants to consider whether the merits of the site are sufficient to justify the application, or to consider what steps might be taken to ensure compatibility with other interests. A third constraint is the need to avoid visual disamenity in the siting of fish farms, and with this in mind it is stated that sites should be inconspicuous to houses, hotels and public viewpoints, or should adopt special techniques in design, management and public relations to avoid scenic intrusiveness. Concerns have been expressed that unsightly fish farms detract from the general amenity of an area for both residents and visitors, especially so where many operations are conducted in attractive and unspoilt rural areas. In response to these concerns the need for sensitive siting is emphasised, and where structures cannot be placed in sites where visual intrusion is insignificant special measures should be followed in the design of farms to minimise conspicuousness.

C.   Separation requirements

After noting the general 'objectives' and 'constraints' which are to be taken into account in granting a lease of a fish farming site, the Crown Estate's *Guidelines* discuss a number of more specific matters which will commonly arise in respect of fish farm lease applications. The first of these is an attempt to provide more detailed guidance upon the separation of fish farms from other interests with which they may conflict. The existence of a supply of uncontaminated water, which must serve as a prerequisite to the establishment of a fish farm, is likely to be impaired by the concentration of too many farms in too small an area or in an area where the circulation of water is insufficient to disperse waste products originating from farms. Similarly, the spread of fish disease, such as furunculosis, between farms is a matter of concern to fish farmers with intensively reared stocks through which disease can progress with rapidity causing major losses. Outside the aquacultural industry a range of other interests need to be respected by preservation of a distance from fish farming operations.

Whilst acknowledging the impossibility of establishing absolute separation distances between fish farms and other interests, the *Guidelines* set out a range of reasonable standard distances whilst stressing that these distances are intended as 'broad and flexible guidance' and not as rigid rules to be followed irrespective of other considerations such as hydrography, topography and existing offshore and onshore interests. With that proviso emphasised, it is indicated that the standard minimum separation distance between one salmon farm and another should be five miles, between a salmon farm and a shellfish farm two miles, and between two shellfish farms one mile. In each case, however, closer siting may be possible between small-scale farms, and in large loch systems or open water. The standard distances between salmon farms and public viewpoints, hotels and tourist centres is one mile, and for houses other than fish farm staff houses half a mile, and in respect of shellfish farms these distances are halved. In each of these cases it is noted that concealment by headlands or woodlands may permit close siting, and the attitudes of residents should be taken into account so that closer siting may be permissible in some areas. In respect of wildlife colonies the separation distance from salmon or shellfish farms is half a mile, and a quarter of a mile for shellfish farms, assuming that effective measures are taken such as the installation of anti-predator nets. With respect to anchorages, approaches and fishing grounds the standard separation distance from salmon and shellfish farms is a quarter of a mile subject to the assessment of the Department of Transport with regard to navigation hazard, and assuming that the fishing grounds concerned are specific productive areas in frequent use.

D. Visual disamenity

Whilst acknowledging that in comparison with some forms of industrial and agricultural development fish farming is an unobtrusive, benign and removable type of development, it is recognised that the novelty of fish farming makes its expansion controversial. For that reason all possible steps must be taken to reduce the intrusive effects of fish farming activity on the landscape and seascape. Accordingly the *Guidelines* stress the need to minimise deterioration of the visual quality of land and sea by avoiding the most accessible parts of designated National Scenic Areas, Regional Areas of Great Landscape Value and Nature Reserves. Visual amenity is also to be preserved by ensuring concealment from public viewpoints on main roads, beaches and popular mountains, or by maintaining adequate distances from such places. The character of the area concerned is a matter to be weighed into consideration in that remote areas famous for their wilderness may be unsuitable, as may areas of great historical or cultural significance. The character of the area may also need to be taken into account in that tourist areas tend to be opposed to intrusive fish farming development whereas crofting townships are likely to be better disposed for economic reasons where it provides a source of local employment. The scale of a fish farming proposal will also be significant in sensitive areas which will be able to accommodate a lesser extent, number and size of installations. Dispersal into smaller sites may be required in some areas to diminish visual disamenity. Likewise, the scale of development may be of special importance in that a large scale development will usually require greater separation distances from other fish farms and conflicting interests. Similarly, concealment from accessible, recreational or residential areas is a factor to be taken into consideration in that conspicuous sites should, wherever possible, be avoided or screened from view. Accordingly, both the natural landscape and vegetation, and the planting of new woodlands, should be utilised to achieve the greatest possible concealment of fish farming installations.

In addition to the matters of siting and landscaping which fall to be considered before a fish farm lease will be granted, the *Guidelines* also provide for a number of matters concerned with the intrinsic appearance of a fish farm. Consideration should be given to the juxtaposition of cages in the light of their appearance from viewpoints. In some sites it may be preferable to place cages in a linear arrangement, whereas in others a dispersed irregular pattern following the outline of the coast will be less intrusive. Cage design is itself a significant factor in avoiding unsightly appearance, and the superstructure of the cages should be kept at a low profile by avoiding tall structures standing above the waterline. Colour is also important in reducing visibility and it is suggested that cages, hoppers and buoyancy floats should be in dark and matt colours to maximise camouflage. Likewise, nets should be black or dark grey, and brightly coloured anti-predator nets should be avoided in conspicuous positions. Only where brightly coloured buoys and floats are necessary for navigation or safety reasons should they be used, and where buoys are used to support shellfish longlines the greatest possible proportion of such markers should be in dark colours.

E.   Future environmental precautions

Finally, the *Guidelines* make provision for a number of operational matters which are related to the future environmental precautions to be taken by fish farmers in the continuing operation of their enterprises under Crown Estate leases. Pollution is a significant matter in this respect, and effluent originating from onshore hatcheries, cleaning and processing activities, and waste food from offshore cages, should be subject to agreed control methods meeting the approval of the appropriate River Purification Boards and Environmental Health Departments. Similarly, acceptable provision should be made for the disposal of dead fish and the cleaning of nets. Likewise measures should be taken where necessary to reduce noise, and action taken to avoid complaints from local residents and roads authorities arising from service traffic causing disturbance and damage to road verges. The maintenance of general tidiness is also a matter of concern, and the use of a purpose-built storage building for the maintenance work and the storage of equipment is preferable in this respect, as are measures to avoid debris and litter originating from onshore installations causing hazard to shipping or becoming an eyesore when washed up on beaches. It is also important to foresee and prevent potential problems arising through wildlife being attracted to fish farms, especially where sites are close to seal colonies, heronries or areas populated by eider duck. From the outset it is better in all respects that predators are deterred or prevented from entering a fish farm *before* they come to treat it as a source of food, and in this matter it is noted that the staff of the Nature Conservancy Council are able to provide useful advice to fish farmers as to appropriate anti-predator measures.

3.05   *The Crown Estate Advisory Committee for Fish Farming Lease Applications*

The procedures for consultation in respect of applications to the Crown Estate for leases for coastal fish farm development have been the subject of a recent review conducted by the Secretary of State for Scotland as to their initial operation. The conclusion of the review was that, in the first two years of their operation, the new consultative procedures were working well and enabled those with an interest in a lease application to make their views known. Criticism had been raised that there was a lack of an overall strategy for the development of the coastal salmon farming industry against which individual applications could be assessed, but no convincing case had been made out for the extension of the planning system to marine fish farming. Nonetheless, the Secretary of State accepted that steps should be taken to enable contentious cases to be discussed more fully and to be subject to an independent element in the decision-making process, and agreed to establish an advisory committee to consider lease applications referred to it.

The Advisory Committee to be established is to include representatives of the relevant district or general planning authority, the Countryside Commission for Scotland, the Nature Conservancy Council, the Highlands and Islands Development Board, the relevant river purification authority and the Department of Agriculture and Fisheries for Scotland. The Committee is to consider applications where a decision which the Commissioners propose to reach encounters objections from one or more of the statutory bodies represented on the Committee which cannot otherwise be resolved. The Commissioners may also put cases to the Committee for consideration where they consider that the advice of the Committee would be of assistance. Applications for leases involving less than 3,000 square metres in cage area, or in sea area for shellfish, will not normally be put before the Committee unless they relate to areas regarded as very sensitive. In any case referred to the Committee the chairman will report to the Commissioners on the outcome of the Committee's discussion and make a recommendation as to whether a lease should be granted, and the Commissioners are to take full account of the recommendation in making their decision on the application (144 HC DEB 1988 Cols. *88* to *91*).

At the time of writing the full details surrounding the operation of the Advisory Committee have not yet been announced. The initial indications are that the Committee will provide an important independent input into the determination of lease applications for fish farms allowing for greater discussion of problematic cases relating to scale and location. This will provide a useful and impartial source of advice to the Commissioners, which will go some way towards meeting criticisms about the lack of an overall strategy for development of the industry.

3.06   *The form of Crown Estate leases*

The end point of the application process for a successful applicant is a lease authorising fish farming or shellfish farming development in accordance with its terms. Although each individual lease is capable of incorporating particular terms reflecting the distinct uses to which the lease relates and the special characteristics of the area concerned, a number of general features of fish farming leases are indicated by the Crown Estates Commissioners in information provided along with lease application forms (Crown Estate: *Marine Fish Farms* and *Marine Fish Farms Application for Lease*, pamphlet A and B, not dated). Hence it is stated that a lease will be for a term of years appropriate to the development and the financing involved, which in practice is usually a term of up to 21 years, and will not be subject to assignment or sub-letting. A condition of the lease will be that the fish farm authorised must be established within two years of the grant of the lease. All leases will be subject to any public rights over the water concerned, and it is stressed that the Commissioners' ownership of the seabed is itself subject to the public rights of navigation and fishing.

Formerly rents for fish farm leases had been held at a low level to encourage the growth of coastal fish farming. With the expansion of the salmon farming industry and establishment of its economic feasibility the rents now payable are directly related to both production and price, and are adjusted annually on that basis. Nonetheless, start up rents, payable for the first three years of a lease, and reduced rents are payable for salmon cages until annual production exceeds 75 tonnes. In the case of shellfish farms the rent moratorium devised to encourage the growth of the industry is still in effect and until the end of 1989 rents are limited to £50 per year.

3.07   *Navigational consents for fish farms*

As has been mentioned previously, a coastal fish farm requires the consent of the Department of Transport as navigational authority. The legal reason for Department of Transport involvement lies in s.34 of the Coast Protection Act 1949, which is concerned with the restriction of works detrimental to navigation. Specifically this section provides that no person may, without the consent in writing of the Secretary of State for Trade and Industry, carry out any of the following operations:

(a)   onstruct, alter or improve any works on, under or over any part of the seashore lying below the level of mean high water springs;
(b)   deposit any object or any materials on any such part of the seashore; or
(c)   remove any object or any materials from any part of the seashore lying below the level of mean low water springs,

if the operation, whether while being carried out or subsequently, causes or is likely to result in obstruction or danger to navigation (s.34(1) Coast Protection Act 1949, as amended by s.36(1) Merchant Shipping Act 1988).

As a condition of considering an application for navigational consent the Secretary of State may require to be furnished with such plans and particulars of the proposed operation as he considers necessary. On receipt of plans and particulars, he may cause notice of the application, and the time and manner in which objections may be made, to be published in such a manner as he considers appropriate for informing persons affected by the proposal. Before granting consent he may, if he thinks fit, direct a local enquiry to be held (s.34(2)). If the Minister is of the opinion that any operation will cause or is likely to result in obstruction or danger to navigation, he must either refuse his consent or give it subject to such conditions as he may think fit, having regard to the nature and extent of the obstruction or danger which it appears to him would otherwise be caused or be likely to result (s.34(3)). A consent provided in accordance with these provisions may continue in force only if the operation for which consent is given is begun or completed within a specified period, and any renewal of consent may be similarly limited (s.34(4)).

Formerly, a difficulty arose in relation to the interpretation of the requirement of consent for the construction of works so that obstruction or danger to navigation is caused or is likely to result. In *Harwich Harbour Conservancy Board* v. *Secretary of State for the Environment* ([1974] 1 Lloyd's Rep. 140) the meaning of the requirement arose in relation to a plan for a marina for 500 yachts in close proximity to a busy commercial harbour. It was decided that the requirement of consent for the works allowed the Minister to consider only the obstruction or danger to navigation which would result from the works *themselves*, and not the issue of whether the increase in traffic caused by yachts using the marina would constitute an obstruction or danger to navigation. This ruling has now been overturned, however, by a recent amendment which allows the consequential effects of works upon navigation to be taken into consideration. Hence in relation to the Secretary of State's consent for operations involving the construction, alteration or improvement of works, the likelihood of the operation resulting in obstruction or danger to navigation is to be construed as including a reference to its being likely to result in a danger to navigation by reason of any *use* intended to be made of the works when constructed (s.34(3A) Coast Protection Act 1949, as added by s.36(3) Merchant Shipping Act 1988).

Other recent amendments of navigational consent requirements under the 1949 Act allow for refinements in the operation of conditions to which a consent for construction work is subject. Hence it is now provided that conditions of this kind may remain in force for a specified period or remain in force without limit of time. Conditions are to bind, so far as is appropriate, any other person who for the time being owns, occupies, or enjoys any use of, the works in question. Conditions relating to the provision of any lights, signals or other aids to navigation, or the stationing of guardships in the vicinity of the works in question, or the taking of any other measures for the purpose of controlling the movements of ships in the vicinity of works, may be varied in the interests of the safety of navigation for the purpose of enhancing their effectiveness (s.34(4A), as added by s.36(4) Merchant Shipping Act 1988).

Amongst a list of exceptions to the requirement of navigational consent is the stipulation that consent will not be required for any work carried out by or in accordance with a licence or permission granted by a conservancy, harbour or navigation authority (defined under s.742 Merchant Shipping Act 1894). A licence or permission of this kind may be provided in pursuance of any Act which requires that, if the approval of the Secretary of State is not previously obtained, other conditions must be complied with, and either the approval has been obtained or the conditions are complied with (s.35(1)(g) Coast Protection Act 1949). This is a reference to the powers of harbour and other authorities, usually constituted under private Acts or local legislation, to authorise works of a kind which would otherwise fall under s.34 of the 1949 Act. This overlap of powers between the Secretary of State and the local harbour authorities has recently been rationalised by the introduction of powers given to the Secretary of State to promote regulations extending the licensing powers of the harbour authorities. Regulations of this kind will allow the necessary consent for coastal works within the jurisdiction of a harbour authority to be granted at local level, subject to a right of appeal to the Secretary of State (s.37 Merchant Shipping Act 1988).

It is an offence for any person to carry out any operation detrimental to navigation without navigational consent, under s.34 of the 1949 Act, or to fail to comply with any condition subject to which consent has been given (s.36(1) Coast Protection Act 1949). The penalty for this offence is, on summary conviction, a fine not exceeding level 3 on the standard scale, presently £400 (s.43). Where works have been constructed without consent, or in breach of a condition of a consent, the Secretary of State may serve a notice on that person requiring him, within a specified period of not less than 30 days, to remove the works or to make such alterations as may be stipulated in the notice. If within the period specified the person upon whom the notice is served fails to comply with it, the Secretary of State may himself remove the object or materials as specified in the notice (s.36(3)). Where it appears *urgently* necessary to do so the Secretary of State may himself remove or alter the works (s.36(2)). In either situation, if the Secretary of State himself removes or alters any works or removes any object or materials, he is entitled to recover the expense of so doing from the person by whom the works were constructed or the object or materials were deposited (s.36(4)). In addition a harbour authority in England and Wales has the power to enforce the provisions of the Act relating to restrictions upon works detrimental to navigation within their jurisdiction (s.36(5)).

The practical effect of navigational consents in relation to coastal fish farming is of considerable importance. It is clear that 'works' will include fish farming equipment such as salmon cages and shellfish rafts and that an offence will be committed where these are positioned where they are likely to cause an obstruction or danger to navigation without the required consent. 'Navigation' is understood to mean the planned and intended passage from one known position to another, but the question as to when obstruction or danger to navigation will be caused is not specified in any enactment, and it would seem that each application is considered by the Department of Transport on its individual merits given the nature of the location and the use of the area by coastal traffic. Consultation on these issues takes place, either as a part of the Crown Estate Commissioners' consultation procedure, or separately, with a range of bodies which will usually include the Royal Yachting Association and the Scottish branch of the Association, the Ministry of Defence through the Navy, and the Ministry of Agriculture, Fisheries and Food or in Scotland the Department of Agriculture and Fisheries. Where the proposed works are considered to cause no interference with navigation the application is returned with the comment 'no observations' since it is only in cases that involve obstruction that consent is required. If some interference with navigation is found, however, the application may either be refused, or the applicant invited to modify the proposal, or the consent granted subject to conditions such as requirements as to the marking or lighting of the works subject to the recommendations of the General Lighthouse Authority.

The recent practice of the Department of Transport has been to grant permanent consents for fish cages and shellfish rafts of substantial construction providing that they are established within a period specified in the consent, whilst smaller items of gear such as shellfish longlines are given a consent which requires renewal every five years. Another practice of the Department of special relevance to fish farming is to grant consent for works to be placed within a given area to allow for the periodic movement of cages to avoid the build-up of debris on the seabed, though it remains the *works*, rather than the area, that are the subject of the navigational consent under the 1949 Act. For that reason the perimeter of an area may be required to be marked along with any fish farming cage or raft within the area.

The difficulty of reconciling aquacultural and navigational interests has recently come before the courts in the case of *Ward* v. *David* (20 January 1989, unreported) which concerned the navigational interference caused by salmon cages placed close to the shore of Scalpay, off the coast of the Island of Skye. The defender was the owner of the salmon cages and had obtained both the consent of the Department of Transport and the Crown Estate for the mooring of the cages in the area concerned. The pursuer, a scallop farmer in the vicinity, did not learn that navigational consent had been granted until application for a lease was made to the Crown Estate, and the 'unfortunate background' to the case was that he had not been consulted or asked to comment on whether the cages would be likely to result in obstruction or danger to navigation. After an intricate examination of the navigational use of the area in which the cages were moored, and the weather conditions to which the locality was subject, it was found that the cages did not constitute a material interference or hazard to navigation which infringed the public right of navigation in the waters concerned, and the declarator which was sought was declined (following *Archibald Orr Ewing* v. *Sir James Colquhoun's Trustees* (1877) 4R (HL) 116). The case establishes that a grant of navigational consent will not by itself serve as conclusive finding that rights of navigation are not infringed, but also illustrates the difficulty of showing material interference with navigation, a matter which depends upon a range of circumstances unique to the location at issue.

Chapter 4

The Environmental Assessment of Salmon Farming

4.01   The Environmental Assessment Directive

In addition to the requirement of obtaining planning permission and the need to obtain a lease and other authorisations for coastal fish farming, a third form of legal constraint applicable to prospective salmon farmers, in either fresh or salt water, is the requirement of 'environmental assessment' for certain kinds of salmon farming project. The origin of this requirement lies in the Directive adopted by the Council of Environment Ministers of the European Communities, in 1985, on the assessment of the effects of certain public and private projects on the environment (EEC/85/337). The purpose of the Directive is the preventative one of seeking to avoid pollution and nuisance at source by providing for the subjection of potentially harmful new development projects to environmental scrutiny before authorisation. This process has been characterised by the Department of the Environment in the following way:

'Formal environmental assessment is essentially a technique for drawing together, in a systematic way, expert quantitative analysis and qualitative assessment of a project's environmental effects, and presenting the results in a way which enables the importance of the predicted effects, and the scope for modifying or mitigating them, to be properly evaluated by the relevant decision-making body before a decision is given.' (Department of the Environment (1988) para.7)

Accordingly, since the Directive became operative in July 1988, member states of the European Community have required that information about the environmental effects of certain types of project must be provided by the developer and taken into account by the competent authority before it is decided whether to grant development consent. In addition, the Directive requires certain bodies with relevant environmental responsibilities to be given an opportunity to comment on certain types of project before consent for development is granted, and for information concerning these projects to be made generally available to the public.

In the first place the Environmental Assessment Directive stipulates that certain kinds of major development projects, listed in Annex I, are invariably to be subject to environmental assessment. These include major industrial and infrastructural projects such as crude-oil refineries, radioactive power stations and motorways. In addition to Annex I projects the Directive provides that a range of projects, specified in Annex II of the Directive, 'shall be made subject to an assessment where Member States consider that their characteristics so require' (Art.4(2) Environmental Assessment Directive). Amongst the matters listed under Annex II is a general heading of 'Agriculture', and under that a specific subheading 'Salmon breeding', which has been understood to extend to salmon farming in general (Annex II 1(g); and Annex B.4 para.3 Department of the Environment (1988), in draft). Although, on one interpretation, the wording of the Directive provides for the permissive or optional extension of environmental assessment to projects of this kind, it has become clear from consultation as to the implementation of the Directive in the domestic law of the United Kingdom, that the general application of environmental assessment to salmon farming is mandatory.

Although the Directive requires the activity of salmon farming generally to be subject to environmental assessment, this does not amount to a requirement that *every* individual development of this kind will be subject to the procedure. The determination as to whether a particular proposal to develop a salmon farm will be subject to assessment depends in each case upon whether the project is likely to have 'significant' effects on the environment' because of its nature, size or location, amongst other things (Art.2(1)). This, in turn, is indicated by the sort of information which is stated to be required where environmental assessment is conducted. In such cases Annex III of the Directive specifies a list of factors which are relevant to the assessment. These include, 'population, fauna, flora, soil, water, air, climatic factors, material assets, including architectural and archaeological heritage, landscape and the inter-relationship between the above factors' (Annex III para.3). The sorts of effects which should be taken into consideration in determining whether environmental assessment is required are those arising from 'the existence of the project, the use of natural resources, the emission of pollutants, the creation of nuisances and the elimination of waste' (Annex III para.4). With these considerations in mind, the Secretary of State for the Environment has taken the view that only a relatively small number of Annex II projects will necessitate environmental assessment. In respect of salmon farming projects it is likely that this category will be restricted to a relatively small number of developments proposed in particularly sensitive or vulnerable locations. In relation to freshwater salmon farming at least, it has been suggested that environmental assessment will not normally apply to developments designed to produce less than 100 tonnes of fish a year (Department of the Environment (1988) Appendix A para.3).

The implementation of the European Directive within the law of the United Kingdom has necessitated the enactment of special legislation in this country where the duties imposed by the Directive are not already a part of the law. In respect of that part of the Environmental Assessment Directive which makes 'salmon breeding' projects which have significant effects upon the environment subject to assessment this has been achieved in Britain by means of three statutory instruments, the Town and Country Planning (Assessment of Environmental Effects) Regulations 1988 (SI 1988 No.1199) applicable in England and Wales, the Environmental Assessment (Scotland) Regulations 1988 (SI 1988 No.1221) Part II of which is of substantially the same effect in relation to planning law in Scotland, and the Environmental Assessment (Salmon Farming in Marine Waters) Regulations 1988 (SI 1988 No.1218) which apply to England and Wales and Scotland.

4.02 Environment assessment in planning law

The Town and Country Planning (Assessment of Environmental Effects) Regulations 1988 serve to incorporate a requirement of environmental assessment, for certain kinds of project, into the planning process in England and Wales. (Since Part II of the Environmental Assessment (Scotland) Regulations 1988, SI 1988 No.1221, is of substantially the same effect in relation to Scotland, the discussion here is confined to the counterpart for England and Wales, but for separate discussion of the position in Scotland see Scottish Development Department (1988).) To that effect it is provided that the local planning authority, or the Secretary of State, is not to grant planning permission for certain kinds of application unless they have first taken the environmental information into consideration (Reg.4(2) Town and Country Planning (Assessment of Environmental Effects) Regulations, SI 1988 No.1199). The provision of environmental information in support of a planning application is the responsibility of the applicant, as an application will not be determined without provision of the appropriate environmental information (Reg.9(1)). Following the plan of the European Directive, the Regulations group the projects for which an environmental assessment is to be provided under two schedules. The second schedule is a list of projects of different kinds for which environmental information is required to support a planning application, where the development is likely to have significant effects on the environment by virtue of factors such as its nature, size or location, and is not exempted by the Secretary of State (Reg.2(1)). Amongst these 'Schedule 2 applications' are developments for the purposes of agriculture, including 'a salmon hatchery' and 'an installation for the rearing of salmon' (Regs. Sch.2 1(d) and (e)). It is clear, therefore, that where new salmon farming developments are taking place on land, and are likely to have a *significant* effect upon the environment, planning applications are to be accompanied by an environmental statement detailing the likely effects of the proposed development upon the environment.

4.03   *Environmental assessment of marine salmon farming*

Because a large number of salmon farming enterprises are conducted in marine waters, outside the general scope of planning law, the Environmental Assessment (Salmon Farming in Marine Waters) Regulations 1988 (SI 1988 No.1218) make separate provision for environmental assessment in these circumstances both for England and Wales and Scotland. These Regulations provide for environmental assessment to be required in support of applications to the Crown Estate Commissioners for consent for salmon farming operations in marine waters (see Chapter 3 above). The principal duty imposed upon the Commissioners is that they are not to grant consent for salmon farming in marine waters where the proposed development will be likely to have significant effects on the environment by virtue, amongst other things, of its nature, size or location, unless they have taken environmental information into consideration (Reg.3(1) Environmental Assessment (Salmon Farming in Marine Waters) Regulations 1988). The issue of whether a project is likely to have such 'significant effects' on the environment is to be determined by the Commissioners (Reg.3(2)).

In order to determine whether a particular application for consent is to be subject to environmental assessment special provision is made for formalities relating to all applications to the Commissioners for consent for salmon farming in marine waters. 'Salmon farming', for these purposes, is defined as meaning the keeping of live salmon (whether or not for profit) with a view to their sale or to their transfer to other marine waters, and the possibility of transfer to non-marine waters is not addressed (Reg.2; contrast the definition of 'fish farming' for registration purposes, discussed in [6.02] below).

It is stated that an application for consent is to be accompanied by:

(a) a plan showing the location and extent of the site of the proposed salmon farm;

(b) a brief outline of the proposed scale of production and the equipment to be installed on the site; and

(c) a statement of the proposed servicing methods and of any intended development on land (Reg.4(1)).

On receipt of an application for a lease for a salmon farming development, the Crown Estate Commissioners are to consider whether the proposed development is one for which environmental information is required. If the Commissioners consider that the applicant has not provided them with sufficient information to enable them to form an opinion as to whether the project should be subject to environmental information they may ask for further information to be provided. Where it appears to the Commissioners that the application is of a kind for which environmental information should be supplied, they must notify the applicant in writing of their view within six weeks, and that without consideration of environmental information they may not grant consent. In coming to a view as to whether consideration of environmental information is required the Commissioners are to consult such of the authorities, bodies or persons listed in a schedule to the Regulations as they consider appropriate (Reg.4(2)).

Where the Commissioners consider that the requirement of providing environmental information is applicable, they are under a duty to inform appropriate authorities, bodies and persons from amongst those listed in a schedule to the Regulations, and the applicant, of certain matters. The Commissioners are to inform the appropriate authorities, first, of the application and the requirement of an environmental statement and, second, that they may be required to make available to the applicant certain information in their possession which he or they consider relevant to the preparation of the environmental statement (Reg.5(a)). The Commissioners are also to inform the applicant, first, of what they have done by way of informing the appropriate authorities; second, of their view that he should provide an environmental statement; and, third, that he is to supply the authorities with such further information about the proposed development as they may request (Reg.5(b)). If requested by the applicant, any of the bodies informed by the Commissioners of the application are to enter into consultation with him with a view to ascertaining whether they have in their possession any information which is relevant to the preparation of the environmental statement. Where an appropriate authority is in possession of relevant information they are to make that information available to him, providing that no disclosure may be required of information which is held by the authority in confidence (Reg.6).

4.04   *Consultation and publicity*

For the purposes of environmental assessment the Crown Estate Commissioners are bound to consult a range of authorities, bodies and persons in respect of an application for a lease for a coastal fish farm which is likely to have a significant effect upon the environment. The list of consultees for the purposes of environmental assessment are stated, in Schedule 2 of the Salmon Farming in Marine Waters Regulations, to be the following:

1. Any planning authority or any local planning authority whose area adjoins the area of marine waters where the proposed development is to be situated.
2. (a) The Secretary of State for Scotland and the Countryside Commission for Scotland, where the proposed development is to be situated in an area of marine waters adjoining Scotland.
   (b) The Secretary of State for the Environment or the Secretary of State for Wales or both as appropriate, and the Countryside Commission, where the proposed development is to be situated in an area of marine waters adjoining England or Wales.
3. The Nature Conservancy Council.
4. Any river purification board whose area comprises or adjoins the area of marine waters in which the proposed development is to be situated.
5. Any water authority in England and Wales whose area comprises or adjoins the area of marine waters in which the proposed development is to be situated [in future, the National Rivers Authority].
6. Where the proposed development is to be situated in marine waters landward of a line drawn between Burrow Head and St Bees Head – (a) both the North West Water Authority and the Solway River Purification Board; and (b) both the Secretary of State for Scotland and the Secretary of State for the Environment and the Countryside Commission for Scotland and the Countryside Commission.

Where an environmental statement is submitted in support of an application to the Crown Estate Commissioners for a seabed lease, explicit provision is made for the publicity of the statement. In particular, the Commissioners are to publish a notice concerning the statement, as soon as possible, in a newspaper circulating in the locality nearest to the proposed development and in the *Edinburgh Gazette* or *London Gazette*. The notice is to specify, first, a Post Office in the locality nearest the proposed development where the application and environmental statement can be inspected; second, the address at which copies of the application and statement can be acquired; third, the cost of a copy of the environmental statement; and, fourth, that representations in writing may be made within a specified period of not less than 28 days from the date of the notice (Reg.7(1)). The cost of this advertisement is to be met by the applicant (Reg.7(2)).

Provision is also made under the Regulations for consultation between the Commissioners and the appropriate authorities from amongst those under Schedule 2, listed above. The Commissioners are under a duty to consult whichever authorities are appropriate in the circumstances, and also any other persons, groups or bodies they consider appropriate, about the environmental statement (Reg.8(1)). Accordingly, the applicant is to supply the Commissioners with enough copies of the statement to enable them to comply with this consultation duty and one additional copy (Reg.8(2)). Where consultation with any authority, body or person takes place, the Commissioners are to allow 28 days' notice that environmental information is to be taken into consideration, and are not to grant consent for the development until after the expiry of that period (Reg.8(3)). However, any authority, body or person which the Commissioners are obliged to consult, in respect of a particular environmental statement, or statements concerning a class of cases, or cases in a specified area, may notify the Commissioners that consultation is not required (Reg.8(4)).

4.05   *The Environmental Statement*

The information to be provided by way of an environmental statement is essentially the same under both the Environmental Assessment (Salmon Farming in Marine Waters) Regulations 1988 and the Town and Country Planning (Assessment of Environmental Effects) Regulations 1988. (The same formula is also followed in relation to Part II of the Environmental Assessment (Scotland) Regulations 1988.) Schedules to the two sets of Regulations (Sch.1 Environmental Assessment (Salmon Farming in Marine Waters) Regulations 1988; and Sch.3 Town and Country Planning (Assessment of Environmental Effects) Regulations 1988) stipulate that an environmental statement is to comprise a document or series of documents prepared by the applicant and providing information termed 'the specified information', which is stated to be as follows:

(a) a description of the proposed development, comprising information about the site, and the design and the size of the proposed development;
(b) the data necessary to identify and assess the main effects which that development is likely to have on the environment;
(c) a description of the likely significant effects, direct and indirect, on the environment of the proposed development, explained by reference to its impact on: A. human beings; B. flora; C. fauna; D. soil; E. water; F. air; G. climate; H. the landscape; I. the interaction between any of the foregoing; J. material assets; K. the cultural heritage;
(d) where significant adverse effects are identified with respect to any of the foregoing, a description of the measures envisaged in order to avoid, reduce or remedy those effects; and
(e) a summary in non-technical language of the information specified above.

In addition to the details which must be provided by way of specified information, an environmental statement *may* include, by way of explanation or amplification, further information on any of the following matters:

(a) the physical characteristics of the proposed development, and any land use requirements during the construction and operational phases;
(b) the main characteristics of any production processes proposed, including the nature and quality of the materials to be used;
(c) the estimated type and quantity of any expected residues and emissions (including pollutants of water, air, or soil, noise, vibration, light, heat and radiation) resulting from the proposed development, when in operation;

(d) (in outline) the main alternatives, if any, studied by the applicant and an indication of the main reasons for his choice, taking into account the environmental effects;

(e) the likely significant direct and indirect effects, (including secondary, cumulative, short, medium and long-term, permanent and temporary, positive and negative effects) on the environment of the proposed development which may result from: (i) the use of natural resources; (ii) the emission of pollutants, the creation of nuisances, and the elimination of waste;

(f) the forecasting methods used to assess any effects on the environment about which information is given under (e); and

(g) any difficulties, such as technical deficiencies or lack of know-how, encountered in compiling any specified information.

Where further information is provided in an environmental statement pursuant to these provisions, a non-technical summary of that information is also to be provided (Sch.1 Environmental Assessment (Salmon Farming in Marine Waters) Regulations 1988; and Sch.3 Town and Country Planning (Assessment of Environmental Effects) Regulations 1988).

4.06   *The Crown Estate's interpretation of the Regulations*

Clearly the Environmental Assessment (Salmon Farming in Marine Waters) Regulations 1988 are formulated in general terms to satisfy the need for comprehensive implementation of the European Directive in the United Kingdom within the sphere of salmon farming. The Regulations offer relatively little detailed guidance as to the precise kinds of salmon farming projects that will be subject to environmental assessment and the specific kinds of environmental information to be provided. To some extent this lack of detail as to the practical effects of the new level of regulation has been complemented by an announcement by the Crown Estate Commissioners. The Commissioners' announcement provides indications as to the threshold criteria, including location, which will be applied in order to ascertain the kinds of project likely to have a significant effect upon the environment by virtue of their type, scale or location. The announcement also provides an outline of the information which will need to be supplied by an applicant for such a project (Crown Estate (1988)).

In respect of the type of salmon farming development which is likely to have a significant effect upon the environment, the specification which is provided by the Commissioners is broadly formulated to encompass marine salmon farming using fixed equipment installed on the Crown Estate seabed within 2 km of the coast. With regard to the scale of projects likely to require environmental assessment, the criteria indicated are projects with a proposed total cage area of over 6,000 square metres within a 2 km radius in specified sensitive locations, or with a total cage area of 12,000 square metres within a 2 km radius in other areas, along with any scale of project or expansion which would raise the total cage area to that amount. The sensitive locations in respect of which the lower area threshold of 6,000 metres is to apply are stated to be, in Argyll, Lochaber, Skye, West Ross and Sutherland, all sea lochs with a length greater than 2 kms, and in the Western Isles to Loch Roag (Lewis), Loch Maddy (North Uist) and Loch Eynort (South Uist).

The 'Commissioners' guidance on environmental assessment of salmon farming developments indicates that the scope and detail required for projects should be adequate to enable the effects of the project to be assessed. It is stressed, however, that a lengthy or costly report is not expected to be provided. The general aim envisaged for such a report is a presentation of the key facts in a concise statement on five matters:

(a) an expansion of the information in the standard application form on the production methods, type of equipment, area required and reasons for the proposed site, plus indications of potential employment;
(b) a description and illustration of the appearance of the installations and of measures to minimise the effects on the landscape and the amenity of the adjoining area, and on other interests and activities;
(c) an outline of the arrangements for construction, servicing, security and disposal of dead fish; proposals for new onshore development or use of existing buildings or jetties etc.;
(d) estimates of the annual level of production and the volume and dispersal of waste etc. on the seabed, taking account of the configuration, depths and hydrology of the area;
(e) an evaluation of the potential effects on marine ecology, local wildlife and conservation areas, and a description of the proposed anti-predator methods.

As an over-rider to the points of guidance offered by the Commissioners on the situations where environmental assessment will be required, and the information which is to be supplied, it is stressed that the thresholds which are given are to be regarded as indicative criteria rather than rigid rules. The application of environmental assessment to particular projects will ultimately be determined from an initial broad appraisal of the nature of the project and the location.

4.07 *Prospects for environmental assessment*

Despite the novelty of the requirement of environmental assessment as a part of the law, and the difficulty of predicting its practical effect, it is worth reiterating that the provisions which are made for environmental assessment of salmon farming under the 1988 Regulations are likely to be applicable to only a relatively small number of developments. Nonetheless, it is clear from the amount of detail for which they provide that the exercise of environmental assessment is intended to permit thorough prior consideration of the effects of all aspects of a proposed salmon farm upon the environment. On the part of the prospective salmon farmer, where a proposal is likely to have a significant effect upon the environment, preparation of an environmental statement will require careful consideration of the potential harmful effects of the venture upon the environment. On the part of bodies and persons concerned about the adverse effects of further expansion of the salmon farming industry, the publicity and consultation procedures will provide an

additional opportunity to have their opinions considered, and to ensure that
development decisions are made on the strength of the most complete set of
environmental data reasonably available.

Chapter 5

Financial Assistance and Advice for Aquaculture

5.01 *Financial assistance and other benefits for aquaculture*

The proven commercial potential of aquaculture has justified both a range of fiscal and financial measures which have sought to promote the growth of the industry, and the provision of direct awards to assist those embarking upon an aquacultural venture. A guiding principle in the support of fish farming has been that grant aid should not encourage the influx of new entrants to the industry who are ill-prepared for the complexities of profitable fish farm management (Ministry of Agriculture, Fisheries and Food (1981) para.40). On the other side of the balance it is clear that the financial and other advantages and incentives that are available for aquaculture must be of sufficient value to provide an inducement for expansion and not be subject to an excessively bureaucratic application procedure.

The plan of this chapter is to consider the various forms of fiscal benefit, grant aid and benefits in kind available for fish farming. This involves providing an overview of the treatment of aquaculture under rating and tax legislation followed by a discussion of the European Community programme for funding for aquaculture developments and the provisions of domestic legislation which complement this scheme. Finally, consideration is given to the legal provision for research, development and advice in relation to fish farming.

5.02 *The rating of fish farms*

Amongst the fiscal provisions bringing significant benefit to the aquaculture industry are valuable concessions made in relation to rating liabilities of fish farms. It has been noted that the de-rating of fish farms represents a major financial contribution for the industry from public funds (Ministry of Agriculture, Fisheries and Food (1981) para.39). The legal mechanism by which this financial redistribution is accomplished in England and Wales is through s.31 of the Local Government, Planning and Land Act 1980, which inserted a new section, s.26A, in the General Rate Act 1967. (Contrast the previous position: see Markson (1976).) The inserted section provides that neither land nor buildings, other than dwellings, are to be liable to rates or to be included in any valuation list if used solely for, or in connection with, fish farming (s.26A(1) Local Government, Planning and Land Act 1967).

Further rating concession is made in relation to the gross value for rating purpose of a dwelling house occupied in connection with land or buildings used solely for, or in connection with, fish farming. The concession applies where a dwelling house in this category is occupied by a person who is primarily engaged in carrying on or directing fish farming operations, or is employed in fish farming operations on the land in the service of the occupier and is entitled to use the house only while so employed. In such a case the ratable value is to be estimated by reference to the rent at which the house might reasonably be expected to be let under agricultural occupancy (s.26A(2)). In relation to the question of whether land or a building is used *solely* in connection with fish farming it is specified that no account is to be taken of any time during which it is used in any other way if that time does not amount to a substantial part of the time during which the land or building is used for or in connection with fish farming (s.26A(3)). The definition of 'fish farming' which is used for the purposes of rating concessions is that of the breeding or rearing of fish or the cultivation of shellfish (including crustaceans and molluscs of any description) for the purpose of producing food for human consumption or for the transfer to other waters. Specifically, however, this is stated not to include the breeding, rearing or cultivation of any fish or shellfish which are purely ornamental, or which are bred, reared or cultivated for exhibition (s.26A(4)).

In Scotland, rating exemptions are differently formulated from those in England and Wales, but in essence the position with regard to fish farms is substantially the same. Rating exemption for fish farms in Scotland is brought about by s.32 of the Local Government, Planning and Land Act 1980 which provides for the insertion of an additional section, s.7A, in the Valuation and Rating (Scotland) Act 1956. This insertion provides that, for the purposes of any rating valuation roll, no lands and heritages used solely for, or in connection with, fish farming, or buildings other than dwelling houses, are to be entered in the roll. Similarly, land occupied together with and used solely in connection with fish farm buildings is not to be entered in the valuation roll (s.7A(2) and (3) Valuation and Rating (Scotland) Act 1956). Reductions of the ratable value of dwelling houses occupied in conjunction with fish farms are also provided for where used by a person engaged primarily in carrying on or directing fish farming operations on the lands concerned, or employed in connection with fish farming on such lands (ss.7(5) to (8) and 7A(4)). For the purposes of these exemptions the definition of 'fish farming' is the same as that applied for rating purposes in England and Wales (s.7A(8)).

5.03   Taxation and fish farming

The tax implications of fish farming are a matter of some complexity and, in some respects, uncertainty, but it appears that a number of general fiscal benefits are available to fish farmers. In the first place a problem of definition arises in that 'farming' is characterised for tax purposes in terms of the husbandry of farm land with no reference to the breeding or cultivation of fish (s.832(1) Income and Corporation Taxes Act 1988). The interpretation of this adopted by the Inland Revenue, however, is that 'husbandry' is to be understood as any method of rearing of livestock or fish on a commercial basis for the production of food for human consumption (Inland Revenue (1980) para.1). This definition has been incorporated into law in relation to agricultural buildings allowances (s.56(4)(c) Finance Act 1986). On another interpretation, however, it has been suggested that 'husbandry' involves some degree of dependence on the land which may be lacking in circumstances where fish are reared in man-made tanks and fed specially prepared food-pellets, and accordingly the scope of fish farming should be limited to activities taking place in natural lakes and rivers (Golding (1987)). The uncertainty surrounding the resolution of this fundamental matter is highly unsatisfactory.

Supposing that fish farming does fall within the 'husbandry' criterion for taxation purposes, a range of fiscal benefits available to farming activities may be claimed in relation to aquaculture. The facility exists for profits and losses to be averaged out over a period of years to even out the effects of different rates of tax applying in years of high and low profitability (s.28 Finance Act 1978). Capital allowances can be claimed in relation to expenditure incurred on the construction, reconstruction or alteration of agricultural buildings at relief rate of 4 per cent per annum (s.56 Finance Act 1986). Alternatively, expenditure on plant and machinery is eligible for relief at 25 per cent per annum where it is established that it serves some functional use in relation to the business. The different rates of relief available for capital and plant and machinery allowances mean that in borderline cases there are advantages in claiming plant and machinery allowances if doubt exists as to the category of the expenditure (Robertson, J.P. (1988)).

Another valuable fiscal allowance which may be claimable in relation to fish farming arises in relation to scientific research expenditure. Where a fish farmer pays a sum to a scientific research institution, which has amongst its objects research into aquaculture, it is possible to reclaim a 100 per cent deduction either as a revenue deduction, or in respect of capital expenditure (s.90 Capital Allowances Act 1968). Similarly, if scientific research is undertaken by a fish farmer himself, or by some person on his behalf, the same 100 per cent allowance will be available (s.91).

Fish farming also has special fiscal implications in relation to the imposition of value added tax. In particular, Item 4 to Group 1 of Schedule 5 to the Value Added Tax Act 1983 specifies that live animals of a kind generally used as food for human consumption are zero-rated supplies for value added tax purposes. The interpretation of this provision was the subject of the somewhat inconclusive recent decision in *Commissioners of Customs and Excise* v. *Lawson-Tancred* ([1988] STC 326) where the fish concerned were live Dinkelsbuhl and Scaly carp which could be used for ornamental purposes or for stocking angling waters. It was the taxpayers' contention, however, that the particular fish were bred for supply to stores and restaurants for human consumption, and the matter turned on the question of whether the fish were of a kind 'generally' used for that purpose. Although the Value Added Tax Tribunal found in favour of the taxpayer, on appeal it was held that the reasoning of the Tribunal was unclear and the matter was remitted for consideration by a fresh tribunal with the direction that the word 'generally' should be applied in its ordinary sense. The principle of zero-rating of live fish for human consumption remains despite this decision, though its precise extent remains to be determined in relation to species of fish such as carp. (See also, Value Added Tax (Imported Goods) Relief Order, SI 1984 No.746, Sch.2, Group 2 Agriculture and Animals.)

5.04   *European financial assistance*

The direct provision of financial assistance for aquaculture projects is the subject of a scheme formulated by the Council of Ministers of the European Communities. Experience having shown that the development of aquaculture has helped to improve fish production in the Community, it was resolved by the Council that further financial encouragement should be provided in this sector. In December 1986 the European Council agreed to a regulation to improve and adapt structures in the fisheries and aquaculture sectors (EEC Council Reg. No.4028/86). On the expiry of previous Community measures for developing aquaculture (Reg. No.2908/83 as amended by Reg. No.3733/85) it was resolved that Community financial assistance should be made available within the framework of a multi-annual budget extending until the end of 1996. The objective behind the aquacultural improvement programme is to achieve a balanced exploitation of internal resources of Community waters and to improve the overall Community deficit in fish products.

Under the 1986 Council Regulation on aquaculture it is provided that member states of the European Community are each to adopt a 'multi-annual guidance programme'. This is a set of objectives for fisheries and aquaculture, together with a statement of means necessary for attaining them, as a guide to the overall long-term development of the sector within the area of the member state. In respect of aquaculture this is specified to involve the development of technically viable and profitable facilities for the farming of fish, crustaceans or molluscs (Art.2 Regulation to improve and adapt structures in the fisheries and aquaculture sectors). As a means to this end the European Commission of the Community may grant financial assistance for the development of aquaculture. This aid may be granted for public, semi-public or private projects relating to physical investments in the construction, equipment, modernisation or extension of aquaculture installations (Art.11(1)(a)). In order to qualify for aid of this kind a particular project must form a part of a national multi-annual guidance programme approved by the Commission, and must involve investment greater than a specified minimum amount (Art.11(2)). In addition, the project must be for a purely commercial purpose, it must be implemented by a person possessing sufficient occupational competence, and must offer a satisfactory assurance of yielding a profit in due course (Art.11(3)). In the case of shellfish farming projects member states are to ensure that such projects are implemented at locations where the water quality is maintained in accordance with the relevant national or Community provisions applicable (Art.11(4); contrast European Community provision on shellfish waters, discussed in [10.06] below).

The financial constraints imposed upon the availability of Community financial assistance provide that an aquaculture project must involve investment totaling more than 50,000 European Currency Units, approximately £32,000, before it is eligible for aid (Art.11(2)). The maximum amount of investment which is eligible for aid is 3 million ECU, approximately £1,907,000, in the case of aquaculture projects comprising the construction of hatchery and on-growing units, and 1.8 million ECU (£1,144,000) in respect of other projects (Art.12(2)). In relation to the amount of eligible investment in each particular project, the aid to be granted by the Community is set at 25 per cent, whilst the financial contribution by the member state concerned is between 10 per cent and 25 per cent in most of the Community. In the case of some regions, classified as 'disadvantaged areas', however, the Commission recognises that there is a need for additional support and allows a higher rate of grant. Hence in disadvantaged areas the amount of Community aid to projects is increased to 40 per cent, with the financial contributions from member states required to be between 10 per cent and 30 per cent. In respect of the United Kingdom, disadvantaged areas include Northern Ireland, and the West of Scotland which, for these purposes, is taken to mean Dumfries and Galloway, the Western Isles, Orkney and Shetland, together with the districts of Caithness, Sutherland, Ross and Cromarty, Skye and Lochalsh, Lochaber, Argyll and Bute, Cunninghame, Kyle and Carrick (Art.12(1) and Annex III). These rates of support are raised by five percentage points in the case of mariculture, mussel farming or shellfish farming projects which are implemented within the framework of redeployment schemes for sea-fishermen and which provide for the scrapping of operational fishing vessels (Art.12(1)).

5.05 The Multi-annual Guidance Programme for Aquaculture

As has been observed, the availability of European financial assistance for aquaculture is dependent upon a project forming a part of the multi-annual guidance programme for the member state concerned. The latest multi-annual guidance programme for aquaculture in the United Kingdom, drawn up within the framework of the European Council's aquaculture improvement Regulation, was prepared and approved by the Commission in 1987 and covers the five-year period to the end of 1991 (Ministry of Agriculture, Fisheries and Food (1987A)). The Programme constitutes a generally formulated account of the overall state of aquaculture in the United Kingdom, the policy priorities for the industry, and the mechanisms by which improvements are to be pursued over the period of the Programme. The existing base of the aquaculture industry in the United Kingdom was identified as the 900 fish farming businesses operating from 1400 sites and employing 3000 persons. The turnover of this sector is estimated to be about £60m in 1986 but is expected to double by 1990. (In some respects this proved to be an under-estimate: see Ministry of Agriculture, Fisheries and Food (1989).) Primarily production is concentrated upon the intensive rearing of salmon and trout, which account for about 90 per cent of present turnover, but also of importance is the rearing of shellfish including oysters, mussels and clams.

The Programme recognises that there are a number of favourable factors in relation to aquacultural development in the United Kingdom. The area has the geographical advantage of an extensive coastline and river systems providing abundant supplies of both salt water and fresh water; there is freedom from serious fish disease; a good supply of healthy young stock; a vigorous research and development programme; concentration on the species most suited to United Kingdom conditions; continuity of supplies from feed manufacturers; and attention to marketing and quality. Despite these advantages it is noted that the United Kingdom is still far from realising its full potential and progress needs to be made through investment and research to encourage diversification, improved farming techniques, and the cultivation of a wider range of species than at present. Alongside these aims for the industry attention has to be given to the problems of coping with competition from imports and reconciling growth with wider environmental considerations such as that of the waste products generated by intensive rearing practices. The potential for the industry is capable of further enhancement by the growing demand for fish, stimulated by awareness of the health and nutritional value of fish, and the promotional activity of a range of fish producing and marketing organisations.

Given the present base of the aquaculture industry and the potential for expansion, the general aims for the sector set out in the Programme are to foster a viable industry; to encourage the industry to exploit the opportunities for future expansion; to promote greater efficiency so that the industry is better able to adjust to the demands of competition; to encourage the uptake of results of research and development; to provide assured supplies of good quality produce, meeting consumer demand at home and overseas and compensating for diminishing supplies from more traditional hunting and gathering sources; to contribute to development and maintenance of the socio-economic structure in the more remote parts of the United Kingdom by providing employment and rural diversification; and to encourage measures to safeguard the environment. Accordingly, priority is to be given to those projects which conform to these aims and, specifically, projects concerned with raising on-farm environmental standards; improving rearing systems and techniques; developing stress- and disease-resistant strains of fish; developing techniques for rearing strains or species of marine fish capable of sustaining profitable growth at lower temperatures; utilizing warm water sources for on-growing, providing hatchery and nursery facilities; and encouraging diversification and more efficient methods of cultivation.

Alongside a fairly detailed account of the present farmed output of fish, and production estimates for the output in 1991 at end of the period of the Programme, it is observed that increased production will partly depend on improving efficiency and techniques as well as on the outcome of continuing research and development programmes. Although the difficulty of estimating the levels of investment which are required to achieve the production targets for 1991 is recognised, it is suggested that the amount required could be in the order of £30 million to £40 million a year. Of this amount it is indicated that national financial support for aquaculture is available under a range of regional industrial and rural development schemes and is guaranteed for all projects which qualify for European Community assistance.

5.06   *The Ministry's explanatory leaflet*

Guidance on the practical implications of the European Community scheme of financial assistance for aquaculture is provided in an explanatory leaflet issued by the Ministry of Agriculture, Fisheries and Food and the other fisheries departments in the United Kingdom, that is, the Department of Agriculture and Fisheries for Scotland, the Welsh Office Agriculture

Department, and the Department of Agriculture for Northern Ireland. The leaflet indicates that applications are restricted to projects for the construction, extension, or modernisation of installations for rearing fish, crustaceans or molluscs which come within the National Multi-annual Programme for Aquaculture, described above. Suitable projects must have a capacity sufficient to ensure sustained commercial operation and offer a satisfactory guarantee of yielding a profit. Hence, in assessing individual projects, specific attention will be paid to their long-term technical practicability and economic profitability. Applicants will need to demonstrate, by reference to a detailed marketing plan, that a market exists or can be secured for any increased production brought about by their enterprise, and that the project will constitute a lasting economic improvement in the structure of the aquaculture industry.

In view of the limited funds available, the Leaflet stresses that particular importance will be attached to a range of factors concerned with improvement in the supply of farmed species or the conditions under which these species are farmed, in determining which projects will receive preference. For example, in respect of trout and carp culture, particular priority will be given to projects which will reduce pollution and mortality in ponds. In addition, account will be taken of the extent to which projects provide for the diversification of economic activity, through the catching or rearing of certain species of fish, crustaceans or molluscs, and the interests of consumers in relation to the project. Also, projects must be carried out by individuals or companies who have sufficient professional competence in the area of aquaculture which is proposed, and importance will be attached to membership of a fishery producers organisation, where one exists.

Qualification for a Community grant is dependent upon both approval by the Government of the United Kingdom, and receipt of a firm offer of a grant of at least 10 per cent from national funds, though in no case must the amount from national funds exceed the maximum amounts allowed by the European Commission. Any grant scheme in the United Kingdom may serve to provide the qualifying grant, but in the event of a project failing to be awarded a grant from any other scheme, the 10 per cent grant may be made available by the appropriate fisheries department within the United Kingdom. In the final outcome, grant aid from a fisheries department is only paid if the project is actually awarded a Community grant, and only then if no other national aid of 10 per cent or more has been obtained by the applicant.

The Commission reserves the right to suspend, reduce or discontinue a grant under certain circumstances. These are, that the project is not carried out as specified; conditions which have been imposed are not satisfied; the beneficiary has not, within one year from the notification of the decision to grant the aid, either begun the work or supplied satisfactory assurances that the project will be carried out; or the project is not completed within two years of commencement. Likewise, payments may be recovered if conditions of the scheme are breached. As a condition of receiving a grant a beneficiary will be required to submit a report on the outcome of the project, particularly the financial results achieved, two years after the payment of grant is made, or five years in the case of coastal marine areas. The report is to be made to the Commission through the appropriate fisheries department.

5.07   *Other sources of financial assistance*

The availability of Community funding for aquacultural projects is, in all cases, dependent upon the applicant having first obtained a minimum 10 per cent of the project cost by way of a financial contribution from national funds. At the other extreme, a project will be ineligible for Community aid if the contribution from national bodies exceeds 30 per cent of the project cost in disadvantaged areas, or 25 per cent of the cost in other areas. Although, as has been noted, it is possible for the contribution from national funds to be met by a grant from the appropriate fisheries department, a grant of this kind will only be available where the applicant has been unsuccessful in obtaining aid from any other public body. Notably, there are a range of possible sources from which funding and low interest loans for aquacultural projects may be obtained, before fisheries departments are approached (Edwards (1987) and (1988)). Amongst the most important alternative souces of aquaculture funding are those made available by the Department of Trade and Industry, and the Highlands and Islands Development Board.

In 'assisted areas' of Great Britain, as provided for under the Industrial Development Act 1982, the Department of Trade and Industry may make available funds for a project where certain criteria of eligibility can be satisfied. Specifically, it must be shown that assistance is necessary for the commencement of a project which will create new, or safeguard existing, jobs, and that the project will be viable. Where these requirements are met, however, care is taken to avoid double-funding from other government departments. The amount which is payable under this scheme is a discretionary amount with no fixed rates specified.

The Highlands and Islands Development Board makes available funding for projects in the following regions of Scotland: Shetland, Orkney, Western Isles, Highland Region, Argyll and Bute District of Strathclyde Region, the Isle of Arran in the Cunninghame District and Cumbrae, and grants at special rates may be available for schemes in the Western Isles offered assistance under the Integrated Development Programme. Within these areas the Board considers applications for the establishment of new fish farms and improvement, expansion or restocking of existing farms. A grant will only apply to projects which are of special development value and to supplement other forms of assistance. In any case applicants are required to raise 50 per cent of the project cost. A grant made available from this source will not normally exceed 30 per cent of the project cost.

There are also a range of bodies that are able to provide smaller amounts of support and loans for fish farming. These include the Council of Small Industries in Rural Areas, the Welsh Office Industry Department, along with other sources such as local authorities who are occasionally in a position to support fish farming ventures.

5.08   *The Fisheries Act 1981*

Two pieces of national legislation link the availability of Community aid for aquaculture and the power of national fisheries departments to make available the necessary element of national funding. The first of these is the Fisheries Act 1981, s.31 of which enables the appropriate Government ministers to make grants for fish farming in accordance with a scheme devised by them for that purpose. The second provision is a statutory instrument, the Fish Farming (Financial Assistance) Scheme 1987 (SI 1987 No.1134) which specifies the details of the scheme for providing financial assistance for aquaculture.

The enabling power under s.31 of the Fisheries Act 1981 commences by stating that the appropriate Ministers may, in accordance with a scheme made by them with the approval of the Treasury, make such grants as appear to them to be desirable for the purpose of reorganising, developing or promoting fish farming in Great Britain (s.31(1) Fisheries Act 1981). The 'Ministers' concerned are, in England, the Minister of Agriculture, Fisheries and Food, and the respective Secretaries of State concerned with fisheries in Wales and Scotland, the involvement of each of whom is dependent upon the availability of grants within their respective countries (s.31(5)). The exercise of this power to provide financial assistance for fish farming may be confined to the making of grants which are necessary to enable persons to benefit from any Community instrument which provides for the making of grants by a Community institution where such grants are also provided by a member State (s.31(3)). That is to say, the scheme may be used by the Ministers as a means to the particular end of rendering persons eligible for Community aquaculture funding who would not otherwise be eligible, rather than as a general scheme for the funding of fish farming enterprises.

Significantly, the ministerial power to make grants for fish farming in accordance with the scheme is to be read in conjunction with the definition of 'fish farming' provided for this purpose. That is, 'fish farming' means the breeding, rearing or cultivating of fish (including shellfish, defined as crustaceans and molluscs of any kind (s.44)) for the purpose of producing food for human consumption (s.31(2)). Notably, this definition of fish farming is narrower than that implicit in the Community Regulation. The Community Regulation providing for aquacultural funding states that appropriate projects must be for 'a purely commercial purpose' (Art.11(3) EEC Council Regulation No.2908/83). In theory, therefore, a project involving the rearing of fish for a commercial purpose other than the production of food for human consumption could fall outside any funding scheme which the Ministers were lawfully empowered to devise. In practice, however, projects are limited to those involving the rearing of fish for food.

As with other areas of the law of aquaculture (see [2.06] above) the problem of ascertaining whether particular fish are actually being produced for human consumption is capable of being a significant, if not insoluble, practical difficulty. As the Earl of Swinton observed in the House of Lords Debate on this point:

'I was also very puzzled by the expression that only fish "for human consumption" was to be eligible for these grants and I wondered how on earth one told the difference between the two. On my trout farm – and I am quite certain that I am not unique in this country – I have trout which go out to stock lakes for fishermen. I suppose that one could say that trout in Pool X are going mostly for the table and those in Pool Y are going for fishing. On the other hand, I get people who ring up in the morning and say that they want so many trout either for a restaurant or else for stocking a pool and, until the things go off in the truck, I have no idea whether those fish have been produced for human consumption or not. I wonder how that is to be got around.' (419 I IL DEB 1981 Cols. 141 to 142)

A number of specific criminal offences are created in relation to the operation of the scheme for provision of grants for fish farming (s.31(8) Fisheries Act 1981). In the first place, it is an offence for a person furnishing information purporting to comply with a requirement imposed by the scheme to make a statement which he knows to be false in a material particular or recklessly to make a statement which is false in a material particular (s.17(a)). Second, it is an offence for a person purporting to comply with a requirement imposed by the scheme to produce a document which he knows to be false in a material particular or recklessly to produce a document which is false in a material particular (s.17(b)). Third, it is an offence wilfully to refuse to supply any information, or to make any return or produce any document when required to do so by or under the scheme (s.17(c)). In respect of any of these three offences, a person found guilty will be liable on summary conviction to a fine not exceeding level 5 on the standard scale, which is presently set at £2,000 (s.17).

5.09   The Fish Farming (Financial Assistance) Scheme

As previously stated, s.31 of the Fisheries Act 1981 is an enabling provision which merely empowers the appropriate ministers to award grants for fish farming in accordance with a scheme of their own devising. It does not, therefore, seek to establish the detailed terms of the scheme for funding fish farming. These are provided for by statutory instrument in the form of the Fish Farming (Financial Assistance) Scheme 1987 (SI 1987 No.1134) which became operative from 4 July 1987, in the place of previous schemes (Marine Fish Farming (Financial Assistance) Scheme 1981, SI 1981 No.1653; and Fish Farming (Financial Assistance) Scheme 1984, SI 1984 No.341). The precise details of the Scheme are now to be found set out in this instrument.

The Scheme provides that the appropriate Minister may make a grant to any person towards expenditure incurred, or to be incurred, in connection with a project for fish farming, if two criteria are satisfied. These are, that a grant appears to the Minister to be desirable for the purposes of the reorganisation, development or promotion of fish farming in England, Scotland or Wales, and to be required to enable the applicant to benefit from Community aid for a fish farming project covered by the Council Regulation on Community measures to improve the aquaculture sector, discussed above (s.3(1) Fish Farming (Financial Assistance) Scheme 1987; and see Arts.11 and 12 EEC Council Regulation No.4028/86).

Applications for ministerial approval of expenditure for the purposes of a grant under the Scheme are to be made in a form determined by the Minister, and it is for the applicant to furnish all the information relating to the application required (s.3(6)). The Minister is not to make a grant, however, unless he has approved the expenditure in writing for the purposes of the grant, and a decision that the project shall receive Community aid has been taken and notified to the United Kingdom in accordance with the Council Regulation (s.3(2), and see Art.35 of the Council Regulation concerning notification). The Minister may approve the expenditure in whole or in part, and approval may be given subject to such conditions as he thinks fit (s.3(3)). Having been approved, any approval of expenditure for the purposes of a grant may be varied or withdrawn by the Minister with the applicant's written consent (s.3(4)). If not withdrawn, any payment by way of a grant under this Scheme may be made at a time, or by instalments at intervals or times, as the Minister may determine (s.3(5)).

Since the primary purpose of the Scheme is to achieve eligibility for Community aquaculture funding for projects in Britain, the amount of a grant is limited to the minimum amount of national funding required to obtain Community aid. Hence the maximum amount of grant which may be paid under the Scheme is 10 per cent of the expenditure incurred, or to be incurred, as approved by the Commission in deciding the amount of Community aid which the project is to receive (s.4(1)). Provision is made for the 'topping up' of grants from other national funds by an additional grant under the Scheme to enable the project to receive Community aid from the Commission (s.4(2)). That is, the Scheme will meet, but not exceed, the shortfall between the other national funds which are available and the overall 10 per cent national grant aid which is required to obtain Community funding for an aquaculture project.

Provision is made in the Scheme for the revocation of approval and recovery of grants for up to six years after payment has been made in certain circumstances. Hence the Minister may revoke the approval in respect of the whole or part of the expenditure and, where any payment has been made he may, on demand, recover all, or a specified part of the payment. The circumstances in which grants may be revoked or recovered are where it appears to the Minister that any of the following criteria is satisfied: first, that any condition subject to which the approval was given has not been complied with; second, that any work in respect of expenditure for which the approval was given has been badly done, or has been or is being unreasonably delayed, or is unlikely to be completed; third, that the person by whom the application for approval, or for the making of any payment, was made gave information on any matter relevant to the giving of the approval or the making of the payment which was false or misleading in a material respect; fourth, that the Commission has decided under Article 44(1) of the Council Regulation to suspend, reduce or discontinue Community aid and to recover any sums paid. In the first three contingencies particular procedures are set out for the Minister to follow in order to revoke or recover grant aid. First, the Minister is to give to the person to whom payment by way of grant would be payable, or from whom it would be recoverable, a written notification of the reasons for the proposed action; second, the Minister is to afford that person an opportunity of appearing before and being heard by a person appointed for the purpose by the Minister; and, third, the Minister is to consider the report by a person so appointed and supply a copy of the report to the person in respect of whom the grant is revoked or reclaimed (s.5).

5.10   Fish farming research, development and advice

As a final form of advantage conferred upon aquaculture it is pertinent to mention the facility which exists for the provision of research, development and advice in relation to fish farming. Section 32 of the Fisheries Act 1981 empowered the Minister of Agriculture, Fisheries and Food and the Secretaries of State respectively concerned with fisheries in Scotland and Wales each to carry out research and development on fish farming. The purpose of this power was stated to be promoting the breeding, rearing or cultivating of fish, including shellfish, for the purpose of producing food for human consumption (s.32(1) Fisheries Act 1981).

In association with the conduct of research and development each of the Ministers is empowered to provide scientific, technical and other advice and instruction on matters relating to the breeding, rearing or cultivation of fish including shellfish. Significantly, however, the provision of advice is not limited to the purpose of producing food for human consumption (s.32(2)). It appears somewhat incongruous that provision is made for advice to be given in areas in which there is no power to conduct research and development, but it is likely that scientific principles involved in rearing fish for human consumption will not differ greatly from those applicable to rearing fish for other purposes. Fees may be charged for any advice or instruction provided in exercise of this power (s.32(3)).

Clearly fisheries research is a significant head of research expenditure, and in relation to fish farming alone it was reported that the Government spent some £3.2 million on research and development in 1988/89, and plans to spend a similar level of expenditure in the following financial year (151 HC DEB 1989 Col. *671*). Much of this money goes to fund the valuable work conducted by the Directorate of Fisheries Research of the Ministry of Agriculture, Fisheries and Food (details of work undertaken are to be found in Ministry of Agriculture, Fisheries and Food (1987B)) and research expenditure of the Department of Agriculture and Fisheries for Scotland. It may be noted also that fisheries research is also undertaken into sea fisheries, and in particular the farming of shellfish, by the Sea Fish Industry Authority, though the position of the authority in relation to fish farming is considered later in the text (see [15.06] below).

Chapter 6

The Licensing and Registration of Fish Farms

6.01   The licensing of fish farms

A common means of exercising legal and administrative control over a potentially harmful activity is to make it subject to prior licensing requirements, and to create criminal offences in circumstances where the requirements are infringed. A less severe method of control, coming closer to a means of keeping an account of the level of participation in the activity, is to subject the activity to a requirement of registration so that those involved in the activity must inform the appropriate administrative authority of the nature of their involvement. Both of these mechanisms exist in relation to the enterprise of fish farming though, for reasons of policy, the licensing power is presently unused. The registration requirement, however, is of considerable importance to those engaged in all kinds of fish farming in Britain.

Considering, first, the unused licensing power, this arises from a somewhat mysterious provision in s.29 of the Salmon and Freshwater Fisheries Act 1975 relating to the licensing of businesses rearing salmon or trout in England and Wales. This provides that the Minister of Agriculture, Fisheries and Food may grant a licence to carry on the business of artificially propagating or rearing salmon or trout in any waters in England or Wales (s.29(1) Salmon and Freshwater Fisheries Act 1975). No further details concerning the nature of the licence which is envisaged by this provision are given other than the stipulation that such a licence may be granted subject to such conditions, if any, as the Minister thinks fit, and may be revoked if he is of the opinion that any condition has not been observed (s.29(2)). Although the Ministerial licensing power arising under this provision is limited to the farming of salmon and trout, it is applicable to the rearing of such fish in 'any waters' and could, therefore, be used to license freshwater or marine fish farming.

The licensing power for fish rearing under the Salmon and Freshwater Fisheries Act is curious in that no indication is provided as to the nature of the licence which is provided for. It does not appear that the holding of a licence of this sort is a prerequisite to carrying on a business of fish farming, or that any offence is committed by failure to obtain such a licence. Moreover it would seem that there are no instances of the use of this provision by the issue of any fish farm licences by the Minister. The Ministry of Agriculture, Fisheries and Food's *Review of Inland and Coastal Fisheries in England and Wales* in 1981, in expressing the general disfavour with which the Government regarded a licensing system governing fish farming, recognised that 'the application of licensing criteria could impose on central Government a responsibility for taking what might be largely subjective decisions on the suitability of new entrants to the fish farming sector' (Ministry of Agriculture, Fisheries and Food (1981) para.32). More recently, the view was iterated in answer to a Parliamentary question that the Government has no plans to extend powers of control over fish farms under the Salmon and Freshwater Fisheries Act 1975, nor to use the provisions under s.29 of the Act (112 HC DEB 1987 Col. 484).

In summary, therefore, it is likely that the fish farm licensing power will remain in abeyance. Although licensing would be a means of exercising considerable control over the expansion of the fish farming industry, it would appear that the Government has no wish to exercise that degree of control. Moreover, the subsequent implementation of the fish farm registration scheme provided for under the Diseases of Fish Act 1983 to facilitate the acquisition of information about fish farming by the fisheries Ministers, discussed below, would seem to render the licensing power under the Salmon and Freshwater Fisheries Act 1975 obsolete and superfluous. Nonetheless, it remains as a legal power capable of being exercised should there be a change of Government policy on fish farming.

6.02   *The registration of fish farms*

A principal objective of the Diseases of Fish Act 1983 was to strengthen the 1937 Diseases of Fish Act in making provision for the control of fish disease. The combined effect of the two enactments in relation to disease control is considered in the following chapter, but it is pertinent to discuss at this point an innovation introduced under the 1983 Act in the form of a scheme of registration of fish farms and the collection of information about fish farms by the Minister with a view to the prevention of the spread of fish disease. The basis of the scheme is that the Minister may exercise a power to require information about various forms of fish farming if it appears necessary to obtain information for the purpose of preventing the spread of disease among fish (s.7(1) Diseases of Fish Act 1983). 'The Minister' means, in relation to England, and any marine waters adjacent to England, the Minister of Agriculture, Fisheries and Food; in relation to Wales and adjacent marine waters, the Secretary of State for Wales; and in relation to Scotland, including the marine waters thereof, the Secretary of State for Scotland (s.7(8)).

The enabling provisions under the 1983 Act permit a Ministerial order to be made for the collection of information about fish farming. An order of this kind may require any person who occupies an inland fish farm for the purposes of a business of fish farming carried on by him, whether or not for profit, to provide certain information. In particular, the following measures are to be taken by the person concerned with regard to the provision of information:

(a) to register the business in a register kept for the purpose by the Minister;
(b) to furnish in writing to the Minister such information as may be specified in the order in relation to the farm and to fish, eggs of fish and foodstuff for fish;
(c) to compile such records as may be specified in relation to the matters mentioned under (b) above; and

(d) to retain for such period, not exceeding three years, as may be specified any records compiled in accordance with (c) above (s.7(2)).

In relation to the provision of this information a number of key terms are explicitly defined. Hence, 'fish farming' is stated to mean the keeping of live fish with a view to their sale or to their transfer to other waters, a broad definition capable of encompassing trade in fish for pet shops as well as conventional fish farming activities. 'Inland fish farm' means any place where inland waters are used for the keeping of live fish with a view to their sale or to their transfer to other waters, whether inland or not. In turn, 'inland waters' means waters within Britain which do not form part of the sea or any creek, bay or estuary or of any river so far as the tide flows (s.7(8)).

Corresponding provisions allow for a Ministerial order to require substantially the same kinds of information to be provided by persons engaged in marine fish farming. Hence any person who owns or possesses any cage, pontoon or other structure which is anchored or moored in marine waters, and is used by him for the purposes of a business of fish farming carried on by him, whether or not for profit, is to take specified measures in providing information (s.7(3)). 'Marine waters' in this context is stated to mean waters, other than inland waters, within the seaward limits of the territorial sea adjacent to Great Britain (s.7(8), and see [3.01] above on the 'territorial sea').

Essentially the same formula is followed in relation to shellfish farming, where any person who carries on a business of shellfish farming, whether or not for profit, may be required under a Ministerial order to provide information relating to similar matters to those detailed in the previous cases (s.7(4)). 'Shellfish farming' is defined to mean the cultivation or propagation of shellfish, whether in marine or inland waters or on land, with a view to their sale or to their transfer to other waters or land. 'Shellfish' includes crustaceans and molluscs of any kind, and includes any brood, ware, half-ware, spat or spawn of shellfish (s.7(8)).

Where a Ministerial order requires a person to register an inland fish farm, or a cage used for the purpose of marine fish farming, or shellfish farming business, under these provisions the order may require the person concerned to pay the Minister a registration fee (s.7(5)). The registration fee is to be an amount determined with the Treasury's approval, but is not to exceed the cost to the Minister of effecting the registration (s.7(6)). In each case, any person authorised by the Minister may, on producing evidence of his authority, on demand, require the production of, and inspect and take copies of, any records which a person is required to retain by virtue of the Ministerial order (s.7(7)).

6.03 *The Registration of Fish Farming Businesses Order 1985*

The provisions under s.7 of the 1983 Act are enabling in that they empower the Minister to make a particular order requiring the registration and provision of information concerning fish farms within the scope provided for by the Act without any compulsion to do so. The Ministerial power has in fact been exercised, however, by the enactment of the Registration of Fish

Farming and Shellfish Farming Businesses Order 1985 (SI 1985 No.1391). This Order requires occupiers of inland fish farms, owners of sea cages used for a business of fish farming and persons carrying on a business of shellfish farming, to register specified particulars of their businesses in the register kept for that purpose by the Minister, within two months of the date on which the business commences. If there is a change in any of the particulars, or the business ceases to operate, this is to be notified to the Minister within one month (Art.3 Registration of Fish Farming and Shellfish Farming Businesses Order 1985). Specifically, the particulars to be provided on registration of the business are stated in Schedule 1 of the 1985 Order to be the following.

Particulars to be notified on registration

Part I

1. The business name, if any.
2. The nature of the business.
3. The name of the person who carries on the business.
4. The address of the business.
5. The telephone number, if any, of the business.
6. The telex number, if any, of the business.
7. The address (or other description) of each site at which fish or shellfish are farmed in the course of business.
8. In relation to each site at which fish or freshwater shellfish are farmed in the course of the business –

   (a) the number and type of fish holding facilities and of shellfish holding facilities;
   (b) the source of the water supply and a statement as to whether that supply is of salt water or fresh water; and
   (c) a statement as to whether effluent water from the site is discharged into any, and if so which, river or other watercourse.

9. In relation to each site at which salt water shellfish are farmed in the course of the business, the number and type of husbandry facilities.

Part II

10. In relation to each site at which fish or shellfish are farmed in the course of the business –

    (a) the name of each species of fish and shellfish that are held at the site;
    (b) in the case of salmon held at the site, a statement whether there are (i) brood fish, (ii) ova, (iii) fry, parr or smolts, and (iv) post-smolts;
    (c) in the case of each species of fish other than salmon held at the site, a statement whether there are (i) brood fish, (ii) ova, (iii) fish weighing up to 5 grams, and (iv) fish weighing more than 5 grams;
    (d) in the case of each species of shellfish held at the site, a statement whether there are (i) larvae or spat, (ii) juvenile shellfish, and (iii) adult shellfish.

The significance of the division of Schedule 1 of the Order into two parts is that if there is any change in the particulars under Part I this is to be notified to the Minister within one month of the change (Art.3(3)). No corresponding notification is required in relation to the matters under Part II. It is notable that though the information to be provided on registration includes details of the fish which are held at a site there is no requirement to disclose the origin of those fish. This is a point of contrast with other information to be provided under the Order which requires the sources of consignments of fish moved onto a site to be disclosed.

The 1985 Order also makes provision for information concerning fish farms to be provided on an annual basis. In respect of each year ending on 30 November, a person who carries on a business of fish farming or shellfish farming is to submit specified information not later than 31 December (Art.4(1)). The information to be furnished on an annual basis is specified in Schedule 2 to the Order as follows.

Information to be furnished annually

Part I: Fish farming business

1. The number of consignments:

    (a) in the case of salmon of (i) ova, (ii) fry, parr or smolts, and (iii) post-smolts, and

    (b) in the case of each species of fish other than salmon of (i) ova, (ii) fish weighing up to 5 grams, and (iii) fish weighing more than 5 grams,

    that were moved on to the site, and from the site for the purpose of stocking other waters.

2. The number:

    (a) in the case of salmon of (i) ova, (ii) fry, parr or smolts, and (iii) post-smolts, and

    (b) in the case of each species of fish other than salmon of (i) ova, (ii) fish weighing up to 5 grams, and (iii) fish weighing more than 5 grams,

    that were moved on to the site, and from the site for the purpose of stocking other waters.

3. A statement whether fish, alive or dead, have been moved on to the site to be eviscerated or processed.

Part II: Shellfish farming businesses

1. In the case of shellfish moved on to the site:

    (a) the number of consignments of each species which have been obtained from hatcheries or nurseries, from shellfish farms, and from wild stocks; and

    (b) the total number or total weight of each species which have been obtained from hatcheries or nurseries, from shellfish farms, and from wild stocks.

2. In the case of shellfish moved off the site for the purpose of stocking other waters:

    (a) the number of consignments of each species; and

(b) the total number or total weight of each species.

Any person carrying on a business of fish farming or shellfish farming, who is required to be registered as such, may be required to furnish a statement as to whether the particulars relating to the business on the register are correct if requested to do so by the Minister. If the particulars on the register are inaccurate the person must, if requested by the Minister, provide accurate particulars in respect of any that are inaccurate (Art.4(2)).

The 1985 Order also makes detailed provision for the keeping of continuing records of fish movements, as envisaged under the Act. Specifically, the Order provides that a person who carries on a business of fish farming or shellfish farming is to compile a record of specified information detailed in Schedule 3 to the Order. The information required for these purpose is as follows.

Particulars to be included in records

Part I: Fish farming businesses

1. In respect of each consignment of fish or ova moved on to the site:

    (a) the date of the movement,
    (b) the species,
    (c) the number,
    (d) in the case of salmon, a statement as whether the consignment consisted of ova, fry, parr, smolts or post-smolts,
    (e) in the case of fish other than salmon, a statement as to whether the consignment consisted of ova, fish weighing up to 5 grams or fish weighing more than 5 grams,
    (f) the source, and
    (g) the name of the carrier.

2. In respect of each consignment of fish or ova moved from the site:

    (a) the date of the movement,
    (b) the species,
    (c) the number,
    (d) in the case of salmon, a statement as to whether the consignment consisted of ova, fry, parr, smolts or post-smolts,
    (e) in the case of fish other than salmon, a statement as to whether the consignment consisted of ova, fish weighing up to 5 grams or fish weighing more than 5 grams,
    (f) the destination, and
    (g) the name of the carrier.

Part II: Shellfish farming businesses

1. In respect of each consignment of shellfish moved on to the site:

    (a) the date of the movement,
    (b) the species,
    (c) the number or weight,
    (d) the average size or weight,

(e) the source, and
(f) the name of the carrier.

2. In respect of each consignment of shellfish moved from the site for the purpose of stocking other waters:

   (a) the date of the movement,
   (b) the species,
   (c) the number or weight,
   (d) the average size or weight,
   (e) the destination, and
   (f) the name of the carrier.

In each case the information is to be entered in the record within 24 hours of the occurrence of the event to which the particulars relate (Art.5(2)). The information recorded is to be retained for three years by the person carrying on the business to which the records relate (Art.5(3)).

6.04   *Enforcement and disclosure provisions*

Contravention of the provisions with respect to the registration of fish farms and provision of information about fish farming is an offence punishable, on summary conviction, by a maximum fine set at level 4 on the standard scale, presently equivalent to £1,000. This offence is committed by any person who:

(a) fails without reasonable excuse to comply with a requirement of a Ministerial order made for the provision of information about fish farming (under s.7 Diseases of Fish Act 1983) other than a requirement as to the payment of a fish farm registration fee, or
(b) in purported compliance with a requirement of a Ministerial order for the provision of information about fish farming (under s.7) knowingly furnishes any information or compiles a record which is false in a material particular, or
(c) knowingly alters a record compiled in compliance with a requirement of a Ministerial order for the provision of information about fish farming (under s.7) so that the record is false in a material particular, or
(d) fails without reasonable excuse to produce information or to allow the inspection or taking of copies of any records required to be retained, by virtue of a Ministerial order for the provision of information about fish farming (under s.7) when required to do so by a person authorised by the Minister, or
(e) intentionally obstructs a person authorised by the Minister requiring the production or inspection or taking copies of any records which are required to be kept by ministerial order (under s.7) in the exercise of his powers (s.8(1)).

Special provision for individual as well as collective culpability is made in respect of offences concerning information about fish farming committed by corporate entities such as limited companies. Hence where an offence is committed by a corporate body and is proved to have been committed with the consent or connivance of, or to be attributable to any neglect on the part of, a director, manager, secretary or other similar officer of the body corporate, or any person who was purporting to act in any such capacity, he, as well as the body corporate will be guilty of the offence and will be liable to be proceeded against and punished accordingly (s.8(2)). In order to avoid difficulties which might otherwise arise in relation to the territorial jurisdiction of courts to hear cases concerning offences committed offshore, explicit provision is made concerning the jurisdiction of courts. Thus it is provided that for the purposes of any magistrates' court, or in Scotland the sheriff, any offence committed in, or in relation to anything in, the territorial sea adjacent to Britain, is to be taken to have been committed in any place where the offender may for the time being be found (s.8(3)).

The information provided under the 1983 Act is likely to be of great assistance in preventing the spread of fish disease and collection of information for that purpose will be of general benefit to the fish farming industry despite the administrative inconvenience to which individual fish farmers may be put in maintaining records of fish, eggs and foodstuff. Given the commercially competitive nature of the fish farming industry it is evident that information relating to the productivity and organisation of fish farms is unavoidably of commercial sensitivity, and should not be made available for purposes other than those for which it was originally provided. In order to safeguard the confidentiality of information provided under a Ministerial order specific offences are created in relation to the improper disclosure of information provided for the purpose of preventing the spread of fish disease. Hence, information obtained in pursuance of a Ministerial order (under s.7) is not to be disclosed except

(a) with the written consent of the person by whom the information was provided, or
(b) in the form of a summary of similar information obtained from a number of persons, where the summary is framed so as not to enable particulars relating to any one person or business to be ascertained from it, or
(c) for the purposes of any criminal proceedings or for the purpose of a report of any such proceedings (s.9(1)), or
(d) for the purpose of enabling the National Rivers Authority to carry out any of its functions under the Diseases of Fish Act 1937 (added by s.38 Salmon Act 1986, and amended by s.141 and Sch.17 para.3 Water Act 1989; on the Diseases of Fish Act 1937 see Chapter 7 below).

The sanction behind this prohibition upon disclosure is that any person who discloses fish farming information in contravention of these provisions will be guilty of an offence and liable to a fine not exceeding level 4 on the standard scale, which presently stands at the sum of £1,000 (s.9(2)).

Chapter 7

Disease Regulation

7.01 The problem of fish disease

Diseases constitute a problem for any intensive form of agriculture, not least
aquaculture. The frequent transfer of fish between farms, and their close
containment in an aquatic medium, facilitate the rapid transmission of
disease through fish farm stock and potentially to and from wild fish in the
vicinity. It is, therefore, of vital importance both to fish farming and to the
general aquatic environment that all practicable measures are taken to
prevent the spread of fish disease. (Practical advice for fish farmers on this
matter is provided in National Farmers' Union (1984A).) The legal provisions
which seek to achieve this objective are the subject matter of this chapter, but
it is to be emphasised that the practical application of this area of the law is
heavily dependent upon the application of a good deal of scientific learning
concerning the nature and varieties of fish diseases and their diagnosis and
treatment. This topic is clearly placed outside the scope of this work and the
interested reader should consult texts providing coverage of the pathological
aspects of the subject. (Useful coverage in relation to trout and salmon is·
provided by Roberts and Shepherd (1986); and generally see Huet (1986)
Ch.XV S.II; and Blake (1983) pp.31 to 35.)

Another feature of the regulation of fish disease which is usefully noted at
this point is the relationship between this chapter and the next, dealing with
controls upon the movement of fish. Clearly the action of restricting the
movement of fish is one of the principal means of preventing the spread of
fish disease. Restrictions on fish movement are also imposed for a variety of
other reasons. For example, the introduction of new species of fish into
waters may constitute an ecological hazard arising through competition with
native species, independently of any threat of disease brought by the
introduced species. Although it is inevitable that there is some overlap
between this chapter and the following one, the broad division of subject
matter is that this chapter is concerned with disease control including
movement restrictions, whilst the next chapter deals with movement
controls arising, primarily, for a range of other purposes.

7.02 The Diseases of Fish Acts 1937 and 1983

The first legal provision concerning fish disease was the Diseases of Fish Act
1937, which was originally passed with the principal object of controlling and,
if possible, eradicating furunculosis in wild fisheries. This disease had first
been recognised early in the century, and was thought to have been imported

from the Continent. It spread rapidly through many of the salmon and trout rivers of England, Wales and Scotland, causing heavy mortality (319 HC DEB 1937 Col. 1567). The original objective of eradicating furunculosis proved to be over-optimistic, in that the disease is now endemic and constitutes a major source of loss in fish farming operations, but the general mechanism of control provided for under the Act was thought to be an effective legal means to prevent the introduction, or minimise the spread, of serious fish disease where containable outbreaks were identified and movement controls applied. The scope of the 1937 Act has subsequently been amended by a series of later orders to permit the same control measures, initially provided for in respect of furunculosis, to be followed in relation to a number of other 'prescribed', or 'notifiable', fish diseases.

In addition to the amendments of the list of prescribed diseases, the 1937 Act has been substantially extended by measures introduced under the Diseases of Fish Act 1983. In addition to providing for the registration of fish farms for disease prevention purposes, described in the previous chapter, the 1983 Act sought to bring the law into alignment with those needs of the modern fish farming industry which had not been envisaged in 1937. For the most part this general objective is realised through modification of the earlier Act and in most contexts it is clearest to examine the 1937 Act as amended by the 1983 Act. The following references to 'Diseases of Fish Acts' are to be understood as refering to the combined effect of the two enactments.

The Diseases of Fish Acts are applicable to England and Wales and to Scotland, and are administered and enforced primarily by the appropriate fisheries Ministers; that is, in respect of England and adjacent marine waters the Minister of Agriculture, Fisheries and Food, in relation to Wales and adjacent marine waters the Secretary of State for Wales, and in relation to Scotland and the marine waters thereof the secretary of State for Scotland (s.10(1) Diseases of Fish Act 1937). References to the National Rivers Authority in England and Wales (s.141 and Sch.17 para.3 Water Act 1989) are to be understood in Scotland to refer to a district salmon fishery board (s.11(b) Diseases of Fish Act 1937, and s.14 Salmon Act 1986). Otherwise the Acts are of the same effect in Scotland as in England and Wales.

A.   Restrictions upon import of live fish

A principal control upon the spread of fish disease in the United Kingdom arises through restrictions upon the import of live fish. There is a cause for concern that a number of serious fish diseases which are quite common in Europe but are virtually unknown in Britain will be transmitted through fish imports. It has been acknowledged that if these diseases were to become established in this country the consequences for both farmed and wild fish would be catastrophic (35 HC DEB 1983 Col. 592). With this concern in mind the Diseases of Fish Acts impose, subject to certain qualifications, a general prohibition upon the import of live fish of the salmon family or freshwater fish, or the eggs of these fish. In practical terms this allows for three kinds of restriction to operate: a prohibition upon imports of salmonids, a restriction upon the import of indigenous freshwater fish subject to import licensing and health certification, and a restriction upon the import of freshwater ornamental species subject to an import licence. It is notable that although the spread of fish disease is possible through the movement of dead fish, for example where fish are imported or moved before the existence of disease is discovered, the import prohibitions and other provisions of the Acts are concerned only with *live* fish. (Contrast the provisions under Animal Health Act 1981, dscussed in [7.04] below.)

The first prohibition imposed under the Acts is upon the import into Britain of any live fish of the salmon family, unless authorised under an order of the appropriate fisheries Minister (s.1(1) and (6) Diseases of Fish Act 1937). For the purposes of this prohibition, 'fish of the salmon family' is defined to include all fish of whatever genus belonging to the family *Salmonidae* (s.10(1)). A Ministerial order permitting the import of salmon, contrary to the general prohibition, may specify fish by reference to the particular species concerned, the place of origin, or any other factor (s.1(7)) in which case the import of such fish is be treated as if the fish were a freshwater fish, and so subject to the controls upon import of freshwater species, discussed below (s.1(8)). The only example of an order of this kind is the Importation of Live Fish of the Salmon Family Order 1986 (SI 1986 No.283) which specifies live fish of the salmon family which have been taken from Northern Ireland and have not at any time been in any other country.

The Diseases of Fish Acts also prohibit the import of any live freshwater fish or live eggs of fish of the salmon family, or freshwater fish (see Anon. (1988D)). Import of any of these items is an offence, unless they are consigned to a person who is licensed to receive them and who produces a licence at the time of the delivery of the consignment (s.1(2) Diseases of Fish Act 1937). 'Freshwater fish' is defined to exclude fish of the salmon family, or any kinds of fish which migrate to and from tidal waters, but otherwise to include any fish living in fresh water. 'Fish', in turn, is defined so as not to include shellfish and thus crustaceans and molluscs of any kind are excluded from the scope of the Acts (s.10(1), but see s.12(3A) Sea Fisheries (Shellfish) Act 1967, discussed in [15.04J] below). 'Delivery' is specified to mean delivery under the enactments for the time being in force relating to customs and excise (s.1(2)).

Prohibition of the import of freshwater fish is subject to a licensing qualification, and an application for the appropriate licence must be made to the appropriate Minister in writing in such form, and containing such information, as he may require. On receipt of an application the Minister is empowered to grant a licence to any person to have consigned to him any fish or eggs of the specified kinds which may be subject to the following conditions:

(a) A licence may be subject to such conditions as the Minister thinks fit as to the quantities or kinds of fish or eggs which may be imported under the licence, as to the disposal, transport, inspection, cleansing and disinfection of the fish or eggs and of the containers or other vessels in which they are to be transported or kept and otherwise as to the precautions which are to be taken for avoiding the spreading of disease among salmon and freshwater fish;

(b) a licence may be granted for any period not exceeding twelve months but may be suspended or revoked by the Minister at any time during its currency (s.1(3)).

In accordance with these conditions a licence to import live fish or the eggs of fish of the salmon family, or of freshwater fish, is to be set out in a prescribed form, provided for under the Diseases of Fish Regulations 1984 (Reg.2(1) and Sch.1, SI 1984 No.455) or as near that form as circumstances permit.

The import of live fish or eggs without a licence, or procuring their import without a licence, or in contravention of any condition of a licence, is an offence (s.1(2) Diseases of Fish Act 1937). In such circumstances a police officer, or an officer of Customs and Excise, or a person appointed by the Minister as an inspector under the Diseases of Fish Acts, either generally or for a particular purpose (s.10(1)) may seize the fish or eggs concerned if he has reason to believe that an offence has been committed. Seizure permits the fish or eggs to be detained by the official pending legal proceedings or until the Minister is satisfied that no proceedings are likely to be instituted (s.1(4)). An exception to this arises, however, where it is shown to the satisfaction of the Commissioners of Customs and Excise that any prohibited or restricted import of live fish or eggs of fish takes place solely for the purpose of re-export. In such a situation the Commissioners, subject to such conditions as they think fit to impose for securing the re-export of the fish or eggs, may allow their import as if the prohibition or restriction did not apply (s.1(5)).

B.   Designation of waters

Along with the prohibition upon import of fish into Britain, a principal mechanism by which the Diseases of Fish Acts seek to prevent the spread of fish disease is through the isolation of fish and disease-carrying materials connected with waters where an outbreak of disease has been identified. As with the quarantine of potentially diseased agricultural stock, this involves the use of a so-called 'standstill notice' preventing fish movements of a kind which might facilitate the spread of the disease into otherwise uninfected areas. Although the important powers exist for preliminary precautions to be taken where disease is suspected (considered in [7.02F] below) the eventual means by which this is achieved is the power of the Minister to 'designate' any inland or marine waters if he has reasonable grounds for suspecting that any waters are, or may become, 'infected waters' (discussed in [7.02C] below). In exercise of this power he may designate the waters concerned, and such land adjacent to them as he considers appropriate in the circumstances, as a 'designated area' for the purposes of taking a range of measures to prevent the spread of disease (s.2(1) Diseases of Fish Act 1937). Pertinently, 'land' is stated to include any land covered by inland waters, and 'waters' means any waters, including any fish farm, which are frequented or used for keeping live fish, live eggs of fish, foodstuff for fish, and includes the banks and margins of any such waters and any buildings used in connection therewith. 'Fish farm', in turn, is defined to mean any pond, stew, fish hatchery or other place used for keeping, with a view to their sale of transfer to other waters, including any other fish farm, live fish, live eggs of fish, or foodstuff for fish, and includes any buildings used in connection therewith, and the banks and margins of any water therein. 'Foodstuff for fish' means any substance used or intended or likely to be used, as food for fish, including natural food (s.10(1)). The combined effect of these comprehensively worded definitions is that the power of designation, in principle at least, is sufficiently broad to encompass premises, such as food storage buildings, which may be some distance from the source of the infection.

Where the Minister has reasonable grounds to suspect that waters are or may become infected waters, he may make an order of such an extent as he considers practicable and desirable for the purpose of preventing the spread of infection among fish. In particular the order may, first, prohibit or regulate the taking into or out of the designated area any specified or described live fish, live eggs of fish and foodstuff for fish and, second, regulate the movement within the area of any of the things specified or described (s.2(2)). Where this is done in England or Wales, any person who is the occupier of any inland water in a designated area, or carries on the business of fish farming in marine waters in a designated area, is entitled, on application, to be supplied by the Minister with a report of the evidence on which the order was made (s.2(3)). For these purposes, 'occupier' means, in relation to any inland waters, a person entitled, without the permission of any other person, to take fish from the waters. 'Inland waters' means waters within Great Britain which do not form part of the sea or of any creek, bay or estuary or of any river as far as the tide flows, and 'marine waters' means any other waters within the seaward limits of the territorial sea (see [3.01] above) adjacent to Britain. 'Business of fish farming' is defined to mean the keeping of live fish, whether or not for profit, with a view to their sale or to their transfer to other waters. In Scotland the corresponding power of the Minister to make a designation order regulating the movement of live fish or other items requires a copy of the report of evidence to be made available, on application, to a person who is the occupier of inland waters, or who carries on the business of fish farming in marine waters, or has a right to fish for salmon in any marine waters, or has a right of fishing in any private non-navigable marine waters (s.2(4) Diseases of Fish Act 1937). Contravention of any provision of a designation order is an offence (s.1(6)).

A Ministerial designation order is to be published in the manner prescribed by regulations and may only be varied or revoked by means of a subsequent order (s.1(5)). Accordingly the Diseases of Fish Regulations 1984 provide that where the Minister has made an order designating waters or land as a designated area, notice of the making of the order is to be published, either in the *London Gazette* in the case of a designated area in England or Wales, or in the *Edinburgh Gazette* in the case of a designated area in Scotland. Notice of the order is to be sent to the National Rivers Authority or district board for the area within which the designated area is situated; the occupier of any fish farm known to the Minister to exist within the designated area; and any person known to the Minister to be carrying on the business of fish farming in any marine waters within the designated area (Reg.3, Diseases of Fish Regulations 1984, SI 1984 No.455).

C. 'Infected waters'

The basis of the Ministerial power to designate waters is, in the terminology of the Diseases of Fish Acts, that the waters are 'infected waters' (s.2(1)). This crucial phrase is defined as waters in which any of a range of prescribed diseases exist among fish, or in which the causative organisms of any of those diseases are present (s.10(1), as amended by the Diseases of Fish Order 1973, SI 1973 No.2093). Originally, as has been noted, the purpose of the Acts was to prevent the spread of furunculosis amongst fish and 'infected' meant merely fish infected with furunculosis (original s.10(1)). It was always acknowledged, however, that the meaning of 'infected' could be modified to encompass other diseases affecting salmon and freshwater fish (original s.13). In the course of time a number of other fish diseases have been identified and found to be so detrimental to fish stocks that disease control measures under the Acts are justified. Accordingly the Minister has made use of the power to make an order to add any disease to, or remove it from, the definition of 'infected' (s.13) on a number of occasions.

In 1966 an Order was made to the effect that the provisions of the Acts would apply in respect of columnaris, a disease affecting fish of the salmon family and freshwater fish, in the same manner as for furunculosis, and that 'infected' was to be understood as meaning infected with either of the two diseases (Art.2, Diseases of Fish Order 1966, SI 1966 No.944). In 1973 the definition was further extended to include infectious pancreatic necrosis (IPN), viral haemorrhagic septicaemia (VHS or Egtved disease), Myxosoma (Lentospora) cerebralis (whirling disease), infectious haematopoietic necrosis (IHN), ulcerative dermal necrosis (UDN) and infectious dropsy of cyprinids (ICD or IAD) in any of its forms including spring viraemia and erythroderma-titis (Art.4, Diseases of Fish Order 1973, SI 1973 No.2093). In 1978 bacterial kidney disease, affecting fish of the salmon family, was added to the list (Art.3, Diseases of Fish Order 1978, SI 1978 No.1022). An Order of 1984 amended the list of diseases by removing from the list furunculosis, columnaris, ulcerative dermal necrosis, and infectious dropsy of cyprinids in any of its forms including spring viraemia and erythrodermatitis. The same Order added furunculosis of salmon and spring viraemia of carp (SVC) to the list (Art.2, Diseases of Fish Order 1984, SI 1984 No.301). Most recently the list has been extended to include gyrodactyliasis caused by *Gyrodactylus salaris* (Art.2, Diseases of Fish Order 1988, SI 1988 No.195).

Taking all the amending orders into account, the present definition of 'infected' under the Act is stated to be as follows: 'infected' means, in relation to fish, infected with any of the diseases respectively known as bacterial kidney disease (BKD), furunculosis of salmon, gyrodactyliasis caused by *Gyrodactylus salaris*, infectious haematopoietic necrosis (IHN), infectious pancreatic necrosis (IPN), spring viraemia of carp (SVC), viral haemorrhagic septicaemia (VHS) and whirling disease (Myxosoma cerebralis) (s.10(1) Diseases of Fish Act 1937, as amended).

D.   Directions and authorisations for the removal of fish

Where an order has been made by the Minister for the designation of an area under the Diseases of Fish Acts a series of additional powers arise in relation to the removal of fish from the area in order to prevent further spread of disease. In particular, the Minister may serve a notice in writing on any occupier of inland waters situated in the designated area, and any person carrying on the business of fish farming in marine waters within the area (s.2A(1)). A notice of this kind may direct the occupier of inland waters to take practicable steps to secure the removal of dead or dying fish from the waters and regulate the manner in which fish, or any parts of fish, removed from the waters are to be disposed of (s.2A(2)). Alternatively, in the case of notice served on a person carrying on the business of marine fish farming, an order may direct that practicable steps are to be taken to secure the removal of dead or dying fish from any cage situated in the waters concerned, and regulate the manner in which any fish, or parts of fish, are to be disposed of (s.2A(3)). 'Cage' is defined in general terms to mean any structure for containing live fish (s.10(1)). The service of a direction to remove fish upon the occupier of inland waters within the area of the National Rivers Authority in England and Wales is limited to fish farms (s.2A(4), as amended by s.141 and Sch.17 para.3 Water Act 1989). It is notable that the Ministerial power in relation to the removal of fish is limited to 'dead and dying fish', and may not apply to all fish infected with a disease. It falls considerably short of a general power to order the slaughter of infected fish in a fish farm, and consequently is without provision for compensation to be awarded to the person against whom the notice is served.

In the event of non-compliance with a Ministerial notice directing the removal of dead or dying fish from a designated area, a back-up power is that the Minister may authorise an inspector appointed under the Acts to take measures to ensure that directions in the order are complied with. To this effect it is provided that if the Minister is satisfied that a direction to secure the removal of fish from a designated area has not been complied with, within a time specified in the notice, he may authorise an inspector to carry out the direction. Where this course is followed any expenses reasonably incurred by the inspector in carrying out the direction are to be recoverable by the Minister from the person upon whom the notice was originally served. If the person upon whom the notice was served does any act which is prohibited by the notice he will be guilty of an offence unless he shows that he did not know that the act was prohibited (s.2A(5)).

To allow greater flexibility in the operation of designation orders for the protection of live fish farm stock subject to a designation order, the Minister is empowered to provide specific authorisation for movements of fish, which would otherwise fall foul of such an order (s.2B(1)). Hence the Minister may authorise an occupier of inland waters situated within a designated area to remove fish, or fish of a specified description, from the waters, and to do so by such agents and by such methods as the Minister considers most expedient for the purpose (s.2B(2)). In prescribing a method for the removal of fish the Minister may authorise the occupier or another person to use methods which are otherwise unlawful, for example, because they amount to prohibited methods of taking fish under general fishery legislation (for example, Salmon and Freshwater Fisheries Act 1975; and Salmon and Freshwater Fisheries (Protection) (Scotland) Act 1951). No authority of this kind may be given, however, in respect of waters in the area of the National Rivers Authority, in England and Wales, which are not a fish farm (s.2B(4) Diseases of Fish Act 1937, as amended by s.141 and Sch.17 para.3 Water Act 1989; and see [7.02E] below).

Analogous provisions are applicable in respect of Ministerial authorisation to remove fish from marine fish farms. Authority may be given to a person carrying on the business of fish farming in marine waters in a designated area to remove fish, or fish of a specified description, from any cage which is owned or possessed by him and used for the purposes of the business. As with inland waters, removal of fish may be authorised by such methods, including methods which are otherwise illegal, as the Minister considers to be most expedient for the purpose (s.2B(3)). In respect of either inland waters or marine fish farms, however, the person authorised to remove fish is to comply with any directions given to him by the Minister as to the manner in which the fish, or any parts of fish, are to be disposed of. In the event of the person intentionally failing to comply with such directions he will be guilty of an offence (s.2B(5)).

E.   Powers and duties of fishery authorities

Under the original provisions of the 1937 Act the authorities with direct responsibility for fisheries, the 'fishery boards', possessed certain powers and duties in respect of fish diseases present in waters other than fish farms. In a succession of reorganisations of fisheries responsibilities in England and Wales, duties were transferred from fishery boards to 'river boards' (under River Boards Act 1948), from river boards to 'river authorities' (under Water Resources Act 1963), from river authorities to 'water authorities' (under Water Act 1973), and finally from water authorities to the National Rivers Authority (s.141 Water Act 1989). At each reorganisation the powers and duties in respect of fish diseases were transferred to the newly constituted body, and hence the present position is that a number of matters relating to fish diseases fall to the responsibility of the National Rivers Authority in England and Wales (s.3, and s.141 and Sch.17 para.3 Water Act 1989). In Scotland these matters fall as responsibilities of district salmon fishery boards (s.11(b), and see s.14 Salmon Act 1986).

The initial duty of the National Rivers Authority is to report any suspicion that inland waters other than fish farms have become infected. Thus where the Authority has reasonable ground for suspecting that any inland waters, which are not a fish farm, are infected waters it is to report the facts forthwith to the appropriate Minister. On receipt of a report of this kind the Minister is to cause an investigation to be made to establish whether the waters are infected. In addition to the duty to report suspicion of disease the National Rivers Authority is empowered to take any practicable steps for the removal of dead or dying fish from the waters (s.3(1)).

Where an order designating infected waters is in force, (under s.2) the Minister has a power to authorise the National Rivers Authority to remove any fish, or fish of a specified description, from any inland water, other than a fish farm, and to use such methods, including methods which are otherwise illegal, as he considers to be most expedient for the purpose (s.3(2)). Whenever fish are removed by the National Rivers Authority in exercise of its powers, or under authorisation from the Minister, the Authority is to destroy or otherwise properly dispose of all fish removed, and send the Minister a return stating the numbers of fish at such times as he may direct (s.3(3)).

F.   Preliminary precautions

Although the ultimate power to designate an area under the Diseases of Fish Acts rests with the Minister, important powers to take preliminary measures where an outbreak of fish disease is suspected are given to inspectors authorised to act by the Minister. Hence if an inspector has reasonable grounds for suspecting that any inland fish farm waters are infected he is empowered to serve a notice, in a prescribed form, upon the occupiers, and where this is done the facts are to be reported to the Minister (s.4(1), and see Reg.4 and Sch.2, Diseases of Fish Order 1984, SI 1984 No.455). The effect of service of a notice of this kind is that no live fish, or live eggs of fish, may be taken into or out of the fish farm, and no foodstuff of fish may be taken out of the farm, without the permission of the Minister. This prohibition applies for a 30-day period from the service of the notice, unless the occupier receives written intimation from the Minister that permission is no longer required (s.4(2)). The period during which movements are prohibited may be extended so that the Minister may, if he thinks it desirable, authorise an inspector to serve a further notice within the 30-day period. If this is done, and no written permission has been given by the Minister to remove the restricted items from the farm, the effect of the second notice is to substitute a period of 60 days for the original 30-day period (s.4(3)). Any person who intentionally takes any fish, eggs or foodstuff into or out of a fish farm while the taking is prohibited is guilty of an offence unless it is shown that he did not know that the taking was prohibited (s.4(4)).

An insight into the practical use which is made of the power of inspectors to take preliminary measures where an outbreak of fish disease is suspected, and the relationship between the exercise of this power and that of the Minister to designate an area as infected, was provided by the Minister of State at the Ministry of Agriculture, Fisheries and Food, Mr Buchanan-Smith, in the debates leading to the passage of the Diseases of Fish Act 1983. Although it is to be noted that some changes have been made to practices since 1983, the Minister described the procedures involved in the following way.

'The fish disease laboratory or one of my Department's veterinary investigation centres is usually the first to learn that a notifiable disease may be present on a site. The information is usually given by a fish farmer, a private veterinary surgeon or a water authority. As soon as we hear that a notifiable disease may be present, arrangements are made for someone from the fish diseases laboratory or from the local veterinary investigation centre to visit the site and, if appropriate, to take samples of fish. The samples are examined at the laboratory and if the presence of a notifiable disease is confirmed, the normal action for that disease is taken. That action will vary in accordance with the disease and the appropriate control. If movement restrictions are necessary the fish disease laboratory will immediately issue a thirty day preliminary precautions notice and perhaps subsequent notices. The notices are sent by recorded delivery, the initial notice being under cover of a letter explaining that a named, notifiable disease has been found and that movement restrictions are being applied. Lists of movements of fish both on and off the infected sites may be required. [These will now be available as a part of the fish farm registration scheme, see [6.03] above.] Attempts are then made to determine whether the disease exists on contact sites. Immediately following the issue of the preliminary precautions notice, the laboratory will, if appropriate, prepare the infected area order. The order declares the specified area to be infected and prohibits the movement of live fish, live eggs of fish and foodstuff for fish from the site without my Department's prior written consent. My

Department will notify the occupier that the order has been made. It will also notify the water authority, the National Water Council [now the National Rivers Authority will be notified] and the National Farmers' Union. A trade notice will be issued. The order is published in the *London Gazette* [in Scotland publication is in the *Edinburgh Gazette*] as required by the Diseases of Fish Regulations 1937.' (41 HC DEB 1983 Cols. 523 to 524.)

A useful and more detailed account of the analogous procedures followed in Scotland is to be found in the Department of Agriculture and Fisheries for Scotland's *Code of Practice* on the operation of the Diseases of Fish Acts (Department of Agriculture and Fisheries for Scotland (undated)).

The power of fish disease inspectors to serve notices prohibiting movements of fish, eggs and foodstuff would be of limited value if they were not in a position to discover that waters are infected, and some duty to communicate suspicions of this kind must be placed upon those with direct charge of waters which might become infected. With that aim in mind it is provided that, in respect of England and Wales, if any person who is entitled to take fish from any inland waters, or employed for the purpose of having the care of any inland waters, has reasonable grounds for suspecting that the waters of a fish farm are infected, it is his duty to report the facts to the Minister forthwith. In respect of waters which are not a fish farm, the written report is to be to the National Rivers Authority. Moreover, it is an offence to fail to report suspicion of this kind without reasonable excuse (s.4(5) Diseases of Fish Act 1937). In Scotland the same duty to report suspicion of disease applies in relation to the Secretary of State, or if the waters are situated in the area of a district board (see ss.1, 14 and 40 Salmon Act 1986) and are not a fish farm, to the district board (s.4(6) Diseases of Fish Act 1937). Clearly this places an important duty upon fish farmers and their employees, water keepers and anglers to take an active role in the reporting of fish disease. Notably, the mere omission to act in reporting suspicions, without reasonable excuse, will constitute a crime under this provision.

Analogous provisions for the issue of notices as to preliminary precautions in respect of suspected infected waters are provided for in respect of marine waters. In the case of suspected infected marine waters an inspector is to serve the prescribed notice upon any person who owns or possesses a cage which is situated in the waters and is used for the purposes of a business of fish farming carried on by him (s.4A(1)). The effect of the notice is to prohibit, subject to Ministerial permission, the moving of live fish or live eggs of fish into or out of the cage, or the taking of foodstuff out of the cage, for an initial 30-day period (s.4A(2)). Again the initial period of the prohibition may be extended to a period of 60 days in total where the Minister thinks this desirable (s.4A(3)). The same duty to report suspicion of the waters being infected waters is imposed upon persons who own or possess fish farming cages in marine waters, or are employed for the purposes of having care of such cages (s.4A(5)). In Scotland, however, the duty to report also extends to persons having the right to fish for salmon in marine waters, or having a right of fishing in any private non-navigable marine waters, or who are employed for the purpose of having the care of such waters, excluding marine waters used for the business of fish farming (s.4A(6)). In any case where the duty arises to report reasonable grounds for suspecting marine waters to be infected it is an offence to fail to do so without reasonable excuse.

G.   Examination of waters and powers of entry

Although it is envisaged that the role of fishery disease inspectors under the Acts will be largely investigative, the initiative to instigate an investigation does not always rest entirely with the Minister. In particular, the Minister is placed under a duty to examine waters on the demand of either the National Rivers Authority or the occupier of inland waters. In such a situation the Minister is to cause an inspector to make an examination of any waters within the National Rivers Authority area, or in the occupier's occupation, with a view to discovering whether they are infected waters. The Minister is then to cause a report of the result of the examination to be furnished to the National Rivers Authority or the occupier free of charge. If the waters are found to be infected the Minister is then to cause the inspector to make a further examination when required to do so by the authority or occupier. This process is subject to the proviso that the Minister is not bound to cause any examination to be made if the period which has elapsed since a previous examination, undertaken on demand, is so short that in his opinion a further examination is not yet necessary (s.5).

To be effective in achieving their purpose of preventing the spread of fish diseases, the offences under the Diseases of Fish Acts must be supported by a collection of ancillary powers permitting inspection of waters and entry upon land for the purpose of investigation. These powers fall into two categories depending upon whether they arise in circumstances where an offence under the Acts is reasonably suspected, or whether they are intended to permit inspectors to perform their general inspection work without impediment. In a situation where there is reasonable cause to suspect that an offence under the Acts has been committed a justice of the peace, upon receiving an information on oath to that effect, may authorise any person named in the warrant to enter on any land, at times mentioned in the warrant. On entry upon the land the authorised person may seize any fish, eggs or foodstuff of fish, or other article which he suspects to have been imported or brought into Great Britain, removed or otherwise dealt with, or to be about to be removed or otherwise dealt with, in contravention of the Act or of any licence granted or order made or notice served under the Act. Such a warrant may also authorise the boarding of, and entry into, a cage situated in marine waters and used for the purpose of fish farming. In any case, however, a warrant of this kind is not to continue in force for more than a week from the date of being granted (s.6(1)). Notably this power is available to authorise the entry of '*any person* named in the warrant'.

A second distinct group of powers are made available only to inspectors authorised by the Minister to act under the Acts. These powers are listed as follows:

(a)   to inspect any inland waters in which fish or the eggs of fish or foodstuff for fish are likely to be found, and to take therefrom samples of any fish or of any such eggs or foodstuff or of water, mud, vegetation or other matter;

(aa) to inspect any cage situated in marine waters and used for the purposes of a business of fish farming, and to take therefrom samples of any fish or of any eggs of fish or of foodstuff for fish or of water or other matter;

(ab) to inspect any marine waters in which fish of the salmon family or freshwater fish or the eggs of such fish or foodstuff for fish are likely to be found, and to take therefrom samples of any such fish, eggs or foodstuff or of water, mud, vegetation or other matter;

(b)   for the purpose of exercising any powers or performing any duties under this Act, to enter, upon production on demand of his authority, on any land;

(c)   for the purpose of exercising any powers or performing any duties under this Act, to board and enter, upon production on demand of the inspector's authority, any cage situated in marine waters and used for the purposes of a business of fish farming.

In each case, any person who refuses to admit or intentionally obstructs an inspector in the exercise or performance of any these powers and duties is guilty of an offence (s.6(2)). Some safeguard is provided to the fish farmer against the excessive use of inspectors' powers to take samples of fish by the imposition of a duty to compensate the farmer for losses sustained in this way. Hence it is provided that if any sample of fish taken from inland waters by an inspector is found not to be infected, the Minister is bound to pay to the occupier of the water, or to such of the occupiers as he considers equitable, a sum equal to the market value of the fish taken in the sample (s.6(3)). Likewise, where a sample of fish is taken from a cage in marine waters by an inspector and found not to be infected, the Minister is to pay the person who owns or possesses the cage, and uses it for the purposes of a business of fish farming, a sum equal to the market value of the fish taken in the sample (s.6(3A)).

In relation to those powers and duties of the National Rivers Authority under the Acts exerciseable outside fish farms (see s.3 discussed in [7.02E] above) any person authorised in writing by the National Rivers Authority will need corresponding powers of entry in order to perform duties imposed upon the authority in exercise of its functions under the Acts. For that purpose a person authorised by the National Rivers Authority may enter, upon production on demand of his authority, on any land within the area of the Authority not being part of a fish farm. Any person who refuses to admit a person so authorised or who intentionally obstructs him in the carrying out of any of his duties will be guilty of an offence (s.6(4)).

H.   Notices, penalties and proceedings

It is apparent that the extensive prohibitions upon the movement of fish and other matters which arise under Ministerial designation orders, and orders issued by fishery inspectors as a preliminary precaution, will be of little consequence unless their content is effectively communicated to the occupiers of the fish farms and cages they concern. To make clear what is required before communication of an order is regarded in law as having been accomplished, the formalities are spelt out in some detail. It is provided where a notice is required or authorised to be served upon an occupier of inland waters it may be served by delivering it to him, or to any servant or agent employed by him for the purpose of having the care of any of the waters (s.7(1)). Where a notice requiring anything to be done by an occupier of inland waters is served by delivery to a servant or agent in this way, the servant or agent is deemed to have the authority of the occupier to do on his behalf, and at his expense, whatever the notice requires to be done in relation to any of the waters (s.7(2)). Alternatively, service of a notice may be brought about by sending it by registered post to the usual or last-known address of the occupier, or, if his address is not known and cannot reasonably be ascertained, by exhibiting the notice addressed to him in some conspicuous place at or near the waters. Where the identity of the occupier of the waters cannot reasonably be ascertained, the notice, addressed to 'The Occupier', and exhibited in this way will be deemed to be addressed to every person who is an occupier of the waters without the need for further name or description (s.7(1)). In the case of a notice required or authorised to be served upon a person carrying on the business of fish farming in marine waters, that notice may be served by delivering it to him or by sending it by registered post to his usual or last-known address (s.7(1A)).

All the offences arising under the Acts are punishable to the same extent in that any person found guilty will be liable, on summary conviction, to a fine not exceeding level 4 on the standard scale, presently £1,000 (s.8(1)). In addition to the imposition of a fine, however, the court before whom a person is convicted of an offence under the Act may order the forfeiture of any fish, eggs of fish, foodstuff of fish or article in respect of which the offence was committed (s.8(1)).

Although the Ministry of Agriculture, Fisheries and Food, and the Welsh and Scottish Offices act as the main prosecuting authorities in relation to the Acts, the power to prosecute for offences arising under the Acts is not their exclusive right. It is provided that in England and Wales the National Rivers Authority is to have the power to take legal proceedings to enforce provisions in respect of inland waters in their area (s.8(2)).

In order to avoid certain difficulties with the territorial jurisdiction of those courts before which prosecutions under the Acts may be brought, it is specifically provided that any offence committed in the territorial sea adjacent to Great Britain is to be taken to have been committed in any place in which the offender may for the time being be found. The purpose of this is to bring matters within the jurisdiction of a magistrates' court in England or Wales or, in Scotland, within the jurisdiction of the sheriff (s.8(4)).

7.03   *Animal health controls*

The powers arising under the Diseases of Fish Acts are usefully contrasted with the wide-ranging powers to regulate for the prevention of the spread of animal disease which are provided to the Minister of Agriculture, Fisheries and Food and the Secretaries of State for Wales and Scotland under the Animal Health Act 1981. Although the Act excludes fish and shellfish from the general definition of 'animal' for most purposes concerned with disease (s.87(3) Animal Health Act 1981) an exceptional situation in which controls may be introduced under the Act concerns the import of live or dead fish. Specifically, the Ministers are empowered to make orders and such provisions as they think fit for the purpose of preventing the introduction or spread of disease into or within Britain. In particular, orders may concern the import of animals and carcasses, and other things, whether animate or inanimate, by or by means of which it appears to the Ministers that any disease might be carried or transmitted (s.10(1)). For these purposes 'animals' is stated to include fish and other cold-blooded creatures (s.10(4)). It follows that the Ministerial power given under this provision allows prohibition or regulation of the import of fish or shellfish and other things, such as water or matter present in water, which are a means by which disease may be carried or transmitted. In addition the Ministers may make further provision for preventing the introduction or spread of disease by the import of fish in respect to persons, animals and other things which may have been in contact with imported fish or other matter (s.10(2)).

There is a clear overlap between the Ministerial powers arising under the Animal Health Act 1981 and the provisions of the Diseases of Fish Acts. In many respects, however, the 1981 Act is more flexible in enabling a specific Ministerial response to a particular disease threat. The 1981 Act is also broader in compass in applying to dead as well as live fish and water and other matter present with fish. An instance of this power being exercised in a fish disease context is to be found in the Salmonid Viscera Order 1986 (SI 1986 No.2265) which prohibits the import into Britain of ungutted salmonids, or any viscera of fish of the family *Salmonidae* whether or not detached from a dead fish, except under the authority of a licence. A licence of this kind may be either general or specific and may be issued subject to such conditions as the Minister considers appropriate for the purpose of preventing the introduction or spreading of diseases of fish into or within Britain (Art.3 Salmon Viscera Order 1986). In addition powers are granted for the disposal of viscera unlawfully imported into Britain and the cleansing and disinfection of premises, vehicles or containers in which unlawfully imported viscera have been present (Arts.4 and 5).

7.04   *Fish health and movement in the European Community*

It is convenient to conclude this chapter, and prelude points taken up for discussion in the next, by giving consideration to imminent developments in the legislation governing fish health and movement which are presently being considered at European Community level. The need for completion of the internal Community market by 1992 necessitates the harmonisation of national trading regulations of Member States and the removal of technical barriers to trade in all kinds of goods including aquacultural products (see [1.04] above). In accordance with this strategy, a proposed Regulation to secure standardisation of the law of the Community with regard to the health conditions governing intra-Community movement of live fish is presently under discussion by the European Commission (Edwards 1989). Although the details of the Regulation are not yet finalised the indications are that it will eventually replace or over-ride all national provisions relating to fish disease in Member States of the Community including the United Kingdom.

Broadly, the proposed Community regulation on health conditions for movement of fishery products seeks to assimilate restrictions upon intra-Community fish movements to those applicable to other kinds of farm livestock. Accordingly, with certain modifications, the movement of live or dead freshwater or saltwater fish, molluscs and crustaceans will be subject to the general strategy devised for the movement of farm livestock within the Community. This involves gradual transition towards the removal of national border checks upon the movement of animals between Member States of the Community. As a counterpart of the removal of border checks authorisation will be conducted in accordance with a system of veterinary checks and certification which it is eventually anticipated will be carried out at the place of dispatch only. Until confidence in this procedure is gained, however, interim measures will allow for checks at the place of destination on the basis of agreed criteria, but it is possible that the checking of animals in transit will only be permitted in the event of a serious presumption of irregularity (8062/88 European Council Regulation concerning veterinary checks in intra-Community trade with a view to the completion of the internal market). In relation to fish and shellfish movements, however, it is apparent that the implementation of this strategy must take account of the presence of different contagious fish diseases in various parts of the Community. Hence the overall objective of free movement of live fish within the Community must be modified to prevent the spread of disease by restricting the movement of fish from an area where a disease is present into an area in which it is absent.

The general mechanism for preventing the spread of fish and shellfish disease alongside the removal of trade barriers envisages the zoning of the Community according to fish disease status. This is to be accomplished by a prohibition upon fish movements from an area of lower disease status to an area of higher status. Broadly the framework for fish disease zoning involves the classification of diseases under three headings. First, there are infections or contagious exotic diseases of a kind not presently occurring in the Community, in relation to which Member States will be required to take immediate eradication measures in the event of an outbreak. Second, there are infectious or contagious diseases present in some parts of the Community and having a major economic impact, in relation to which fish movements will only be permitted into areas of equivalent or lower disease status. Third, there are infectious or contagious diseases with a lesser economic impact, in relation to which a certain amount of discretion is permitted to the governments of Member States to operate disease controls at an individual fish farm level by allowing movements only between approved farms within the Community (Edwards (1989)).

In relation to imports of fish into the European Community from non-Member States the details of the Community strategy have still to be finalised but the indications are that imported fish will have to have come from approved sources and will have to meet standards which are at least as stringent as those applicable to movements within the Community. Regulation of Community imports will be made subject to requirements of veterinary inspection and health certification at designated points of entry into the Community before being allowed into free circulation or being placed under a customs procedure. Alternatively, importation into the Community will be prohibited if fish are found to have come from a country from which import is prohibited, or are suspected of being infected or contaminated with an infectious or contagious disease, or certification or other conditions are not complied with. Detailed provisions for these, and other matters arising under the Regulation, are to be supplied by a Community Standing Veterinary Committee.

The eventual Community Regulation which gives effect to the proposals

for fish health and movements will be directly applicable in the United
Kingdom, and is clearly intended as a comprehensive measure governing the
movement of fishery products into and within the Community. Moreover, in
the event of inconsistency, the Regulation will take precedence over current
provisions contained in the Diseases of Fish Acts, discussed above. It is vital,
therefore, that the Community strategy for fish movements is accompanied
by stringent operational controls to ensure that, amongst other matters, the
basis upon which veterinary certification is provided at the point of dispatch
of a consignment of fish is conducted in a uniformly rigorous manner
throughout the Community. In addition, mechanisms will need to be devised
whereby standardisation of transportation procedures, water changes, and
disinfection measures are achieved throughout the Community. Beyond
these operational considerations, attention will need to be given to the
relationship between the proposed Community Regulation and wider
ecological issues which may be involved in the relaxation of constraints upon
the introduction of live fish into waters (Howarth (1989D). The legislation
dealing with this matter is considered in the following chapter.

Chapter 8

Controls upon the Movement of Fish

8.01 *Provisions on the import and movement of fish*

This chapter continues the examination of restrictions of various kinds which are imposed upon the movement of fish. Whereas the last chapter concentrated upon movement controls arising through the need to prevent the spread of fish disease, this chapter groups together a miscellaneous collection of provisions which restrict movements for a variety of other reasons (see Howarth (1989C); and generally Blake (1983) at pp. 23 to 30). It is apparent that many of these provisions have incidental fish disease control implications, though in some instances their objectives are not entirely clear, it is suggested that in most respects their primary purpose is to restrict the movement of fish for reasons other than the control of fish disease. Broadly the plan of the chapter is to consider, first, those measures which relate to the import and export of fish and, second, measures dealing with transfers of fish between waters in Britain.

8.02 *The Import of Live Fish Acts*

The Diseases of Fish Acts 1937 and 1983 impose important restrictions upon the import of live salmon and freshwater fish and the eggs of such fish. As has been previously noted, however, it is significant that the purpose of these controls is the prevention of the spread of disease amongst salmon and freshwater fish. By contrast, it is doubtful whether these provisions will always serve to prevent other kinds of threat which are posed to indigenous species by the import or introduction of species from abroad. The shortcomings of the disease control legislation were made apparent by an incident in 1976 when a consignment of Pacific Coho salmon, *Oncorynchus kisutch*, was imported into Scotland (see Ministry of Agriculture, Fisheries and Food (1979)). The import of eggs of the Coho salmon was permitted under a conditional licence issued by the Secretary of State for Scotland under the Diseases of Fish Act 1937 (s.1(3) Diseases of Fish Act 1937, discussed in [7.02A] above). The fish were kept in absolute quarantine, with effluent sterilised in order to ensure that no live fish or diseased organisms could escape to the outside environment. Regular monitoring took place under the supervision of the Department of Agriculture and Fisheries for Scotland, and no trace of disease was found. It was recognised by the Minister, however, that if the salmon matured to broodstock and spawned, without disease being identified, there was a problem in that there were no clear powers in the existing legislation on disease control to restrict movement of the progeny of the imported fish eggs. (Now see s.24 Salmon Act 1986, and s.14 Wildlife and Countryside Act 1981, considered in [8.06] and [8.07] below.) The probability of damage to native stocks through competition, or genetic integration, with an introduced strain of Coho salmon was a considerable one, and yet the law contained no clear provision to prevent the introduction of the new species (389 HL DEB 1978 Col. 1547).

The case of the imported Coho, moreover, was illustrative of a collection of broader difficulties relating to the import and introduction of 'exotic' and other non-native species of fish. The fear raised by these possibilities is, not merely that a new species may carry disease to which native species lack immunity, but rather that the interloper may become established and have a detrimental competitive effect upon the environment of indigenous species. An example of this having happened is to be found in the establishment of the predatory Zander, *Stizostedion lucioperca*, in East Anglia to the detriment of native species. In response to the perceived threat posed by the introduction of new species Parliament provided the appropriate Ministers with an enabling power to prohibit or regulate the import or release of foreign fish or their eggs into waters in Great Britain. Perhaps because of the introduction of subsequent legislation (discussed below) only one use of the Ministerial power has yet been made, in relation to Scotland only, but the power remains a legal provision which may be used to prevent damage being caused by imported species.

For reasons of Parliamentary pragmatics rather than legal principle, the law of Scotland was changed by the Import of Live Fish (Scotland) Act 1978 before that of England and Wales, which was subsequently amended under the Import of Live Fish (England and Wales) Act 1980. It was accepted, however, that the later enactment was intended to bring the law of England and Wales into line with that of Scotland. The form of the two enactments is substantially the same, and in the following discussion the two Acts are considered together as the 'Import of Live Fish Acts' (although differences in section numbers are indicated in parenthesis).

The Import of Live Fish Acts 1978 and 1980 are stated to be without prejudice to the fish import prohibitions which arise under the Diseases of Fish Acts. The 1978 and 1980 Acts permit the Secretary of State for Scotland, (s.1(1) Import of Live Fish (Scotland) Act 1978), the Minister of Agriculture, Fisheries and Food in relation to England, and the Secretary of State for Wales in relation to Wales (s.4 Import of Live Fish (England and Wales) Act 1980), to exercise certain powers over the import of fish or fish eggs. In particular, the appropriate Minister may, by order, forbid either absolutely or except under a licence, the import into, or the keeping or the release in any part of Great Britain of live fish, including shellfish, or the live eggs of fish, of certain species of fish (s.1(1) of both Acts, definitions under s.1(6) 1978 Act and s.4 1980 Act). The species concerned are those which in the opinion of the Minister might compete with, displace, prey on or harm the habitat of any freshwater fish, shellfish or salmon in Great Britain (s.1(1) of both Acts). For these purposes, 'freshwater fish' means any fish living in fresh water including eels and the fry of eels, but excluding salmon; 'shellfish' includes crustaceans and molluscs of any kind and any spat or spawn of shellfish; and 'salmon' includes all migratory fish of the species *Salmo salar* and *Salmo trutta*, commonly known as salmon and sea trout respectively (s.1(6) 1978 Act, and s.4 1980 Act). It is evident, therefore, that the concern underlying this enactment is not merely the spread of infectious disease between fish but rather the damage to native species which may be brought about by the introduction of non-native competitors.

The Ministerial power to make an order, either to forbid the import of non-native species of fish absolutely or to make import subject to a licensing requirement, is not to be exercised without consultation. In particular, the Minister must first consult with the Nature Conservancy Council (established under the Nature Conservancy Act 1973), and any other person with whom the Minister considers that consultation is appropriate (s.1(2) of both Acts). It is notable that no explicit provision was made for consultation with the water authorities (now the National Rivers Authority) in England and Wales and it was suggested that, in view of the power of these authorities to decline to authorise the release of fish into waters in their area (s.30 Salmon and Freshwater Fisheries Act 1975, discussed in [8.04] below) this was an omission. In response to this criticism, however, it was conceded in the Parliamentary debates that the power of the Minister to consult before an order was made was a broad one, and an assurance was given that the Government would, 'seek advice from the widest possible range of interests, including fishing and fish farming interests' (407 HL DEB 1980 Col. 1230).

After consultation the Minister may, subject to such conditions as he thinks fit, grant a licence to any person to import, keep or release, live fish, or the live eggs of fish of a species specified in an order. Having granted a licence of this kind the Minister retains the power to revoke or vary the licence (s.1(5)(b) of 1978 Act, and s.1(3) 1980 Act). With the consent of the Treasury, an order which is made in exercise of these powers may authorise the making of a charge for the licence and specify a maximum charge for the licence (s.1(4) of both Acts) and in Scotland a licence may be granted subject to such other conditions as the Secretary of State thinks fit (s.1(4) of 1978 Act). In any case the power conferred to make orders prohibiting or licensing the import of non-native species is to be exercisable by statutory instrument, subject to annulment in pursuance of a resolution of either House of Parliament (s.1(5) of both Acts).

In the event of the Minister exercising his power either to forbid or to grant a licence for the import, keeping or release of non-native species of fish, certain powers of entry and inspection are given to any officer commissioned by the Commissioners of Customs and Excise or a person authorised by the Minister. These persons may at all reasonable times, on production of authority if required, enter and inspect any land occupied by a person holding a licence, and any other land upon which the inspector has reason to believe that live fish, or the eggs of fish, of a species specified in the order, are being kept or may be found (s.2(1) of both Acts). Notably, however, although the definition of 'land' which is applicable for these purposes includes land covered by water it does not include a dwelling-house (s.2(2) of both Acts).

A power of seizure arises in the event of an officer commissioned by the Commissioners of Customs and Excise, or a person authorised by the Minister, having reason to believe that an offence under the Acts has been committed in relation to any fish or eggs of fish. This power permits the person exercising the power of entry or inspection to seize the fish or eggs and detain them pending the determination of any proceedings to be instituted, or until the Minister is satisfied that no such proceedings are likely to be instituted (s.3(4) of both Acts).

A number of offences arise in relation to the Ministerial power with regard to the import of fish. It is an offence to import, or attempt to import, keep or release any live fish, of a species specified in a Ministerial order where the order forbids absolutely the import, keeping or release of such species. Where a Ministerial order forbids the import, keeping or release of live fish of specified species except under licence, it is an offence to do so without having a valid licence authorising the import, keeping or release concerned (s.3(1)(a) of both Acts). It is an offence for the holder of a licence granted pursuant to a ministerial order to act in contravention of, or to fail to comply with, any term of the licence (s.3(1)(b) of both Acts). It is also an offence to obstruct any person from entering or inspecting any land in pursuance of his powers of inspection (s.3(1)(c) of both Acts). In respect of any of the offences, a person found guilty will be liable, on summary conviction, to a fine not exceeding level 4 on the standard scale of fines, which presently is set at £1,000 (s.3(1) of both Acts). Moreover the sheriff, or court, by whom a person is convicted of an offence involving the unlawful import, keeping or release of fish or eggs under the Act may order any fish or eggs in respect of which the offence was committed to be forfeited and destroyed (s.3(4) of both Acts). By way of an exception, no person will be guilty of an offence under the Act in respect of any act which is done for a scientific or research purpose authorised by the Minister (s.3(2) of both Acts).

By way of a general observation upon the Import of Live Fish Acts 1978 and 1980, it is to be noted that both Acts are enabling in character. They enable the appropriate Minister to introduce particular orders prohibiting the import, keeping or release of specified species of fish and shellfish. The Ministers are not placed under any obligation to make orders of this kind, and without there being an order in existence no legal prohibitions or criminal offences arise. This is essentially the position in England and Wales because no orders have been introduced under the 1980 Act. In Scotland only one order has been introduced, the Import of Live Fish (Coho Salmon) (Prohibition) (Scotland) Order 1980 (SI 1980 No.376). This Order states that, after the necessary consultation, the Secretary of State for Scotland has exercised his power to prohibit the import into, or the keeping or the release in Scotland of live fish or the live eggs of fish of the Coho salmon species except under licence. The reason why the powers arising under the 1978 and 1980 Acts have remained unused apart from the single instance of the 1980 Order is that they have become largely redundant due to the creation of an overlapping provision in the offence of introducing new species of fish into the wild arising under the Wildlife and Countryside Act 1981 (s.14(1) Wildlife and Countryside Act 1981, discussed in [8.07] below). For most purposes the need for a Ministerial Order is made unneccessary by the enactment of the later offence.

8.03   *The import and export of endangered species*

Another legal mechanism regulating the import and export of fish for quite different reasons arises through the operation of the Endangered Species

(Import and Export) Act 1976. This enactment gives effect to the Convention on International Trade in Endangered Species of Wild Fauna and Flora, referred to as CITES, which was signed in Washington in 1973 and came into force in the United Kingdom in 1976 (Cmnd. 5459). The purpose of CITES is to reduce the over-exploitation of species that are in danger of extinction by subjecting international trade in such species to strict regulation and allowing authorisation of such trade only in exceptional circumstances. The basis of these measures is the recognition that peoples and States are the best protectors of their own wild fauna, but that international cooperation is also essential for the protection of certain threatened species.

Although CITES has been ratified by the United Kingdom, and is given effect through the 1976 Act, the European Council has also made a Regulation on the implementation of the Convention in order to ensure uniformity in the application of the Convention throughout the European Community (European Council Regulation EEC No.3626/82, as amended). The Community Regulation has direct applicability in United Kingdom law, and would take precedence if a conflict were to arise, but because both the Regulation and the 1976 Act follow CITES fairly closely there is unlikely to be inconsistency. However, the Regulation provides for stricter controls to be imposed under national law than arise under the Regulation and this is done under the 1976 Act by the inclusion of controls upon trade in certain species that are not included in CITES (Haigh (1987) p. 308). In summary, therefore, the position is that though both the 1976 Act and the Community Regulation serve to give effect to CITES in the United Kingdom, in some respects the Act is stricter than the Regulation in the controls which it imposes upon the international trade in endangered species.

The main intention behind the 1976 Act is to prevent the trade in endangered species, and to that effect its most significant feature is the prohibition of import or export of any live or dead animal listed under Schedule 1 to the Act to or from the United Kingdom (s.1(1)(a) Endangered Species (Import and Export) Act 1976). 'Animal' in this context is understood to encompass all animals other than man, (s.12(1)) and a range of uncommon species of fish and molluscs are specifically included in Schedule 1 to the Act and listed below. The prohibition of import or export of scheduled species is made subject to the exception that it does not apply to the import or export of any animal under, and in accordance with, the terms of a licence issued by the Secretary of State (s.1(1) and (2)). Accordingly the Secretary of State is to submit any application for a licence of this kind to whichever of the scientific authorities he considers is best able to advise him as to whether a licence should be issued and, if so, its terms, before he issues or declines to issue the licence (s.1(3)). Alternatively, the Secretary of State need not submit an application to the appropriate scientific authority if it is an application of a kind that the scientific authority has previously advised as to whether licences of that kind should be issued and, if so, their terms (s.1(3A), as amended). For the purposes of advising on these matters the Secretary of State is empowered to establish any body or bodies, consisting of such members as he may appoint, or assign any existing body the duty of advising on the administration of the Act and giving general advice on the import or export of animals which are, or are likely to become, endangered (s.2).

A number of offences arise under the 1976 Act in relation to the wrongful import or export of animals. It is an offence for a person to make a statement or representation, or furnish a document or information, which he knows to be false in a material particular, or recklessly to make a statement or representation, or furnish a document or information, which is false in a material particular. The penalty for this offence is, on summary conviction, a fine not exceeding the prescribed sum, presently £2,000, and on conviction on indictment to imprisonment for a term not exceeding two years or a fine of unlimited amount, or both (s.1(5)). In addition, any licence issued after the commission of this offence will be void (s.1(7)). Moreover, where an animal is being imported or exported the person having possession or control of the animal may be required to provide proof that the import or export is lawful. If proof is not furnished to the satisfaction to the Commissioners of Customs and Excise the animal will be liable to forfeiture (s.1(8), and Customs and Excise Management Act 1979).

In addition to the basic prohibition upon import or export of animals under the Act a number of additional prohibitions apply in relation to the sale and movement of endangered animals unless authorised by a licence issued by the Secretary of State (s.4(1B)). It is an offence to sell, offer or expose for sale, have in possession for sale, or transport for the purposes of sale, or display to the public any animal which has been unlawfully imported under the Act (s.4(1)). In addition it is an offence to sell, offer or expose for sale, or have in possession for sale or transport for the purpose of sale any live or dead animal which is listed in Schedule 4 to the Act, considered below, unless it has been imported before the passing of the Wildlife and Countryside Act 1981 (s.4(1A), as amended). For the purposes of assisting the discovery of any unlawful import of a live animal under the Act, the Secretary of State may make an order prohibiting the import by sea or by air of specified animals, or restricting the import by sea or air other than at ports specified in relation to animals of that kind (s.5(2)).

Separate provision arises under the Act for the Secretary of State, after consultation with the appropriate scientific authority (s.7(1)) to impose restrictions on the movement of certain live animals after import. Hence when a licence has been issued or applied for in respect of a live animal falling under Schedule 1, after consulting with one or more of the scientific authorities, the Secretary of State may give a direction as to restrictions upon movement of the animal after import (s.6(1)). Where a direction of this kind has been given in relation to an animal, the animal is to be kept at the premises specified under the direction (s.6(2)). In such circumstances it is an offence for anyone who knows, or ought to know, that a direction has been given, knowingly to take the animal, or permit it to be taken, to premises other than those specified in the direction. Alternatively, the offence is committed where the animal is moved from premises which are specified under the direction, with knowledge that the removal is not authorised, to keep the animal in premises which are known not to be specified by the direction. The penalty for this offence is, on summary conviction, a fine not exceeding level 5 on the standard scale, presently £2,000 (s.6(3)).

The species of fish the import and export of which are restricted under the Act are specified in Part II of Schedule 1 to the Act to be as shown in Table 8.1. It is to be noted that the second column of this table, giving a common name or names for the species, where available, is stated to be included by way of

Table 8.1

Restricted kind	*Common name or names*
Sturgeons	
Acipenser breviostrum	Shortnose sturgeon
Acipenser fulvescens	Lake sturgeon
Acipenser oxyrhynchus	Atlantic sturgeon
Acipenser sturio	Common sturgeon
Bonytongues	
Arapaima gigas	Arapaima
Scleropages formosus	Asiatic bonytongue
Salmon	
Coregonus alpenae	Longjaw cisco
Salmo chysogaster	Mexican golden trout
Stenodus leucichthys leucichthys	Inconnu
Carps and suckers	
Caecobarbus geertsi	Blind cave fish
Chasmistes cujus	Cui-ui
Plagopterus argentissimus	Woundfin
Probarbus julliene	Ikan temoleh
Ptychocheilus lucius	Colorado squawfish
Rhodeus sericeus	Bitterling
Toothcarp	
Cynolebias constanciae	
Cynolebias marmoratus	
Cynolebias minimus	Annual killifish
Cynolebias opalescens	
Cynolebias splendens	
Xiphophorus couchianus	Monterey platyfish
Coelacanths	
Latimeria chalumnae	Coelacanth
Australian lungfish	
Neoceratodus forsteri	Australian lungfish
Catfish	
Pangasianodon gigas	Giant catfish
Silurus glanis	Wels (European catfish)
Perch	
Ambloplites rupestris	Rock bass
Lepomis gibbosus	Pumpkin seed (sunfish)
Micropterus salmoides	Large-mouthed black bass (sand perch)
Stizostedion lucioperca	Zander
Stizostedion viterum glaucum	Blue walleye
Drumfish	
Cynoscion macdonaldi	Drumfish

guidance only, and in the event of any dispute or proceedings only the first name is to be taken into account.

8.04   *Introduction of fish into waters in England and Wales*

Turning from restrictions upon import of fish into Britain to restrictions upon transfers of fish between waters, in England and Wales, the release of fish into inland waters amounts to a fishery offence, the responsibility for enforcement of which falls to the National Rivers Authority. Section 30 of the Salmon and Freshwater Fisheries Act 1975 makes it an offence to introduce any fish or spawn of fish into an inland water, or for a person to possess any spawn of fish with the intention of introducing it, unless he first obtains the written consent of the National Rivers Authority. In practical terms this must be an important offence for fish farmers supplying coarse or game fish for restocking to keep in mind, since the restocking of a water without National Rivers Authority permission will be an offence which will be committed by the person who 'introduces' the fish into the water. The maximum penalty for the offence is a fine at level 4 on the standard scale of fines, presently equivalent to £1,000 (Sch.4 para.1(2) Salmon and Freshwater Fisheries Act 1975).

For the purposes of the offence of introducing fish into inland waters, 'inland water' is defined to mean any of the following:

(a) any river, stream or other watercourse, whether natural or artificial and whether tidal or not;
(b) any lake or pond, whether natural or artificial, and any reservoir or dock in so far as these do not fall within (a);
(c) so much of any channel, creek, bay, estuary or arm of the sea as does not fall within (a) or (b) (s.41(1) Salmon and Freshwater Fisheries Act 1975 and s.135(1) Water Resources Act 1963, as amended by s.128 and Sch.13 para.31(1) Water Act 1989).

In addition to the broad definition of 'inland water', the offence of introducing fish into inland waters is also broadly formulated in that the offence is committed in respect of the release of 'any fish'. Notably this expression does not serve to limit the scope of the offence to fish within any particular category, such as freshwater fish, salmon, eels, or seafish. Indeed, though it may not correspond with the interpretation of the provision generally adopted by those enforcing it, there are judicial dicta to the effect that where the word 'fish' is used in an unqualified sense it is capable of applying to shellfish as well as finfish. Hence in *Caygill* v. *Thwaite* ((1885) 49 JP 614) it was decided that crayfish were 'fish' in the absence of any indication to the contrary, so that a statute which made it unlawful to take fish applied equally to crayfish as to other kinds of floating fish.

8.05   *Introduction of fish into fish farms in England and Wales*

In relation to the development of the fish farming industry the Government's expressed policy objective has been stated to be the achievement of a fish farming industry unhindered by unnecessary constraints, and the removal of unnecessary statutory restrictions as a means to that end (Ministry of Agriculture, Fisheries and Food (1981) para.29). Pursuant to this policy it was proposed that the power then exercised by water authorities (now the National Rivers Authority) to restrict the movement of fish, by refusal to grant written permission to introduce fish into inland waters, should be limited to the movement of fish into public waters and waters discharging into public waters. Specifically, the Government's proposal was that the introduction of fish into the private waters of a fish farm should cease to require water authority authorisation, as should the introduction of fish into fish farms discharging water into public waters, providing that such discharges took place in accordance with discharge consent granted by a water authority (para.38, and see [11.02E] below on discharge consents). The requirement of obtaining written water authority permission on every occasion when fish were brought into a fish farm was perceived as a source of unnecessary inconvenience where frequent movements of fish took place, and a consequent relaxation in the law was thought desirable by the fish farming industry.

Although not as extensive as had been originally envisaged, some relaxation of the offence of introducing fish into inland waters was brought about under the Salmon Act 1986. Originally it was proposed that the offence would not be committed where fish or spawn of fish were introduced into any fish farm. ('Fish farm' was given the same meaning as under the Diseases of Fish Act 1937, see [6.02] above.) The original proposal to remove fish farms from the scope of the offence gave rise to concern that this might result in a serious decline in the general aquatic environment through the spread of fish disease. In response to this concern, the original clause was modified to limit the relaxation of the law to those fish farms which either do not discharge into another inland water, or do so by means of a specially constructed or adapted conduit. It was in this form that the provision passed into law as s.34 Salmon Act 1986. Although it is not entirely clear what precise interpretation will be placed upon the requirement of a 'specially constructed or adapted conduit' in practice, it seems that an effective means is required to prevent the escape of fish, or organisms which may cause disease in fish, from fish farms. Consequently, the exemption will be unavailable in the case of fish farms consisting of cages placed in inland waters where the degree of isolation required to prevent the spread of fish disease is not present.

It is to be noted that though authorisation from the National Rivers Authority is no longer needed for the introduction of fish into fish farms in England and Wales, information about fish movements is required to be supplied to the Ministry of Agriculture, Fisheries and Food under the fish farm registration scheme (see [6.03] above). This information may be made available to the National Rivers Authority for the purpose of enabling the Authority to carry out any of its functions under the Diseases of Fish Act 1937 (s.9(1)(d) Diseases of Fish Act 1937 and s.38 ,Salmon Act 1986, as amended by s.141 and Sch.17 para.3 Water Act 1989). It follows that the Authority have access to information about fish movements into fish farms where this is needed for disease control purposes (see s.3 Disease of Fish Act 1937, considered in [7.02E] above, on the powers and duties of the National Rivers Authority in relation to fish disease).

8.06   Introduction of salmon into waters in Scotland

The restrictions imposed upon the introduction of fish into waters under the Salmon and Freshwater Fisheries Act 1975 are applicable only to England and Wales, but a narrower counterpart to the power to control the entry of fish into inland waters has recently been provided for in relation to Scotland under the Salmon Act 1986. Section 24 of the 1986 Act states that a person who intentionally introduces any salmon or salmon eggs into inland waters in a salmon fishery district for which there is a salmon fishery board, is guilty of an offence and liable on summary conviction to a fine not exceeding level 2 on the standard scale, presently £100. The basic prohibition upon introduction of salmon or salmon eggs is, however, made subject to two exceptions. First, no offence is committed if the person concerned has the previous written consent of the district salmon fishery board for the salmon fishery district in which the waters are situated. Second, the offence is not committed where the waters constitute or are included in a fish farm within the meaning of the Disease of Fish Act 1937 (see [6.02] above). So far as salmon are concerned, therefore, the position in Scotland is analogous to that in England and Wales with the fishery authority having a regulatory power to prevent the introduction of salmon where they consider such introduction undesirable.

8.07   Introduction of new species

An extensive restriction upon the introduction of new species of fish into waters in England and Wales and Scotland arises under s.14 of the Wildlife and Countryside Act 1981. This provision states that a person will be guilty of an offence if he releases, or allows to escape into the wild, any animal which is, either of a kind which is not ordinarily resident in and is not a regular visitor to Great Britain in a wild state, or is included in Part I of Schedule 9 to the Act (s.14(1) Wildlife and Countryside Act 1981). Likewise, an attempt to commit this offence, or the possession of anything capable of being used in committing the offence, is punishable to the same extent as the main offence (s.17). A person found guilty of the offence is liable, on summary conviction, to a fine not exceeding the statutory maximum, presently set at £2,000, and on conviction on indictment, to a maximum fine of unlimited amount (s.21(4)). In addition, the offence is accompanied by various powers of forfeiture which may be exercised by a court convicting a person of the offence. Specifically, a convicting court is bound to order the forfeiture of the animal in respect of which the offence was committed, and *may* also order the forfeiture of any vehicle, or boat, used to commit the offence, and any animal of the same kind as that in respect of which the offence was committed found in the possession of the convicted person (s.21(6) and s.27(1)).

The offence of introducing a new species of animal is capable of covering a range of situations where non-native species of fish are introduced into waters. 'Animal' for the purposes of the offence includes fish, and hence the release of species of fish that are not ordinarily resident in Great Britain would come within the offence. Beyond the introduction of new species, however, there are a number of non-native species which, to some degree, have become established in Great Britain and the release of such species is made an offence through the listing of these species in Part I of Schedule 9 to the Act. At the time of enactment that part of the Schedule included the following species of fish which are already established in the wild: the Large-mouthed Black Bass (*Micropterus salmoides*), the Rock Bass (*Ambloplites rupestris*), the Pumpkinseed, otherwise known as Sun-fish or Pond-perch, (*Lepomis gibbosus*), the Wels, otherwise known as European catfish, (*Silurus glanis*) and the Zander (*Stizostedion lucioperca*). This list may, however, be subject to variation from time to time in that the Secretary of State may by order, either generally or with respect to particular areas in Great Britain, add the name of any animal to, or remove it from, the Schedule (s.22(5)).

The offence of introducing new and 'scheduled' species of fish into the wild is subject to two explicit defences. The first defence is that the provision creating the offence of releasing new species is stated not to apply to anything done under, and in accordance with, a licence granted by the Secretary of State (s.16(4) and (9)). In this respect the Minister has been advised by the Nature Conservancy Council that any species that has not bred successfully in the wild should nonetheless be subject to the prohibition. Accordingly, the introduction to waters outside fish farms, of species such as the Rainbow Trout (*Salmon gairdneri*), Portuguese Oysters (*Crassostrea angulata*) and Pacific Oysters (*Crassostrea gigas*) is, in principle, required to be licensed. However, the potential difficulty constituted by the widespread introduction of these species has been avoided by the Minister making them subject to a general licence authorising their introduction for the purposes of the 1981 Act (Newbold, Hambrey and Smith (1986) p. 143).

The second defence to the offence of introducing new species is that the accused took all reasonable steps and exercised all due diligence to avoid committing the offence (s.14(3) Wildlife and Countryside Act 1981). Where, however, this defence involves an allegation that the commission of the offence was due to the act or default of another person, the person charged will not, without leave of the court, be entitled to rely on the defence unless prior notice of the intention to raise this defence is given. Accordingly the accused person seeking to raise the defence must, within a period ending seven clear days before the hearing, serve on the prosecutor a notice giving information identifying or assisting in the identification of the other person concerned (s.14(4)). Clearly the intention behind this provision is that the act or default of another person should not be introduced as a last-moment defence without the prosecution having sufficient opportunity to consider the genuineness of the claim.

A person authorised by the appropriate Secretary of State may, at any reasonable time and, if required to do so, upon producing evidence that he is so authorised, enter any land other than a dwelling for the purpose of ascertaining whether the offence of introducing new species is being, or has been, committed on that land (s.14(5)). Anyone who intentionally obstructs a person acting in the exercise of this power of entry upon land is guilty of an offence (s.14(6)). In addition to the powers given to persons authorised by the Secretary of State special powers of enforcement are given to police constables, (s.19(1)) and for the purpose of exercising these powers, a constable who with reasonable cause suspects that a person is committing the offence of introducing new species may enter any land other than a dwelling house (s.19(2)). If a justice of the peace, or sheriff, is satisfied by information given on oath that there are reasonable grounds for suspecting that an offence of introducing new species has been committed, and that evidence of the offence may be found on any premises, he may grant a warrant to any constable, with or without other persons, to enter upon and search those premises for the purpose of obtaining evidence (s.19(3)). Legal proceedings for the offence of introducing new species may be instituted by a local authority in England and Wales for any offence committed in their area (s.25(2)).

Despite the apparent breadth of the offence of introducing new species under s.14 of the 1981 Act, two key difficulties surround its operation. First it is to be noted that the offence is formulated in terms of the introduction of fish of a 'kind' that are not ordinarily resident, and the listed species in the Schedule. The word 'kind' is somewhat ambiguous in this context in that it could mean 'species', or alternatively a particular part of a species distinguished by genetic characteristics. The marginal note to the section indicates that it is 'species' that are intended to be the measure of whether fish are of the same 'kind' or not, and it follows that matters such as genetic difference between the introduced fish and the existing stock of that species are not relevant. If this interpretation is correct then the offence would not be committed in a situation where fish of a native species are introduced even though such fish are of a significantly different genetic make-up from the existing population of that species in a water. At a time when fishery biologists are becoming increasingly concerned about the need to preserve genetic integrity of native stocks, and farmed fish are being selectively bred for qualities which might not commonly be found in natural populations, it may be a shortcoming that the provision is concerned only with the species and not with the potentially undesirable genetic character of the fish concerned. Alternatively it could be maintained that if 'species' had been intended that word should have been used in the section rather than 'kind' and, therefore, it was envisaged that genetic differences would be taken into account. The difficulty with this argument lies in the question of what constitutes a distinct genetic 'kind' since, in the final analysis, it may be shown that all creatures are genetically unique.

A second difficulty inherent in the prohibition upon introduction of new species lies in the formulation of the offence as that of allowing the 'release' of fish into the 'wild'. The meaning of this expression is not defined in the Act and again presents a serious difficulty of interpretation. For example, it might be argued that the release of fish into an enclosed pond is not a release into the 'wild' because of the element of containment. If that argument were to be accepted it would not seem to matter, in principle, that the water concerned was a large one, and as a result the offence would become difficult to prove in many situations. Similarly the point at which 'release' into the wild takes place is not without difficulty. For example, modern shellfish rearing practices may involve shellfish being fixed to rafts and lines by some means before being placed in waters and arguably this does not constitute a 'release' for the purposes of the provision since control is retained by the owner. If shellfish held in this way were allowed to deposit spat, however, a release into the wild will have been 'allowed', but the precise point at which the offence is committed will be extraordinarily difficult to determine in such circumstances.

Chapter 9

The Supply of Water

9.01 Rights to water

A supply of water is an essential prerequisite of fish farming, and yet the right to this commodity for aquacultural purposes is capable of giving rise to legal difficulties concerning both common law and statutory provisions. Although the supply of a sufficient quantity of water is not likely to give rise to practical or legal problems for fish farms in coastal waters, or for freshwater cage culture operations, in all other circumstances, the viability of aquaculture depends upon the availability of water. This, in turn, depends upon the possession of a legal right to abstract, divert or impound enough water to accommodate the farmed population of fish.

For practical purposes the supply of water means the supply of an amount of water which is maintained at a sufficiently high quality to support the type of fish which are to be farmed. In law, however, matters of water quantity and quality are, in important respects, the subjects of separate systems of regulation, and accordingly are best considered separately. The approach taken here is to devote this chapter to the general principles of law relating to the right to a supply of water for a fish farm, whilst leaving matters relating to water quality to be considered in the two chapters which follow. Hence abstraction, diversion and impoundment of water for fish farms fall for discussion here whilst issues of water pollution, relating to either water taken into, or discharged from, fish farms are deferred for consideration in the subsequent chapters.

An initial point to note is that the main concern of the law is with water *rights*, rather than the *ownership* of water in any strict sense. Water which is found in watercourses is not normally the subject of private ownership. Such water may be taken and used by anyone who has the legal right to abstract or make particular uses of the water, either as a matter of common law or under statute. After use, however, the water will be returned to the watercourse where it is available for use by others with the right to do so, once again without the user gaining any continuing property right in it which excludes its future use when returned to the watercourse. It is only where water is in some way 'appropriated' for private use that the possessor acquires the right to exclude others from using it, and only then is it capable of being stolen from the possessor by another person (*Ferens* v. *O'Brien* (1883) 47 JP 472; and in Scotland *Morris* v. *Bicket* (1864) 2M.1082 and 4M.44). Other than when appropriated by being contained within a tank or pool, however, water is public rather than private property and the subject of rights of use which fall short of ownership.

9.02   Riparian rights

As a matter of common law the right to a supply of water brought by a watercourse derives from ownership of the 'riparian' land forming the bank of a stream or river. Although modified by a range of statutory provisions, the riparian rights of waterside owners amount to a collection of traditional interests in the enjoyment of a natural stream. Hence it has been observed that,

> 'It has now been settled that the right to the enjoyment of a natural stream of water ... belongs to the proprietor of the adjoining lands as a natural incident of the soil itself; and that he is entitled to the benefit of it as he is to all the other advantages belonging to the land of which he is the owner. He has the right to have it come to him in its natural state, in flow, quantity and quality, and to go from him without obstruction.' (Lord Wensleydale in *Chasemore* v. *Richards* (1859) 7 HL Cas.349, at p.382.)

In addition to the right to the flow of water in its natural state, each riparian owner has the right to make certain uses of water from the stream. Traditionally these include rights to abstract, divert and impound water for specified purposes. The purposes for which water is legitimately taken have been termed 'ordinary' and 'extraordinary' uses. The distinction between these two is that, whilst ordinary use of water is unrestricted in that abstraction is permissible even to the extent that it brings about the total exhaustion of the stream, extraordinary use must be reasonable and water which is taken must be restored to the stream substantially undiminished in volume and unaltered in character (*McCartney* v. *Londonderry and Lough Swilly Railway* [1904] AC 301, Lord Macnaghten at pp. 306 to 307). Despite the significant legal differences between ordinary and extraordinary uses of water the distinction has never been clearly and comprehensively stated. It would seem that ordinary uses encompass the taking of water for domestic purposes and for watering cattle, whilst extraordinary purposes have been suggested to include water 'used for producing power, or for a fish farm, or for cooling, or for such irrigation as does not affect the quantity of the flow' (Newsom and Sherratt (1972) p. 6). The categorisation of water use for fish farming purposes as an extraordinary purpose within the riparian right of abstraction, means that this use is only permissible where the activity is for a reasonable purpose in relation to the riparian property, and the water which is taken is restored to the stream substantially unaltered in either quantity or quality. (Illustrations of this principle in respect of other extraordinary uses are to be found in *Swindon Waterworks Co.* v. *Wilts and Berks. Canal* (1875) 33 LT 513; and *Attwood* v. *Llay Main Collieries* [1926] Ch 444.)

The riparian rights of diversion and impoundment follow the same general principles as those relating to abstraction in that, to be permissible, any re-routeing or holding-back of water must be both reasonable in relation to the riparian property and involve no sensible diminution in the quantity or quality of the water eventually received by lower riparian proprietors. Hence, as a matter of common law, it is permissible for a riparian owner to construct an artificial channel carrying some part of the flow of water in a stream away from the main channel for purposes relating to the riparian land. It is this power that is exercised where water is taken as a source of supply to a fish farm and yet, it must be stressed, the power must be exercised in such a manner as to cause no impairment to the supply of water provided to other riparian owners. In practice, therefore, this means that the water, after diversion or impoundment, must be returned to the main channel within the boundaries of the land held by the diverting or impounding riparian owner.

In respect of a proposed diversion or impoundment of a stream particular consideration may need to be given to adverse consequences upon navigation and fisheries. Where a right of navigation exists upon the stream it is not permissible to remove water from a stream to such an extent that navigation is impaired. Thus in *Attorney-General* v. *Great Eastern Railway Co.* ((1871) 35 JP 788) it was decided that a railway company was not entitled to take such a large quantity of water for use at its station as would impede navigation. In respect of fisheries, it has been held that a lower riparian owner is not permitted to divert the flow of water in a stream to the extent that interference will be caused to the free passage of migratory fish, and in such a situation an upper riparian owner will be entitled to a remedy to prevent the diversion (*Pirie and Sons Ltd.* v. *Kintore (Earl)* [1906] AC 478; and *Fraser* v. *Fear* (1912) 107 LT 423).

A recent decision providing a pertinent illustration of riparian rights to water in a fish farming context is *Swan Fisheries Ltd* v. *Holberton* (unreported, Queen's Bench Division, 14 December 1987), where the importance of the common law right to a continuing supply of water was conclusively reaffirmed. The essential facts were that the supply of river water to a trout farm was interrupted for a period of six hours as a result of the closure of a sluice on the river by an upstream riparian proprietor who sought to impound a quantity of water to abstract for irrigation purposes. The effect of the sluice closure was to reduce the flow of the river to a negligible amount so that the river bed became virtually dry apart from some of the larger pools. The water flow fell below the level of the trout farm inlet, and despite the strenuous efforts of the proprietors of the farm to pump water through the trout ponds, a large quantity of fish died through oxygen starvation.

In an action by the trout farm proprietors based upon nuisance and negligence on the part of the upstream abstractor (see [10.03B] and [10.03D] below), it was observed that a riparian proprietor may only use water in a reasonable manner, so as not to cause material injury or annoyance to downstream neighbours (citing *Embrey* v. *Owens* 6 Ex. Ch. Rep. 353). Although irrigation, as an instance of extraordinary use of water, is permissible provided it is reasonable, the use which had here been made did not fall into that category, the defendant's conduct in interrupting the flow of the stream by closing the sluice went beyond the bounds of their entitlement to make use of the river for irrigation purposes. Because the death of the trout was a foreseeable consequence of the closure of the sluice it was found that the defendant was liable in both negligence and nuisance for the consequences of his act. Accordingly, damages of £18,500 plus interest were awarded to the plaintiff both to cover the value of the trout which were lost and the expense of steps taken in an attempt to mitigate the damage, including summoning the local fire brigade to pump water into the fish farm.

9.03   *The Water Resources Act 1963*

Although common law riparian rights remain of considerable importance in establishing the relative legal entitlements of owners of a watercourse, in a great many contexts these rights have been superseded by Parliamentary enactments or are to be read subject to statutory modifications. In respect of water abstraction, diversion and impoundment, this is markedly so. In respect of England and Wales some, though not all, of the common law rights of riparian owners have been abrogated by the provisions of the Water Resources Act 1963, as recently amended by the Water Act 1989. Notably the 1963 Act does not apply to Scotland where, with a few exceptions, the law relating to water abstraction continues to be provided under the common law. (The exceptions applicable to Scotland arise under s.17 Water (Scotland) Act 1980, concerning abstraction orders made by the Secretary of State; under s.10 Electricity (Scotland) Act 1979, concerning abstraction by electricity boards; under Spray Irrigation (Scotland) Act 1964, providing for the safeguard of public rights in relation to spray irrigation; and under Private Acts of Parliament.)

The overall purpose of the Water Resources Act 1963 was to promote measures for the conservation, augmentation and proper use of water resources in England and Wales, and, amongst other things, this was to be accomplished by the imposition of controls upon the abstraction of water. Administrative responsibility for these controls was originally entrusted to river authorities, but was later transferred to water authorities (under s.10 Water Act 1973) and now rests with the National Rivers Authority. Accordingly it is now the duty of the National Rivers Authority, in accordance with directions from the Secretary of State for the Environment, to take all such actions as it considers to be necessary or expedient for the purpose of conserving, redistributing or otherwise augmenting water resources, and securing the proper use of water resources, in England and Wales (s.125 Water Act 1989).

In relation to the functions of the National Rivers Authority in relation to water resources, 'water resources' are stated to be, in relation to any area, the water for the time being contained in any source of supply in the area of the Authority. 'Source of supply' means any inland water which discharges into other waters or underground strata in which water is or at any time may be contained (s.2(1) Water Resources Act 1963, as amended by s.128 and Sch.13 para.2 Water Act 1989). The requirement that water discharges into other waters is specifically stated to exclude any inland waters which are a lake, pond or reservoir which do not discharge into other waters, or one of a connected group of such waters where none of the group discharges into inland waters outside the group (s.2(3)). 'Inland water' is broadly defined to include rivers, streams and other watercourses, lakes, ponds and reservoirs, and estuaries and arms of the sea (s.135(1), as amended by s.128 and Sch.13 para.31(1) Water Act 1989; for the full definition see [8.04] above). 'Watercourse' is stated to include all rivers, streams, ditches, drains, cuts, culverts, dykes, sluices and passages through which water flows, except certain mains and water fittings, local authority sewers and adits and passages (s.135(1), as amended by s.128 and Sch.13 para.31(1) Water Act 1989). The upshot of this chain of definitions is that the National Rivers

Authority are to take responsibility for almost all of the waters in which freshwater fish farming is likely to take place, and as a general principle the use of these waters will come within the Authority's power to impose controls upon abstraction and other uses of water.

A.   Control of water abstraction

The control of abstraction of water under the Water Resources Act 1963, as amended, is achieved through the creation of a criminal offence of unauthorised abstraction of water. 'Abstraction' is defined to include doing anything whereby water in the area of the National Rivers Authority is removed from the source of supply, whether temporarily or permanently (s.135(1), as amended by s.128 and Sch.13 para.31(1) Water Act 1989), and will, therefore, include such matters as the diversion of a stream through the pools of an inland fish farm, even though the water is eventually returned to the stream. Unauthorised abstraction is, however, made subject to specified exceptions, the most important of which is the possession of an abstraction licence issued by the National Rivers Authority. Thus the basic offence is that no person is permitted to abstract water from any source of supply or cause or permit it to be abstracted, except in accordance with a licence to abstract granted by the National Rivers Authority (s.23(1), as amended by s.128 and Sch.13 para.5 Water Act 1989). Contravention of the licensing requirement, or failure to comply with a condition or requirement imposed in a licence is an offence, and on summary conviction the maximum penalty for this offence is a fine of the prescribed sum, which is presently set at £2,000 (s.49).

The general requirement of obtaining a licence to authorise the abstraction of water is made subject to a number of exceptions relating to small abstractions of less than five cubic metres; abstractions for domestic and agricultural purposes; land drainage operations; mining and other operations; water transfer by navigation, harbour or conservancy authorities; abstractions by vessels; fire fighting; and abstraction under an order of the Secretary of State for the Environment or the Secretary of State for Wales or both (ss.24 and 25, as amended by s.128 and Sch.13 paras.6 and 7). Of these, the only exception to the licensing requirement which is likely to be of general relevance to fish farms is the exception grounded upon abstraction for agricultural purposes.

The exception from the abstraction licensing requirement for agricultural purposes is available in the case of limited abstractions from inland waters by an occupier of land contiguous to the water at the point of abstraction, where the water is to be used on that land or other land held with it for agricultural purposes other than spray irrigation (s.24(2)(b)). In this context, 'agriculture' is defined to include the breeding and keeping of livestock, including any creature kept for the production of food, wool, skins or fur (s.135(1), and see [2.06] above). As a consequence of the reference to any creature kept for the production of food, it follows that fish farming activity will be exempt from the licensing requirement only in so far as it involves the keeping of creatures for the production of food. Implicitly, therefore, the farming of species for sporting or ornamental purposes will fall outside of the agricultural abstraction exemption and be subject to the requirement of abstraction licensing (see [2.06] and [5.08] above). Although previously the amount of water that could be abstracted within the agricultural licensing exception was unlimited, the position has been radically changed by the Water Act 1989. Under the amendments to the Water Resources Act 1963 brought about by the 1989 Act the qualification has been introduced that the amount of water abstracted for agricultural purposes is not to exceed twenty cubic metres, in aggregate, in any period of twenty-four hours (s.128 and Sch.13 para.31(3) Water Act 1989). The effect of this is that all but the very smallest fish farming operations will be brought within the abstraction licensing requirement.

In the unlikely event of a fish farm's operations now falling within the agricultural purposes exemption from water abstraction licensing, it is worth noting that the apparent freedom which this provides may not be as valuable as it appears at face value. This is because the farmer who is free to abstract water for agricultural purposes may not be equally free to *discharge* the same water back into the stream after use. Curiously, although exemption is available for agricultural abstractions, no corresponding exemption is given for agricultural discharges of the same water after use. As will be seen in Chapter 11 below, the discharge of such water by returning it to the stream will require a discharge consent, issued by the National Rivers Authority, under Part II Chapter I of the Water Act 1989 (see [11.02E]). Such a licence may stipulate, amongst other things, a maximum quantity of water which may be discharged and a maximum rate of discharge. As a practical matter, it follows that unless a fish farming abstractor is in the unlikely position of having the facility of being able to store a large amount of abstracted water indefinitely, the amount of water which can be abstracted will be determined by the amount which may be discharged in accordance with the discharge consent. Depending upon the precise terms upon which the National Rivers Authority issues a discharge consent, it may be that, in practical terms, one fish farmer rearing fish for food is not in a greatly different overall position from another rearing fish other than for food, notwithstanding the former's legal privilege of exemption from water abstraction licensing.

An incidental but related point to be noted concerns the significance of discharge consents in relation to abstraction in Scotland. Abstraction is not subject to statutory licensing requirements in Scotland, but discharge *is* subject to a requirement of authorisation by the river purification authorities. The ability of river purification authorities to grant discharge consents for discharges from fish farms, under Part II of the Control of Pollution Act 1974, as amended by the Water Act 1989, means that once again abstraction may be determined by the authorisation for discharge granted under the discharge consent. That is, although a fish farm in Scotland does not need an abstraction licence, as a practical matter abstraction may be limited by other legal means.

B.   Application for an abstraction licence

The lawfulness of water abstraction, other than on exempted grounds, is dependent upon the grant of a National Rivers Authority abstraction licence. A range of provisions are specified in relation to an application for such a licence. Initially, the person seeking the licence must be a person who is either the occupier of land contiguous to inland water, or a person who will have a right of access to such land at the time when the proposed licence is to take effect (s.27(2) Water Resources Act 1963). 'Occupier' of land is broadly interpreted to include a person who satisfies the Authority that he has entered into negotiations for the acquisition of an interest in land such that, if the interest is acquired, he will be entitled to occupy that land (s.27(4)(a), as amended by s.1(2) Water Resources Act 1968). Hence it would be open to a person negotiating to purchase a waterside site as a prospective fish farm to seek an abstraction licence without it needing to be shown that an interest in the site had actually be acquired.

An application for a water abstraction licence having been made, the proposal is then subject to a publication procedure which involves a notice of the details appearing in the *London Gazette* and, for each of two successive weeks, in one or more of the newspapers circulating in the locality of the proposed abstraction (s.28(1)). This notice is to include details of the planned abstraction and a statement as to where a copy of the application, and any map or plan or other document which has been submitted by the applicant, can be inspected free of charge (s.28(2)(a)). In addition the notice is to state that any person may make representations in writing to the National Rivers Authority with respect to the application at any time before the end of a specified period (s.28(2)(b)). The period for representations is specified to be not less than 25 days from publication in the *London Gazette*, and not less than 28 days from publication in the other newspaper circulating in the locality (s.28(2)(b) and s.28(3)). The National Rivers Authority is not to determine the application until this period has elapsed.

In determining whether to grant a licence the National Rivers Authority is to have regard both to any written representations which have been properly made concerning the application, and to the reasonable requirements of the applicant (s.29(3)). When the 1963 Act was originally enacted it was envisaged that it would be possible to determine water quantity criteria for each inland water, in accordance with what was termed 'minimum acceptable flow', and that abstraction licensing would take place against the need to maintain this level of flow (s.19(3)(b), now replaced by s.127 Water Act 1989). In practice, however, minimum acceptable flow levels have not been formulated. Nonetheless the National Rivers Authority is bound to have regard to the same criteria as would be relevant to the determination of minimum acceptable flow in considering applications for abstraction licences (s.29(5)). Stated explicitly, this means that the Authority is to have regard to the flow of water from time to time, the character of the water and its surroundings, and water quality objectives for the water. The amount of water flow specified as a minimum acceptable flow is to be not less than that needed for safeguarding public health and for meeting, both in respect of quantity and quality, the requirements of existing lawful uses of the water, whether for agriculture, industry, water supply or other purposes, and the requirements of land drainage, navigation and fisheries, both in relation to that water and to other waters whose flow may be affected (s.19(5), as amended by s.127(4) Water Act 1989).

If the National Rivers Authority decides to grant an abstraction licence, it must contain a number of specified provisions. In particular, it is to make provision as to the quantity of water authorised to be abstracted during a period or periods specified in the licence, including provision as to the way in which the quantity is to be measured, and provision for determining what quantity of water is to be taken to have been abstracted during the period of the licence (s.30(1)). The licence is to indicate the means whereby water is to be abstracted (s.30(2)), the land on which, and the purposes for which, the abstracted water is to be used (s.30(3)), and the person to whom the licence is granted (s.30(4)). The licence is also to state whether it is to remain in force until revoked, or whether it is to expire at a time specified in the licence (s.30(5)). Different provisions may be made, however, for the abstraction of water during different periods, or from the same source of supply but at different points or by different means, or for different purposes (s.30(6)).

If an applicant for an abstraction licence is dissatisfied with the decision of the National Rivers Authority in determining the application, a right of appeal exists to the Secretary of State (s.39(1)). The right of appeal is exercisable by notice in writing to the Minister within 28 days from the date of notification of the Authority's decision to the applicant, with service of a copy of the notice of appeal on the Authority (s.39(2)). Where an appeal of this kind is made the Minister may allow or dismiss the appeal, or may reverse or vary any part of the Authority's decision, and may deal with the application as if it had been made to him in the first instance (s.39(3)). In the event of written representations having been made in relation to the original application, the Minister is to require the National Rivers Authority to serve a copy of the notice of appeal on each of the persons who made representations, and to take into account any further representations in determining the appeal (s.30(4)). The Secretary of State may, and must if requested by the Authority or the applicant, hold a local enquiry or hearing before determining the appeal (s.30(5)). The decision of the Secretary of State is final and where his decision is to grant, vary or revoke a licence, the decision will include a direction to the Authority accordingly (s.39(6)).

C. Consequences of an abstraction licence

As has been observed, a key feature of the Water Resources Act 1963 is the creation of an offence of unauthorised abstraction of water (s.23(1)). The main consequence of the National Rivers Authority granting a licence to abstract water is that the licence provides a defence to any legal action brought on account of the abstraction other than a breach of contract or negligence (s.31).

Another key feature of abstraction licensing which has been changed by the Water Act 1989 relates to charges for abstraction licensing. Although legal provision was previously available for charges for abstraction licensing imposed by the licensing authority (s.30 Water Act 1973) no use was made of the provision. Under s.129 of the 1989 Act, however, it is provided that where an application is made for an abstraction licence, or for a variation of the conditions of a licence, or where a licence is granted or varied, or is for the time being in force the Authority may require the payment of such charges as may be specified under a scheme for abstraction charges made by the Authority (s.129(1) Water Act 1989). Charges are to be payable by the person making the application, or to whom the licence is granted, or to the person holding a licence which is varied or is in force. Provision made under a scheme of this kind may impose a single charge in respect of the whole period for which a licence is in force or separate charges in respect of different parts of the period, or both a single charge and separate charges (s.129(2)). Charging schemes for abstraction licensing are subject to the approval of the Secretary of State and the consent of the Treasury (s.129(3)).

The requirements dealing with the creation of charging schemes for abstraction licensing require the Authority to publish a notice setting out its proposals for a charging scheme in an appropriate manner for bringing the scheme to the attention of persons likely to be affected by it before submitting the scheme to the Secretary of State. A period is to be specified within which representations or objections may be made to the Secretary of State (s.129(4)). When submitted to the Secretary of State, it is his duty, first, to consider any representations duly made to him and not withdrawn; second, to have regard to the desirability of ensuring that the amounts recovered by the Authority under the scheme are appropriate to attribute to the expenses of the Authority in carrying out its water resources functions; and third, to have regard to the need to ensure that no undue preference is shown and that there is no undue discrimination in the fixing of charges under the scheme (s.129(5)). When made, it is the duty of the Authority to take appropriate steps to bring the provisions of the scheme to the attention of persons likely to be affected by it (s.129(8)).

The provisions for charging schemes in relation to water abstraction licences are made subject to a number of exceptions (s.129(9)). Hence the National Rivers Authority may, after having regard to material considerations, make an agreement with any person providing for exemption from payment of charges, or payment at a reduced rate (s.60(1) and (2) Water Resources Act 1963). Notably, no charges are to be levied in respect of water authorised to be abstracted from underground strata in so far as that water is to be abstracted for use for agricultural purposes other than spray irrigation (s.60(5)). If the Authority refuses to make an agreement exempting or reducing charges for abstraction, or makes an agreement which the applicant considers to be unsatisfactory, the question may be referred by either party to the Secretary of State (s.60(4)). The decision of the Secretary of State is final (s.60(5)). If charges payable under a licence are not paid within 14 days after written demand has been served on the licence-holder, the Authority may, after giving written notice, suspend the operation of the licence until the outstanding charges are paid (s.64).

Although at the time of writing no proposed scheme for abstraction licensing charges has been prepared the implications of the recent changes in the law for fish farmers are clear. The provision for charges means that water supply costs, depending upon the precise terms of the scheme devised, are capable of becoming a significant head of expenditure. It may be noted, however, that the special circumstances of aquacultural water use, involving the return of water to a watercourse with a minimum diminution to quantity and quality, ought properly to be taken into account. If special charging arrangements for fish farms are not devised, the large quantities of water which are used by such farms might make water abstraction economically prohibitive.

D. Control of impoundment

In addition to controls upon abstraction from inland waters, the Water Resources Act 1963 imposes analogous restrictions upon the construction of impounding works on such waters. Hence it is an offence for any person to begin, or to cause or permit any other person to begin, to construct or alter any impounding works at any point in an inland water, unless authorised by licence granted by the National Rivers Authority to obstruct or impede the flow at that point. Where an impounding licence has been granted the works are not to obstruct or impede the flow of the water except to the extent, and in the manner, authorised by the licence (s.36(1), as amended by s.128 and Sch.13 para.12 Water Act 1989). 'Impounding works' are defined as any dam, weir or other works in an inland water, whereby water may be impounded, and any works for diverting the flow of an inland water in connection with the construction or alteration of any dam, weir or other works in an inland water by which water may be impounded (s.36(6)). The offence of unlicensed impoundment is punishable on summary conviction by a fine not exceeding the prescribed sum, which is presently set at £2,000 (s.49).

As with the provisions relating to abstraction, the possession of a National Rivers Authority licence to impound water is a defence in a prosecution for unlawful impounding. Equally the possession of a licence will serve as a defence in any legal action, other than for negligence or breach of contract, providing the terms of the licence are complied with. Hence a person will be exonerated in any action arising from an obstruction or impoundment of flow providing that the obstruction or impediment are brought about in pursuance of the licence, in a manner specified in the licence, and to an extent not exceeding that specified in the licence, and that any other requirements of the licence have been complied with (s.37(2)). In circumstances where an impounding licence is required for the purpose of constructing or altering impounding works in an inland water in order to abstract water, it is possible to apply to the National Rivers Authority for a combined licence to impound and abstract (s.37(3)).

As an incidental point on the impoundment of water it is to be noted that large reservoirs are subject to special regulation for safety reasons. 'Large raised reservoirs', capable of holding more that 25,000 cubic metres of water above the natural level of land adjoining the reservoir, are subject to the Reservoirs Act 1975, which requires the local authorities in England and Wales and the regional and islands councils in Scotland to establish and maintain a register containing specified information about reservoirs. Generally the Act makes the construction or enlargement of large raised reservoirs subject to the supervision of a qualified engineer (s.6 Reservoirs Act 1975). Similarly, the undertakers responsible for reservoirs will be required to have them inspected, within 10 years of the last inspection, by an inspecting engineer and a report submitted as to their safety (s.10). Amongst other things the failure to have a reservoir surveyed, or to carry out any recommendation of the engineer included in his report in the interests of safety, as soon as practicable, will be an offence (s.22). Although the obligations upon reservoir owners are capable of being considerable in financial terms, the size specifications at which these duties arise is sufficiently large to exclude most fish farms.

E.   Revocation, variation and registration of licences

A number of provisions are made under the Water Resources Act 1963 for the revocation, variation and registration of licences to abstract or impound water. First, it is possible for the holder of a licence under the Act to apply to the National Rivers Authority to revoke the licence (s.42(1) Water Resources Act 1963). Alternatively, the holder may apply to the Authority to vary the licence, in which case the procedures for publication, determination by the Authority, reference to the Secretary of State, and appeals are the same as for initial licence applications (s.42(2)). Where the application for variation is for the reduction of the quantity of water, however, the provisions concerning publicisation of the application, and inviting and considering written representations in appeals against the Authority to the Secretary of State, do not apply (s.42(3)).

A second situation which is provided for is where the National Rivers Authority or the Secretary of State seeks to revoke or vary a licence. Where it appears to the Authority that a licence should be revoked or varied, the Authority may formulate proposals for revoking or varying the licence (s.43(1)). Alternatively the Secretary of State may, where he is of the view that a licence ought to be reviewed, direct the Authority to formulate proposals for revocation or variation (s.43(2)). In either case notice of the proposals are to be served on the holder of the licence and publicised in a prescribed manner (s.43(3)), naming a place in the locality where a copy of the proposals are available for public inspection and stating that written objections and representations may be made to the Authority before the end of the publicity period (s.43(4)). If, before the end of that period, the holder of the licence gives notice in writing to the Authority of objections to the proposals, the proposals are then to be referred to the Secretary of State with a copy of the notice of objection (s.43(6)). If no notice of objection is received before the end of the period the Authority may proceed with the proposals. Where, however, the proposals are for variation, rather than revocation, of a licence the Authority is to determine the matter according to considerations which apply to an initial application for a licence, including the need to have regard to representations which have been made and the need to secure minimum acceptable flow (s.43(7)).

Where the holder of a licence objects to National Rivers Authority proposals for the revocation or variation of the licence and the matter is referred to the Secretary of State he must consider the proposals along with the objections and any written representations which have been made. It is then for the Secretary of State to determine whether the licence should be revoked, or if the proposals were for variation, to determine whether the licence should be varied either in accordance with the proposals or, with the consent of the holder of the licence, in any other way (s.44(1)). Before determining the matter, however, the Secretary of State may, or must if a request is made by the holder of the licence or the Authority, cause a local inquiry to be held, or afford to the holder and the Authority an opportunity of appearing before a person appointed by the Secretary of State for the purpose (s.44(2)). The decision of the Secretary of State is final and, where it is to the effect that a licence should be revoked or varied, it is to include a direction to the Authority to revoke or vary the licence accordingly (s.44(3)).

Provision is made for the payment of compensation by the National Rivers Authority to the holder of a licence where revocation or variation takes place after the proposal has been referred to the Secretary of State for determination. In such a case compensation is payable by the Authority for expenditure incurred in carrying out work rendered abortive, and other loss or damage directly attributable to the revocation or variation (s.46(1)). Although compensation is payable for expenditure incurred in the preparation of plans and other similar preparatory matters (s.46(2)), no compensation will be paid for other work carried out before the grant of the licence which is revoked or varied (s.46(3)). No compensation will be payable in respect of a licence to abstract water if it is shown that no water has been abstracted under the licence during a period of seven years ending with the date on which the proposals for revocation or variation were served on the holder of the licence (s.46(4)).

A final matter relating to revocation or variation of an abstraction licence concerns applications initiated by the owner of fishing rights in the inland water concerned. In this context 'fishing rights' are defined to mean any right, whether it is an exclusive right or a right in common with one or more other persons, to fish in a water, where the right in question either constitutes an interest in land or is included in an interest in land or is exercisable by virtue of an exclusive licence granted for valuable consideration (s.47(11); and generally on fishing rights see Howarth (1987A)). The owner of fishing rights may apply to the Secretary of State for the revocation or variation of an abstraction licence on the ground that he has sustained loss or damage directly attributable to abstraction under the licence. Applications of this kind cannot be made within a year of a licence being granted, or where the owner of fishing rights is himself entitled to a protected right to abstract in respect of the water, or where the loss or damage is attributable to a breach of statutory duty on the part of the National Rivers Authority (s.47(1) and (2)). Where an application is made by the fishery owner under this provision, notice is to be served on the licence holder and the Authority stating that each is entitled to make representations to the Secretary of State within a specified period (s.47(3)). The Secretary of State may revoke or vary the licence where he is satisfied of the grounds for the application, and that the loss or damage which has been sustained justify it and were not wholly or mainly attributable to exceptional shortage of rain or to an accident or other unforeseen act or event not caused by, and outside the control of, the Authority (s.47(4)).

The public availability of information concerning abstraction and impoundment licences, and applications for such licences, is secured through this information being included in public registers kept by the National Rivers Authority. In this respect, the Authority is required to keep registers containing information relating to applications made to the Authority for the grant, revocation or variation of licences, including information as to the way in which such applications have been dealt with (s.53(1), as amended by s.128 and Sch.13 para.17 Water Act 1989). The Authority registers containing this information is to be available for inspection by the public at all reasonable hours (s.53(3)).

9.04   Gratings

A final issue which is pertinently considered alongside matters of water supply concerns the installation of gratings to prevent the entry of native fish into fish farms abstracting from, or discharging into, inland watercourses. It is mutually beneficial to fish farmers and fishery owners both to prevent the entry of wild fish into fish farms and to prevent the escape of farmed fish into the wild. From the point of view of the fish farmer the effective isolation of stock prevents interloping species taking feed intended for farmed fish or causing predation of the farmed species, and also prevents the loss of stock through escape. From the perspective of fishery interests sharing the same watercourse, preventing the entry of wild stocks into fish farms is a means of avoiding loss of native fish and preventing damage to the fishery by escapes of farmed fish (Lucas (1988)).

In England and Wales the provision of gratings to prevent the entry of salmon or migratory trout into diverted waters is provided for under the Salmon and Freshwater Fisheries Act 1975. (Generally see Howarth (1987A) sections 4.20 to 4.23.) For the purposes of these provisions, a 'grating' is defined to mean a device approved by the Minister of Agriculture, Fisheries and Food for preventing the passage of salmon or trout through a conduit or channel in which it is placed (s.41(1) Salmon and Freshwater Fisheries Act 1975). Hence where water is diverted from waters frequented by salmon or migratory trout by means of any conduit or artificial channel, and the diverted water is used for the purpose of a water undertaking or mill, the owner of the undertaking is to place and maintain, at his own cost, a grating across the conduit or channel for the purpose of preventing the descent of salmon or migratory trout (s.14(1)). Likewise the owner of the undertaking is to place and maintain a grating across the outfall of the conduit or channel for the purpose of preventing salmon or migratory trout entering (s.14(2)). In either case, however, exemptions may be granted by the National Rivers Authority. With Ministerial consent the National Rivers Authority may cause a grating of such form and dimensions as they may determine to be placed in a suitable place in any watercourse, mill race, cut, leat, conduit or other channel for conveying water for any purpose from any waters frequented by salmon or migratory trout. In such a case the Authority may cause the watercourse to be widened or deepened to compensate for the diminution of flow caused by the placing of the grating. Where the grating is placed and maintained, or the watercourse widened or deepened, by the Authority, this is to be done at the Authority's expense (s.15(1)).

Although regulations exist for securing the passage of salmon in relation to mill dams in Scotland (under s.6(6) and Schedule G. Salmon Fisheries (Scotland) Act 1868 and s.3(7) Salmon Act 1986) there is presently no provision for the screening of water diversions to prevent the passage of fish into or from fish farms. It is proposed, however, that regulations will be introduced to cover the matter in the near future (Department of Agriculture and Fisheries for Scotland (1988)). Under s.3 of the Salmon Act 1986 powers are given for the regulation of salmon fisheries, and the Secretary of State is specifically empowered, after consulting with such persons as he considers appropriate, to make regulations with respect to the construction, alteration and use of screens for the control of the passage of salmon in off-takes from inland waters and structures associated with such screens (s.3(2)(f) Salmon Act 1986).

In accordance with the power of the Secretary of State to make regulations in relation to screens in off-takes in inland waters in Scotland, it is envisaged that forthcoming regulations will lay down basic requirements in relation to sluices and screens. In particular there will need to be a sluice to control the flow of water at all off-takes to limit the quantity of water abstracted to that required for use by the abstractor. At the intake of every off-take there is to be installed a screen or barrier, the bars, mesh or operation of which are adequate to prevent migrating smolts from entering. At the point of return of a diverted supply there is to be placed a heck or grating, the bars of which are not to be more than 2 inches apart to prevent the entry of migrating salmon (Department of Agriculture and Fisheries for Scotland (1988) para.2.3).

As a final matter of relevance to the installation of gratings in inland fish farms, it would appear to have been the past practice of the water authorities in England and Wales to make use of powers to impose conditions in fish farm discharge consents to require outlets to be suitably screened to retain fish in fish farms (see Water Authorities Association (1984) Condition 2, cited in [11.03] below). Although the legal basis of this stipulation is not made explicit, it is probably referable to the power to impose 'such conditions as the Authority may think fit' in discharge consents (s.113 and Sch.12 para.2(3) Water Act 1989). The general basis on which discharge consents for fish farms are granted is discussed in Chapter 11 below.

Chapter 10

The Quality of Water Supply

10.01 The quality of water supply and discharge

In addition to the requirement of a supply of a sufficient quantity of water considered in the previous chapter, the viability of any kind of aquaculture must depend upon the availability of water of satisfactory quality. A contaminated source of supply may result in fish or shellfish becoming tainted and unfit for consumption, or in an extreme case will be a cause of fish mortality. In the past the major sources of water pollution have included industrial pollution, involving a range of chemicals and sources of physical pollution as diverse as the processes involved, and pollution arising from the inadequate treatment of sewage which has a severe deoxygenating effect upon the receiving waters. To the traditional categories of pollution may now be added an alarming increase in the amount of pollution of agricultural origin arising through the inadequate disposal of slurry and silage liquor (Water Authorities Association (1989)) and frequent incidents arising from accidents involving the movement of hazardous substances (Landless (1984A and B); and see *Welsh Water Authority* v. *Williams Motors* (1988) *Times* 5 December 1988). In a work of this kind it is impossible to give anything approaching a comprehensive account of the range of pollutants that may affect fish farms and the distinct effects upon fish stocks to which they give rise, but generally the legal principles involved are similar regardless of the nature of the pollutant concerned (generally see Howarth (1988A)).

In addition to the need for a pure supply of water fish farmers, as water users, will be appreciative of their obligations to other users in avoiding contamination of water through their own activities. It follows, therefore, that matters of water quality relating to fish farming are of two kinds. The first issue is that of permissible pollution of the water supply *received* by fish farmers, or the water environment in which fish farming takes place, whilst the second issue concerns the extent to which fish farm *discharges* may feature as a source of pollution. These different facets of the relationship between fish farming and water quality are reflected in differences in the legal principles relevant to the two different kinds of situation. For that reason matters of water quality of supply and water quality of discharge are considered separately, with this chapter concerned with the former and Chapter 11 with the latter.

As a broad generalisation, the difference between pollution received by fish farms and pollution discharged by fish farms follows the distinction drawn between the civil and the criminal law of water pollution. Where a fish farm receives polluted water causing a fish kill, or some other form of damage, the main concern of the farmer will be with entitlement to compensation for the injury caused to the enterprise. In addition he may be concerned with entitlement to a court order, termed an injunction, or in Scotland an interdict, to prevent further damage being caused by a recurrent or continuing source of pollution. These are essentially matters of civil law concerned with the respective rights and duties arising between different users of the shared water resource. By contrast, the most direct legal constraints imposed upon fish farmers and other persons discharging potentially polluting matter into a watercourse, or into coastal waters, arise by virtue of the criminal law making it an offence to pollute waters in particular circumstances.

There may be situations in which the civil and criminal law of water pollution both apply, as where a pollution incident which causes damage to a fish farm, for which compensation is payable, also amounts to a criminal offence on the part of the person causing the discharge, for which the polluter may be prosecuted. In such a case it would be possible for a single incident to give rise to both civil proceedings for compensation for the damage caused, and criminal proceedings to punish the accused. In more typical cases, however, the concern is usually one-sided, either to compensate the recipient of pollution or to prosecute the discharger. This chapter deals with the quality of water supply and is also primarily about the civil law of water pollution, whilst Chapter 11 is concerned with the criminal law. In actual instances it is conceded that matters of civil and criminal law are often interwoven, but for the purposes of this exposition it is clearer to deal with the main legal features involved separately.

10.02   *The basis of liability for water pollution at common law*

The basic purpose of the civil law of water pollution is to provide a remedy where a right to an uncontaminated supply of water has been infringed. The general common law principles upon which this branch of the law is based, and which are broadly the same in England and Wales and in Scotland (Ferguson (1907) p. 364; and Taylor (1928) p. 15) were evolved long before the development of commercial aquaculture. Nonetheless these principles serve to vindicate the present water quality interests of fish farmers. The common law continues to form the basis of entitlement to the two principal remedies of compensation for damage or loss caused by pollution, and the granting of an injunction or interdict to prevent continuation or recurrence of water pollution originating from a specified source.

Setting aside the pollution of coastal waters for later discussion (in [10.05] below) it is most convenient to consider the operation of the common law of water pollution in relation to the rights of owners of waterside land. As was noted in the preceding chapter, riparian ownership confers a range of common law rights in relation to the use of a stream, river or other watercourse. Most freshwater fish farms are located alongside rivers or streams and make use of an abstracted or diverted part of the flow of the watercourse, or in some cases impound the full flow of smaller streams. In situations of this kind the waterside location of the fish farm will normally carry with it the rights associated with riparian ownership. Only in exceptional circumstances when water is taken such a distance from the watercourse that the land on which it is used no longer 'abuts' the main watercourse will the land concerned cease to be riparian land (*Stockport Waterworks Co.* v. *Potter* (1864) 159 ER 545). Although freshwater lakes and ponds may sometimes be used for aquacultural purposes when fish cages are placed in open still water, in the absence of clear authority it has been suggested that the owner of the lake or pond will possess the same riparian rights as would the owner of land bounded by flowing waters (Wisdom (1979) p. 56).

Most pertinently amongst the collection of riparian rights enjoyed by the owners of waterside land is the right to receive the flow of water in the stream, 'in its natural state, in flow, quantity and quality' (Lord Wensleydale in *Chasemore* v. *Richards* (1859) 7 HL Cas. 349 at p. 382; on water quantity see Chapter 9 above). Traditionally this right has been of importance to those riparian owners using a watercourse as a fishery, or as a source of water for abstraction for agricultural or industrial purposes. Equally, the same right serves to protect the riparian interest of a fish farmer who abstracts from, or diverts, a source of supply for an aquacultural purpose.

The riparian right to an unpolluted supply of water was given its most complete and authoritative formulation in the speech of Lord Macnaghten in *John Young and Co.* v. *Bankier Distillery Co.*, where it was said,

> 'A riparian proprietor is entitled to have the water of the stream on the banks of which his property lies, flow down as it has been accustomed to flow down to his property, subject to the ordinary use of the flowing water by upper proprietors, and to such further use, if any, on their part in connection with their property as may be reasonable under the circum-stances. Every riparian owner is thus entitled to the water of his stream in its natural flow, without sensible diminution or increase, and without sensible alteration in its character or quality. Any invasion of this right causing actual damage, or calculated to found a claim which may ripen into an adverse right, entitles the party injured to the intervention of the court.' ((1893) [1891-4] All ER 439, at p. 441.)

The direct implications of Lord Macnaghten's principle for an activity such as fish farming, which is fundamentally dependent upon a continuing supply of uncontaminated water, are self-evident. Nonetheless a number of particular features of the principle deserve comment.

A. Ordinary and extraordinary uses of water

In the first place it is to be noted that under Lord Macnaghten's principle the right to the accustomed flow of water in its natural state of quantity and quality is subject to upstream riparian owners making 'ordinary use' of the water, and such additional use 'in connection with their property as may be reasonable under the circumstances'. 'Ordinary' uses of water by upper proprietors have been taken to encompass domestic and certain agricultural uses such as the watering of cattle, and for these purposes the proprietor is, at common law (contrast statutory provisions limiting abstraction discussed in Chapter 9 above) entitled to take water without restriction even if this has the effect of exhausting the stream completely. 'Extraordinary' uses of water are only permissible to the extent that they are reasonable in relation to the riparian land concerned, and also that the water which is taken and used for such purposes is returned 'substantially undiminished in volume and unaltered in character' (*McCartney* v. *Londonderry and Lough Swilly Railway* [1904] AC 301, at p. 307).

Alongside the common law categorisation of ordinary and extraordinary uses of water, it is evident that fish farming falls outside the narrow range of ordinary uses of water, and to be permissible, therefore, must come within the compass of extraordinary uses. As such, taking water for the purpose of fish farming must satisfy the constraints that it is a reasonable use of the water in relation to the land concerned, and that the water is restored to the stream substantially undiminished in volume and unaltered in character after use. Although this matter has not yet been the subject of an authoritative ruling by the courts, it has been suggested that, in principle at least, the use of water for a fish farm would be permissible as an extraordinary use of water (Newsom and Sherratt (1972) p. 6). Since the water which is abstracted or diverted for fish farming use is eventually returned to the stream it would not involve any diminution of volume. (Contrast spray irrigation, see *Rugby Joint Water Board* v. *Walters* [1966] 3 All ER 497; and Spray Irrigation (Scotland) Act 1964.) If it could be shown, however, that in any instance the addition of waste products of a fish farm brought about a *significant* change in the quality of the returned water then this would take the use outside those permitted at common law. Clearly there may be fine points of fact to be determined as to when the polluting effect of a fish farm exceeds that permitted by common law relating to riparian water use.

B.   Sensible alteration of the quality of water

A second key point arising from Lord Macnaghten's guiding principle on riparian water rights is the stipulation that a riparian owner is entitled to the 'natural' flow of water in the stream 'without sensible alteration in its character or quality'. It is notable that this formulation declines to relate the riparian owner's entitlement to any absolute physical or chemical standard of purity. Because natural waters vary so greatly in physical and chemical characteristics, the only meaningful comparison which can be drawn is the relative contrast between the stream with, and without, the presence of a man-made contamination which is complained of. At common law, therefore, water pollution is to be judged by the test of 'sensible alteration of quality' rather than by reference to any absolute physical or chemical measure of the polluted state of the water concerned.

Despite the reluctance of the common law to specify precise standards of water purity, the extensive case law in which the phrase 'sensible alteration of quality' has been at issue has served to clarify its meaning with some precision. Hence, in the later Victorian period water pollution litigation established that the most prevalent and harmful kinds of water pollution consequent upon industrialisation and concentrations of people in the major manufacturing centres came within the scope of the common law principles. Accordingly, numerous successful civil actions were brought against polluters causing water contamination through a diverse range of industrial processes, and against many local authorities failing to discharge their duty to prevent sewage pollution adequately.

The versatility of the common law principle governing water pollution was also demonstrated by its successful application to other forms of pollution which are not readily classified as chemical or organic in character. Thus, for example, it has been established that the principle is applicable to situations where the complaint arises, not because of any change in the chemical character of the water, but merely because of the alteration of a physical characteristic of a water supply. An action under the principle may, therefore, be grounded on the water temperature having been significantly changed due to thermal pollution through use of the water for industrial cooling purposes (*Tipping* v. *Eckersley* (1855) 69 ER 179). Similarly actionable would be the addition to a watercourse of matter which changes the colour or natural turbidity of the water (Mills (1976)) though in every case the need to show 'sensible alteration' of the water quality allows for the possibility that trivial interferences will be held insufficient to ground an action. Hence in one instance it was decided that the making of water temporarily muddy was too insignificant in its effect to support an action (*Taylor* v. *Bennet* (1836) 173 ER 146). On the other hand, it is established that it is no defence for a person whose actions cause sensible deterioration in water quality to claim that his actions were only one amongst many causes of pollution of a watercourse. In situations where pollution is a cumulative result of a number of polluters, each one making an appreciable contribution to the overall pollution will be liable under the principle (*Blair and Sumner* v. *Deakin* (1887) 52 JP 327).

C.   Actual damage and adverse rights

A final feature of Lord Macnaghten's principle worthy of comment is the concluding observation about remedies for water pollution, 'invasion of this right causing actual damage, or calculated to found a claim which may ripen into an adverse right, entitles the party injured to the intervention of the court'. This is a reference to the two legal objectives which may underlie an action for water pollution (see remedies discussed in [10.04] below). In the first kind of case an action may be brought where damage or loss has been suffered as a consequence of the pollution, in which case the usual purpose of the claim is to obtain monetary compensation and perhaps an order to prevent recurrence of pollution. In the second kind of case a claim arises because the polluter purports to be exercising a right to which he has no genuine entitlement, in which case the purpose of the case is to obtain a court declaration, termed declarator in Scotland, to prevent an unauthorised action becoming legitimated by long use or prescription. In the past it was possible to acquire a legal right, termed an easement, to pollute water by showing that the right had been exercised for a sufficiently long period of time without objection being raised by those riparian owners legally entitled to object. In law the continued and unopposed exercise of a right of this kind was presumed to rest upon a legitimate foundation. Today the acquisition of an easement to pollute water in this manner is of less relevance because of the stricter controls upon water pollution which arise in the criminal law, and the fact that an easement cannot be acquired through the continuation of behaviour which amounts to a criminal act. Nonetheless, in principle at least, it remains possible to bring an action without the need to show actual damage where such an action is brought to prevent another acquiring an adverse right to pollute water.

10.03   Common law actions for water pollution

Having considered the broad general formulation for redress which is provided for fish farmers and other riparian owners under the common law it must be added that any particular action concerning water pollution must be grounded upon a recognised head of civil liability. The branch of civil liability most relevant to water pollution is the law of tort, termed delict in Scotland, which is concerned with rights and duties in relation to injuries of all kinds arising outside the terms of any contract which may exist between the parties. The recognised head of tortious liability on which an action for water pollution may potentially be brought are trespass, nuisance, the rule in *Rylands* v. *Fletcher*, and negligence. The requirements for these different kinds of tortious action are considered under the following subheadings.

A.   Trespass

The tort of trespass arises in relation to water pollution where an unauthorised person brings about the direct entry of polluting matter into the water of the plaintiff without lawful justification. Trespass would be committed where, for example, a person placed poisoning matter in the water of a river, or fish enclosure, for the purposes of taking fish. Although the use of this method of taking fish would be a criminal offence against fishery law, (under s.4 Salmon and Freshwater Fisheries Act 1975; and s.4(b) Salmon and Freshwater Fisheries (Protection) (Scotland) Act 1951) it would also amount to a civil wrong for which the owner of the fishery, or fish farm, could sue the wrongdoer for compensation for loss suffered as a consequence of the trespass. Notably, however, an action in trespass may be brought without the need to show that any actual loss has been suffered. For that reason the action is especially appropriate to a situation where the plaintiff seeks to gain a declaration that the defendant has behaved wrongly in order to prevent continuation of a polluting activity, or to establish that no right to pollute exists in law.

Despite the initial attraction of the tort of trespass as a basis for a civil action for water pollution, its operation is limited in a number of ways which, in combination, have the effect of severely restricting its general utility. In the first place trespass, as it relates to water pollution, is inextricably linked to the ownership of land, and so would only be available to a person having the freehold ownership of riparian land or to a person occupying the land under a lease (*Jones* v. *Llanrwst U.D.C.* [1908–10] All ER Rep. 922). Second, trespass, though traditionally concerned with direct rather than indirect forms of tortious injury (see *Prior of Southwarks's Case* (1498) YB 13 Hen 7 p. 26, cited by Denning L.J. in *Southampton Corporation* v. *Esso Petroleum Co.* [1954] 2 All ER 561 at p. 570) is now thought only to lie in circumstances where damage arises through fault on the part of the defendant (Street (1988) p. 69). Given that fault involves showing either intention to pollute or negligence on the part of defendant, in most circumstances it will be simpler to pursue an action for negligence (considered in [10.03D] below) rather than trespass. Finally, and most problematically, the requirement of directness of injury which must be shown before an action for trespass can be maintained serves to rule out the majority of situations where water pollution damage is sustained to a fishery or fish farm. This is because in most cases concerning water pollution the pollutant is not directly deposited into the water alongside the plaintiff's land but, more likely, is carried down to the land by mediation of the flow of the river from a point of entry some distance upstream. Because the pollutant is carried on to the land the element of directness required for trespass is unlikely to be established. This view is supported by a leading case in which oil pollution contaminating a beach was held not amount to trespass because oil which had been jettisoned at sea by a foundering vessel was held to have been 'committed to the action of wind and wave' rather than being discharged directly onto the foreshore. The indirect means by which the oil reached the shore amounted to a denial of the directness of injury required for trespass (*Esso Petroleum Co. Ltd.* v. *Southport Corporation* [1955] 3 All ER 864).

B. Nuisance

A more appropriate basis for the kind of water pollution problem likely to be encountered by fish farms is a tortious action grounded in nuisance. Nuisance, properly termed private nuisance, is an action available where there has been an intentional or negligent act which causes unjustifiable and substantial interference with the enjoyment of land, including riparian land and water. As with trespass, therefore, it is an action which is only available to persons with an interest in land, either as a freeholder or leaseholder. In contrast to the action for trespass, however, actual damage needs to be shown for an action for nuisance to succeed. Another distinctive feature of nuisance of relevance to a water pollution action is the need to establish respective landholding by both parties to the proceedings. Hence it has been said that 'the ground of responsibility is the possession and control of the land from which the nuisance proceeds' (*Sedleigh-Denfield* v. *O'Callaghan* [1940] 3 All ER 349, at p. 364 per Lord Wright). Consequently, in the case referred to above where oil was discharged from a tanker causing pollution it was held that the action for nuisance was not available because it did not involve the defendants' misuse of land because the pollution originated from a ship at sea rather than a land-based source (*Southport Corporation* v. *Esso Petroleum Co.* [1955] 3 All ER 864, at p. 871). The significance of this is that a nuisance action would not be appropriate, for example, if a road accident caused the spillage of polluting matter which passed into a watercourse and through the waters of a fish farm, for the reason that the necessary interest in land on the part of the defendant would be lacking (see discussion of negligence in [10.03D] below).

Despite the potential difficulty of establishing landholding interests in some situations, the action for nuisance has traditionally proved to be an effective means of obtaining redress in cases of water pollution. In particular there are numerous instances in which it has formed the basis of successful actions for compensation for damage to fisheries. The most decisive of these was the decision in *Price of Derby Angling Association* v. *British Celanese Ltd. and Others* ([1953] 1 All ER 179) where an angling association complained of the deterioration of their fishery on the River Derwent as a consequence of pollution from a combination of sources. British Celanese, the principal defendant, discharged heated effluent containing suspended organic matter into the river, Derby Corporation discharged effluent consisting of inade-

quately treated sewage matter, and the British Electrical Authority aggra-
vated the problems caused by the presence of these pollutants by discharging
large quantities of heated effluent from their generating station. The
combined effect of these discharges was that the part of the river on which
the angling association held the fishing rights supported few, if any, fish.
Although arguments were raised on behalf of the local authority to the effect
that they were under a statutory duty to operate the sewage works
responsible for causing pollution, it was decided that that duty did not
authorise the discharge of inadequately treated effluent. The decision of the
Court of Appeal was that the angling association were entitled to compensatory damages in respect of the loss suffered to the fishery. In addition,
injunctions were granted against all three defendants to prevent further
pollution, though in the case of the local authority and the electricity
authority the operation of the injunctions was suspended for a period of time
to enable improvement work to be done to bring water treatment facilities up
to standard.

The *Pride of Derby* decision is of exceptional importance in reaffirming the
appropriateness of the action for nuisance to situations involving water
pollution. Although the plaintiffs' interest in the waters concerned was in
respect of their fishery value, it is clear that other kinds of interest in the
enjoyment of land can be protected by the same legal means. For this reason
it would, in many situations where water pollution is complained of, be open
to a fish farmer to bring an action against an upstream riparian proprietor in
the tort of nuisance for compensation for damage to fish stocks and an
injunction to prevent recurrence of pollution (see remedies discussed in
[10.04] below).

C.   The Rule *Rylands* v. *Fletcher*

Worthy of incidental mention amongst the forms of tortious action which
may ground an action for water pollution is a principle, closely related to
nuisance, usually referred to as the rule in *Rylands* v. *Fletcher*. The principle
involved, as originally stated, is that if a person for his own purposes brings
onto his land and collects or keeps there anything which is likely to do
mischief if it escapes he is, on the face of things, liable for all the damage which
is the natural consequence of its escape if it does so (*Rylands* v. *Fletcher* (1866)
LR 1 Ex. 265, and (1868) LR 3 HL 330). Initially this rule was applied to a
situation where water escaped from a reservoir, without any fault on the part
of the owner, and caused damage to neighbouring land. Despite the absence
of fault on the part of the owner, the application of the principle resulted in
his being found strictly liable for the damage which was suffered as a
consequence of the escape of water.

Stated in general terms the original rule annunciated in *Rylands* v. *Fletcher*
looks pertinent to many situations where an accumulation of noxious matter
on land subsequently 'escapes' causing water pollution as a natural consequence of the escape. The attractiveness of the principle from the plaintiff's
perspective is enhanced by its applicability being independent of any fault
being established on the part of the defendant. Because of a series of
subsequent decisions interpreting the rule, however, its apparent breadth
must be severely restricted to a narrow range of situations where land is used

for exceptionally hazardous activities which are not justifiable by reference to any generally beneficial purpose. Amongst other limitations upon the applicability of the principle, it has been stressed in later interpretations that it is to be restricted to 'non-natural' uses of land, a phrase which has been understood to mean activities bringing increased danger to others and not merely the ordinary use of land for the general benefit of the community (*Rickards* v. *Lothian* [1913] AC 263, at p. 280). Accordingly, subsequent decisions have found that the accumulation of industrial waste (*British Celanese Ltd* v. *A.H. Hunt Capacitors Ltd* [1969] 2 All ER 1252), the operation of sewage disposal works by a local authority (*Pride of Derby Angling Association* v. *British Celanese Ltd and Others* [1953] 1 All ER 179, at p. 203), and the operation of a munitions factory during wartime (*Read* v. *Lyons and Co. Ltd* [1946] 2 All ER 471) have not amounted to 'non-natural' uses of land. The overall indication is that, despite the initial attractiveness of the principle in relation to many situations where an action for water pollution is to be pursued, the scope for its application in these contexts is very limited indeed.

D. Negligence

Although of relatively modern origin compared to the torts discussed above, negligence today forms the most comprehensive basis upon which tortious liability, including liability for water pollution, may be founded. The abstract basis of negligence has been expressed as the imperative that reasonable care must be taken to avoid acts and omissions which can reasonably be foreseen would be likely to injure persons who are so closely and directly affected that they ought reasonably to have been in contemplation in relation to the act or omission (*Donoghue* v. *Stevenson* [1932] AC 562, Lord Atkin at p. 580). Alternatively, negligence can be said to arise wherever one person owes a duty of care to avoid acts or omissions which may cause injury or damage, and such loss is suffered by a person within the duty of care as a consequence of a breach of the duty. However stated, negligence is clearly a form of tortious liability of broad compass which since its first general formulation in 1932 has provided the legal basis for liability in a diverse range of situations where persons have caused injury by failing to adhere to the standard of behaviour expected of a reasonable person. It is a fair generalisation to suppose that in most situations where a person causes significant water pollution without legal justification this action would come within the bounds of negligence. It follows that where the consequence of water pollution is damage to fish farm stock then the losses suffered by the fish farmer would be compensatable under the tort of negligence.

Not only is negligence such a broad principle that it will cover most situations where pollution damage is sustained to a fish farm, it also has certain advantages from the plaintiff's point of view over the other potential forms of legal action. In the first place it is not limited to action by, or between, landholders, as are trespass and nuisance. Hence, for example, a tanker driver who causes the negligent spillage of noxious chemicals into a watercourse leading to a fish farm may be liable for the consequent damage caused in negligence, though not in trespass or nuisance. Moreover, another advantage of negligence is that where the circumstances which give rise to the pollution are solely within the custody of the defendant, the plaintiff may raise the plea of *res ipsa loquitur*, meaning the thing speaks for itself (*Scott* v. *London and St. Katherine Docks Co.* (1865) 3 H&C 596). The effect of this plea is that by showing that the incident could not have happened without negligence on the part of the defendant the onus is placed upon him to show that he was *not* negligent in causing pollution. The advantages of such a plea in a case of water pollution, where the precise cause of the incident may be known only to the defendant, are considerable (*Southport Corporation* v. *Esso Petroleum Co. Ltd* [1954] 2 All ER 561, Denning L.J. at pp. 573 to 574).

Given the breadth and strategic advantages of negligence it is somewhat surprising that there have been few authoritative decisions in which this form of legal action has been pursued by victims of water pollution. (Contrast the United States decision in *Union Oil Co.* v. *Oppen* 9 CA (1974) 501 F 2d 558.) One recent decision which hints at the potential of negligence to provide redress in situations of this kind in the future is *Scott-Whitehead* v. *National Coal Board* ((1987) 53 P&CR 263, and Tromans (1987)) where the defendants discharged a solution of chlorine into a river during a drought. At a point downstream water was removed by a farmer for irrigation purposes under an abstraction licence granted by the water authority for the area (under Water Resources Act 1963, see Chapter 9 above). Due to insufficient dilution of the chlorine, the water used for irrigation was saline and caused damage to the crops to which it was applied and an action was brought by the farmer for negligence against both the dischargers and the water authority. It was held that the dischargers were not liable, first, because it could not reasonably be expected that they would know that the concentration of chlorine was so great as to cause harm to crops and, second, because they were entitled to rely upon the water authority to issue a warning of the hazard. With respect to the water authority, however, it was held that they were liable in negligence in failing to warn the farmer of the danger to crops in using the water in accordance with the licence which they had issued.

The *Scott-Whitehead case* establishes, in principle at least, that a discharger of pollution is capable of being liable to other water users to whom damage is caused. On the facts of the case, the exceptional low water conditions and the level of technical knowledge required to appreciate that damage to crops might be caused, pollution damage of this kind was unforeseeable on the part of the discharger and liability was not found. In that respect, however, the circumstances may have been exceptional, since in most pollution incidents a reasonable person would appreciate that pollution will cause damage to other water users, such as mortality to fish farm stock. In a more typical case, therefore, liability in negligence on the part of the polluter would be likely to be found. Another feature of the case worthy of emphasis is the potential for liability on the part of persons other than the actual discharger where it can be shown that they have a responsibility to avoid damage being caused by water pollution. The administrative responsibilities of the water authority placed them in this category, and their failure to act by drawing the hazard to the attention of the farmer was an omission which possessed all the elements necessary to ground a claim in negligence. Although the plaintiff was not a fish farmer, his predicament well illustrates the potential application of negligence to situations in which water pollution damage is caused to fish farms.

10.04   Remedies for water pollution

As has been mentioned, the usual purposes of a civil action for water pollution are to gain either a compensatory award of damages or an injunction, known as an interdict in Scotland, to prevent continuation of pollution. There may be some exceptional situations in which the object of the proceedings are to vindicate a claim of entitlement to pollute, in which case one party will be satisfied with a declaration of the court that the discharge in question was legally justified, but actions of this kind are uncommon. In the vast majority of situations the plaintiff seeks a substantial award of damages, or an injunction, or both.

It is to be noted from the outset of this discussion of remedies for water pollution that compensatory damages and injunctions serve quite distinct legal purposes and are appropriate to markedly different circumstances. A typical case where damages alone are properly awarded is where an isolated pollution incident results in a fish kill but is unlikely to be repeated. In such a situation a court would normally be unwilling to grant an injunction. By contrast, where the complaint concerns a continuing or recurring source of pollution, which perhaps causes a relatively small amount of damage at any particular time but has, or is likely to have, a harmful cumulative effect upon a watercourse, then an injunction is the appropriate remedy. The terms upon which the injunction is granted will be such as to compel the discharger to discontinue the polluting activity and to prevent further damage. Broadly, therefore, an award of damages is retrospective and compensatory in character, whilst an injunction is prospective and prohibitive. In practice, there are many situations which justify both kinds of remedy, though the different bases upon which each is granted must always be recognised.

A.   Damages

A claim for a substantial award of damages is intended to compensate the plaintiff for loss suffered as a result of water pollution for which the defendant is found to be liable. The counterpart of this is that damages awarded under this part of the civil law are not intended to punish the defendant for his malice or foolhardiness, since, in general, these are functions of the criminal rather than the civil law (generally, see Chapter 11 below). It is the extent of the plaintiff's loss, rather than the behaviour or predicament of the defendant, which is used as the measure of damages. Accordingly, the objective of the court is to determine what sum of monetary compensation will place the plaintiff in the same financial position as he would have been in had the injury not been suffered.

Assessment of the precise amount of damages to award to a victim of water pollution is frequently a matter of some complexity, and there may be respects in which no award of money provides genuine recompense for unquantifiable losses which have been suffered. In general, however, a fish farmer will normally be entitled to claim for the value of stock which are lost as a result of pollution. This loss may arise either through direct mortality or because the contaminating effect of the pollutant is such that the fish become commercially worthless and have to be destroyed. The costs of clearing up and the disposing of dead fish would also be recoverable. In addition, certain kinds of pollution may cause damage to fish farming equipment which may require replacement or special cleaning as a result, or may cause tainting of ponds which require costly decontamination treatment, and the expenses of these operations would be granted in an award of damages (*James* v. *Bedwellty U.D.C.* (1910) 00 JP 192). It is sound practical advice to suggest that detailed note should be taken of the precise extent and cost of each of these heads of loss as soon as possible after they arise, and to advocate that wherever possible they should be verified by independent and knowledgeable persons to avoid subsequent evidential difficulties (Landless (1984B) and Institute of Fisheries Management (1981)). Likewise there may be situations in which preserving marked samples of dead fish by freezing, in order to allow a report of a pathologist to be made as to the cause of mortality, and taking photographs of the damage done by water pollution, may serve a useful purpose in later establishing the grounds and extent of liability (Mills (1979)).

Another significant factor in the general quantification of tortious damages is the extent to which reasonable action has been taken by the victim to mitigate the loss suffered. It follows that a fish farmer suffering a water pollution incident will need to show that he has behaved reasonably in seeking to minimise losses arising from the incident and has avoided doing anything that has the effect of exacerbating the damage. Accordingly a fish farmer would be refused compensation for losses suffered as a result of his failure to take steps reasonably open to him to prevent fish mortality. For that reason it is advisable, if reasonably possible, to take measures such as isolating ponds from an affected water supply, or utilising an alternative supply if available, or making use of any available aerators if a deoxygenating form of pollutant is suspected (Mills (1979)). Likewise, failure to mitigate loss may mean that later trading losses will not be compensatable where they are due to an omission to act with expediency in purchasing replacement stock and restoring the venture to a going concern as soon as reasonably practicable after the incident.

The exercise of establishing tortious liability and quantifying the consequent loss from water pollution incidents has been followed on numerous occasions by lawyers determining out of court settlements in order to save the expense of pressing a dispute to a full court hearing. By comparison to the number of settlements of this kind, however, the number of instances in which damages have been judicially determined in relation to fish farms are relatively few. One example illustrating the difficulties of establishing liability for this kind of loss, however, is the 1921 House of Lords decision in *Dulverton R.D.C.* v *Tracy* ((1921) 85 JP 217). The plaintiff in this case was described as the owner of a 'fishery', which actually consisted of 'fishery ponds' used for hatching trout, terminology which perhaps indicates the novelty of the idea of farming fish at the time of the decision. On an occasion of heavy rainfall, the defendant Council's sewage works, which was 'by common admission not constructed on the most modern and efficient principles' and lacked any facility for dealing with storm water, discharged crude sewage into the river two miles upstream from the plaintiff's premises. Shortly afterwards the plaintiff's trout crowded towards the inlets in their ponds, a fact that was recognised to be indicative of an oxygen deficiency of the kind attributable to organic pollution such as sewage, and eventually suffocated. Despite the strength of these indications as to the cause of the pollution incident, ingenious arguments were raised by the defendants to the effect that the death of the fish may have been caused as a consequence of cattle manure entering the river, or as a result of salmon disease, or through fungus of the gills. At the first hearing it was found that, despite the high probability that the fish died as a result of the sewage, the matter was not conclusively proven and the plaintiff's action failed. On appeal, however, and in the final determination before the House of Lords, it was held that the evidence was sufficient to establish liability on the part of the defendants. Damages were assessed at £100, at 1921 money values, but because of the exceptional circumstances which gave rise to the incident, the abnormally heavy rainfall, and the unlikelihood of recurrence, it was held that no injunction would be granted.

Granby (Marquis of) v. *Bakewell U.D.C.* ((1923) 87 JP 105) is another leading case in which detailed judicial consideration was given to the measure of damages appropriate to compensate losses caused to a game fishery due to water pollution. The action, based on nuisance, arose out of the pollution of the plaintiff's fishery, and the death of large numbers of trout, following more than one discharge of noxious liquid from a drain-pipe issuing from the defendants' gasworks. The polluting effect of the discharges was disputed by the defendants. The gasworks manager drank some of the effluent sample without ill effects and considered that this demonstrated it was harmless, but as the judge commented, 'I am not trying the question whether the effluent was poisonous to human beings, and ... I fail to see how such an experiment assists me to determine the question which I have to decide', which was whether the discharge had caused the death of the fish. The plaintiff, however, was able to support his contention by the findings of an analysis of samples of the discharged liquid, and water from the river below the drain-pipe, which were found to contain ammoniacal liquor in a concentration which was highly poisonous to fish. This evidence was supported by the testimony of experts that the cause of the fish mortality had been the discharge from the gasworks. The defendants' liability having been established, the plaintiff was awarded an injunction to prevent recurrence of the discharges and an award of damages.

Although the finding of liability in this case was the outcome of a well prepared and conclusively supported argument with exemplary presentation of evidence by a range of witnesses and technical experts, the decision is of most relevance to present concerns in relation to the argument about the measure of damages for a loss of this kind. Although the general character of the interest which had been damaged was that of right of fishery (*Fitzgerald* v. *Firbank* [1897] 2 Ch. 96) the task of quantifying compensation has some common features with the measurement of losses that would be suffered by a fish farm in a similar predicament. The consequence of the polluting discharges was the death of a large number of fish, and although the plaintiff had no property in the fish until their capture (see [14.06] below) the destruction of the fish had a directly prejudicial effect upon the value of the fishery. It was recognised, however, that in the circumstances of a natural river fishery the number of fish which had been killed was difficult to ascertain because not all the dead fish were visible. The judge was prepared to make allowance for this difficulty in assuming that for each dead fish seen there were at least two more dead fish that could not be observed, and based his estimate of the total loss of 450 fish on that supposition.

Having reached a figure for the number of fish killed, the judge then confronted the question of the value of those fish to the fishery. Although it was accepted that it would be possible to restock the river with hatchery-reared fish of the same average size as those that had perished for a specified price, the judge reasoned that such fish, having been reared by hand-feeding in a stew, would not be so wary and would offer less good sport than the wild fish which they were to replace. This matter was legitimately taken into account in assessing the damages. In addition it was found that another effect of the the pollution was to cause the destruction of a quantity of the natural fish food in the river such as crustaceans, molluscs and nymphs. This also was a matter to be taken into account. In total it was held that along with his costs, the plaintiff was entitled to the sum of £150, at 1922 money values. Clearly the extent of fish mortality, and the sums of money needed to compensate such losses, would be far greater in the circumstances of a pollution incident affecting a modern fish farm of any size than were awarded in *Granby (Marquis of)* v. *Bakewell U.D.C.*. The principles according to which compensatory damages are calculated, however, will be in accordance with this precedent. The overall objective remains that of awarding the pecuniary sum which will make good the loss suffered as a natural and probable consequence of the defendant's misdeed so as to place the plaintiff in the financial position he would have been in had the damage not been suffered.

A final point of relevance to the compensatory aspects of water pollution claims is the possibility of an award being made by way of a compensation order in criminal proceedings arising out of the same incident (generally, see Chapter 11 below). Where a polluter is prosecuted for a pollution offence which has caused damage to another person, such as a fish farmer, it is open to the convicting court to impose a compensation order requiring the offender to pay compensation to a person suffering loss or damage arising from the offence (s.35 Powers of the Criminal Courts Act 1973, as amended by s.67 Criminal Justice Act 1982; and Bathers (1986)). The amount of such an award is to be such amount as the court considers appropriate, having regard to the evidence and to any representations made, and up to a specified upper limit. In circumstances where a pollution incident gives rise to criminal proceedings in which a compensation order is made, any subsequent compensation from civil proceedings will be reduced by any amount paid under a compensation order (s.38). In effect the total amount of compensation which is payable is unchanged, but there may be circumstances where full compensation is recoverable under a compensation order without the need for further civil proceedings to be pursued to obtain adequate compensation.

B.   The injunction or interdict

Whereas damages serve to compensate fish farmers and others for past injuries sustained through water pollution, the injunction is a prohibitive order of a court which serves to prevent future pollution. The ultimate sanction behind an injunction, or interdict in Scotland, is that disobedience amounts to a contempt of court for which the court is allowed to order sequestration of the offender's assets or, in an extreme case, imprisonment

(Contempt of Court Act 1981). The prospective character of the injunction means that it is appropriate to situations where there are reasonable grounds to suppose that substantial pollution will otherwise be suffered, or a prescriptive right to pollute will be acquired by continuation of a polluting discharge (see [10.02C] above). Overall, it is significant that the injunction is a form of equitable remedy which is granted at the discretion of the court where, taking all the circumstances into account, it is thought appropriate to do so.

Traditionally, the availability of an injunction in relation to anticipated water pollution is said to depend upon the 'balance of convenience' in granting the injunction, meaning that a range of factors are to be weighed into consideration. An injunction will not be granted, for instance, where damages are thought to be an adequate remedy for the plaintiff's loss, and so an injunction would normally be declined where the nuisance complained of has ceased by the time that the action is brought and is unlikely to recommence (*Batcheller* v. *Tunbridge Wells Gas Co.* (1901) 65 JP 680). Likewise, if the matter complained of is of a temporary or trivial character an injunction will probably not be granted (*Attorney-General* v. *Metropolitan Board of Works* (1863) 27 JP 597). Providing that a source of pollution is continuing and substantial, however, the determination of whether an injunction is to be granted involves an evaluation of all the interests involved. Ultimately private interests will prevail over public, so that pollution caused by sewage treatment at a publicly operated treatment works cannot be justified where it causes intolerable interference with a private riparian owner's enjoyment of land (*Goldsmid* v. *Tunbridge Wells Improvement Commissioners* (1866) 14 LT 154). Conversely, the balance of convenience may favour important public works to be completed against minor complaints which do not materially interfere with the plaintiff's enjoyment of his property (*Lillywhite* v. *Trimmer* (1867) 16 LT 318).

Where the immediate removal of an actionable nuisance is physically impossible, a common practice of courts is to defer the operation of an injunction for a period of time in order to allow the defendant to take steps to rectify the problem. This procedure is not uncommon where the source of pollution is a major installation such as a sewage treatment works where substantial measures need to be taken to bring discharged effluent up to standard. Alternatively, suspension of an injunction has sometimes been allowed because of special circumstances preventing improvements, such as the difficulties of obtaining labour during wartime (*Great Central Railway* v. *Doncaster R.D.C.* (1917) 82 JP 33). Occasionally an extension to the period of deferment of an injunction will be allowed, but in such a case further deferment will not be granted automatically and the polluter must show that all reasonable measures have been taken to remedy the nuisance within the time initially allowed. (*Pride of Derby Angling Association* v. *British Celanese Ltd and Others* (1953) 117 JP 52, at p. 77). It may also be thought proper by the court to increase an award of damages in order to cover the period during which the injunction is suspended (*Owen* v. *Faversham Corporation* (1908) 73 JP 33).

10.05   *Pollution of coastal waters*

In comparison with the problems of freshwater pollution the capacity of the sea to disperse and assimilate pollutants has, until relatively recent times, been imagined to be almost unlimited. Marine pollution has frequently been dismissed as a problem of enclosed bays and harbours having insufficient circulation to disperse pollutants from onshore points of discharge. Over recent years, however, the extent of marine pollution has become disturbingly apparent. Amongst the first indicators of the true extent of the problem have been stocks of shellfish reared in inshore waters. Because of the accumulation of many forms of pollution upon the sea bed, and the sedentary nature of these species, they have proved to be especially vulnerable to certain kinds of pollution. In law, however, litigation concerning damage to shellfish has served to establish the bases on which civil liability for marine pollution damage to fish stocks may be found. The outcome of these proceeding was to establish that the common law principles of liability for freshwater pollution are in most respects applicable to the circumstances of marine pollution, and to corresponding damage sustained by aquaculture operations taking place in the marine environment.

The applicability of the common law of water pollution to marine pollution affecting coastal fish farming was established in a trio of cases decided in the early years of this century concerning damage to shellfisheries through sewage discharges. (Contrast the position in the United States, discussed in Kane (1970) pp. 74 to 76.) Bivalve molluscs such as oysters and mussels, as sedentary species that feed by filtration of particulate matter present in surrounding water, are particularly prone to accumulate large quantities of bacteria in waters polluted by sewage. These accumulations have clear public health implications in that disease may be transmitted through consumption of shellfish which have not been properly purified or sterilised and today special regulations govern shellfish constituting a public health hazard (see Pain (1986); and [16.03] and [16.04] below). The danger of disease being transmitted by shellfish contaminated by sewage first became a matter of general public concern after an incident in 1902 in which contaminated shellfish supplied for a banquet at Winchester caused a serious outbreak of typhoid fever resulting in the death of a number of the guests (Royal Commission on Sewage Disposal (1904)).

In the first case in which civil liability for sewage pollution of shellfish was considered, *Hobart v. Southend-on-Sea Corporation* ([1906] LT 337), the plaintiff was a lessee of oyster beds in an ancient several fishery (see [15.04C] below) where oysters and other shellfish were deposited until required for sale. The defendants, as the local sanitary authority, discharged untreated sewage into the Thames estuary from a number of outfalls which, it was alleged, caused contamination of the plaintiff's oysters to such an extent that their sale was forbidden in London by the Fishmongers' Company (see [16.07] below) because they were found to be unfit for human consumption.

A number of distinct arguments were raised on behalf of the Corporation as to why they should not be held liable in nuisance for damage caused by pollution to the shellfish beds. In the first place it was contended that there were a number of points along that part of the coastline from which sewage was discharged by persons and bodies other than the defendants, and therefore it could not be established that it was their discharges that were the cause of the pollution. On this contention there was detailed discussion as to the overall effect of the range of eddies and cross currents to be found at different stages of the tide in the estuary upon the dispersal of discharged matter. The analysis entered into by the court provides a clear illustration of the difficulties involved in relating damage caused by marine pollution to a particular source of discharge. Nonetheless it was found that, on the balance of expert evidence and witness testimony, pollution from the Corporation's outfalls had caused contamination of the plaintiff's shellfish.

A second argument raised by the Corporation was that duties imposed under public health legislation (Public Health Acts 1848 and 1875) placed them under a statutory duty to dispose of sewage in the manner which had caused the shellfish contamination and that this provided a defence to the action. On closer examination of the powers of the Corporation as a sanitary authority, however, it was found that an explicit proviso stated that, for the purpose of disposing of sewage, no nuisance was to be created by the exercise of those powers (s.49 Public Health Act 1848 and s.23 Public Health Act 1875). It followed that the statutory obligation to make provision for sewage treatment on the part of the defendants did not permit the creation of a nuisance of the kind that had arisen. Moreover, though not directly at issue, two provisions under fishery law made the discharges which had taken place amount to criminal offences. The Sea Fisheries Act 1868 imposed a penalty upon persons who knowingly disturbed or injured any oyster bed (s.53 Sea Fisheries Act 1868, and now see [15.04G] below). The Sea Fisheries Act 1888 authorised local fisheries committees to regulate coastal fisheries by making byelaws (s.2 Sea Fisheries Act 1888, and now see [15.08] below) and in the circumstances of the case the appropriate local fisheries committee had in fact created a byelaw prohibiting the discharge of any substance detrimental to sea fish. Accordingly the discharge of sewage which had taken place was not only beyond the statutory powers of the Corporation, but was also forbidden as a criminal offence under fishery law.

Having determined that the plaintiff was entitled to bring the action, that the pollution was caused by the defendants' failure to discharge their duties as a sanitary authority, and that the pollution was otherwise unjustified by common law or statutory authority, a finding of liability for nuisance was inevitable. The appropriate remedy was held to be an injunction to restrain the defendants from causing further pollution during the term of the plaintiff's lease of the shellfishery, along with an award of damages. The award of damages took into account that the plaintiff had been unable to sell any shellfish other than small amounts supplied with a warning that they should be sterilised by cooking for a certain time before consumption. Also taken into account was the fact that the plaintiff was bound to continue paying rent, rates, wages and other incidental expenses during the period when shellfish were contaminated. Taking these and other factors into consideration, damages were assessed at £1500, at 1906 money values.

Following *Hobart's Case* the second of the three cases establishing liability for sewage pollution of shellfisheries was the Court of Appeal decision in *Foster* v. *Warblington U.D.C.* ((1906) 70 JP 233) where the facts were similar. The defendant District Council discharged sewage through an outfall into a tidal estuary causing contamination of oysters stored in the plaintiff's oyster beds on the foreshore. It was oysters from these beds which had been the cause of the typhoid outbreak following the Winchester banquet referred to earlier. In these circumstances it was held that the plaintiff had a right to maintain the action for nuisance by virtue of his ownership of the oyster beds and the right of several fishery, and that the defendants had neither a common law nor statutory justification for causing the pollution. In the final decision of the trio, *Owen* v. *Faversham Corporation* ((1908) 73 JP 33), similar reasoning was followed, and reaffirmed on appeal to the Court of Appeal, that the defendants were liable for the nuisance caused by their discharge and the plaintiff was entitled to damages and an injunction, though the injunction was suspended for a period to allow improvements in the state of the discharge to be made. The three cases serve to establish the application of the common law principles to marine as well as freshwater pollution. In principle at least it follows that an analogous action might be brought in circumstances where salmon in sea cages are destroyed by pollution. Perhaps because of the relative newness of this form of aquaculture, however, no authoritative decisions have been reported concerning water pollution resulting in this kind of loss.

Having recognised that in principle the common law of water pollution is applicable to all kinds of waters, the practical difficulties involved in applying these provisions to coastal waters must also be appreciated. Despite the theoretical existence of tortious liability in respect of the pollution of sea water, the nature of marine pollution is such that issues of causality are very much more difficult to establish. Where polluted water enters a riverside fish farm there is little alternative but to conclude that it has originated from an upstream point of discharge. By contrast, the turbulence of the sea and the range of onshore and offshore locations from which pollution may have originated mean that the evidential problem of linking pollution damage to a particular offending discharge may frequently be a matter of difficulty (as in *Hobart's case* discussed above). In more general terms an obstacle confronting fish farming in some coastal locations is that of the overall problem of the water quality of the local marine environment, rather than a particular complaint about any specific discharge. Against this background it can be seen that preferable solutions to the problem of securing satisfactory standards of water quality for fish farming require a broader approach to the effective utilisation of coastal waters for aquaculture than permitted by the case by case approach provided for in civil litigation. Attempts to adopt such an approach in relation to the quality of both freshwater and saltwater are provided for under European Community provisions relating to water quality for freshwater fish and shellfish discussed in the following section.

10.06   Directives on freshwater fish and shellfish waters

The strategy of establishing target values for water quality, in relation to the content of various pollutants and the uses to which the water concerned is to be put, is mainly a product of the European Community programme of environmental legislation (generally see Haigh (1987)). As was observed earlier, the traditional approach of the common law towards water pollution is the relativist approach of enquiring whether a particular discharge results in a 'sensible alteration' to the natural water quality, rather than making any comparison between actual water quality and an absolute standard of acceptability for water of that kind. The European approach to water quality has been embodied in a series of Directives relating to the pollution of waters by particular substances. These have included water quality Directives regulating the amounts of detergents (73/404/EC), 'dangerous substances' (76/464/EC), and particularly harmful pollutants such as titanium oxide waste (78/176/EC) and mercury (82/176/EC). Alongside these, additional Directives specify quality criteria for water to be used for particular purposes such as drinking water (75/440/EC and 80/778/EC) and bathing water (76/160/EC).

Of greatest potential importance to aquaculture are the European Council Directive on the quality of fresh waters needing protection or improvement in order to support fish life (78/869/EC) and the Council Directive on the quality required of shellfish waters (79/923/EC). Although the Directive on fresh water to support fish life is expressly stated not to apply to waters within natural or artificial fish ponds used for intensive fish farming (Art.1(2) 78/869/EC), it is unavoidable that measures affecting rivers and streams providing the source of supply for fish farms will have direct consequences upon water quality for freshwater aquaculture use. The fresh waters Directive aims to protect or improve the quality of running or standing waters, within the member states of the Community, which are capable of supporting fish life in the form of either indigenous species offering a natural diversity or species the presence of which is judged to be desirable for management purposes (Art.1(3)). In order to protect or improve such waters member states are placed under an obligation to designate waters as either salmonid or cyprinid waters, and to set values for physical and chemical water quality parameters in accordance with those provided for in the first Annex to the Directive. Having so designated waters for these purposes, member states are to establish programmes to reduce pollution and to ensure that designated waters conform with the relevant water quality criteria set for each particular water.

In broad terms the shellfish waters Directive follows the approach of the fresh waters Directive. The Directive concerns the quality of coastal and brackish shellfish waters designated by member states of the Community as needing protection or improvement in order to support bivalve and gastropod molluscs and to contribute to the quality of shellfish products for direct human consumption (Art.1 79/923/EC). Notably this objective is somewhat ambivalent in that it is not clear whether the purpose of the directive is purely environmental in nature, or whether it serves a public health purpose. If the latter is the case the measure looks incongruous in its application to the United Kingdom where the public health aspects of shellfish quality are provided for under separate legislation from that dealing with matters of water quality (see [16.03] below). Taking the main purpose of the Directive to be predominantly environmental in nature, member states are placed under an obligation to designate waters as shellfish waters within the terms of the Directive, and to set values for a range of water quality parameters set out in the Annex to the Directive (Art.3(1) 79/923/EC). The Annex specifies a range of physical and chemical parameters as either 'imperative' values which must be observed in every case, or 'guide' values which member states are to 'endeavour to observe' (Art.3(2)). The parameters listed concern matters such as temperature, coloration, suspended solids, salinity, dissolved oxygen and the presence of harmful substances such as petroleum hydrocarbons, organohalogenated substances and metals. In addition parameters are provided for in relation to faecal coliforms, a measure of the level of sewage pollution, and substances affecting the taste of shellfish. In relation to most of the parameters methods of analysis to determine conformity are stated and minimum sampling and measuring frequency are stipulated (Annex).

In principle the European approach to water quality amounts to an admirably rational strategy for ensuring acceptable standards of water purity for aquaculture and safeguarding the water environment generally. Undeniably, the method for specifying water quality objectives in relation to water to be used for particular uses has much to commend it by comparison to the fragmentary case-by-case approach to water pollution provided for under the common law. Nonetheless there have been sizable difficulties in putting European Directives concerning water quality into practice (Wathern, Young, Brown and Roberts (1987)). In relation to the fresh waters and shellfish waters Directives a major hindrance has arisen through the ambivalent specification of the duty of member states to designate waters for these purposes. Contrary to the initial impression that a binding obligation to designate is intended, it has been understood that the Directives allow for *discretion* on the part of member states to determine whether or not designations should be made. As a result it appears that some member states have declined to make any designations whatsoever of waters for the purposes of the Directives. In the case of the United Kingdom, designations have tended to be of only those waters that already meet the appropriate standards at the time of implementation of the Directives, rather than the Directives being used as an independent mechanism for achieving general improvements in water quality (Haigh (1987) ss.4.5 and 4.6). Despite the considerable potential of the Directives, therefore, in practice they have had little or no effect on water quality in the United Kingdom.

An indication of the minimal compliance approach to the shellfish waters Directive in the United Kingdom is provided by the initial designation of only 29 waters throughout the United Kingdom as protected shellfish waters. The locations of the designated areas are as follows:

England: Holy Island; Norton Creek; Bulteley River; Pyefleet Channel; River Blackwater; Walton Blackwater; River Rouch; Calshot/Stanswood Bay; Lepe Middle Bank; Sowley Ground; Yarmouth Road; Newtown Bank and Harbour; Poole Harbour; Portland Harbour; Helford River; Percuel; Turnaware.
Wales: Menai Strait.
Scotland: Dornoch Firth; Arbroath Coast; St.Andrews/Fife Ness Coast; Fife Ness/Elie Coast; North Berwick/Dunbar Coast; Loch Ryan; Ayrshire Coast; Kyles of Bute; Loch Fyne coastal strip; Loch Long/Loch Goil.
Northern Ireland: Strangford Lough. (Royal Commission on Environmental Pollution (1984) p. 96.)

Although many uncertainties remain to be clarified, the restricted application which has been given to the shellfish waters Directive may have a number of significant legal implications. In the first place it has been noted that if other member states of the Community were to place greater emphasis upon the public health aspects of the Directive they might seek to accept imports of shellfish only from designated waters, in which case the commercial effect upon the shellfish industry would be serious (Royal Commission on Environmental Pollution (1984) para.4.76). Second, the list of designated shellfish waters appears to be unrelated to those waters in respect of which several and regulated shellfisheries exist. An incongruous consequence of this is that official authorisation may, therefore, be given for the husbandry of shellfish in waters which are probably failing to meet the appropriate environmental standards (see [15.04] below). Third, the requirement of financial assistance for aquaculture projects, including shellfish farming, from Community funds is subject to the approval of the project, including amongst other things the acceptability of the water quality in the location in which it is planned (see [5.04] above). It is incongruous that a proposed shellfish farming project submitted for Community financial assistance might be planned for waters that have not been designated for that purpose.

10.07   *Insurance and water pollution*

It is evident from the legal complexities concerning water pollution that have been discussed that establishing liability and gaining the appropriate remedy are rarely simple and straightforward either as a matter of law or practice. Even where fault is apparently self-evident, the pitfalls of litigation mean that the process of obtaining a legal remedy remains slow, costly and uncertain. Having surmounted all the legal obstacles, for example, a plaintiff may still find the defendant in an impecunious state with no prospect of meeting a proven claim for damages against him. Opportunities to avoid the future of a fish farming business hinging on fine points of forensic detail and legal hazard are prudently avoided by taking out insurance cover. The normal effect of insurance is that legal rights to sue for water pollution are subrogated to the fish farmer's insurer. This means that the insurer takes on the problems and risks of gaining a remedy from the polluter, and though some insurers may take longer than others to settle a claim (Mills (1979)) claims will normally be settled with considerably greater expedition than can be expected of the legal process.

Having drawn attention to the advantage of insurance cover for pollution losses, the difficulties and costs of the insurance dimension need to be weighed into the balance. The advantages of peace of mind brought by an all-risks policy are immediately apparent in that coverage would normally extend, according to the precise terms of the policy, to losses suffered by cases which might not be actionable as pollution. Hence it would be possible to recover under an all-risks policy for damage caused, for example, through natural increases in the load of suspended solids in a water supply, or exceptionally warm conditions causing deoxygenation, that may not be related to any particular pollution incident. On the other hand, an all-risks policy will be more costly, and the preference of many fish farmers is for cheaper policies covering specified risks such as pollution damage only. If that option is chosen it may serve as a partial means of avoiding difficulties, but may mean also that a fish farmer needs to establish, to the satisfaction of the insurer, that pollution was in fact the cause of damage which has been suffered. Nonetheless, even this is inevitably a much simpler option than the alternative of litigation against a polluter (Landless (1984A)).

Although not concerned with water pollution insurance, an interesting example of the operation of insurance in an aquacultural context is provided by the recent House of Lords decision in *Forsikrings Vesta* v. *Butcher* ([1989] 1 All ER 402). The case arose out of an insurance policy taken out by a Norwegian fish farmer covering the loss of his stock of trout and salmon as a result of any cause whatsoever. The policy was taken out with a Norwegian insurance company but was underwritten by London underwriters for 90 per cent of the risk. Originally it had been a condition of the insurance policy and the contract for reinsurance between the insurance company and the underwriters that a 24-hour watch should be kept on the fish cages in which the farm's stock was held, and that failure to comply with this term would render the contract null and void. The owner of the fish farm was not able to comply with the 24-hour watch condition and he informed the insurers of that fact, but because of inadequate communication between the insurers and underwriters, the underwriters did not learn of the waiver of the condition. Six months later a violent storm severely damaged the fish farm causing the loss of over 100,000 fish during a period when the cages were not being watched. It was conceded, however, that nothing could have been done to prevent loss by storm even if the cages had been watched at the time of the disaster.

Although the Norwegian insurers settled the farmer's claim relatively quickly, a dispute then arose between the insurers and the London underwriters. The substance of the dispute was the underwriters' contention that they were not bound to indemnify the insurers for 90 per cent of the risk because of the failure of the fish farmer to satisfy the condition requiring 24-hour watching of the farm which, they alleged, had the effect of rendering the underwriting contract null and void. The difficulty in resolving this dispute lay in a crucial difference between Norwegian and English insurance law. In English law the failure to satisfy a condition in a contract of insurance was capable of invalidating the contract even where that failure had no connection with the loss which had been suffered, as was the case on the facts which had arisen. In Norwegian insurance law, however, the failure to satisfy a condition in an insurance contract would only have the effect of invalidating the contract if that failure had caused or in some way contributed to the loss, as had not happened here. The ultimate question to be decided by the court, therefore, was that of whether the agreement between the insurers and the underwriters was governed by Norwegian or English law. On this issue the House of Lords held that the implication was that the underwriting contract should follow the insurance contract, and therefore the non-compliance with the 24-hour watch condition did not invalidate the insurers' claim against the underwriters and so recovery was allowed.

The principal issue in the *Forsikrings Vesta case* was the relationship between the insurers and underwriters of a contract for aquaculture insurance, but the case also has some direct implications for fish farmers who are party to a contract of insurance of this kind. Most notably, had the fish farm in question been in England rather than Norway the operation of the English law of insurance would mean that a contract of this kind, if not modified by agreement between the fish farmer and his insurer, would be invalid in protecting the fish farmer if any condition to which it was subject was not satisfied. Thus a failure to adhere to the 24-hour watch condition would render the policy ineffective in protecting the fish farmer in the event of loss to his stock, even if there was no causal connection between failure to watch and the damage suffered. Likewise, though not contested in the case itself, failure on the part of the fish farmer to adhere to another requirement of the contract, to maintain regular written stock control records and make them available to the underwriters or their representatives for their inspection at all times, would also have the effect of rendering the policy of insurance inoperative in English law. The clear message for the fish farmer is that he has to be scrupulously careful in complying with *all* the conditions to which his insurance cover is subject, since failure to do so is capable of having drastic consequences.

Chapter 11

The Quality of Water Discharge

11.01 Pollution from fish farms

As has been previously observed, fish farms are both receivers and dischargers of pollution. The civil law of water pollution is the main recourse for a fish farmer where a water supply is impaired by pollution, though an alternative might be to instigate criminal proceedings against the polluter or press the authority responsible to do so. Equally, the civil law can be used against a fish farmer whose activities cause diminution of water quality which is actionable by lower riparian owners. In relation to the water quality of discharges, however, fish farmers are themselves subject to the criminal law of water pollution and this chapter deals with the operation of this branch of the law as it concerns discharges into the aquatic environment. Fish farm discharges contain a range of pollutants originating from food waste, fish excrement and general detritus, which have the effect of deoxygenating the receiving waters and increasing the levels of suspended solids and ammonia (Alabaster and Lloyd (1980); and Solbe (1987 and 1988)). Discharges may also contain amounts of medicines and other potentially harmful chemicals used in fish farming which are subject to pollution controls in addition to their use being subject to separate legal controls which arise independently of their polluting effect (discussed in Chapter 13 below).

Until recently the criminal law of water pollution, as it was likely to affect fish farmers throughout Britain, was contained in a single enactment, the Control of Pollution Act 1974, Part II of which provided for the main criminal offences. This position has been significantly changed, however, by the enactment of the Water Act 1989 which facilitates the division of the water industry in England and Wales into private water utility companies and the public regulatory body, the National Rivers Authority. In substance the Water Act 1989 has made relatively few changes in the criminal law of water pollution, but nonetheless the provisions applicable to England and Wales, which formerly appeared under Part II of the 1974 Act, have now been re-enacted under Chapter I of Part III of the 1989 Act. In relation to Scotland Part II of the 1974 Act is retained as the principal enactment governing the criminal law of water pollution, but substantial amendments have been made to assimilate its provisions to those applicable in England and Wales. The outcome of the recent amendments, therefore, is that England and Wales are subject to a different enactment from Scotland, but the provisions of the two are of broadly equivalent effect. For ease of exposition the following discussion is couched in terms of the provisions arising under the Water Act 1989, with contrasts being drawn from the law of Scotland where significant distinctions arise, but notes in parenthesis indicate the equivalent section numbers under the amended 1974 Act applicable to Scotland. All references to Control of Pollution Act 1974 are to the Act *as amended* by s.168 and Sch.23 Water Act 1989.

11.02 Water pollution under the Water Act 1989

Considered from an aquacultural perspective, Chapter I of Part III of the Water Act 1989, comprising ss.103 to 124, creates two main offences concerning water pollution in England and Wales. (In Scotland the equivalent is Part II Control of Pollution Act 1974, ss.31 to 56, as amended by s.169 and Sch.23 Water Act 1989.) The first of these, under s.107(1)(a) (s.31(1)(a) Control of Pollution Act 1974) involves the entry of poisonous, noxious or polluting matter into water, and is most commonly applicable to situations in which an isolated entry gives rise to a distinct pollution incident, as where a person brings about water pollution through the purposeful dumping of polluting matter into a watercourse. The second offence, under s.107(1)(d) (s.32(1)(a) Control of Pollution Act 1974) arises where there is a sustained discharge of effluent into waters, as might typically occur in the course of continuing activity, such as the disposal of an unwanted by-product of an industrial process, and the emission is not authorised by a discharge consent. Either of these offences is capable of being committed in the context of fish farming. Moreover, the regime for control of water pollution provides comprehensive coverage in relation to 'controlled waters' including almost all kinds of waters in which fish farming is likely to take place, encompassing inland waters, estuaries, tidal rivers, the sea within a three mile limit and specified underground water (s.103(1) Water Act 1989; and s.30A(1) Control of Pollution Act 1974). It follows that there is no significant legal distinction between causing pollution of fresh water and causing pollution of the sea in that both are capable of amounting to the same offence under the 1989 Act.

A.   The entry of polluting matter into waters

Section 107(1)(a) of the Water Act 1989 (s.31(1)(a) Control of Pollution Act 1974) sets out the offence of causing or knowingly permitting the entry of polluting matter or any solid waste into waters. Subject to specified exceptions, this offence is committed where a person causes or knowingly permits, any poisonous, noxious or polluting matter to enter any controlled waters. A person found guilty of this offence is liable, on summary conviction, to imprisonment for a term not exceeding three months or a fine not exceeding the statutory maximum, presently £2,000, or both, and, on conviction on indictment, to imprisonment for a term not exceeding two years or a fine or both (s.107(6) Water Act 1989; and s.31(7) Control of Pollution Act 1974).

In relation to fish farming contexts, the 'controlled waters', in respect of which the offence of causing or knowingly permitting the entry of matter may be committed, are defined in the following ways. 'Relevant territorial waters' are waters extending seaward for three nautical miles from the baselines from which the breadth of the territorial sea is measured (s.103(1)(a) Water Act 1989; and s.30A(1)(a) Control of Pollution Act 1974).

'Coastal waters' are waters which are within the area which extends landward from those baselines as far as the highest tide, or as far as the fresh-water limits (s.103(1)(b) Water Act 1989; and s.30A(1)(b) Control of Pollution Act 1974). 'Inland waters' are waters of any lake or pond which discharges into a river or watercourse, or of so much of any river or watercourse as is above the fresh-water limit other than public sewers or drains (s.103(1)(c) Water Act 1989; and s.30A(1)(c) Control of Pollution Act 1974). 'Ground waters' include waters contained in any underground strata, or any well, borehole or excavation (s.103(1)(d) Water Act 1989; and s.30A(1)(d) Control of Pollution Act 1974).

An important feature of the offence of causing or permitting the entry of poisonous, noxious or polluting matter or any solid waste to enter waters, is that the meaning of 'poisonous, noxious or polluting' matter is nowhere defined in the 1989 Act. The suggestion has been offered that 'poisonous, noxious or polluting matter' is wide enough to include waste that is harmful to fauna, or possibly to flora, even if it is harmless to human beings (Garner (1975) p. 17). In the interpretation of previous legislation which employed the same phrase, (s.2(1)(a) Rivers (Prevention of Pollution) Act 1951) it was suggested that, "poisonous" implies destruction of life, human or animal; "noxious" is lower in degree, and signifies some injury, but not of necessity immediately dangerous to life; "polluting" will include both the other qualities and also what is foul and offensive to the senses, except innocuous discoloration' (Simes and Scholefield (1954) p. 5158 note e). Other than in accordance with these general observations, however, the question of what constitutes 'poisonous, noxious or polluting' awaits an authoritative determination by the courts.

B.   'Causing or knowingly permitting' polluting matter to enter waters

An important legal aspect of the offence relating to the entry of polluting matter into waters is that it is committed where a person 'causes or knowingly permits' the entry of the matter concerned. The precise meaning of the phrase 'cause or knowingly permit' has been a matter of recurring difficulty which has occupied the attention of courts on a number of occasions. Significantly, 'cause' and 'knowingly permit' contemplate what are essentially two distinct situations. The difference between the two was expressed in general terms by Lord Wright who observed that:

> 'To cause ... involves some express or positive mandate from the person "causing" to the other person, or some authority from the former to the latter, arising in the circumstances of the case. To "permit" is a looser and vaguer term. It may denote an express permission, general or particular, as distinguished from a mandate ... However, the word also includes cases in which permission is merely inferred.' (*McLeod* v. *Buchanan* [1940] 2 All ER 179, at p. 187.)

Because of this crucial distinction, which has been judicially reaffirmed on several occasions, the circumstances in which it is maintained that entry of polluting matter is caused must be assessed on a different basis from those in which it is alleged to have been knowingly permitted.

The leading authority on the meaning of 'causing' pollution is the House of

Lords decision in *Alphacell Ltd* v. *Woodward* [1972] 2 All ER 475 where water which had been used to wash raw materials at a paper works was piped into settling tanks alongside a river. Although the tanks were equipped with a pump designed to switch off automatically in order to prevent overflows into the river, the pump failed to operate through becoming clogged by refuse and polluted water from the tanks overflowed into the river. On an appeal against a charge of *causing* polluting matter to enter the river (under s.2(1) of the Rivers (Prevention of Pollution) Act 1951) it was held that, despite the absence of knowledge, intention or negligence on the part of the accused, they had nonetheless caused the entry of the polluting matter into the river.

The irrelevance of knowledge, intention or negligence to the issue of causation is reaffirmed by the decision in *Wrothwell Ltd* v. *Yorkshire Water Authority* ([1984] Crim. L.R. 43) where a director of the defendant company deliberately poured 12 gallons of a concentrated herbicide, known to be toxic to fish life, into a drain. The director's expectation had been that the liquid would pass through the drain, and the sewer system, to the public sewage works. It transpired, however, that the drain was not connected to the public sewer, but to a system of pipes through which the herbicide passed and was discharged into a nearby stream causing extensive fish mortality. In an appeal against a conviction of causing poisonous matter to enter a stream, it was argued that the actual result of the act of disposing of the herbicide had been so different from its expected result, that the entry of the poison into the stream could not be said to have been 'caused' in the sense required by the offence. It was held on appeal, however, that 'cause' is a word in everyday usage which is to be understood according to its ordinary meaning, and despite his ignorance of the consequences of his act, the director had 'caused' the liquid to enter the stream.

Having established that cause is not to be understood as incorporating an intention to pollute into the offence, it is clear that the offence of causing pollution requires some positive act on the part of the accused, and this may occasionally be lacking where his behaviour has been 'passive' with respect to bringing about pollution of water. Hence in *Price* v. *Cromack* ([1975] 2 All ER 113) the appellant had entered into an agreement to allow effluent created by an industrial company to pass on to his land where it was contained in two lagoons which had been built by the company. After two breaches in the containing walls of the lagoons had allowed the effluent to escape into a nearby river it was held that the notion of 'causing' pollution involved some active operation as opposed to mere tacit standing by and looking on. Since the appellant was contractually bound to receive the effluent in the lagoons, and there was no positive act causing the pollution on his part, he could not be said to have 'caused' the entry of the polluting matter into the stream and was found not guilty of the offence. (See also *Moses* v. *Midland Railway Co.* (1915) 113 LT 451; and *Southern Water Authority* v. *Pegrum* (1989) *Guardian* 22 February 1989 p. 47.)

Other contexts in which it may be found that the element of causation is lacking arise where there has been an intervention of a person other than the accused or due to an extraneous factor which is the true cause of the entry of the polluting matter. A situation of this kind is illustrated by *Impress (Worcester) Ltd* v. *Rees* ([1971] 2 All ER 357) where the appellants had placed a fuel oil storage tank on their premises near to a river. After an unauthorised person, trespassing on the premises at night, opened a valve on the tank oil escaped into the river. The act of the trespassing third party served to initiate a distinct chain of causation which justified the finding that the tank owner had not caused the pollution. Likewise, it has been suggested that in extreme circumstances an act of God may be held to break the chain of causation and amount to the 'cause' of an incident of pollution, though the circumstances in which this is likely to arise are uncommon. (*Alphacell Ltd* v. *Woodward*, discussed above, at p. 488.)

Turning from the situations where the entry of pollution is alleged to have been 'caused' by the accused the alternative formulation of the offence is committed where a person 'knowingly permits' the entry of polluting matter. The key phrase in this formulation has been said to involve a failure to prevent pollution which must be accompanied by knowledge (*Alphacell Ltd* v. *Woodward*, discussed above, per Lord Wilberforce at p. 479). It is apparent, therefore, that the offence involves an express or implied element of permission which may not be present where a person lacks control over the circumstances giving rise to pollution, or where a person simply fails to act to prevent pollution entering a watercourse where it is within his power to do so. Nonetheless 'knowingly permitting' pollution requires knowledge on the part of the accused, so that in *Impress (Worcester) Ltd* v. *Rees* (discussed above), proceedings on the basis that the accused had committed an offence of knowingly permitting pollution were dismissed at an early stage. The fact that the pollution at issue had been 'caused' by an unknown trespasser entering the premises at night was sufficient to place the circumstances outside the *knowledge* of the owners of the tank.

C.   Exceptions to the offence of polluting waters

The offence of causing or knowingly permitting poisonous, noxious or polluting matter to enter waters is subject to a number of exceptions. Of these, those that may be appropriate to fish farming contexts are the following. First, a person is not to be guilty of the offence of causing or knowingly permitting poisonous, noxious or polluting matter or any solid waste to enter waters if the entry in question is authorised by a discharge consent granted by the Secretary of State or the National Rivers Authority, or in Scotland a river purification authority (s.108(1)(a) Water Act 1989; and s.31(2)(a) Control of Pollution Act 1974) in pursuance of the Act, and the entry is in accordance with the conditions, if any, to which the consent is subject. Discharge consents relating to fish farms are considered below in [11.03]. The second exception is available where an entry of polluting matter takes place under statutory authorisation. A particular instance where this exception may be relevant to fish farming activities arises under Part II of the Food and Environment Protection Act 1985 which allows for the granting of licences in relation to the disposal of substances at sea (s.108(1)(c) Water Act 1989; and s.31(2)(b)(iii) Control of Pollution Act 1974). The operation of this exception is considered later in [11.05]. In Scotland a third main exception arises where the polluting matter in question is trade effluent discharged in a specified manner (s.32(2)(d) Control of Pollution Act 1974). The reason for this exception is that discharges of trade effluent are separately provided for, and the exception serves to avoid overlap between the offence of polluting waters and the control of discharges of trade effluent.

D. Discharges of trade effluent into waters

Whilst the first key offence under the 1989 Act is concerned with pollution of waters by the entry of poisonous, noxious or polluting matter or any solid waste, the second is concerned, amongst other things, with pollution brought about by the discharge of trade or sewage effluent (s.107(1)(c) and (d) Water Act 1989; and s.32(1)(a) Control of Pollution Act 1974). The particular offence which is most likely to arise in relation to fish farming is where a person causes or knowingly permits (the meaning of 'cause or knowingly permit' was discussed previously in [11.02B]) any trade effluent or sewage effluent to be discharged into any controlled waters (the meaning of 'controlled waters' was discussed previously in [11.02A]). The maximum penalty provided for the offence of discharging trade effluent is, on summary conviction, imprisonment for a term not exceeding three months or to a fine not exceeding the statutory maximum, presently £2,000, or both, or, on conviction on indictment, to imprisonment for a term not exceeding two years or a fine or both (s.107(6) Water Act 1989; and s.32(7) Control of Pollution Act 1974).

'Trade effluent' is defined to include any effluent which is discharged from premises used for carrying on any trade or industry, other than surface water and domestic sewage (s.124(1) Water Act 1989; and s.56(1) Control of Pollution Act 1974). For the purpose of this definition any premises wholly or mainly used (whether for profit or not) for agricultural purposes or for the purposes of *fish farming* or for scientific research or experiment is deemed to be premises used for carrying on a trade (s.124(3)). In relation to Scotland it is added that the deeming of fish farms to be trade premises is that they are deemed 'always to have been' trade premises, confirming the past practice of river purification authorities to regard fish farms as trade premises (s.56(3) Control of Pollution Act; and see [11.04] below).

The offence involving discharge of trade effluent is not committed where the discharge is made with the consent of the Secretary of State or the National Rivers Authority (s.108(1)(a) Water Act 1989; s.32(1) Control of Pollution Act 1974; and see [11.02E] below on discharge consents). Where a consent of this kind is given for the discharge it must be in accordance with the conditions, if any, to which the consent is subject. Another exception arises under the power of the Secretary of State to make regulations exempting certain categories of discharge (s.113(2) Water Act 1989; and s.32(3) Control of Pollution Act 1974). In addition a defence which may be relevant to discharges from fish farms is that the offence concerning discharge of trade effluent is not to apply to any discharge which is authorised by a licence granted under Part II of the Food and Environment Protection Act 1985 (s.15(4)(a) Food and Environment Protection Act 1985, considered in [11.05] below).

E. Consents for discharges

Both the offence of causing the entry of polluting matter into waters and the offence of discharging trade effluent under the 1989 Act are made subject to the exception that they will not be committed where the entry or discharge is in accordance with a discharge consent granted by the Secretary of State or the National Rivers Authority (ss.108(1) 113 and Sch.12 Water Act 1989; and ss.31(2)(a), 32(1) and 34 Control of Pollution Act 1974). In practical terms the facility for authorisation of what would otherwise amount to water pollution offence, by a grant of discharge consent, is of considerable importance to fish farms which make their discharges subject to such consents. The system of discharge consents allows the National Rivers Authority and river purification authorities, who are responsible for the determination of most of the consents, to regulate potentially polluting emissions with reference to the particular characteristics of the receiving waters and general policies for the aquatic environment. For example, the use of appropriately formulated discharge consents may be used to realise water quality objectives (provided for under s.105 Water Act 1989; and s.30C Control of Pollution Act 1974) and European Community water quality standards (see [10.06] above) or to secure conservation objectives (under s.8(1) Water Act 1989). It may be added, however, that though a defence to criminal proceedings, the possession of a discharge consent will not necessarily serve as a defence to civil proceedings against a person who causes water pollution by making a discharge within the scope of a discharge consent (s.122 Water Act 1989; s.105(2)(c) Control of Pollution Act 1974; and see Chapter 10 above on civil liability generally).

In outline, the procedure to be followed in obtaining a discharge consent for a fish farm involves, in the first place, the provision of all the information the National Rivers Authority may reasonably require being provided by the person seeking a discharge consent (s.113 and Sch.12 para.1(1) Water Act 1989; and s.34(1) Control of Pollution Act 1974). It is an offence for a person making an application for consent to make any statement which he knows to be false in any material particular, or recklessly to make any statement which is false in a material particular. The maximum penalty for this offence, on summary conviction, is a fine not exceeding the statutory maximum, presently £2,000, or on conviction on indictment, to a fine of unlimited amount (s.175(1) Water Act 1989; and s.34(5) Control of Pollution Act 1974).

On receipt of an application, it is the duty of the National Rivers Authority, to give the consent either unconditionally or subject to conditions or to refuse it (s.113 and Sch.12 para.2(1) Water Act 1989; and s.34(2) Control of Pollution Act 1974). An application is deemed to have been refused if consent is not given within a period of four months beginning on the day on which the application is received, or such longer period as may be agreed in writing between the Authority and the applicant, unless the matter is to be determined by the Secretary of State (s.113 and Sch.12 para.2(2) Water Act 1989; and s.34(2) Control of Pollution Act 1974; and see [11.02F] below).

The National Rivers Authority may give its consent for a discharge subject to 'such conditions as the Authority may think fit' (s.113 and Sch.12 para.2(3) Water Act 1989; and s.34(4) Control of Pollution Act 1974). A number of particular conditions which may be included in a discharge consent are specified as follows:

(a) as to the places at which the discharges to which the consent relates may be made and as to the design and construction of any outlets for the discharges;

(b) as to the nature, origin, composition, temperature, volume and the rate of the discharges and as to the periods during which the discharges may be made;

(c) as to the steps to be taken, in relation to the discharges or by way of subjecting any substance likely to affect the description of matter discharged to treatment or any other process, for minimising the polluting effects of the discharges on any controlled waters;

(d) as to the provision of facilities for taking samples of the matter discharged and, in particular, as to the provision, maintenance and use of manholes, inspection chambers, observation wells and boreholes in connection with the discharges;

(e) as to the provision, maintenance and testing of meters for measuring or recording the volume and rate of the discharges and apparatus for determining the nature, composition and temperature of the discharges;

(f) as to the keeping of records of the nature, composition, temperature, volume and rate of the discharges and, in particular, of records of readings of meters and other recording apparatus provided in accordance with any other condition attached to the consent; and

(g) as to the making of returns and the giving of other information to the Authority about the nature, origin, composition, temperature, volume and rate of the discharges (s.113 and Sch.12 para.2(3) Water Act 1989; and s.34(4) Control of Pollution Act 1974).

It is to be emphasised that this list of conditions is not intended to be exhaustive (Royal Commission on Environmental Pollution (1984) p. 206) and it is made explicit that conditions which are imposed in a discharge consent may be varied in respect of different periods (s.113 and Sch.12 para.2(3) Water Act 1989; s.34(4) Control of Pollution Act 1974; and see also *Trent River Authority* v. *Drabble and Sons Ltd* [1970] 1 All ER 22).

F. Reference to the Secretary of State

Applications for discharge consent are normally determined by the National Rivers Authority, but provision is made for contentious applications to be referred to the Secretary of State for determination. The Secretary of State may call in applications for consideration, either as a result of representations made to him or at his own initiative. In exercise of this power he may direct the National Rivers Authority to transmit to him for determination a specified application for consent or applications of a specified kind (s.113 and Sch.12 para.4(1) Water Act 1989; and s.35(1) Control of Pollution Act 1974). Where this is done it becomes the duty of the Authority to comply with the direction and to inform the applicant that his application has been transmitted to the Secretary of State (s.113 and Sch.12 para.4(2) Water Act 1989; and s.35(1) Control of Pollution Act 1974).

Where an application for discharge consent is transmitted to the Secretary of State for determination by the National Rivers Authority, it may become the subject of a public inquiry. Accordingly, the Secretary of State may, if he thinks fit, and must, if a request to be heard is made to him by either the applicant or the Authority, cause a local enquiry to be held into the application, and afford both the applicant and the Authority an opportunity of appearing before, and being heard by, a person appointed by the Secretary of State for the purpose (s.113 and Sch.12 para.4(4) and (5) Water Act 1989; and s.35(2) Control of Pollution Act 1974). The Secretary of State must also afford an opportunity, to appear and be heard, to any person who has made representations in respect of the application (s.113 and Sch.12 para.4(6) Water Act 1989; and s.35(3) Control of Pollution Act 1974). The Secretary of State is to determine any application for a discharge consent transmitted to him by the Authority whether or not a public enquiry takes place. This is to be done by directing the Authority to refuse its consent or to give consent either unconditionally or subject to such conditions as are specified in the direction. It is the duty of the Authority to comply with the direction (s.113 and Sch.12 para.4(6) Water Act 1989; and s.35(4) Control of Pollution Act 1974).

G.   Publicity for discharge consents

A distinctive policy objective underlying the provisions under Chapter I of Part III of the 1989 Act is that of securing general public availability of information about the aquatic environment, and specifically the availability of information concerning discharge consents (see also [11.02J] below). In accordance with the policy of environmental openness, a duty is imposed upon the National Rivers Authority, on receiving an application for a discharge consent, to take certain measures with respect to publicity, and to receive representations concerning the discharge before determining the application. Specifically, the Authority is required to publish notice of the application in newspapers circulating in the area in which the place of discharge is located and areas in which there are waters which are likely to be affected by the discharge, and in the *London Gazette*, or in Scotland the *Edinburgh Gazette* (s.113 and Sch.12 para.1(3) Water Act 1989; and s.106(8) Control of Pollution Act 1974). In addition, copies of the application are to be sent to each local authority in whose area a discharge is proposed to be made, or in the case of an application relating to coastal waters (see, for example, discussion in [11.04] below) to the Secretary of State and the Minister of Agriculture Fisheries and Food (s.113 and Sch.12 para.1(3) Water Act 1989; and s.36(1) Control of Pollution Act 1974, requiring the information to be sent to the Secretary of State for Scotland). The Authority is entitled to recover costs incurred in the publication of the application from the applicant (s.113 and Sch.12 para.1(6) Water Act 1989; and s.36(3) Control of Pollution Act 1974). After having so publicised the application, the Authority is to consider any written representations which are made within six weeks of the publication of the notice of the application in the *London Gazette* (s.113 and Sch.12 para.1(5) Water Act 1989; and s.36(1) Control of Pollution Act 1974).

By way of exception to the general requirements for the publicity of discharge consent applications the National Rivers Authority is allowed to disregard the need for publicity where an application for discharge consent is considered to have 'no appreciable effect' upon the receiving waters. If, however, the dispensation is for consent to a discharge into coastal waters, the National Rivers Authority must still send copies of the application to the Secretary of State and the Minister of Agriculture, Fisheries and Food (s.113 and Sch.12 para.1(4) Water Act 1989; and s.36(4) Control of Pollution Act 1974, requiring the information to be sent to the Secretary of State for Scotland).

A difficulty with the dispensation from publicity for this reason lies in the precise meaning of the phrase 'no appreciable effect' on receiving water. Guidelines on the operation of the exemption have been given in a

Department of the Environment Circular (Department of the Environment (1984) Annex 3 para.3) where the view was taken that applications should normally be advertised, but exemption on the ground of 'no appreciable effect' may be given where three criteria are satisfied. These are:

(i)   the discharge should not affect an area of amenity or environmental significance (a beach, marine nature reserve, shell fishery, fish spawning area, or site of special scientific interest); and

(ii) the discharge should not result in a major change in the flow of receiving waters; and

(iii) taken together with previously consented discharges, the discharge should not result in such a change to water quality as to (a) damage existing or future uses of the waters (whether or not resulting in a change of water quality classification), or (b) alter by 10 per cent or more the concentration in the receiving waters of any substance which is of importance for the quality of the water and the well-being of its flora and fauna, e.g. dissolved oxygen, B.O.D. (biochemical oxygen demand, a measure of the deoxygenation effect of polluting substances), suspended solids, ammonia, nitrates, phosphates and dissolved metals.

In circumstances where the National Rivers Authority proposes to give consent to an application for discharge consent in respect of which written representations have been made (under s.113 and Sch.12 para.1(5) Water Act 1989; and s.36(1)(c) Control of Pollution Act 1974) then it is the duty of the Authority to serve notice of the proposal to give consent on persons who made representations. In the notice a statement is to be included to the effect that the representer may, within a period of 21 days, request the Secretary of State to direct that the application should be transmitted to him for determination (under s.113 and Sch.12 para.3(3) Water Act 1989; and s.35(1) Control of Pollution Act 1974). In effect, therefore, a right of appeal is provided against the granting of a discharge consent in that it is the duty of the Authority not to give consent in consequence of the application before the expiration of the 21 day period. If within that period, the representer serves notice that the application should be transmitted to the Secretary of State for determination, the Authority is not to give consent in pursuance of the application unless the Secretary of State has given notice to the Authority that he declines to comply with the request (under s.113 and Sch.12 para.3(4) Water Act 1989; and s.36(6)(c) Control of Pollution Act 1974).

A discharge consent granted by the Authority is not merely a personal right afforded to the successful applicant since the authorisation extends to discharges of the kind permitted by the consent where they are made by *any* person (s.113 and Sch.12 para.2(4) Water Act 1989; and s.36(7) Control of Pollution Act 1974). Because of this the benefit of a discharge consent may pass to successors in title, or tenants, of the original grantee of the consent. It follows that a purchaser of a fish farm, for example, would not need to reapply for a discharge consent.

H.   Revocation and alteration of consents

In order to provide for reconsideration of the terms of a consent, the National Rivers Authority issuing a consent is bound to review it from time to time together with the conditions, if any, to which it is subject. Accordingly the

Authority is empowered to serve a notice on the person making the discharge revoking the consent, where it is reasonable to do so, or otherwise make reasonable modifications to conditions to which it is subject. Likewise in the case of an unconditional consent, the Authority may provide that it is to become subject to reasonable conditions specified in the notice (s.113 and Sch.12 para.6(1) and (2) Water Act 1989; and s.37(1) Control of Pollution Act 1974). To the same effect, the Secretary of State may, in consequence of representations made to him or otherwise, direct the Authority to serve a notice of this kind, and where this is done the Authority is bound to comply with the the direction (s.113 and Sch.12 para.6(3) Water Act 1989; and s.37(2) Control of Pollution Act 1974).

Whilst the power to revoke or vary a discharge consent may be justified by the need to bring about improvements in water quality, the power is capable of causing hardship where a discharge consent has been relied upon in making capital expenditure, as where a fish farm has been established on the basis that a right to discharge will continue for a reasonable period. The potential conflict of interests is reconciled by a stipulation that a discharge consent should normally operate for a specified minimum duration, and that a discharge consent is to specify a period during which no notice of revocation of consent, or alteration or imposition of conditions is to be imposed without the written agreement of the person making the discharge. The period during which a discharge consent is not to be revoked or varied without a written agreement is a period of not less than two years beginning with the day on which the original consent, or modified consent, takes effect (s.113 and Sch.12 para.7(1) to (3) Water Act 1989; and s.38(1) and (2) Control of Pollution Act 1974).

I.   Appeals to the Secretary of State

Whilst entitlement to a discharge consent is in most cases initially determined by the National Rivers Authority, a right of appeal to the Secretary of State is provided for. Hence it is provided that an applicant, and any person who has made representations concerning an application for discharge consent, are to be afforded the right to make further representations to the Secretary of State. Specifically, the Secretary of State may hear an appeal where the Authority has refused a consent for discharges, made a consent subject to conditions, revoked a consent, or specified a period during which revocation or variation of a consent will not take place (s.113 and Sch.12 para.8(1) Water Act 1989; and s.38(1) and (2) Control of Pollution Act 1974, where slightly different grounds for appeal are on the basis that the action of the river purification authority is 'unreasonable'). In the event of the Secretary of State deciding an appeal against the Authority, he may give the Authority such direction as he thinks fit and it is the duty of the Authority to comply with it (s.113 and Sch.12 para.8(4) Water Act 1989; and s.36(4) Control of Pollution Act 1974).

J.   Registers of information

A key feature of the general policy for information about water quality under Chapter I of Part III of the 1989 Act is that information of this kind should be made publicly available wherever possible (see also [11.02G] above). In accordance with this, policy provision is made for public access to registers, maintained by the National Rivers Authority and river purification authorities, containing details about effluents and water quality (s.117 Water Act 1989; s.41 Control of Pollution Act 1974; and Department of the Environment (1985)). The matters to be recorded in an Authority register include particulars of: applications for consents made under Chapter I of Part III of the 1989 Act; consents given under Chapter I and the conditions to which they are subject; certificates exempting applications, consents or discharges from the publicity provisions under Chapter I (discussed below); samples of water taken by the Authority (see s.147(1) on the power of the Authority to enter premises to take samples of water) and information produced by analyses of the samples; information with respect to samples taken by any other person; and steps taken in consequence of information produced by analyses of samples of water (s.117(1) Water Act 1989; and s.41(1) Control of Pollution Act 1974). The Authority is to ensure that the register is open to inspection by the public free of charge at all reasonable hours and that members of the public are afforded reasonable facilities for obtaining from the Authority, on payment of reasonable charges, copies of entries in the register (s.117(2) Water Act 1989; and s.41(2) Control of Pollution Act 1974).

A significant exception to the general principle of public access to information about discharge consents and water quality is that, occasionally, genuine grounds exist for not making certain types of information publicly available. For this reason a person who proposes to make, or has made, an application to the National Rivers Authority for discharge consent is permitted to apply to the Secretary of State to secure exemption from publicity requirements. Certification by the Secretary of State may also confer exemption from publicity in Authority registers in respect of a consent granted and the conditions imposed in it, and details of a sample of effluent taken from a discharge or information produced by analysis of such a sample (s.113 and Sch.12 para.1(7) Water Act 1989; and s.42(1) Control of Pollution Act 1974).

The dispensation from publicity requirements will not be readily granted, since over-use of this power would undermine the general policy objective of public availability of information concerning the water environment. For that reason the applicant must satisfy the Secretary of State that disclosure of information would either prejudice to an unreasonable degree some private interest by disclosing information about a trade secret, or would be contrary to the public interest (s.113 and Sch.12 para.1(7)(b) Water Act 1989; and s.42(1)(b) Control of Pollution Act 1974). Although it is conceivable that a fish farmer might argue that disclosure of information about a discharge was commercially confidential, because it might reveal information about his enterprise to a competitor, the scope for this kind of claim is narrow. In practice it would appear that relatively little use is made of the possibility of exemption from publicity on this ground (Royal Commission on Environmental Pollution (1984) para.2.68; and Department of the Environment (1986B)).

K. Charges for applications and consents

Amongst the substantial changes in the law relating to discharge consents brought about under the Water Act 1989 is the introduction of new powers for the National Rivers Authority and the the river purification authorities to impose charges in respect of discharge consents (s.113 and Sch.12 para.9 Water Act 1989). Although general provision existed previously for the imposition of charges by water authorities (under s.30 Water Act 1973) no use was made of this provision. As a part of the privatisation programme for the water industry in England and Wales it was decided that the Authority should, wherever possible, charge those to whom its services are provided. Accordingly, provision has been made for the imposition of charges in relation to abstraction licensing (s.129(1) Water Act 1989; discussed in [9.03C] above) and analogous provision made in relation to the imposition of charges in respect of discharge consents. Corresponding amendments to the Control of Pollution Act 1974 have the effect of making similar provision for the imposition of charges in relation to discharge consents granted by the river purification authorities in Scotland (s.53 Control of Pollution Act 1974).

The new charging provisions provide that where an application for discharge consent is made to the National Rivers Authority, or discharge consent is granted, or a discharge consent is for the time being in force, the Authority may require payment of charges specified in, or determined by, a scheme of charges (s.113 and Sch.12 para.9(1) Water Act 1989; and s.53(1) Control of Pollution Act 1974). The persons liable to pay charges are those making an application, upon whom an instrument granting consent is served, or who make a discharge in pursuance of a consent to which the scheme of charges relates (s.113 and Sch.12 para.9(2) Water Act 1989; and s.53(2) Control of Pollution Act 1974).

A discharge consent charging scheme for these purposes is not to be made without the approval of the Secretary of State, and the consent of the Treasury (s.113 and Sch.12 para.9(3) Water Act 1989; and s.53(3) Control of Pollution Act 1974). Before submission to the Secretary of State for approval the Authority is to take steps to bring the proposed scheme to the attention of persons likely to be affected by it. Thus it is to publish a notice setting out its proposals and specifying the period within which representations or objections may be made to the Secretary of State (s.113 and Sch.12 para.9(4) Water Act 1989; and s.53(4) Control of Pollution Act 1974). The Secretary of State is to consider any representations or objects made and not withdrawn, and is to have regard to specified factors in determining whether or not to give approval to the proposed scheme (s.113 and Sch.12 para.9(5) Water Act 1989; and s.53(5) Control of Pollution Act 1974). In particular he is to take into account the desirability of ensuring that the amount recovered by the Authority by way of charges does not exceed any amount reasonably attributable to the expenses incurred by the Authority in carrying out its functions in relation to discharge consents. The Secretary of State is also to have regard to the need to ensure that no undue preference is shown, and that there is no undue discrimination in the fixing of charges under the scheme (s.113 and Sch.12 para.9(6) Water Act 1989; and s.53(6) Control of Pollution Act 1974). When made and approved by the Secretary of State it is the duty of the Authority to take appropriate steps to bring the provisions of the charging scheme to the attention of persons likely to be affected (s.113 and Sch.12 para.9(8) Water Act 1989; and s.53(8) Control of Pollution Act 1974).

Although precise details of charging schemes in relation to discharge consents have not yet emerged the implications of the new provisions for inland fish farmers are clear. Depending upon the particular mechanism for determining charges devised, the cost of a discharge consent for a fish farmer may become a significant, and in some cases perhaps economically prohibitive, head of expenditure. As with the earlier discussion of charges for abstraction licensing (in [9.03C] above), the point is deservedly made that though large amounts of water are discharged by many fish farms, the diminution of water quality caused by this diversion and return of water is relatively small, and that this factor is justifiably taken into account in determining discharge consent charging schemes. Consideration will also need to be given to the inter-relationship between the abstraction charging and discharge charging schemes, since a failure to take account of a payment already having been made by a fish farmer for abstraction, in charging for a discharge consent, would result in a duplication of charges for essentially the same use of water.

11.03 *The operation of discharge consents*

Turning from the detailed legal controls which regulate the granting of discharge consents to the use which is made of those powers by the licensing authorities, it is pertinent to examine how those powers are used to restrict potentially polluting discharges from fish farms. Taking the predicament of an inland fish farm where water is abstracted from a stream to be used in a fish farm before being returned to the stream (contrast the cage rearing situation, discussed in [11.04] below), it is apparent that the formulation of discharge consents for such farms, which are adequate both to protect the aquatic environment and to allow the farm to operate efficiently, is not a simple exercise.

The pollution load of organic waste originating from a fish farm will vary according to the level of stock contained in the farm, and this is likely to vary considerably at different times of the year depending upon stock movements. Moreover, the capacity of the receiving waters to accommodate effluent without significant detriment will depend upon other uses of the stream and a range of factors which may be uncontrolled such as the rate of flow and the temperature of the stream. Clearly it would be inadequate to set a level of discharge of deoxygenating material by reference to rates of flow which are not maintained during summer periods when the stream is at its lowest and its capacity to receive effluent least. Alternatively a discharge consent set by reference to a historically determined summer minimum flow rate would mean, in many cases, that farms would be unable effectively to utilise the pollution-neutralising capacity of the stream at other times of the year, and in extreme cases would be unable to maintain production at a level enabling commercial viability to be sustained (Tervert (1981); and Blake (1983) pp. 36 to 42).

A report of the Water Authorities Association Fish Farming Working Party in 1984, considered the difficulties involved in determining discharge consents for fish farms with a view to obtaining greater uniformity throughout the United Kingdom (Water Authorities Association (1984)). The

Working Party recognised the difficulty in setting any absolute standards for some determinands where a fish farm takes water directly from the flow of a river, since the quality of the discharged water will inevitably be dependent upon the quality of the water initially abstracted. A preference was expressed, in some respects, for differential conditions measuring the deterioration of water quality between the inlet and outlet of individual fish farms. In relation to biochemical oxygen demand suspended solids, ammonia, turbidity and colour, therefore, the Working Party declined to specify precise standards for fish farms but made a number of observations. First, changes in biochemical oxygen demand (B.O.D.) should not result in a fall in the general river classification of the river; second, it was stressed that the B.O.D. and suspended solids determinands have to be stringently controlled; and third, the ammonia limit should be determined so that the river downstream complies with appropriate EEC requirements (see [10.06] above) and does not cause a problem with oxygen uptake or public water supplies. Other than in respect of these unspecified determinands, and the matter of antibiotic content on which the Working Party thought that the available evidence was insufficient to allow them to make any definite recommendation, the set of standard consent conditions shown in Table 11.1 were proposed for a fish farm taking water from a watercourse and discharging back into that watercourse.

Table 11.1

Consent conditions

Name and address of person
to whom this consent is given

Reference No:
Date of Application:
Plans:

Full address or description of
the land or premises to which
the consent relates

Receiving watercourse:

Map reference of outlet:

CONSENT CONDITIONS
1. The outlet shall be used only for the discharge of fish-farm effluent.
2. The outlet shall be suitably screened to retain fish on the fish farm.
3. The sampling point agreed for the purposes of obtaining representative samples of effluent discharged from the fish farm shall be marked on the attached plan.
4. The point agreed for the purposes of obtaining representative samples of water entering the fish farm shall be a suitably designed sampling point, marked on the attached plan.
5. Facilities approved by the Water Authority shall be provided to allow representative samples to be obtained at both sampling points.

6. The composition of the effluent discharged from the fish farm as sampled at the agreed sampling point shall not be changed relative to the influent water with respect to the corresponding determinand or determinands by amounts greater than specified below:
   (i)   the Biochemical Oxygen Demand (nitrification suppressed 5 days at 20°C) shall not be increased by more than ... milligrams per litre (mg/l).
   (ii)   The total Suspended Solids content (dried at 105°C) shall not be increased by more than ... mg/l.
   (iii)   The total Ammonia content (expressed as Nitrogen) shall not be increased by more than ... mg/l.
   (iv)   The turbidity (expressed in Formazin Turbidity Units) shall not be increased by more than ... units.
   (v)   The colour (expressed in Hazen Units) shall not be increased by more than ... units.
   (vi)   The pH shall not be changed by more than 0.5 pH units.
7. The effluent shall at no time contain:
   (i)   A free Chlorine concentration greater than 0.1 mg/l.
   (ii)   A Cationic Detergent concentration greater than 0.1 mg/l.
   (iii)   A Malachite Green concentration greater than 0.1 mg/l. and in addition:
   (iv)   Antibiotics – no standard recommendation but this may be reviewed in the light of further information.
   (v)   Visible oil shall be absent.
   (vi)   The discharge shall not contain less that 60% of the air saturation value of Dissolved Oxygen.
   (vii)   The effluent shall not contain material in sufficient quantity to cause significant visible fungal growth in the receiving watercourse downstream of the outlet.
   (viii) Copper compounds shall not be present at a concentration greater than 0.05 mg/l Cu.
   (ix)   Phenolic compounds shall not be present at a concentration greater than 0.005 mg/l expressed as C_6H_5OH.
   (x)   Formaldehyde shall not be present at a concentration greater than 1.0 mg/l.
8. The total flow discharged from the fish farm shall be taken as the flow measured at the outlet marked on the attached plan, or at any other measurement point agreed with the Water Authority.
9. A suitable measuring device shall be installed at the above location and shall be approved in writing by the Water Authority before the discharge commences.
10. The total flow of effluent discharged from the fish farm as measured at the agreed point shall not exceed ... megalitres per day and the maximum rate of discharge shall not exceed ... litres per second.
11. The agreed sampling points and agreed flow measurement points shall be accessible at all times to the Authority's Officers for the purposes of taking samples or measuring flows.

   Dated the ......

Despite the attempt of the Water Authorities Association's Working Party on Consent Conditions for Fish Farms to suggest respects in which discharge consent conditions might achieve greater uniformity, it would appear that the practices of water authorities towards consent formulation have remained rather variable. Whilst some authorities have made use of all or part of the model consent, others have not, and it has not yet reached the point of becoming standard throughout the water industry, though it is probable that standardisation of practice will be brought about in future by the National Rivers Authority. Whether adhered to or not, however, it is of fundamental importance that the basis upon which the comparison between influent and effluent is to be made is precisely stipulated if legal proceedings for breach of a discharge consent are to be pursued. Departures from the model consent, which are presently incorporated into particular consents issued by some authorities, are undesirably ambiguous as to the manner in which differences between influent and effluent are to be ascertained (Beck (1988)).

An illustration of legal proceedings being pursued for breach of a fish farm's discharge consent is to be found in *Wansford Trout Farm* v. *Yorkshire Water Authority* (unreported, Queen's Bench Division, 23 July 1986) where a trout farmer appealed against a conviction before magistrates for discharging trade effluent contrary to discharge consent conditions (imposed under s.7(14) Rivers (Prevention of Pollution) Act 1951, the forerunner to discharge consent conditions now provided for under s.113 and Sch.12 Water Act 1989). Specifically, the farm concerned diverted almost the total flow of the stream on which it was located, and discharged effluent which failed to meet the minimum dissolved oxygen content of 5 milligrams per litre specified amongst the conditions in its discharge consent. As a result some fish in the stream below the point at which the fish farm water was returned were found to be dead, and others in a distressed condition, as a result of a lack of oxygen.

Amongst the legal issues which were raised by the appeal, it was contended that the discharge was not of 'trade effluent', nor was it discharged from 'land or premises', within the wording of the enactment under which the offence of breaching discharge consents arose. (On this point now see s.124(3) Water Act 1989, discussed in [11.02D] above.) On this point the court was clearly of the view that the discharge was of 'trade effluent' and that the discharge took place from 'land or premises'. An additional issue to which attention was given was the admissibility of evidence of dissolved oxygen levels taken by the Water Authority from measurements provided by a dissolved oxygen meter. The taking of water samples for analysis by a water authority is subject to an explicit rule of admissibility whereby evidence of water quality will not be admitted in court unless a procedure is followed involving a part of the sample being made available to the occupier for independent analysis (under s.113 Water Resources Act 1963, now provided for in relation to the National Rivers Authority under s.148 Water Act 1989). Despite the absence of a means by which the occupier might check the measurements of the dissolved oxygen meter, however, the court held that admissibility of this kind of evidence was not dependent upon the provision of a sample to the occupier since the use of the meter did not involve the taking of any sample for the purposes of analysis. (See also, *Trent River Board* v. *Wardle Ltd* [1957] Crim. L.R. 196.) Moreover, because the machine which had been used to make the measurement of dissolved oxygen was reliable and correctly operated by an experienced officer of the Water Authority there was no reason to exclude it as evidence of the offence. Conviction for breach of the discharge consent was affirmed on appeal. In addition the court affirmed a separate conviction against the appellant for causing to flow into waters containing fish liquid matter causing the waters to be poisonous or injurious to fish, which constitutes a distinct offence under the Salmon and Freshwater Fisheries Act 1975 (s.4 Salmon and Freshwater Fisheries Act 1975).

Although not concerning fish farm discharges, another recent decision of general relevance to the operation of the discharge consent system is *Severn-Trent River Authority* v. *Express Foods Group Ltd* ([1989] Crim. L. Rev. 226). Here the accused Company had a discharge consent allowing the discharge of trade effluent, consisting of milk processing waste, subject to certain conditions. After an emission contravened several of the conditions of the discharge consent, they were charged with a number of offences each of which consisted of a breach of a separate condition in the same discharge consent. It was held on appeal that the offence at issue was that of causing or knowingly permitting the discharge of effluent without the consent of the Water Authority (under s.32 Control of Pollution Act 1974, now see ss.107(1)(c) 108(1)(a) Water Act 1989) and that this could not be construed as a series of separate, and separately punishable, offences. Accordingly, only one offence was committed by each offending emission regardless of the number of conditions of the discharge consent which were infringed by the emission.

More general issues concerning the duty of water authorities, and in future the National Rivers Authority, to pursue action against fish farms causing pollution by contravening discharge consents also arose for consideration in *R* v. *Wessex Water Authority, ex parte Cutts*, (unreported, Queen's Bench Division, 18 March 1988) where an action for judicial review was brought by a riparian owner against a water authority for allegedly failing to take effective action to stop pollution of a river, specifically, by prosecuting fish farms. Whilst recognising the general pollution control responsibilities of the Authority, and the statutory duty to 'maintain, improve and develop' fisheries in the river (under s.28(1)(a) Salmon and Freshwater Fisheries Act 1975, now the responsibility of the National Rivers Authority under s.141(1)(a) Water Act 1989) the court found that in relation to the particular complaints that were raised the Authority had not been guilty of any dereliction of its statutory duties. It had done all within its power to tackle pollution in the river and could not conscientiously have brought proceedings against the allegedly offending fish farms with any reasonable prospect of success. Although unsuccessful on the facts of this case, the point of the proceedings remains, that the failure of a water authority, and now the National Rivers Authority, to act in accordance with its statutory duty to enforce pollution control legislation will, in principle at least, amount to a legal ground for judicial review of an authority's failure to act and will provide the basis for a court order compelling statutory duties to be properly performed by the authority.

11.04 Cage culture under the Water Act 1989

The provisions of Chapter I of Part III of the Water Act 1989 (Part II Control of Pollution Act 1974, as amended by s.168 and Sch.23 Water Act 1989, in

Scotland) have clear application to situations where fish farming takes place in inland waters, as where water is abstracted from a stream to supply a trout farm and returned in a polluted state. In relation to situations where fish are reared in cages, as with the culture of salmon in coastal waters, the application of the provisions under the 1989 Act are less clear in their effect. The following discussion explores some of the difficulties.

Setting aside the use of medicines and other regulated chemicals in salmon farming (discussed in Chapter 13 below), cage culture methods have well established effects upon water quality. Estimates of food wastage from cages range from 5 per cent to 40 per cent of the total amount fed to fish (Philips and Beveridge (1986) p. 17). Of that which is consumed it has been suggested that a tonne of solid organic waste, containing large amounts of phosphorus and nitrogen, is generated from each ten tonnes of food pellets (Anon. (1987B); Brown, Gowan and McLusky (1987); and Scottish Wildlife and Countryside Link (1988) pp. 15 to 28). The extent of the pollution problem resulting from these sources clearly depends upon a range of factors including the extent, intensity and duration of the operation and the depth and circulation of waters in which it takes place. Nonetheless, the potential for pollution from salmon cages is widely acknowledged.

An initial accumulation of a nutrient-rich deposit on the sea bed beneath salmon cages is likely to produce enhanced plant growth through nutrient-enrichment or 'eutrophication'. The continued build-up of a sediment of decaying organic matter, however, has the effect of reducing the diversity of benthic invertebrates in the locality of sea cages. The longer term effects of sediment accumulation include the emission of gaseous by-products of decomposition, and a general deoxygenating effect brought about by the bacteriological action of organic decay (Philips and Beveridge (1986)). This is accompanied by the possibility of sudden increases in toxic algal growth, termed 'algal bloom', as a consequence of excessive nutrient enrichment (Cobham Resource Consultants (1987) para.6.8; and Anon (1988B) and (1988C)).

The application of the controls under Chapter I of Part III of the Water Act 1989 to pollution originating from salmon cages is a matter of some legal difficulty. As has been stated, the 1989 Act provides for the main offences relating to water pollution in Britain and is applicable to the pollution of inland waters and coastal waters to a distance of three nautical miles from the coastal baselines (see [11.02A] above). The two offences under the Act which might potentially arise in relation to cage culture of salmon are, first, the offence of causing or knowingly permitting any poisonous, noxious or polluting matter to enter any relevant waters (under s.107(1)(a) Water Act 1989, and see [11.02B] above) and, second, the offence of causing or knowingly permitting any trade effluent to be discharged into any relevant waters (s.107(1)(c) Water Act 1989, and see [11.02D] above). A number of legal difficulties have arisen in relation to the application of these offences to pollution from salmon cages.

In respect of the first offence, of causing or knowingly permitting poisonous, noxious or polluting matter to enter waters, the difficulty lies in the mechanism by which the pollution occurs. Although there may be high food wastage in some situations capable of having a polluting effect, if not consumed by wild species in the vicinity of fish cages, the larger part of the problem lies in sediment produced by fish excrement and general fish detritus. It follows that the matter which *enters* the water, that is, the food pellets fed to the caged fish, is not in itself the matter which causes the pollution. Arguably, the matter which causes the pollution is the fish waste products produced by the fish which are *already* in the water. If this analysis is correct it follows that, in law, the element of 'entry' of the poisonous, noxious or polluting matter required for the commission of the offence may be lacking.

In view of the recent re-definition of 'trade effluent' (discussed in [11.02D] above) making it explicit that premises used for fish farming are 'trade premises' (s.124(3) Water Act 1989; and in relation to Scotland s.56(3) Control of Pollution Act 1974, as amended by s.168 and Sch.23 Water Act 1989) it is more likely that the main offence committed in relation to pollution from fish cages is that of causing or knowingly permitting the discharge of trade effluent (s.107(1)(c)). The problematic aspect of this subsumption, however, is the question of whether the undesirable by-products of the industry can be said to be 'discharged' into the marine environment. 'Discharge' is an awkward term to characterise the emission which takes place. At one extreme the term 'discharge' seems an apt one to apply to discreet sources of pollution such as pipelines and sea outfalls, but at the other extreme it appears an inappropriate term to apply to diffuse sources of pollutant such as water pollution arising through atmospheric pollution or the general run-off of pollutants from land. Organic waste products from fish cages, carried by gravity and the action of water current, fall awkwardly between these two extremes, and the difficulty of determining whether this kind of emission amounts to a 'discharge' awaits authoritative resolution.

It is pertinent to note that the Highland River Purification Board, the authority with responsibility for an area in which a large number of salmon farms are situated, has made use of its power to grant discharge consents (Scottish Wildlife and Countryside Link (1988) para.8.2) in relation to cage discharges. The practical effect of this is that, providing fish farmers comply with the terms of their discharge consents, the difficulties of determining what offence would otherwise be committed do not arise. The underlying legal difficulty remains, however, as to which, if any, of the offences would be committed if a discharge consent were to be breached, and the general area of law is one which is in great need of clarification.

11.05   Part II of the Food and Environment Protection Act 1985

In addition to Chapter I of Part III of the Water Act 1989, water pollution from fish farms in coastal waters is capable of being subject to measures intended to regulate the deposit of waste at sea which arise under Part II of the Food and Environment Protection Act 1985. Although specific exemptions under the later enactment apply to fish farming, the general effect of the 1985 Act, and its relationship to the 1989 Act warrant discussion.

Amongst other objectives (see [13.07] below on Part III of the Food and Environment Protection Act 1985 concerned with pesticides) the Food and Environment Protection Act 1985 regulates the deposit of waste at sea and gives effect to obligations arising under international conventions including the Oslo Convention for the Prevention of Marine Pollution by Dumping from Ships and Aircraft of 1972 (Cmnd. 4984) and the London Convention for the Prevention of Marine Pollution by Dumping of Wastes and Other Matter of 1972 (Cmnd. 5169). The basic mechanism of Part II of the 1985 Act is to subject all deposits of substances and articles in the sea to a licensing requirement. Hence a licence is required for the deposit of substances and articles in the sea within United Kingdom waters from any vessel or marine structure, or from a structure on land constructed or adapted wholly or mainly for the purpose of depositing solids in the sea (s.5(a) Food and Environment Protection Act 1985). Associated with the licensing require-ment is the sanction that it is an offence to do anything for which a licence is required other than in pursuance of a licence and in accordance with its terms, or to cause or permit any other person to do so. Alternatively it is an offence, for the purpose of procuring a licence, to make a statement known to be false in a material particular, or recklessly to make a statement which is false in a material particular, or intentionally to fail to disclose any material particular (s.9(1)).

The general subjection of all deposits of substances and articles in the sea to licensing enables the licensing authority to have regard to the need to protect the marine environment, the living resources which it supports and human health, and to prevent interference with legitimate uses of the sea (s.8(1)). In relation to specific cases, however, the Ministers are empowered to make an order specifying those operations which do not need a licence, or are exempt from licensing where certain conditions are satisfied (s.7(1)). Accordingly the Minister of Agriculture, Fisheries and Food acting jointly with the Secretary of State have exercised this power in making the Deposits in the Sea (Exemptions) Order 1985 (SI 1985 No.1699). This Order states that a licence is not needed for operations listed in the Schedule to the order provided that specified conditions are satisfied (Art.3 Deposits in the Sea (Exemptions) Order 1985). Of the range of operations not needing a licence listed in the Schedule the following may be relevant to fish farming operations:

Para.8: Deposit (by way of return to the sea) of fish or shellfish or parts thereof in the course of fishing operations or fish processing at sea.

Para.9: Deposit (by way of return to the sea) by a fishing vessel of any article (other than a fish or shellfish) taken from the sea by the vessel in the course of normal fishing operations.

Para.10: Deposit of any substance or article (otherwise than for the purpose of disposal) in the course of, for the purpose of, or in connection with, the propagation or cultivation of fish or shellfish.

Para.11: Deposit (by way of return to the sea) of any substance or article dredged from the sea-bed in connection with the propagation or cultivation of shellfish.

Para.24: Launching of vessels or marine structures (Schedule).

The effect of these exemptions is to place most normal activities which take place in the course of marine fish farming outside the licensing requirements imposed under the 1985 Act.

An interesting legal puzzle arising from the licensing exemption under the 1985 Act concerns the permissive character of the exemption. The 1985

Order states that 'a licence is not needed' for specified operations including the activities listed above, but does not indicate whether a licence would be issued if applied for in relation to the stated activities. Although not necessary for the purposes of the licensing requirement under the 1985 Act the possession of such a licence has important implications in relation to water pollution offences arising under the Water Act 1989. Both the offence relating to the entry of polluting matter into waters (s.107(1)(a) Water Act 1989, discussed in [11.02B] above) and the offence relating to the discharge of trade effluent (s.107(1)(c) discussed in [11.02D] above) are subject to the exception that they will not be committed where the entry or discharge concerned is authorised by a licence granted under Part II of the 1985 Act (s.108(1)(c)). It would appear to follow from this that if a licence under the 1985 Act were to be available, though not required by the 1985 Act, it would provide a potentially important defence to the offences under the 1989 Act.

Chapter 12

Predator and Pest Control

12.01 The problem of predation

The intensification of aquacultural activity brings with it some major difficulties in relation to the control of predators and pests. The confinement of large numbers of fish in a relatively small enclosure, or the concentration of shellfish in cultivated beds or rafts, constitute a strong allurement to birds and other animals for which the farmed species would naturally constitute a source of food. Predator species are generally regarded as a threat to aquacultural productivity, but in some instances are subject to special legal protection as uncommon or rare species. A number of problematic issues of law and policy arise in determining whether species protection or fish farm productivity should be given priority in authorising destructive methods of predator and pest control.

At least four distinct effects of predation can be discerned. First, there is the direct loss of stock by consumption and damage which occurs as a result of a predator attack. Second, fish which are wounded by a predator become highly susceptible to disease either as a result of an infection transmitted by the predator, or as a result of increased vulnerability to water-carried diseases such as furunculosis, which are common in fish farms and difficult to contain or eradicate once established. Third, a predator attack, or even the presence of predator in the vicinity of a fish enclosure, has been shown to induce a state of 'stress' in fish which disrupts feeding and brings about hormonal changes which reduce the resistance of stock to disease. Fourth, where stock is contained in net enclosures in the sea or inland waters a predator attack may result in damage to nets which allows the escape of stock into the wild (Ross (1988) at p. 22). The particular predators which will constitute a problem for any individual fish farmer will depend upon the type of fish which are farmed, the effectiveness of anti-predator measures and the location in which farming takes place. The differing combinations of these factors which arise in particular circumstances mean that for some fish farms predation is an insignificant problem whilst for others it is a very serious difficulty resulting in major financial losses (Ross (1988) at p. 24).

The mammalian predators of greatest significance are mink, otters and seals, whilst major bird predators include herons, cormorants, shags and, in relation to shellfish farms, eider duck (Ross (1988) at p. 4). A range of other predators are also capable of taking or destroying fish farm stock (Huet (1986) Ch.XV S.I; and Ross (1988) at p. 34). Although prudent fish farmers take extensive measures to deter or scare these predators from their sites, and to prevent their entry into areas containing fish through anti-predator nets, these methods frequently fail to prevent losses. As a last resort destructive methods of predator control including trapping and shooting are applied. In some cases the species involved are protected by law and may not be killed without special authorisation. In this context two enactments are of particular importance, the Conservation of Seals Act 1970, and the Wildlife and Countryside Act 1981.

In this discussion of the control of predators and pests it is to be noted that the species which are discussed do not encompass interloping fish species as either predators or pests. It is recognised that piscivorous species of fish within a fish farm may prey upon stock, and almost any unfarmed species may become a pest by taking food intended for the farmed species. At this point it may be observed that, in some situations, it may be permissible to use methods to remove or control the unwanted fish species which would otherwise be contrary to the general fishery law. These issues are considered in Chapter 14 dealing with the relationship between fish farming and fishery law.

12.02   The Conservation of Seals Act 1970

Seals are a major predator species on coastal salmon farms where a recent survey indicated that, until recently, the shooting of seals was a widespread form of control practised on the majority of such farms (Ross (1988) at p. 59). In England and Wales and Scotland killing of seals is regulated by the Conservation of Seals Act 1970 which makes it an offence to kill grey seals, *Halichoerus grypus*, or common seals, *Phoca vitulina*, by certain methods and at certain times of the year. Due primarily to the present epidemic of seal disease, provisions of the 1970 Act have been extended by Orders concerned with the conservation of seals. This section examines the general extent and operation of the provisions of the 1970 Act, but it is to be read subject to [12.03] below, which deals with the Orders made under the Act.

The Conservation of Seals Act 1970 imposes a basic prohibition upon certain methods of killing seals so that, subject to certain exceptions, it is an offence to use, for the purpose of killing or taking any seal, any poisonous substance, or any firearm other than a rifle using ammunition having a muzzle energy of not less that 600 foot-pounds and a bullet weighing not less than 45 grains (s.1(1) Conservation of Seals Act 1970). The offence of using a prohibited method to kill a seal is subject to two exceptions. First, there is the 'mercy killing' exception that a person will not be guilty of the offence where the killing is of a seal which had been so seriously disabled otherwise than by this act that there is no reasonable chance of its recovering (s.9(2)). Second, a person will not be guilty of the offence where the killing or taking of the seal takes place pursuant to a licence granted by the Minister of Agriculture, Fisheries and Food in England, or the respective Secretary of State in Wales or Scotland (s.10, discussed below). These Ministers are also empowered to make orders amending the types of firearm and ammunition which may lawfully be used for the purposes of the prohibition (s.1(2)).

The technical provisions relating to firearms apply in the same way as provided for under the Firearms Act 1968 (s.15). Accordingly, a 'firearm' means a lethal barrelled weapon of any description from which any shot, bullet or other missile can be discharged and includes certain specifically prohibited weapons, components of such weapons, and accessories of such weapons designed or adapted to diminish the noise or flash caused by firing the weapon (s.57(1) Firearms Act 1968). 'Ammunition' includes ammunition for any firearm and also grenades, bombs and other like missiles, whether capable of use with a firearm or not, and certain specifically prohibited ammunition (s.57(2)). The 1968 Act also requires a person possessing a firearm to be in possession of a firearm certificate (s.1). It is a legal prerequisite of the use of a firearm to shoot seals, or any other form of predator, that firearm certification requirements are complied with.

Subject to the prohibition upon the use of certain methods of killing or taking seals, described above, the killing of seals is lawful only when in season. During close seasons it is an offence for any person wilfully to kill, injure or take a seal. For grey seals the close season extends from 1 September to 31 December, both dates inclusive. For common seals the close season extends from 1 July to 31 August, with both dates inclusive (s.2(1) Conservation of Seals Act 1970).

The offence of wilfully killing, injuring or taking a seal during the close season is subject to exceptions either where it is in compliance with a Ministerial licence (s.10, discussed below) or where it is provided for under the category of 'general exceptions'. The latter category provides for the unseasonable killing, injury or taking of seals in four circumstances. The first general exception is where there is a taking or attempted taking of a seal which has been disabled, otherwise than by the act of the person taking it, for the purpose of tending it and releasing it when no longer disabled. The second exception arises where the unavoidable killing or injuring of any seal occurs as an incidental result of a lawful action. The third exception covers the killing or attempted killing of any seal by a person to prevent it from causing damage to a fishing net or fishing tackle in his possession, or any fish for the time being in the fishing net, provided that at the time the seal was in the vicinity of such net or tackle (s.9(1)). A final exception covers the killing of any seal which has been so seriously disabled otherwise than by the act of the person killing it that there was no reasonable chance of it recovering (s.9(2)).

It is notable that the control of seal predators attacking salmon cages fits awkwardly alongside any of the general exceptions provided to the offence of unseasonable killing of seals. It is conceivable, though open to dispute, that the unseasonable killing of a seal might amount to a lawful protection of farmer's property under the second of the exceptions. Of similar uncertainty is the applicability of the third exception, that the destruction of a seal might be justified to prevent damage to a fishing net or fishing tackle where a seal is in the vicinity of such a net or tackle. Here, however, difficulty surrounds the question of whether the net of a salmon cage can properly be described as a 'fishing net' for these purposes. The application of the general exceptions to the situation of unseasonable killing of seals as a means of fish farm predator control is, therefore, a matter of some legal difficulty which has not yet been authoritatively resolved.

If, after consultation with the Natural Environment Research Council (provided for under s.3(3) Science and Technology Act 1965) it appears to the Secretary of State necessary for the proper conservation of seals, he may by order prohibit the killing, injuring or taking of either grey seals or common seals, or both, in any area specified in the order (s.3(1) Conservation of Seals Act 1970). If any person wilfully kills, injures or takes a seal in contravention of an order of this kind he will be guilty of an offence, subject to the same exceptions which arise in relation to the unseasonable killing of seals, discussed above (s.3(2)). The Ministerial orders presently in operation are considered in the following section.

All the offences arising under the 1970 Act so far considered are punishable on summary conviction by a fine not exceeding level 4 on the standard scale, presently £1,000 (s.5(2)). Equally, an attempt to commit an offence under the Act is an offence punishable to the same extent (s.8(1)). Possession, for the purpose of killing seals, of any poisonous substance or any firearm or ammunition the use of which is a prohibited method is also an offence (s.8(2)). A court by which a person is convicted of an offence under the Act may also order the forfeiture of any seal or seal skin in respect of which the offence was committed, or of any seal, seal skin, firearm, ammunition or poisonous substance in the possession of an offender at the time of the offence (s.6). To allow courts jurisdiction to deal with offences which may fall outside their area, any offence under the Act committed at a place on the sea coast or at sea is deemed to have been committed at the place where the offender is found or to which he is first brought after the commission of the offence (s.7).

As has been noted, the three main offences under the 1970 Act, of using a prohibited method of killing seals, killing seals during the close season, and killing seals in contravention of a Ministerial order, are subject to the exception that they are not committed where the acts concerned are in accordance with a licence granted by the appropriate Minister. A licence of this kind may authorise the killing or taking of a number of seals by specified means, other than the use of strychnine, for scientific or educational purposes or by any specified means for the purposes of any zoological gardens or collection specified in the licence. Also, a licence may be granted for the killing or taking in certain areas, by any means other than the use of strychnine, for the prevention of damage to fisheries, the reduction of a population of seals for management purposes, the use of a population surplus of seals as a resource, or the protection of flora or fauna in areas of special environmental significance (s.10(1) and (4)). These include nature reserves (under s.15 National Parks and Access to the Countryside Act 1949), areas notified as sites of special scientific interest (under s.28(1) Wildlife and Countryside Act 1981), areas where there is special protection for certain areas of special scientific interest (under s.29(3) Wildlife and Countryside Act 1981) and areas designated as marine nature reserves (under s.36 Wildlife and Countryside Act 1981). In relation to these areas and except in relation to the prevention of damage to fisheries, the Minister is not to issue a licence to kill or take seals without the consent of the Nature Conservancy Council. In all cases the Minister is to consult with the Natural Environmental Research Council (s.10(3)).

Relating the Ministerial licensing powers to the circumstances of seal control in the vicinity of salmon farms, the use of these powers in that context is somewhat uncertain. The most pertinent provision lies in the power of the Minister to grant licences for the 'prevention of damage to fisheries' (s.10(1)(c)(i)). Although it appears that in practice the Minister exercises his powers to authorise the shooting of seals for this reason, the ambiguity of whether a fish farm constitutes a 'fishery' for these purposes has never been authoritatively determined.

12.03   The Conservation of Seals Orders 1973 and 1988

Of the three Orders which have been made under the Conservation of Seals Act 1970, the first is the Conservation of Seals (Scotland) Order 1973 (SI 1973 No.1079). This Order was made by the Secretary of State for Scotland in exercise of the powers conferred under ss.3 and 14 of the 1970 Act, and after consultation with the Natural Environment Research Council. The effect of the Order is to prohibit the killing, injuring or taking of common seals in the County of Zetland and the territorial water adjacent thereto.

It has been suggested that the present epidemic of seal disease, termed 'seal plague', may have had dramatic effects upon populations of common and perhaps grey seals, and the indications are that high levels of mortality have been suffered (Lightowlers (1988)). As a result of this situation Ministers have extended the protection of seals through the mechanism of two recent Orders, the Conservation of Seals (Common Seals) Order 1988 (SI 1988 No.2023) and the Conservation of Seals (England and Wales) Order 1988 (SI 1988 No.2024). Both of these orders came into operation on 19 December 1988 and expire two years after that date unless revoked before that time.

The Conservation of Seals (Common Seals) Order 1988 prohibits the killing, injuring or taking of common seals within the seaward limits of the territorial waters (see [3.01] above) adjacent to Britain (Art.2 Conservation of Seals (Common Seals) Order 1988). The Conservation of Seals (England and Wales) Order 1988 prohibits the killing, injuring or taking of grey seals within the seaward limits of the territorial waters adjacent to England and Wales (Art.2 Conservation of Seals (England and Wales) Order 1988). The territorial waters adjacent to England and Wales are stipulated to be: on the east coast, the territorial waters south of a line drawn at 055 degrees true from the point on the mainland at 55 degrees 48'.67 North latitude and 02 degrees 02'.0 West longitude; and on the west coast, the territorial waters south of a line drawn at 050 degrees true from Point of Ayre light on the Isle of Man to the Barnkirk Point light near Annan, provided that any waters which are nearer to any point on the coast of Scotland than to any point on the coasts of England or Northern Ireland are to be deemed to be north of that line (Art.3).

The effect of the 1988 Orders is to extend the close season for common seals in Britain and grey seals in England and Wales, so that it covers the whole year. Significantly, however, the Orders apply subject to the general exceptions and licensing provisions under the Act. This is because the Orders are both made under s.3(1) of the 1970 Act which, as has been noted, allows the Secretary of State to prohibit the killing of seals when this is necessary for their proper conservation, but an offence will only arise under an order of this kind subject to the general exceptions and licensing provisions in the Act. As previously discussed, the general exceptions allow the taking of disabled seals, the unavoidable killing of seals as a result of lawful action, and the killing of seal to prevent damage to a fishing net or fishing tackle (s.9 Conservation of Seals Act 1970). The licensing exception empowers the Secretary of State to grant a licence, amongst other things, to authorise the killing of seals to prevent damage to fisheries (s.10).

12.04   The Wildlife and Countryside Act 1981

The most extensive general protection for potential fish predator species is provided for under the Wildlife and Countryside Act 1981, which imposes wide-ranging prohibitions upon the killing or taking of birds and other wild animals. In relation to birds (generally, see British Field Sports Society (1985)) the 1981 Act creates an offence where any person intentionally kills, injures or takes any wild bird, subject only to specific exceptions provided for under the Act(s.1(1)(a) Wildlife and Countryside Act 1981; and see *Kirkland* v. *Robinson*, *Times* 4 December 1986, on strict liability for this offence). Although a more severe penalty is provided in respect of certain rare species of birds, the general penalty for the offence of killing wild birds is, on summary conviction, a fine not exceeding level 3 on the standard scale, presently £400 (s.21(1)). The most general exceptions to the offence cover matters such as the killing of listed game birds and 'pest' species, including certain gulls, at specified times of the year (s.2). In general, however, the control of major predator species of birds of a kind which are likely to be problematic on fish farms, such as herons, is rendered unlawful subject to two exceptions which might be applicable to fish farms.

The first exception to the general prohibition upon the killing of wild birds which might avail a fish farmer is an exception allowing for the killing or injury of a wild bird, other than certain rare species which are specially protected under the Act, by an 'authorised person' for the purpose of preventing serious damage to livestock or fisheries. An 'authorised person' means the owner or occupier, or any person authorised by the owner or occupier, of the land on which the killing or injury of a bird takes place (s.27(1)). 'Livestock' is defined to include any animal which is kept for the provision of food, or for the provision or improvement of fishing (s.27(1)) and, therefore, would clearly include farmed fish whether reared for food or for sporting purposes. (On this point see [2.06] above.) Uncertainty surrounds this exception, however, in relation to the requirement that the purpose of the killing is to prevent serious damage. What constitutes 'serious damage' is a matter of inevitable imprecision and subjectivity, and yet a mistake made in evaluating the gravity of damage may constitute the crucial difference between a fish farmer committing the offence and coming within the exception. (See *Robinson* v. *Whittle* [1980] 3 All ER 459 for an illustration of the difficulty.)

The second exception to the prohibition upon killing wild birds which may be applicable to fish farming situations is where the killing is authorised by an appropriate licence. Accordingly, the offence will not apply to anything done for the purpose of preventing serious damage to livestock or fisheries when done under and in accordance with the terms of a licence granted by the appropriate authority (s.16(1)(k) Wildlife and Countryside Act 1981). The 'appropriate authority' is the Minister of Agriculture, Fisheries and Food or the Secretaries of State for Wales and Scotland respectively (s.16(9)(d) and s.27(1)). The appropriate agriculture Minister is bound from time to time to consult with the Nature Conservancy Council as to the exercise of his functions in granting licences of this kind. Specifically, the Minister is not to grant a licence of any description unless he has been advised by the Council as to the circumstances in which, in their opinion, licences of that description should be granted (s.16(10)).

Turning from the protection of birds to the protection of other wild animals, a general contrast in the approach of the 1981 Act is to be discerned. As has been seen, the Act provides comprehensive coverage for the protection of wild birds, by commencing with the initial stipulation that it is an offence to kill any wild bird and allowing departures from this principle only where recognised grounds to do so are established. In respect of other animals, however, the presumption which applies is the converse of this. An offence is only committed if a person intentionally kills, injures or takes any wild animal if it is amongst those animals specifically listed in a schedule to the Act (s.9(1) and Sch.5). The penalty for this offence is, on summary conviction, a fine not exceeding level 5 on the standard scale, presently £2,000 (s.21(2)). Of those animals scheduled for this purpose the only one which is likely to be a fish farm predator is the otter. Other than in the case of the otter, therefore, it is generally lawful to employ humane (s.11 prohibits the use of certain methods of killing animals) destructive methods of predator control in relation to wild animals other than birds.

The protected status of otters means that it is an offence intentionally to kill, injure or take them, subject to a narrowly formulated exception. The exception is that an authorised person, such as the owner or occupier of a fish farm, will not be guilty of the offence if he shows that the action was necessary for the purpose of preventing serious damage to livestock or fisheries (s.10(4)). To restrict the application of this exception, however, a person will not be allowed to rely upon this defence if it had become apparent, before the time when the action was taken, that the action would prove necessary for the purpose of preventing serious damage to livestock or fisheries and certain preliminary actions were not taken. The preliminary actions which must be shown are that either a licence from the Agriculture Minister authorising the action had been applied for as soon as reasonably practicable after the need to prevent serious damage had become apparent, or an application for such a licence had been determined (s.10(6)). The effect of this is that in all but the most exceptional cases a person will only be able to rely upon the exception if the agriculture Minister has granted a licence authorising the killing in accordance with the procedure discussed previously (s.16).

12.05   The control of pests

In addition to the problems involving predator species, which kill and feed upon farmed fish, aquacultural activity suffers adversities arising from a range of other smaller pests. Pests include birds, such as gulls, crows and starlings, that take fish pellets from feeder hoppers and damage food bags causing untidiness and creating a general hygiene risk (Ross (1988) at p. 34). Similarly rodents, of all kinds, may be attracted to fish farms as a potential source of food, and are capable of constituting a vermin problem if measures are not taken to restrict their entry or control their numbers (Huet (1986) Ch.XV S.I; and generally see Sandys-Winsch (1984) Chapter 11). Shellfish farming is susceptible to a range of invertebrate pests and predators which include starfish and crab, though modern methods of raft production make these less of a problem by holding shellfish stock above the sea bed where they are less vulnerable in this respect. Most of these species are capable of being kept under control by the use of deterrents and, as a last resort, destructive methods, and raise no substantial legal difficulties in that they enjoy no special protection under the Wildlife and Countryside Act 1981.

In a serious case of infestation it is within the powers of the appropriate agriculture Minister to issue a pest control order, if it is thought to be expedient for the purpose of preventing damage to, amongst other things, animal foodstuffs and livestock, a term including fish kept for the production of food (s.109(3) Agriculture Act 1947, and see [2.06] above). In such circumstances the order is to specify steps to be taken, by a person with the right to do so, for the killing, taking or destruction of the animal or bird to which it applies (s.98(1)). Specifically, the power to make an order of this kind applies in relation to rodents and wild birds other than those listed under Schedule 1 of the Wildlife and Countryside Act 1981 as being protected by special penalties (s.98(4), and see [12.04] above). A person who fails to comply with a requirement imposed under a pest control order is liable, on summary conviction, to a fine not exceeding level 2 on the standard scale, presently £100, and a further fine not exceeding £5 for each day after conviction on which the failure continues (s.100(1)). In addition, the Minister may authorise a person to enter the land to which the order relates and take such steps as the Minister directs to secure compliance with the order. In such circumstances the reasonable cost of taking those steps is to be recoverable from the person on whom the requirement was imposed under the original order (s.100(2)).

In relation to rats and mice specific pest control duties fall to local authorities. Accordingly it is the duty of every local authority to take such steps as are necessary to secure, so far as practicable, that their districts are kept free from rats and mice. In particular, local authorities are bound to carry out such inspections as may be necessary to keep their districts free from rats and mice, and to enforce the duties of owners and occupiers of land in relation to control of these pests (s.2(1) Prevention of Damage by Pests Act 1949). If it appears to an authority that steps should be taken for the destruction of rats or mice, or otherwise for keeping land free from rats and mice, they may serve on the owner a notice requiring him to take such reasonable steps for this purpose as may be specified (s.4(1)). If any person on whom a notice is served by the local authority fails to take any of the steps required by the notice the local authority may themselves take those steps and recover from him any expenses reasonably incurred by them in doing so (s.5(1)). In addition, a person who fails to take the steps required of him in a notice served by the local authority is guilty of an offence and liable, on summary conviction, to a fine not exceeding level 3 on the standard scale, presently £400 (s.5(2)).

Chapter 13

Medicines and other Chemicals

13.01 Controls upon chemicals used in fish farming

The use of medicines, pesticides, and other chemicals in fish farming prompts discussion of two distinct kinds of legal issue. (In general, see National Farmers' Union (1984B).) The first of these is the problem of water pollution and the contamination of the general aquatic environment by fish farming chemicals. The second is the matter of controls upon the lawful use of a range of chemicals for medicinal, pesticidal and other uses in aquacultural contexts. The general problem of water pollution caused by fish farming has been considered earlier in Chapter 11 and will not be reconsidered at this juncture. The use of medicines, pesticides and other controlled chemicals in fish farming falls for discussion in this chapter.

An introductory illustration of the environmental and legal difficulties in the use of chemicals to control infestation by small pests on fish farms is provided by recent concerns about the use of pesticides to eradicate fish parasites. In intensive forms of aquaculture the transfer of parasites and other infestations between large numbers of fish in close proximity becomes a serious problem without counterpart in the wild. For example, the common presence upon salmon of the copepod crustacea known by anglers as 'sea lice' is generally regarded as a welcome sign on a wild fish caught in freshwater, indicating that it has only recently left the sea. In natural populations of salmon sea lice are rarely a major problem since it is uncommon for any fish to suffer severe or debilitating infestation. Amongst sea-caged populations of salmon the high stocking densities involved mean that the parasite multiplies rapidly and is readily transferred between fish. As a result the problem of sea lice infestation may become a serious one in cage culture and at present allows few options for the salmon farmer other than the use of chemical treatment with an appropriate pesticide.

The problem of sea lice infestation of caged salmon has been widely tackled in the Scottish salmon farming industry by the use of an organophosphorus pesticide known as Nuvan 500 EC (generally, see Ross and Horsman (1988)). The use of this substance has been a matter of concern on account of its general toxicity in the environment and in particular its toxicity to shellfish. This concern has been intensified by reports that some users have applied the pesticide by direct mixing with the water in fish cages at times of slack tide, rather than isolating the cage water by surrounding cages with tarpaulins, as officially recommended (Scottish Wildlife and Countryside Link (1988) p. 23: and Ross and Horsman (1988) pp. 4 to 6). Such practices may have direct pollution implications in law (see Chapter 11 above). In addition, the use of Nuvan as a substance for external application in the treatment, control or prevention of ectoparasites on fish is classified as a veterinary drug, and along with many other medicinal products used to prevent fish disease, is subject to controls arising under the Medicines Act 1968 (although ectoparasite treatments may be classified as pesticides for some purposes; see [13.07] below).

13.02 The Medicines Act 1968

The Medicines Act 1968 imposes controls upon the sale and use of medicinal products of all kinds, for the treatment of either humans or animals, including fish, and is administered jointly by the Health and Agriculture Ministers throughout the United Kingdom (generally see Dale and Appelbe (1989)). Medical products are those used for a 'medicinal purpose', which is defined to include the treatment or prevention of disease, diagnosis of disease, anaesthesia and interference with the normal operation of physiological function (s.130 Medicines Act 1968). It is a significant feature of the purposive definition of medicinal products that a particular substance may, or may not, come within the definition depending upon the use to which it is put. The same substance, for example, may be classified as either a pesticide or a medicine depending upon the manner in which it is used.

Any medicinal product which is manufactured, sold, supplied, imported or exported for the purpose of being administered to animals, but not for the purpose of being administered to human beings is classified under the Act as a 'veterinary drug' (s.132(1)). All drugs used for the medical treatment of fish are, therefore, veterinary drugs. (For a general account of veterinary drugs used to treat fish diseases see Roberts and Shepherd (1986); Anon. (1987A); and Smith (1988).) Animal feed stuffs which incorporate a medicinal product, despite appearing to be within the definition of veterinary drugs, come under separate provisions of the 1968 Act. Hence, by special order, the Minister of Agriculture, Fisheries and Food, and the respective Secretaries of State for Wales and Scotland may provide that a medicated feeding stuff is, or is not, to be treated as a medicinal product for the purposes of the Act (s.130(3A) Medicines Act 1968, as amended). In this discussion medicinal feeding stuffs for fish are considered separately from medicinal products.

The general approach of the 1968 Act involves the subjection of any medicinal product or veterinary drug to a requirement of product licensing. This involves a licence being issued before a medicinal product may be sold, supplied or manufactured in the United Kingdom (s.7). Applications for product licences are submitted to the appropriate Ministerial licensing authority in a prescribed form (ss.1, 6 and 18) along with full supporting data relevant to the determination of the application relating to the safety, efficiency and quality of the product for the purposes for which it is to be used (s.19). Specifically, in relation to the consideration of safety, the authority is to consider the capacity of the substance to cause danger to the health of the community, or to animals generally, or the harm which it may induce to the animal to which it is administered, or the harmful residue which it may leave in the carcass of the animal, or the capacity of the substance to interfere with the treatment, prevention or diagnosis of disease, or the extent to which the substance may be harmful to the person administering it (s.132(2)).

Despite the normal requirement of product licensing in respect of the sale and use of veterinary drugs, and the requirement arising under a European Community Directive that no veterinary product may be marketed or used unless authorised by a competent authority (Art.4 European Council Directive of 1981 on the approximation of the laws of the Member States relating to veterinary medical products, 81/851/EEC), an exception to the product licensing requirement arises in the case of products specially prepared under a veterinary surgeon or veterinary practitioner's prescription. This is that a vet is permitted to prescribe any medicinal product, termed a 'veterinary special', which is specially prepared for administration to particular animals under his care. This allows a vet to sell or supply, or procure the sale or supply, of a product to a person having the possession or control of an animal which is under the care of the vet (s.9(2)(a) Medicines Act 1968). 'Under his care' has been understood to mean that the vet should be acquainted with the animals concerned to the extent that he has seen them recently or has sufficient personal knowledge of their state of health to be able to diagnose or prescribe properly for them (Cooper (1987) at p. 115). Notably, the ectoparasite treatment Nuvan, discussed earlier in relation to the treatment of sea lice on salmon, has only recently gained a product licence (154 HC DEB 1989 Col. 563 to 564; and on product licences generally see National Office of Animal Health (1988)). The lack of a product licence in relation to drugs used to prevent and treat disease in fish farming is not uncommon (Scottish Wildlife and Countryside Link (1988) pp. 22). In part, however, this may be due to veterinary medicine manufacturers or suppliers being unwilling to take the administrative steps necessary to obtain a licence. There may be economic reasons for this. For example, amongst the most common medicines used in relation to freshwater fish farming are substances such as formalin, common salt and malachite green. (On the use of malachite green in fish farming see, Ministry of Agriculture, Fisheries and Food (1982A).) These substances are so readily available for medicinal as well as non-medicinal purposes that there is little economic incentive for a manufacturer to undertake the expense involved in the application procedure for a product licence.

The sale of licensed medicinal products, of a kind that are likely to be used on fish farms, are regulated according to their category. (For a brief summary, see Alderman (1988).) The most restricted amongst veterinary drugs are 'Prescription Only Medicines' which may only be sold or supplied in accordance with a prescription issued by a vet, or sold or supplied by a vet for administration to an animal or herd under his care (s.58 Medicines Act 1968, and Medicines (Veterinary Drugs) (Prescription Only) Order 1985, SI 1985 No.1288, listing prescription only medicinal products for animal use). A second category of medicinal products and veterinary drugs are 'Pharmacy Medicines' which do not require the prescription of a vet, but can only be supplied by, or under the supervision of, a registered pharmacist (s.52, and Medicines (Pharmacy and General Sale – Exemption) Order 1980, SI 1980 No.1924), or a vet where the sale is for administration by him, or under his direction, to an animal or herd which is under his care (s.55(3)). Third, are those veterinary drugs on the 'Pharmacy and Merchants List' which may be supplied to a person having charge of animals for business purposes by an approved agricultural merchant, involved in the retail sale of agricultural requisites, without the need for a vet's prescription (Medicines (Exemptions from Restrictions on the Retail Sale or Supply of Veterinary Drugs) Order 1985, SI 1985 No.1823, as amended). Finally, the 'General Sale List' specifies those medicines and veterinary drugs which in the opinion of the appropriate Ministers can be sold or supplied otherwise than by, or under the supervision of, a pharmacist or vet (s.51, and Medicines (Veterinary Drugs) (General Sale List) Order 1984, SI 1984 No.768, listing veterinary drugs for general sale).

13.03   *Medicated feeding stuffs*

For most purposes medicated feeding stuffs for animals are dealt with separately under the Medicines Act 1968 in that the Agriculture Ministers may provide that specified kinds of medicinal feeding stuff are not to be treated as medicinal products (s.130(3A), as amended). For the purposes of such an order a medicated feeding stuff means any substance which is manufactured, sold, supplied, imported or exported for use by being fed to animals for a medicinal purpose, or for use as an ingredient in the preparation of a substance which is to be fed to animals for a medicinal purpose (s.130(3B), as amended). Accordingly the Ministers may prohibit any person, in the course of business, incorporating a medicinal product of any description in an animal feeding stuff unless incorporated in accordance with a product licence or animal test certificate (under s.32, authorising the use of a substance in medicinal tests on animals) or incorporated in accordance with a written direction given by a vet (s.40, as amended).

The regulations which have been made by exercise of the Ministerial powers to make special provision for medicated animal feeding stuffs, are the Medicines (Medicated Animal Feeding Stuffs) Regulations 1988 (SI 1988 No.976). In general these Regulations give effect to the requirement that medicinal products are not to be incorporated into animal foods other than in accordance with a product licence, animal test certificate or veterinary written direction, and impose a general registration requirement upon persons who compound medicated animal feeding stuffs. In relation to things done in the course of business as a fish farmer, however, exemptions are provided in relation to all the major obligations under the Regulations (Reg.3(1)(b) Medicines (Medicated Animal Feeding Stuffs) Regulations 1988). For these purposes a fish farmer is defined as a person carrying on the business of fish farming or shellfish farming which is registered in a register kept for the purposes of an order made under s.7 of the Diseases of Fish Act 1983 (discussed in [6.02] and [6.03] above). It follows, perhaps because of the relatively small number of medicated fish feed suppliers and the remoteness of many fish farms (Alderman (1988) at p. 12) that the specific Regulations governing medicated feeding stuffs presently impose no stricter obligations upon fish farmers than arise under the general provisions relating to medicinal products under the 1968 Act, though further controls are planned.

13.04   *Withdrawal periods*

It is clear that there may be potentially harmful effects to human beings if animals to which veterinary drugs have been administered were to be slaughtered directly for human consumption. Consequently, where this hazard arises a specified minimum period of time, referred to as a 'withdrawal period', should be allowed to elapse between the administration of a substance and the slaughter of the animal for human consumption (generally, see European Inland Fisheries Advisory Commission (1988)). The importance of a statement of a withdrawal period amongst the labelling requirements for veterinary medicines is recognised by the European Council Directive on the approximation of the laws of Member States relating to veterinary medicinal products (81/851/EEC). This Directive seeks to subject all veterinary products to authorisation by the competent authority in the relevant member state of the Community (Art.4 European Council Directive 81/851/EEC). As a part of the authorisation process the applicant is to provide specified information relating to the product concerned. Amongst the information to be provided is an indication of the withdrawal period necessary. This is stated to be the period necessary between the last administration of a veterinary medicinal product to animals under normal conditions of use, and the production of food stuffs from such animals, in order to ensure that such foodstuffs do not contain any residues which might constitute a health hazard to the consumer (Art.5(8)).

In accordance with the Community Directive, withdrawal periods are made an explicit requirement by regulations governing the labelling of veterinary drugs in the United Kingdom. Specifically, the Medicines (Labelling of Medicinal Products for Incorporation in Animal Feeding Stuffs and of Medicated Animal Feeding Stuffs) Regulations 1988 (SI 1988 No.1009, and ss.85 and 86 Medicines Act 1968) make provision for labelling requirements in respect of withdrawal periods relating to medicinal products and medicated feeding stuffs. In most cases the withdrawal period is that provided for in the product licence for the substance concerned, but where the product licence does not specify a withdrawal period for a prescription only medicine the period is that stated in the veterinary written direction relating to the prescription. In a case where a medicinal product which is not subject to a product licence is incorporated into a medicinal feeding stuff the appropriate withdrawal period is specified as the 'standard withdrawal period', or any longer period specified in a veterinary written direction in relation to the incorporation of the product in the feeding stuff (Reg.7(2)). In relation to fish the standard withdrawal period is stated to be a number of days ascertained by measuring once on each day following treatment with the medicinal product the temperature of the water in which the fish are kept and summing the daily temperatures until the cumulative total temperature is, at present, at least 200°C (Regs. Sch.1). This 200 'degree day' period reflects the cold-blooded nature of fish. Their metabolic rate, and consequently the speed at which medicinal products are metabolised or excreted, is directly dependent upon water temperature (Anon. (1987A)).

13.05   Feed additives

Substances which are added to feeding stuffs to promote growth and to maintain fish health are separately regulated as either medicinal products or ingredients in feeding stuffs. Into the latter category fall nutritional food additives such as vitamins and minerals. In addition, widespread use is made of pigments to colour the flesh of farmed trout and salmon to transform the otherwise commercially unacceptable grey flesh of farmed fish into a more attractive pink colour reminiscent of wild fish. In each instance, however, the use of additives to fish feeding stuffs must be in accordance with detailed regulations specifying the substances which may be added, conforming with the European Council Directive of 1970 concerning additives in feeding stuffs (70/524/EEC). The 1970 Directive is founded upon the need to standardise provision for feeding stuff additives within the Community in order to avoid harm to animal or human health, and proceeds on the basis that only named additives may be incorporated into feeding stuffs in accordance with the requirements of the Directive. After substantial amendment to the original list of permitted additives, the present provisions of the 1970 Directive are implemented (also implemented are other Directives such as the 1974 Council Directive concerning undesirable substances and products in animal nutrition 74/63/EEC) by means of the Agriculture Act 1970 and the Feeding Stuffs Regulations 1988 (SI 1988 No.396; and see also provisions under SI 1985 No.1823).

The Agriculture Act 1970 makes it an offence to sell, or possess for the purpose of selling in the course of trade, any material for use as feeding stuff which is found to contain any ingredient which is deleterious to animals of various kinds including farmed fish (s.73(1) Agriculture Act 1970, and Reg.3 Feeding Stuffs Regulations 1988). Likewise, it is an offence to sell, or possess for sale, any material for use as a feeding stuff which is shown to be unwholesome for, or dangerous to, animals, including farmed fish (s.73A(1), as amended, and Reg.3). More specific provision for control of substances contained in feeding stuffs is made under the Feeding Stuffs Regulations 1988, which provide a detailed listing of permitted additives where the substances concerned are neither medicinal products nor used in accordance with a veterinary written direction (s.74A, as amended and Reg.15). Hence, provision is made under a schedule to the Regulations for permissible antioxidants, colourants, emulsifiers, binders, vitamins, trace elements, and other substances which may legitimately be added to feeding stuffs (Regs. Sch.4). Taking a pertinent example from amongst the permitted colourants, the Regulations state that the carotene pigments canthaxanthin and astaxanthin, at a maximum content of 100 mg per kg, may be used in relation to trout and salmon from the age of 6 months onwards (Regs. Sch.4 para.3 and Part II).

13.06   *Antibiotics, hormones and residues*

In other countries where intensive fish farming is practised the widespread and increasing use of antibiotics as an additive to feeding stuffs to treat and prevent disease has become a matter of concern. In the Norwegian fish farming industry it has recently been calculated that the antibiotic consumption in aquaculture exceeds the combined intake of human and veterinary medicine in the country as a whole (Anon.(1988A)). The extent of antibiotic use is a matter of disquiet, initially, because of the low proportion of antibiotics which are actually administered to fish when incorporation in feed

pellets is the method of delivery adopted. Because of low rates of absorption
through the intestines of fish, and the inefficiency of the method of
application, only an estimated one-tenth of antibiotics actually reach their
intended destination, with the remainder passing into the general aquatic
environment. Beyond this, there are medicinal grounds for concern about the
possibilities of residues in fish, the effects on those handling antibiotics, and
the general spread of resistance to antibiotics (Anon. (1988A) at p. 9).
Amongst the unknown effects of introducing such large quantities of
antibiotics into the marine environment is the possibility that marine
organisms will develop resistance to antibiotics. This resistance may
eventually be transferred to human pathogens, with the eventual
consequence of impairing the effective medicinal use of antibiotics in humans
(generally, see Anon. (1988A)).

In Britain the scale of antibiotic use in fish farming is smaller than in
Norway, and controls appear to be stricter, but concerns about the effects of
antibiotic discharges upon the aquatic environment remain. In relation to the
freshwater rather than the marine environment, it has been observed that
biologically active chemicals such as antibiotics may be added to waters in fish
farms to treat disease and improve growth. Residues of chemicals may then
pass into a watercourse which serves as a source of public water supply, or is
abstracted to irrigate crops which are grown for human consumption
(Freeman (1984); reply by Saunders-Davies (1984)). There is, therefore,
ample reason for vigilance over the misuse of antibiotics in the British fish
farming industry (Scottish Wildlife and Countryside Link (1988) at p. 23).

In law the position with respect to the use of antimicrobial agents, including
antibiotics, in fish farming is that their use is subject to the general controls
upon veterinary drugs, discussed above. As previously noted (in [13.02]), the
Medicines Act 1968 includes amongst the meanings of 'medicinal purpose',
that of preventing or interfering with the normal operation of a physiological
function, whether by way of terminating, reducing or postponing, or
increasing or accelerating the operation of that function (s.130(2)(e)
Medicines Act 1968). This covers the use of antibiotics to promote fish
growth, and when administered for medicinal purposes antibiotics would
come within the medicinal purpose of treating or preventing disease
(s.130(2)(a)). Accordingly antibiotics will be subject to the product licensing
system, previously considered, unless specially supplied under veterinary
prescription (discussed in [13.02] above).

Although a less immediate practical issue, the possibility of fish being fed
hormones in order to improve growth is at least as contentious as the misuse
of antibiotics. At the European level, measures which prevent the use of
hormonal substances in fish farming include the prohibition of hormones as
an additive to feedstuffs. The European Council Directive concerning
additives to feeding stuffs (84/587/EEC; feeding stuffs, discussed in [13.03]
above), allows that only specified additives may be incorporated into feeding
stuffs for animals belonging to species normally nourished and kept or
consumed by humans. Despite the provision for certain derogations from the
list of permitted additives under the Directive, it is expressly stated that the
power of derogation given to member states is not to apply to substances
having a hormonal effect (Art.4(1)(b)).

If hormones were to be used for promoting fish growth they would be classified as veterinary drugs under the Medicines Act 1968, and be administered under a vet's prescription. The general dangers of misuse of hormones has been recognised by a European Council Directive which prohibits certain substances having a hormonal or thyrostatic action from being administered to farm animals, excluding fish, other than for therapeutic uses. Beyond this, however, the Directive prohibits other substances having similar effect from being administered to any species of animal absolutely (81/602/EEC). This ban has been implemented in the United Kingdom by regulations under the Medicines Act 1968 (s.62 Medicines Act 1968) which make unlawful the sale or supply of the prohibited substances as a medicinal product for an animal, or as a part of a medicated animal feeding stuff (Medicines (Stilbenes and Thyrostatic Substances Prohibition) Order 1982, SI 1982 No.518). For the purposes of the Regulations 'animal' includes any kind of fish, (s.132 Medicines Act 1968) and hence the ban encompasses any use of the prohibited substances in fish farming.

A more exacting approach to the problem of preventing fish flesh for human consumption becoming contaminated by harmful substances would be to institute a system of checking slaughtered fish to ascertain the levels of residues of undesirable substances which they contain. This is the method adopted within the European Community to ensure the purity of meat for human consumption (under the European Council Directive on trade in fresh meat, 64/433/EEC, as amended by later Directives including 71/118/EEC, 77/99/EEC and 86/469/EEC). This system of control, however, extends only to the meat of certain kinds of farm animals and does not include fish. It follows, therefore, that the comprehensive and detailed system of controls designed to give effect to European requirements on permissible residue contents of meat (Meat Inspection Regulations 1987, SI 1987 No.2236, and Animals and Fresh Meat (Examination for Residues) Regulations 1988, SI 1988 No.848) have no application to fish or fish products.

Specific powers exist to authorise the making of regulations governing the quantities of pesticides which may remain in any food for human consumption, and to direct that foods exceeding specified pesticide contents may be seized and disposed of (s.16(2)(k) and (l) Food and Environment Protection Act 1985). However, no regulations of this kind have yet been made. Nonetheless, public health departments of local authorities possess a general responsibility to ensure that any fish which is offered for sale is not rendered unwholesome by chemical contaminants (generally see Food Act 1984, discussed in [16.02] below). In respect of most contaminants the precise meaning of 'unwholesomeness' is not clearly specified, though exceptionally there are definite standards laid down by law. Thus in the case of lead contamination of food in England and Wales, the maximum proportion of lead which is permissible is 2 milligrams per kilogram in fish and 10 milligrams per kilogram in shellfish (Reg.4 and Sch.1 Lead in Food Regulations 1979, SI 1979 No.1254, as amended).

13.07   *Pesticides*

In addition to medicines and substances incorporated in fish feeding stuffs a range of other chemicals are used in fish farming. It is convenient to consider the controls upon non-medicinal chemicals in the remainder of this chapter. As with medicines and food additives, it is to be noted that many of these kinds of products are capable of causing water pollution and may be subject to separate regulation as a result of their pollutant effects (see Chapter 11). It is also worth reiterating the point that classification of substances as pesticides rather than medicines depends upon the *purpose* to which they are put rather than their chemical composition. The same substance may be a medicine in relation to one application but a pesticide when put to a different use.

A significant category of non-medicinal chemicals used in fish farming is that of pesticides, which are used for a range of miscellaneous purposes. For example, herbicides may be used to control the growth of weeds in or near water in freshwater fish farms (generally, see Ministry of Agriculture, Fisheries and Food (1985A); and Seagrave (1988)) and occasionally, and with Ministerial authorisation, piscicides may be used to remove unwanted species of fish from a water (see s.5(1) and (2) Salmon and Freshwater Fisheries Act 1975; and ss.4(b) and 9 Salmon and Freshwater Fisheries (Protection) (Scotland) Act 1951). More generally perhaps, poisons are used to control smaller pests and infestations, and particularly rodents which, in the case of rats, constitute a special hazard because they carry Weil's Disease, which is a risk to which those working near water or on farms are exposed (see also [12.05] above).

The control of pesticides in England and Wales and Scotland, including those that are used on fish farms, is provided for under Part III of the Food and Environment Protection Act 1985. The object of Part III of the 1985 Act is stated to be the protection of health of human beings, creatures and plants, safeguarding the environment, and securing safe, efficient and humane methods of controlling pests (s.16(1) Food and Environment Protection Act 1985). These purposes are to be achieved, amongst other means, by requiring Ministerial approval of pesticides in accordance with regulations, and the imposition of prohibitions upon sale and use in relation to specified pesticides (s.16(2)). For the purposes of these controls a 'pest' is defined as any organism harmful to plants or to wood or other plant products, any undesired plant, and any harmful creature (s.16(15)) where a 'creature' means any living organism other than a human being or a plant (s.24(1)). Accordingly a 'pesticide' is any substance, preparation or organism prepared or used for destroying any pest (s.16(15)). Alternatively, the controls under the Act may be applied to other substances, preparations or organisms which are used for pesticidal purposes as if they were a pesticide. These purposes are, the protecting of plants or wood or other plant products from harmful organisms; regulating the growth of plants; giving protection against harmful creatures; rendering such creatures harmless; controlling organisms with harmful or unwanted effects on water systems, buildings or other structures, or on manufactured products; and protecting animals against ectoparasites (s.16(16)).

The general mechanism for the control of pesticides under the 1985 Act is through a system of authorisation whereby the agriculture Ministers may give their approval for sales, use and other matters in relation to the handling of pesticides, which otherwise would be contrary to prohibitions upon pesticides (s.16(2)(a) and (b)). In imposing such controls the Ministers are to have regard to the interests of persons supplying information relating to the authorisation or prohibition of pesticides (s.16(5)) and an Advisory Committee on Pesticides has been established to advise the Ministers on the matters relating to the control of pests and the furtherance of the general purposes of Part III of the Act (s.16(7) and Sch.5, and Control of Pesticides (Advisory Committee on Pesticides) Order 1985, SI 1985 No.1516). The Ministers are to consult the Committee as to regulations which they contemplate making, the approval of pesticides and any conditions to which approval is subject (s.16(9)).

The authorisation of a specific pesticide under the approval scheme involves the conduct of any examinations and tests which in the opinion of the Minister are necessary or expedient to enable an application for authorisation of a pesticide to be determined (s.18(2)). The reasonable costs of expenses incurred in conducting such examinations may be required to be met by the applicant, along with a reasonable fee in respect of the administrative expenses of processing the application (s.18(1)). Enforcement of authorisation requirements is through a Ministerial power to direct that there has been a breach of any of the specified prohibitions upon pesticides, or of any condition relating thereto, and a power to take action in such circumstances. Specifically, the Minister is empowered to seize and dispose of the pesticide in relation to which the direction is issued, or anything treated with it, or to direct that any remedial action is to be taken which is necessary as a result of the contravention (s.16(2)(g)).

Detailed effect is given to the pesticides approval scheme by the Control of Pesticides Regulations 1986 (SI 1986 No.1510) which impose specific prohibitions upon pesticides and substances used for pesticidal purposes. Notably, the Regulations do not apply to substances which are covered under other legislation (Reg.3(2)(b)) such as the Medicines Act 1968 (discussed in [13.02] above) concerned with medicinal products and medicated feedstuffs, the Part IV of the Agriculture Act 1970 (discussed in [13.03] above) concerned with animal feeding stuffs, the Food Act 1984 (discussed in [16.02] below) concerned with controls upon food, and the Food and Drugs (Scotland) Act 1956, which makes equivalent provision for Scotland (discussed in [16.06] below). In addition, the Regulations exclude substances prepared for the purpose of disinfecting, bleaching or sterilising any substance, including water, other than soils, compost or other growing medium (Reg.3(2)(c) Control of Pesticides Regulations 1986). It follows, therefore, that non-pesticidal disinfectants used in fish farming may fall outside pesticide controls (see [13.09] below).

Within the scope of the pesticides approval scheme, the Regulations set out a series of prohibitions in relation to pesticides. These prohibitions relate to the advertising, sale, supply, storage and use of pesticides (Reg.4 Control of Pesticides Regulations 1986). In respect of the use of pesticides, it is stated that no person is to use a pesticide unless the Ministers have given approval of it, by way of an experimental permit or a provisional or full approval, and the conditions of approval relating to use are complied with (Regs.4(5) and 5(1)). Infringement of the provisions under the Regulations prohibiting use of an unapproved pesticide, or misuse of an approved one, is an offence under Part II of the 1985 Act (s.16(12) Food and Environment Protection Act 1985) and a person found guilty of this offence is liable, on summary conviction, to a fine not exceeding the statutory maximum, presently £2,000, or on conviction on indictment to a fine of an unlimited amount (s.21(3) and (4)).

13.08   *Anti-foulants: tributyltin*

A specific use of pesticides in fish farming is as anti-foulants, and one particular kind of anti-foulant, tributyltin, warrants special discussion. The accumulation of algal growth on fish cages is capable of being particularly problematic to coastal fish farmers because of the increased resistance to tidal flow on cage nets, the reduction of water flow through cages and increased likelihood of disease transmission. Consequently the use of anti-foulants to prevent algal accumulation is a convenient alternative to the disruption involved in frequent cleaning of nets by conventional methods. Until recently the most common, and most notorious, anti-foulant used in fish farming was tributyltin, an organotin compound which had its major use as an ingredient in anti-fouling paints applied to boats to prevent infestation by barnacles. It was found that, used in any form, tributyltin is highly toxic in the marine environment (Wood (1986)) and in even minute concentrations can cause serious damage to shellfish populations (Davies, Bailey and Moore (1987)). It is also found to accumulate in the flesh of farmed salmon (Davies and McKie (1987)).

The eventual appreciation of the dangers of tributyltin resulted in the adoption of a strict set of legal controls to prevent further use of the substance. In the first place, because the substance is a form of pesticide it is subject to the pesticides approval scheme under Part III of the Food and Environment Protection Act 1985, discussed above. Summarising the discussion in the previous section, this means that the Control of Pesticides Regulations 1986 make it unlawful, amongst other things, to use pesticides which are without Ministerial approval, and consequently unapproved use of tributyltin will amount to an offence under the 1985 Act.

In addition to the regulation of tributyltin under pesticide controls, the full appreciation of the seriousness of its toxic effects (Anon. (1987C)) prompted further legislative measures. These were introduced by the Secretary of State for the Environment and the Secretaries of State for Wales and Scotland, in exercise of their powers under the Control of Pollution Act 1974 to regulate the importation, use and supply of any substance to prevent damage to persons, animals or plants, or pollution of air, water or land (s.100 Control of Pollution Act 1974). Accordingly the Control of Pollution (Anti-Fouling Paints) Regulations 1987 (SI 1987 No.783, replacing SI 1985 No.2011 and SI 1986 No.2300, and see Department of the Environment (1987)) which apply to England and Wales and Scotland, make unlawful the supply for retail sale, or by way of retail sale, of an anti-fouling paint, or anti-fouling treatment, containing a tri-organotin compound (Reg.4). Specifically, an anti-fouling treatment is defined to include a treatment containing a chemical compound which has the effect of inhibiting the growth of, or having other detrimental effects on, freshwater, estuarial or marine life, and which is intended for application in a liquid or semi-liquid form to any net, cage, float or other apparatus used in connection with the propagation or cultivation of fish or shellfish (Reg.2). Contravention of these provisions is an offence the punishment for which is a fine not exceeding £2,000 on summary conviction, or a fine of an unlimited amount on indictment, subject to the defence that it can be proved that the person charged can show that he took all reasonable steps and exercised all due diligence to avoid committing the offence (Reg.5).

Despite the comprehensive outlawing of tributyltin as an anti-foulant treatment for fish farming nets, it has been suggested that treated equipment has continued in use after the imposition of the ban (Scottish Wildlife and Countryside Link (1988) p. 20). In addition there was evidence of a lack of knowledge as to the proper methods for disposal of unused quantities of the substance, the retention of which became unlawful as a result of the ban. In one graphic incident, a fish farmer was fined £600 for dumping a 45-gallon drum containing tributyltin over a cliff in Shetland (*Shetland Times*, 31 December 1987, noted by Scottish Wildlife and Countryside Link (1988) at p. 21).

13.09 Other chemicals used in fish farming

In addition to the categories of substance discussed previously in this chapter, a range of miscellaneous chemicals have diverse applications within fish farming. (For a list of health and hygiene products available to fish farmers see Anon. (1987A) at p. 43). Most notable are those products which are used to maintain general hygiene in fish farms and particularly those which serve as disinfectants or fungicides. For example, recommended disinfectants for fish farming purposes are chlorine, sodium hydroxide, iodophors, quaternary ammonium compounds, and calcium oxide (Ministry of Agriculture, Fisheries and Food (1978)). Also of importance are iodophor disinfectants (Ministry of Agriculture, Fisheries and Food (1985B)). These substances would normally be applied to equipment and working surfaces to ensure cleanliness and to prevent the spread of disease. They are, however, in many cases extremely toxic and capable of causing serious harm to fish, or to persons handling them, if misused.

In addition to regulations applicable to medicines, food additives or pesticides, substances used in fish farming may be the subject of other legal controls. Notably the Health and Safety at Work etc. Act 1974 imposes a general duty upon every employer in England and Wales and Scotland to ensure, so far as reasonably practicable, the health, safety and welfare of all his employees (s.2(1) Health and Safety at Work etc. Act 1974). Amongst other things the employer's duty extends to arrangements for ensuring safety and the absence of risks to health in connection with the use, handling, storage and transport of articles and substances (s.2(2)(b)). Similarly, the Act imposes a duty upon every self-employed person to conduct his undertaking in such a way as to ensure that he, and other persons who are not his employees but who may be affected by the undertaking, are not exposed to risks to their health or safety (s.3(2)).

Ministerial powers arising under the Health and Safety at Work etc. Act 1974 permit the making of regulations for any of the general purposes of the Act concerned with safety at work (s.15(1)). Accordingly, the Packaging and Labelling of Dangerous Substances Regulations 1984 (SI 1984 No.1244) make special provision for the packaging of dangerous substances, including pesticides, requiring a clear indication to be given as to the toxicity category of the substance concerned (Regs.5(4)(a) and Sch.3). Other regulations under the 1974 Act govern the use of poisonous substances in agriculture (Poisonous Substances in Agriculture Regulations 1984, SI 1984 No.1114; see also SI 1988 No.1657). In this context, 'agriculture' is stated to encompass livestock breeding and keeping, and 'livestock' includes any creature kept for the production of food, and the Regulations would, therefore, cover most fish farming activities (Reg.2(1), and see [2.06] above). Amongst other safety requirements to be followed where poisons are used for agricultural purposes, the Regulations require specified protective clothing to be worn where certain operations are conducted. For example, where a container containing a listed substance is opened approved respiratory protective equipment, a coverall, a rubber apron, rubber boots and gloves must be worn (Reg.4, and Sch.1). Amongst the listed substances for these purposes is the substance Dichlorvos (Regs. Sch.2) which is the active ingredient in the pesticide Nuvan used for removal of sea lice in salmon farming (discussed above in [13.01]).

Chapter 14

Fish Farming and Fishery Law

14.01 Conservation and harvesting

This chapter deals with two aspects of the relationship between aquaculture and fishery law. The first area of concern is the exemptions and defences from fishery offences provided in relation to fish farming in England and Wales and Scotland arising under s.33 of the Fisheries Act 1981, and the related provisions applicable in Scotland under s.7 of the Freshwater and Salmon Fisheries (Scotland) Act 1976. The second area to be discussed is the effect of the restrictions upon possession and selling fish in England and Wales and Scotland created by the Salmon Act 1986 and imposed upon those producing and dealing in salmon.

The traditional aim of most freshwater and sea fishery legislation has been that of conservation. Given the limited replacement capacity of natural fish populations and the need to avoid over-cropping, the bulk of fishery enactments share the objective of seeking to prevent exploitation exceeding the maximum sustainable yield for a species. In some situations the mechanism to achieve this objective is quite finely tuned, with legislation imposing quotas upon the quantity of a species which can be harvested in a particular region during a particular period. In other respects the aim is pursued by making unlawful those methods of taking fish which have proved to be too efficient, or too wasteful, in the past (generally see Hunter (1963) and (1965)). Although the need for conservation is a self-evident principle of rational management for a naturally sustained, but exploited, population of fish, the same principle does not apply where the fish are the product of aquaculture. Where fecundity, growth, mortality and harvesting can be controlled to a high degree, in an environment isolated from wild populations of fish, there is no need for the external imposition of conservation constraints upon the enterprise. The objective of maintaining long-term aquacultural production at an optimum level is generally secured with negligible adverse effect upon natural stocks.

Not only is the imposition of conservational objectives upon aquaculture inappropriate, it is also capable of being highly obstructive. For example, the uncontrolled use of nets is capable of decimating stocks of wild fish in freshwater, so justifying close controls where the use of a net is permitted as a commercial fishing method. By contrast, the use of a net to remove fish from a tank or rearing pool is such a commonplace occurrence in fish farming that, were its use to be legally constrained, the resulting inconvenience would be considerable. Likewise, though prohibitions upon taking undersized or unseasonable fish serve useful purposes in conserving wild stocks, without modification, they might also serve to prevent a fish farmer meeting a market demand at an optimum time. With these comparisons in mind, alongside the Government's expressed wish to see development of the fish farming industry unhindered by unnecessary statutory or administrative restrictions and constraints (Ministry of Agriculture, Fisheries and Food (1981) at para 29) measures were introduced under the Fisheries Act 1981 to exempt fish farming from conservation provisions intended for the protection of wild fish stocks.

14.02   *Exemptions and defences under conservation legislation*

Section 33 of the Fisheries Act 1981 brings about a degree of separation between fishery law and the law of fish farming, first, by enabling the Minister to confer exemptions in certain situations and, second, by allowing a defence to certain fishery offences of showing that the fish concerned were the product of fish farming. In relation to fishery offences arising in England and Wales under the Salmon and Freshwater Fisheries Act 1975, the 'Minister' empowered to confer exemptions is the Minister of Agriculture, Fisheries and Food, except in the former area of the Welsh Water Authority where the Secretary of State for Wales is responsible. In relation to Scotland the power is possessed by the Secretary of State for Scotland. In respect of fishery offences concerned with sea fishing, the 'Minister' is the Minister of Agriculture, Fisheries and Food, except in respect of Wales or Scotland, where the responsibilities are those of the respective Secretaries of State concerned with fisheries in those countries (s.33(4) Fisheries Act 1981).

For the purposes of the exemptions from, and defences to, the general fishery law under s.33 of the Fisheries Act 1981, the general meaning of 'fish farming' is stated to be the breeding, rearing or cultivating of fish, including shellfish, meaning crustaceans and molluscs of any kind (s.44), whether or not for the purpose of producing food for human consumption (s.33(6)). This is a significantly wider definition of fish farming than has been adopted in other contexts (see [2.06] and [6.02] above) and serves to include the rearing of fish for sporting purposes or for ornamental purposes. Nonetheless it is an appropriate definition since most of the fishery offences from which dispensation is given are equally capable of being committed in relation to fish which are not intended for human consumption as those which are intended for human consumption.

As has been indicated, the approach which is taken to the displacement of fishery law in the context of fish farming under s.33 of the Fisheries Act 1981 is two-pronged. First, in relation to a list of fishery offences set out in Part I of Schedule 4 to the Act a person is not to be guilty of an offence where it is the subject of an exemption conferred by the Minister. Specifically, no offence will be committed by reason of anything done or omitted to be done in the course of fish farming if done or omitted by the authority of an exemption conferred by the Minister and in accordance with any conditions attached to the exemption (s.33(1)). In this respect the Minister is empowered to make regulations making different provisions for different methods of fish farming and other different circumstances, and to specify conditions to which the exemptions are subject (s.33(2)). At the time of writing, however, no regulations have yet been made by exercise of this Ministerial Power, and

consequently none of the potential exemptions from conservation legislation
are presently available.

In addition to exemptions capable of arising under Ministerial regulations,
the second prong of s.33 provides a direct defence to certain offences
concerned with possession and sale of fish and related matters without the
need for any further measures to be taken by the Minister. Accordingly, in
respect of a range of fishery offences listed in Part II of Schedule 4 to the Act,
it is a defence for a person charged to show that he believed, on reasonable
grounds, that the fish with respect to which the offence is alleged to have
been committed were produced by fish farming (s.33(5)). 'Fish farming' for
these purposes specifically excludes fish bred, reared or cultivated in captivity
which have later been released to the wild (s.33(6)). It may be a point of
contention, however, whether release into the 'wild' takes place where fish
are released into ponds in which they are contained without a means of escape
(see discussion of this point in [8.07] above).

14.03   *Exemptions under conservation legislation*

Part I of Schedule 4 to the Fisheries Act 1981 specifies the fishery offences in
relation to which the Ministerial power of exemption by regulations for fish
farming arises. These offences are placed under two headings, the first
concerned with offences in England and Wales under the Salmon and
Freshwater Fisheries Act 1975, and the second concerned with offences
relating to sea fishing in England and Wales and Scotland. As chronologically
enumerated in the Schedule, the offences in respect of which Ministerial
exemptions can be created are as follows.

Offences under the Salmon and Freshwater Fisheries Act 1975

1. Any offence under s.2(2)(a) of the Salmon and Freshwater Fisheries Act
   1975, concerned with the taking, killing or injuring or attempting to take,
   kill or injure, unclean or immature fish.
2. Any offence under s.3 of the Salmon and Freshwater Fisheries Act 1975,
   concerned with restrictions on shooting or working seine or draft nets in
   certain waters and prohibition on use of certain nets.
3. Any offence under s.5(1) of the Salmon and Freshwater Fisheries Act
   1975, prohibiting the use of explosives, poison or electrical devices to take
   or destroy fish, relating to the use of a noxious substance or electrical
   device, and any offence under s.5(4) relating to the possession of such a
   substance or device.
4. Any offence under s.19 of the Salmon and Freshwater Fisheries Act
   1975, concerned with fishing for, taking or killing or attempting to take
   or kill fish during close seasons or close times.
5. Any offence under s.27 of the Salmon and Freshwater Fisheries Act
   1975, concerned with fishing for or taking fish without a licence or
   possession of equipment with intent to use it for an unlicensed purpose.
6. Any offence under s.28(7) of the Salmon and Freshwater Fisheries Act
   1975, concerned with infringement of byelaws, consisting of a
   contravention of a byelaw made for a purpose mentioned in any of the
   following paragraphs of Schedule 3 to the 1975 Act:

(a) paragraph 21 or 25, concerned with descriptions of nets and other instrument which may be used for taking fish, and restrictions on their use;

(b) paragraph 23 or 24, concerned with restrictions on carrying certain nets;

(c) paragraph 26, concerned with taking or removing fish from water without lawful authority;

(d) paragraph 28, concerned with taking fish of less than the prescribed size.

Offences relating to Sea Fishing

7. Any offence consisting of a contravention of a byelaw made under s.4 of the Sea Fisheries (Scotland) Amendment Act 1885, concerned with byelaws prohibiting or regulating methods of fishing.

8. Any offence under s.6(1) of the Herring Fishery (Scotland) Act 1889, concerned with prohibition of beam or otter trawling in certain areas, and any offence consisting of a contravention of a byelaw made under s.7(1) of that Act, concerned with the power to prohibit beam or otter trawling in certain other areas.

[Para.9 related to offences under s.1 of the Trawling in Prohibited Areas Prevention Act 1909 of landing fish caught by beam or otter trawling within a prohibited area, but this has now been repealed by s.1(1) and Sch.1 Part XI Statute Law (Repeals) Act 1986.]

10. Any offence consisting of a contravention of a byelaw made under s.5 of the Sea Fisheries Regulation Act 1966, concerned with byelaws for the regulation of sea fishing.

11. Any offence under s.17 of the Sea Fisheries (Shellfish) Act 1967 of taking an edible crab or landing a lobster in a condition prohibited by s.17(1) or (3).

12. Any offence under s.1(1) or (3) of the Sea Fish (Conservation) Act 1967, concerning landing or carrying fish smaller than a prescribed size.

13. Any offence under s.3(5) of the Sea Fish (Conservation) Act 1967, concerning contravention of an order regulating nets and gear.

14. Any offence under s.4(3) or (9A) of the Sea Fish (Conservation) Act 1967, concerning contravention of an order prohibiting fishing without licence and failure to return sea fish caught in contravention of such a prohibition.

15. Any offence under s.4A(3) of the Sea Fish (Conservation) Act 1967, concerning contravention of an order prohibiting trans-shipment of fish without licence.

16. Any offence under s.5(1) or (6) of the Sea Fish (Conservation) Act 1967, concerning contravention of an order prohibiting fishing and failure to return sea fish caught in contravention of such a prohibition.

17. Any offence under s.6 of the Sea Fish (Conservation) Act 1967, concerning landing or trans-shipping fish in contravention of an order.

It deserves iteration that despite this diverse collection of provisions, in respect of which Ministerial exemption from general law of fisheries can be brought about by statutory instrument, the Minister has not yet brought in such an instrument and, therefore, the offences in the above list presently apply to fish farming in the same way as for fishing.

14.04   *Defences under conservation legislation*

In contrast to the presently unused enabling provisions noted above, a number of defences have *actually* been provided to fishery offences in circumstances where a person believes, on reasonable grounds, that the fish in respect of which the offence is alleged to have been committed was produced by fish farming and not subsequently released to the wild. The offences in respect of which this defence is available are listed in Part II of Schedule 4 to the 1981 Act and, following their enumeration in the Schedule, they are as follows.

Offences relating to freshwater fish and salmon

18. Any offence under s.XI of the Solway Act 1804, concerned with possessing, selling or offering or exposing to sale of certain fish out of season, and certain fish at any time.
19. Any offence under s.LXXIV of the Tweed Fisheries Act 1857 of wilfully selling, purchasing or possessing smolt, fry, or young brood or spawn.
20. Any offence under s.X of the Tweed Fisheries Amendment Act 1859, concerned with possession during close season of fish taken or caught in the river, and selling or offering for sale or exchange fish caught between 15 September and 14 February.

[Paras.21 to 23, related to offences under s.3 of the Salmon Acts Amendment Act 1863 and ss.20 and 21 of the Salmon Fisheries (Scotland) Act 1868, but have been repealed by s.41 and Sch.5 Salmon Act 1986.]

24. Any offence under s.1 of the Freshwater Fish (Scotland) Act 1902 of having possession of trout during the close season.
25. Any offence under s.2 of the Trout (Scotland) Act 1933, concerning the purchase, sale, exposing or consigning for sale, export or consigning for export, of trout under 8 inches in length or between 1 September and 31 March.
26. An offence under s.2(2)(b) of the Salmon and Freshwater Fisheries Act 1975, concerning buying, selling, exposure for sale or possession of unclean or immature fish or parts of such fish.
27. Any offence under s.22(1) of the Salmon and Freshwater Fisheries Act 1975, concerned with buying, selling, exposure for sale or possession for sale of fish at prohibited times of year.
28. Any offence under s.23(3) of the Salmon and Freshwater Fisheries Act 1975 of entering for export or exporting fish contrary to s.23(1), concerned with unclean fish and fish caught at a time when their sale is prohibited.

Offences relating to sea fishing

[Para.29 related to offences under s.1 Trawling in Prohibited Areas Prevention Act 1909, of selling fish caught by beam or otter trawling within a prohibited area, but this has now been repealed by s.1(1) and Sch.1 Part XI Statute Law (Repeals) Act 1986.]

30. Any offence under s.16 of the Sea Fisheries (Shellfish) Act 1967, concerned with the sale, exposure for sale, buying for sale or consignment for the purpose of sale of oysters at prohibited times of the year.

31. Any offence under s.17(1) of the Sea Fisheries (Shellfish) Act 1967 of possessing, selling or offering for sale, buying for sale or consigning for the purpose of sale an edible crab in a condition prohibited by that subsection.

32. Any offence under s.17(3) of the Sea Fisheries (Shellfish) Act 1967 of selling, exposing or offering for sale, or possessing for the purpose of sale a lobster in a condition prohibited by that subsection.

33. Any offence under s.1(2) of the Sea Fish (Conservation) Act 1967, concerned with selling, exposing or offering for sale, or possessing for the purpose of sale fish smaller than the prescribed size.

34. Any offence under s.2 of the Sea Fish (Conservation) Act 1967, concerned with possession for use in the course of a business of fish prohibited from being sold under s.1(2) of that Act.

It has been noted that because no regulations have been made by exercise of the Ministerial power to confer fish farming exemptions from the general fishery law, the matters listed under paragraphs 1 to 17 above are, for the present at least, of no practical effect. For that reason they will not be discussed at any greater length. By contrast, the defences provided to offences under the fishery law, under paragraphs 18 to 34 above, are of considerable present significance in affording defences in relation to possession and sale of farmed fish. For that reason the nature of legal privilege which they confer is worth outlining in each case. These defences are available within the compass of the relatively broad definition of 'fish farming' incorporated in s.33 of the Fisheries Act 1981. That is, the defences arise where the person charged believed, on reasonable grounds, that the fish in respect of which the offence is alleged to have been committed were produced by 'fish farming', defined as the breeding, rearing or cultivating of fish of all kinds, including shellfish, but excluding any fish which has later been released to the wild.

Section XI Solway Act 1804 (Para.18)

The Solway Act 1804 (44 Geo.III c.XLV) was originally stated in its preamble to be, 'An Act for better regulating and improving the Fisheries in the Arm of the Sea between the County of Cumberland and the Counties of Dumfries and Wigton, and the Stewartry of Kircudbright, and also the several Streams and Waters which run into, or communicate with, the said Arm of the Sea'. This objective, however, was later curtailed by the Annan Fisheries Act 1841, which withdrew the River Annan from the purview of the 1804 Act, and the Salmon Fisheries Act 1861, which repealed the 1804 Act in so far as it applied to the English side of the Solway. Moreover, it has been suggested that although the provisions of the 1804 Act have not been superseded, coverage of the same matters under subsequent general fishery legislation means that the provisions of the local Act are unlikely to be invoked (Tait (1928) p. 227;

though contrast Stewart (1892) in Ch.XVIII). Nonetheless, s.XI of the Solway Act 1804 remains in force and creates an offence concerned with possessing, selling or offering or exposing for sale certain fish out of season, and certain fish at any time. The defence provided under s.33(5) of the Fisheries Act 1981 means that the offence will not be committed in relation to fish which are believed, on reasonable grounds, to have been produced by fish farming.

Section LXXIV Tweed Fisheries Act 1857 (Para.19)

The Tweed Fisheries Act 1857 consolidates and amends early fishery legislation intended 'for the more effectual preservation and increase of salmon and the regulation of the fisheries in the River Tweed' (Preamble, Tweed Fisheries Act 1857). To that effect it regulates fisheries in tributary streams and the main River Tweed to its mouth, and incorporates a range of conservational measures applicable to the fishery. Amongst these provisions s.LXXIV is intended to prevent the destruction of spawn or fry of salmon by unsporting methods. Amongst other things, the section creates an offence where a person wilfully sells, purchases, or has in his possession, any smolt, fry or young brood or spawn of salmon. The penalty for the offence was originally a fine not exceeding £25, and an additional penalty equivalent to 10p for each of the smolts, fry, or young brood of salmon found in the possession of the offender, and all nets, tackle, and engines whereby the same have been taken or killed, and the hampers, baskets, or packages wherein the same may be found, are to be seized and forfeited. Although the offence under s.LXXIV is broadly formulated it is likely that the greatest practical importance of the defence provided under the Fisheries Act 1981 in respect of fish farming will concern transactions involving the sale of farmed fish, such as sales of live salmon eggs or fry between fish farmers. The effect of the Fisheries Act 1981 is that no offence will be committed under the 1857 Act where the fish concerned are reasonably believed to have been produced by fish farming.

Section X Tweed Fisheries Amendment Act 1859 (Para.20)

The Tweed Fisheries Amendment Act 1859 sought to extend the fishery conservation powers provided under the 1857 Act, in particular by an alteration of the annual close times for fishing. In accordance with the amended close times an offence is provided for in respect of having or selling fish caught during that time. That is, it is an offence for a person to have in his possession during the annual close times salmon known to have been taken or caught in the River during the annual close times, or to sell or offer or expose for sale or exchange any salmon known to have been caught in the River between 15 September in any year and 14 February in the year following, both days inclusive. The original penalty for the offence was a fine not less that 50p and not exceeding £25 for each salmon possessed, or sold or offered or exposed for sale. Any boat, cart, basket or package in which the salmon was found may be seized and forfeited, and the proof that the salmon was not taken contrary to the provisions of the Act is to lie upon the person in whose custody the fish was found. The defence to this offence provided under the Fisheries Act 1981 will mean, for example, that during the annual close time on the Tweed fishmongers who sell fish that are believed, on

176 The Law of Aquaculture

reasonable grounds, to have been produced by fish farming will not commit any offence under the 1859 Act.

Section 1 Freshwater Fish (Scotland) Act 1902 (Para.24)

The Freshwater Fish (Scotland) Act 1902 has as its purpose the better protection of freshwater fish in Scotland, and to that effect imposes a close time for fishing for trout. During the close time, between 7 October and 14 March in the year following, both dates inclusive, it is unlawful to have possession of 'common trout', *Salmo fario*. Any person possessing trout at any time within the dates, will on summary conviction forfeit and pay a sum not exceeding £5 for each offence. Within s.1 of the 1902 Act there is an exception in favour of stews and artificial hatcheries in respect of which the section is stated not to apply to the owner, occupier or lessee of any water where trout are kept in captivity or artificially reared and fed, or to any person employed by them for the rearing or feeding of trout, or to any person to whom such trout may be consigned by them for sale or otherwise, for the purpose of stocking ponds, rivers or other waters. However, this is subject to the proviso that if trout are taken from the waters during the close time, except for scientific or breeding purposes or to be removed in a living state to other waters, an offence will be committed under the section. In summary therefore, the possession of trout by a fish farmer during the close time will not amount to an offence, but certain transfers of the fish during the close time will amount to an offence in respect of farmed fish. The effect of the Fisheries Act 1981 on this provision is to provide a comprehensive defence to s.1 of the 1902 Act in respect of *any* alleged offence involving possession of trout during the close time where such fish are believed, on reasonable grounds, to have been produced by fish farming.

Section 2 Trout (Scotland) Act 1933 (Para.25)

The Trout (Scotland) Act 1933 has as its purpose the better protection of trout, other than rainbow trout and sea-trout, and related purposes in Scotland. In pursuance of this, s.2 of the Act makes it an offence to purchase, sell, expose or consign for sale, or export or consign for export, first, trout under 8 inches in length and, second, trout at any time between 1 September and 31 March, both inclusive. Any person who contravenes these provisions is to be guilty of an offence and liable on summary conviction to a penalty which was originally stated not to exceed £5. There is an explicit saving in the Act, however, to the effect that is not to apply to live trout sold or disposed of for the purpose of stocking any river, loch, or water whatsoever, or artificial propagation. Nonetheless, the effect of the Fisheries Act 1981 on this provision is that the offence will not be committed in respect of undersized or unseasonable trout which are believed, on reasonable grounds, to have been produced by fish farming.

Section 2(2)(b) Salmon and Freshwater Fisheries Act 1975 (Para.26)

The Salmon and Freshwater Fisheries Act 1975 is the principal statute governing sporting and commercial fishing for salmon and freshwater fish in England and Wales. Section 2(2)(b) of the Act provides that any person who buys, sells, exposes for sale, or has in his possession any salmon, trout or freshwater fish, excluding eels, which is unclean or immature, or any part of any such fish, is guilty of an offence. 'Unclean' for the purposes of this offence is defined to mean any fish which is about to spawn, or has recently spawned and has not recovered from spawning. 'Immature', in respect of salmon, means that the salmon is of a length of less than 12 inches, measured from tip of the snout to the fork or cleft of the tail. In relation to other fish, 'immature' is stated to mean fish of a lesser length than prescribed by the National Rivers Authority (s.41(1) Salmon and Freshwater Fisheries Act 1975). The maximum penalty for this offence is, on summary conviction, a fine of level 4 on the standard scale, presently set at £1,000 (Sch.4 para.1(2)).

The offence of selling unclean or immature fish is subject to an explicit exception in respect of any act done for the purpose of the artificial propagation of salmon, trout or freshwater fish or for some scientific purpose, or for the purpose of the preservation or development of a private fishery and the previous permission in writing of the National Rivers Authority (s.2(5)). It may be that many sales of fish between fish farmers are already within the general defence in that they are for purpose of artificial propagation, as where live fish are purchased as brood stock. Otherwise, the effect of the defence under the Fisheries Act 1981 is that fish farmers and others, such as fishmongers, will be able to buy unclean or immature salmon, trout and freshwater fish, which are reasonably believed to have been produced by fish farming, without committing any offence under s.2(2)(b) of the 1975 Act.

Section 22(1) Salmon and Freshwater Fisheries Act 1975 (Para.27)

Section 22(1) of the Salmon and Freshwater Fisheries Act 1975 prohibits the sale of salmon and trout, or parts of these fish, in England and Wales, at certain times of the year. Specifically, it is an offence to buy, sell, or expose for sale or have in possession for sale, any salmon between 31 August and the following 1 February or, any trout other than rainbow trout between 31 August and the following 1 March. A distinctive feature of the offence relates to the burden of proof involved. This is that the burden of proving that any salmon or trout bought, sold, exposed for sale or in the possession of any person for sale during the prohibited time is not bought, sold, or exposed for sale or in possession for sale in contravention of the provision, is to lie on the person buying, selling or exposing it for sale, or having it in his possession for sale. That is, it is for the possessor of a fish during the prohibited time to prove that the possession was lawful. This might be proved, for example, by showing that a fish possessed during the prohibited period was intended to be sold at a later date when the sale was not prohibited (*Birkett* v. *McGlassons* [1957] 1 All ER 369). The maximum penalty for this offence is, on summary conviction, a fine of level 4 on the standard scale, presently set at £1,000 (Sch.4 para.1(2) Salmon and Freshwater Fisheries Act 1975).

The offence of selling salmon and trout at unseasonable times is, however, made subject to a list of exceptions, so that it does not apply to:

(a) any salmon or trout which has been canned, frozen, cured, salted, pickled, dried or otherwise preserved outside the United Kingdom; or

(b) any salmon which has been canned, frozen, cured, salted, pickled, dried or

> otherwise preserved in the United Kingdom between 1 February and 31 August; or
>
> (c) any trout which has been canned, frozen, cured, salted, pickled, dried or otherwise preserved within the United Kingdom between 1 March and 31 August; or
>
> (d) any salmon or trout, other than an unclean salmon or trout, caught outside the United Kingdom; or
>
> (e) any salmon or trout, other than an unclean or immature salmon or trout, caught within the United Kingdom, if its capture by any net, instrument or device was lawful at the time and in the place where it was caught (s.22(2)).

To this list of exceptions is added another to the effect that a person will not be guilty of the offence in respect of trout for any act done for the purpose of the artificial propagation of fish, or the stocking or restocking of waters, or for some scientific purpose (s.22(3)). It follows in respect of artificial propagation, therefore, that a trout farmer may enjoy a defence not shared by a counterpart farming and selling salmon for the purpose of artificial propagation.

Despite the range of exceptions to which the offence under s.22(1) of the 1975 Act is subject, it is likely that the defence provided under the Fisheries Act 1981 is of greater practical importance than any of those incorporated in the 1975 Act. Indeed, the large and increasing proportion of salmon and trout that are produced by fish farming means that the majority of sales will be of fish, reasonably believed, to have been produced by fish farming within the defence under the 1981 Act, and only a relatively small proportion of such sales, relating to wild fish, will be subject to the seasonal prohibition.

Section 23(1) and (3) Salmon and Freshwater Fisheries Act 1975 (Para.28)

Section 23(1) of the Salmon and Freshwater Fisheries Act 1975 imposes further restrictions upon the distribution of unlawfully caught salmon and trout by making it an offence to export unclean salmon or trout, or to export salmon or trout caught during the time when sale of the fish is prohibited at the place where caught. This offence involves a stipulation that all salmon or trout intended for export between 31 August and the following 1 May are, before shipment, to be entered for that purpose with the proper officer of Customs and Excise, at the port or place of export (s.23(2)). If any salmon or trout is entered for export, or exported, or brought to any wharf, quay or other place for export and is not entered for export, the salmon or trout and any package containing it is to be deemed to be goods liable to be forfeited. The person entering or exporting the salmon or trout, or bringing it for export, or failing to enter the salmon or trout for export as required commits an offence (s.23(3)). As with the prohibition of sale of salmon and trout at certain times of the year, the burden of proving that any salmon or trout entered for export is not entered in contravention of the prohibition is to lie with the person entering the fish for export (s.23(5)). The maximum penalty for this offence is, on summary conviction, a fine of level 4 on the standard scale, presently £1,000 (Sch.4 para.1(2)).

In the same way that most sales of fish within the prohibited times of year under the 1975 Act are likely to involve farmed fish, it is probable that the preponderance of exported salmon and trout will be produced by fish farming. As a consequence most exports of unclean or unseasonable salmon or trout, or failures to conform to the requirements relating to entry for export, will come within the defence under the Fisheries Act 1981 that the fish concerned are reasonably believed to have been produced by fish farming.

Sections 16, 17(1) and 17(2) Sea Fisheries (Shellfish) Act 1967 (Paras.30, 31 and 32)

The Sea Fisheries (Shellfish) Act 1967 is the main consolidating enactment relating to shellfisheries and shellfish in England, Wales and Scotland. The provisions of the Act and the offences provided for under ss.16, 17(1) and 17(2) are discussed elsewhere (in [15.04N] and [15.04O] below). In relation to all three offences it is a defence to show that the shellfish concerned were believed, on reasonable grounds, to be produced by fish farming.

Sections 1(2) and 2 of the Sea Fish (Conservation) Act 1967 (Paras.33 and 34)

Sections 1(2) and 2 of the Sea Fish (Conservation) Act 1967 impose restrictions upon the landing and sale of under-sized sea fish in Great Britain, and the use of such fish in the course of business. These matters are discussed in detail elsewhere (in [15.05] below). In each case it will be a defence under s.33(5) of the Fisheries Act 1981 to show that the fish concerned were reasonably believed to have been produced by fish farming.

14.05 *Exceptions for fish farming in Scotland*

The exceptions and defences from fishery law provided for in respect of fish farming by the Fisheries Act 1981 arise in relation to England and Wales and Scotland, depending on the extent of operation of the various enactments for which an exemption or defence is provided. In relation to Scotland alone, however, special provision is made for exemption from particular fishery offences under the Freshwater and Salmon Fisheries (Scotland) Act 1976. Hence s.7 of the 1976 Act provides that persons are not to be guilty of contravention of certain enactments set out in Part I of Schedule 3 to the Act in respect of any act or omission carried out within a fish farm in the course of the operation of a fish farm. The basic meaning of 'fish farm' is taken to be the same as defined under the Diseases of Fish Act 1937, that is, any pond, stew, fish hatchery or other place used for keeping, with a view to their sale or to their transfer to other waters including any other fish farm, live fish, live eggs of fish, or foodstuff for fish, and includes any buildings used in connection therewith, and the banks and margins of any water therein (s.10(1) Diseases of Fish Act 1937, discussed in [6.02] above). In addition to the basic definition of fish farm, however, it is specified that the act of selling or exporting fish by or on behalf of a person who has reared the fish in a fish farm is to be deemed to be an act carried out within a fish farm in the course of operation of that farm (s.7(3) Freshwater and Salmon Fisheries (Scotland) Act 1976). Further extension of the meaning of 'fish farm' is brought about by a stipulation that in any proceedings under enactments specified in Part II of Schedule 3 to the 1976 Act, in relation to a boat or other thing mentioned in the enactments concerned, which is not in a fish farm, it is to be a defence for the person charged to prove that the act or omission complained of was necessary for the purpose of the operation of a fish farm (s.7(4)).

The offences in relation to which a person is not to be guilty in respect of acts or omissions carried out within a fish farm in the course of operation of the farm are specified in Part I of Schedule 3 to the 1976 Act in the following way.

1. In the Solway Act 1804:
    (a) section I, imposition of close time;
    (b) section II, requirements to remove boats, etc;
    (c) section XI, selling fish out of season, and having fish in possession;
    (d) section XV, regulation of size of mesh of nets.

2. In the Tweed Fisheries Act 1857:
    (a) section XLV, prohibition against use of any pout net or net during close season;
    (b) section LXXII, requirement to return unclean fish to river;
    (c) section LXXIV, prohibition against destruction of spawn or fry.

3. In the Tweed Fisheries Amendment Act 1859:
    (a) section VI, offence of fishing in close season;
    (b) section X, offence of having in possession during close season salmon taken or caught in the river;
    (c) section XI, boats, nets etc. to be removed in close season;
    (d) section XIII, prohibits drawing or using in the river nets with mesh less than prescribed size.

[Para.4 was repealed by s.41 and Sch.4 para.15(2)(a) Salmon Act 1986.]

5. In the Salmon Fisheries (Scotland) Act 1868:
    (a) section 15(1), fishing for salmon in close season other than by rod and line;
    (b) section 15(2), fishing for salmon in weekly close time;
    (c) section 15(4), fishing for salmon with a net having a mesh contrary to any byelaw;
    (d) section 20, buying, selling, taking or possessing unclean or unseasonable salmon;
    (e) section 21, buying, selling, exposing for sale or having in possession salmon taken in close season;
    (f) section 23, boats, nets etc. to be removed in close season.

6. In the Freshwater Fish (Scotland) Act 1902, section 1, fishing for or having possession of trout in close season.

7. In the Trout (Scotland) Act 1933, section 2, purchase or sale of trout under 8 inches or between 1 September and 31 March.

8. In the Salmon and Freshwater Fisheries (Protection) (Scotland) Act 1951:
    (a) section 2, fishing for salmon and freshwater fish by illegal methods;
    (b) paragraphs (b) and (c) of section 4, prohibition against using poisons and electrical devices for destruction of fish;
    (c) section 13, fishing for salmon in weekly close time.

8A. In the Salmon Act 1986, regulations made under s.3(2)(a) or (d), general
regulations (added by s.41 and Sch.4 para.15(2)(b) Salmon Act 1986).

In relation to these exemptions it may be noted that the offences under the
Solway Act 1804, the Tweed Fisheries Act 1857 and the Tweed Fisheries
Amendment Act 1859, are offences which are of local application arising
under enactments the general effects of which have been considered
previously (in [14.04]). Likewise the general nature of the offences under s.1
of the Freshwater Fish (Scotland) Act 1902 and s.2 of the Trout (Scotland) Act
1933 are now also the subject of fish farming exemptions granted under the
Fisheries Act 1981 (discussed in [14.04] above) which apply throughout
Britain.

Although the 1981 Act also provides exemptions for offences under the
Salmon Fisheries (Scotland) Act 1868, the exemption here provided for in
relation to fish farming in Scotland is wider than under the 1981 Act in that
offences under ss.15 and 23, relating to fishing for salmon and the removal of
boats during the close season, are also exempted. Of broader application, and
not provided for under the 1981 Act, are the offences under ss.2, 4(b) and (c)
and 13 of the Salmon and Freshwater Fisheries (Protection) (Scotland) Act
1951, relating to fishing for salmon and freshwater fish by illegal methods,
the use of poisons and electrical devices for destruction of fish and fishing for
salmon in the weekly close time. Notably, though, the exemption for the use
of poisons and electrical devices for destruction of fish is qualified in that the
exemption only applies where the act is carried out with the consent of the
Secretary of State (s.7(2) Freshwater and Salmon Fisheries (Scotland) Act
1976).

In addition to the provision of direct exemptions from fishery offences in
relation to fish farming under s.7 and Part I of Schedule 3 of the Freshwater
and Salmon Fisheries (Scotland) Act 1976, separate provision is made for
offences arising in relation to the use of boats in fish farming. Hence it is
provided that in proceedings for an offence under any of the enactments
specified in Part II of Schedule 3 to the Act, in relation to a boat or other thing
mentioned in any such enactment which is not in a fish farm, it is to be a
defence for the person charged with such an offence to prove that the act or
omission complained of was necessary for the purpose of the operation of a
fish farm. The enactments to which this dispensation applies are listed in Part
II of Schedule 3 as follows.

9. In the Solway Act 1804, section II, requirement to remove boats, etc.
10. In the Tweed Fisheries Amendment Act 1859, section XI, boats, nets etc.
to be removed in close season.
11. In the Salmon Fisheries (Scotland) Act 1868, section 23, boats, nets etc. to
be removed in close season.

14.06   *Escapes from fish farms*

Following on from the exemptions from fishery law granted to fish farms, it
is convenient to discuss the legal issues relating to escapes of fish from fish
farms. Not uncommonly, due to vandalism, accident or exceptional weather
conditions (see, for example, *Forsikrings Vesta* v. *Butcher* [1989] 1 All ER 402,

discussed in [10.07] above) stock from a fish farm escapes from rearing ponds into a river, or from fish cages into coastal waters. In such circumstances two key legal issues arise. First, there is the question of who owns the farmed fish which are at large in the river or coastal waters. Second, there is the related question of what steps can be taken by a fish farmer to recover lost stock without falling foul of fishery laws concerning prohibited methods of taking fish.

The issue of property rights over fish is illustrative of a somewhat peculiar aspect of the common law dealing with the ownership of wild creatures. In this respect the ownership of fish is in sharp contrast to the ownership of other kinds of farmed animals. If, for example, an animal farmer were to lose cattle or sheep by their straying from an enclosure, it would not be concluded that the first person to find a straying animal would thereby be entitled to claim ownership over it. Normally ownership of cattle or sheep is retained by the farmer despite the loss of custody. The position in relation to escaped fish, however, is quite different as a consequence of the the legal classification of living creatures.

At common law the animal kingdom is divided into two categories, domestic animals, termed *domitae naturae*, and wild animals, termed *ferae naturae*. (Generally, see, Williams (1939); and North (1972).) Although this classification is of special importance in relation to liability for damage caused by animals (generally, see Animals Act 1971 and Animals (Scotland) Act 1987), it is also important in determining rights of ownership over animals. Specifically, the distinction between domestic and wild animals corresponds to the difference between those animals in which the possessor has an 'absolute' right of ownership, and those where the right is merely that of 'qualified' ownership. The difference between absolute and qualified rights of ownership is crucial in situations where an animal escapes from custody. In the case of a domesticated animal the absolute right of ownership means that ownership is retained despite the escape. In the case of qualified ownership of a wild animal, ownership is maintained only for so long as the animal is retained in the custody of the owner. Because of the legal categorisation of fish as wild creatures, it follows that the legal interest of their possessor is only that of qualified ownership and this is lost where possession is lost.

The basis of the distinct property rights subsisting in domesticated and wild animals is to be found in the statements of the legal authority Blackstone, who observed:

'In all creatures reclaimed from the wildness of their nature the property is not absolute but defeasible; a property that may be destroyed if they resume their antient wildness and are found at large. For if ... the fishes escape from the trunk, and are seen wandering at large in their proper element, they become *ferae naturae* again and are free and open to the first occupant that has the ability to seize them. But while they thus continue my qualified or defeasible property they are as much under the protection of the law as if they were absolutely and indefeasibly mine.' (Blackstone, (1766) Vol.2 p.393.)

The same principle of the common law relating to animal ownership is incorporated in the present law of theft, where it is explicitly provided that

'Wild creatures, tamed or untamed, shall be regarded as property; but a person cannot steal a wild creature not tamed nor ordinarily kept in captivity, or the carcase of any such creature, unless either it has been reduced into possession by or on behalf of another person and the possession of it has not since been lost or abandoned, or another person is in the course of reducing it into possession.' (s.4(4) Theft Act 1968; and see [15.02] and [17.04] below.)

Essentially the same principle, referred to as *res nullius*, amounting to an affirmation that creatures which are not owned cannot be the subject of theft, is also to be found in Scots criminal law (Stair, (1832) Book II Title 3 para.76; Gordon (1978) at p. 476; *John Huie* (1842) 1 Broun 383; *Scott* v. *Everitt* (1853) 15 D. 288; and see [15.03] and [17.04]).

The application of these longstanding principles of property law concerning wild creatures to the circumstances of an escape of fish from a fish farm entails that, as wild creatures, the qualified ownership which they admit is lost when they escape from a rearing pool or cage. Blackstone at one point seems to concede a principle of immediate pursuit, in suggesting that qualified property is retained in a deer which is chased out of a park and instantly pursued by the keeper. This qualification would appear to be of narrow compass, however, as it is followed by a decisive statement that if wild animals stray without knowledge of their former possessor it becomes lawful for any stranger to take them, and at another point it is suggested that qualified property 'instantly' ceases when wild animals regain their natural liberty (Blackstone (1766) Vol.2 at p. 392). This, therefore, would probably be the usual position in relation to escapes of fish from fish farms. Whilst fish are contained within ponds or cages they are the property of the owner of the farm and it will be theft for any person to take them dishonestly. If they escape, however, the right of qualified property in the fish is lost, they become wild creatures in law, and may be appropriated by any person who has the lawful means to do so.

The second question for discussion in this section concerns the steps that can legitimately be taken by a fish farmer to recover lost stock without falling foul of fishery laws concerning prohibited methods of taking fish. In the first place this depends upon the scope of the exceptions to general fishery law which are provided under the exemptions discussed in the preceding sections of this chapter. Hence, in relation to England, Wales and Scotland, there are general exceptions and defences which arise in relation to fish farming under s.33 of the Fisheries Act 1981 (discussed in [14.03] above). It was noted, however, that though some of the exceptions which are provided for under s.33(1), and listed under Part I of Schedule 4 to the Act, would provide exemption from offences under the Salmon and Freshwater Fisheries Act 1975 in England and Wales, no Ministerial exemptions have yet been granted. It follows that, for example, the use of a net to recover escaped fish would constitute a fishery offence unless it was a licensed instrument within the provisions of the 1975 Act (s.27 Salmon and Freshwater Fisheries Act 1975). Remarkably, the inference to be drawn is that a fish farmer seeking to recover escaped stock using other than a permitted fishery method will commit a criminal offence by so doing unless special dispensation from ordinary licensing requirements is provided by the National Rivers Authority.

In relation to Scotland additional exemptions from general fishery law for fish farming are more broadly formulated under s.7 of the Freshwater and Salmon Fisheries (Scotland) Act 1976 (see [11.05] above) in that defences are provided for acts that would otherwise constitute offences under the general fishery law in relation to the use of prohibited methods for taking fish. However, it is to be noted that, other than in relation to certain matters concerning the use of boats, these defences are only available in relation to acts or omissions carried out *within a fish farm* in the course of operation of a fish farm (s.7(1) Freshwater and Salmon Fisheries Act 1976). A situation where fish have escaped from a fish farm is inevitably one in which recapture must take place *outside* the fish farm, and consequently these defences to fishery offences would not be available in such circumstances.

More hopeful, however, in relation to the recapture of escaped salmon from fish farms in Scotland is the wide power given to the Secretary of State or, in certain cases, the district salmon fishery board for a salmon fishery district, to provide written exemption for acts or omissions which would otherwise amount to a fishery offence. This power is made available for the purpose of protecting, improving or developing stocks of fish, or conserving any creature, under s.28 of the Salmon Act 1986 (see also [17.05] below). Although some expedition might be required to obtain the necessary written permission before the dispersal of the escapees, this power would appear to be sufficiently broadly formulated to provide the necessary exemptions from fishey law in relation to escapes of salmon from fish farms. Analogous powers arise in relation to freshwater fish, including trout, under s.9 of the Salmon and Freshwater Fisheries (Protection) (Scotland) Act 1951. This allows for a defence to fishery offences arising under the Act in relation to acts done for the purpose of protecting, improving or developing stocks of fish where the previous permission of the Secretary of State has been obtained in writing.

The main concern of this section, it is to be noted, has been with *escapes* of fish from fish farms where the rights and obligations of the fish farmer are at issue. In a situation where fish have been intentionally or negligently released there are other legal considerations which may become of relevance. Within the criminal law, for instance, the unauthorised introduction of fish into waters may constitute an offence in England and Wales under the Salmon and Freshwater Fisheries Act 1975 (s.30 Salmon and Freshwater Fisheries Act 1975; see [8.05] above) or in Scotland where salmon are released without authorisation (s.24 Salmon Act 1986; see [8.06] above). In either jurisdiction an offence will be committed where a person releases or allows to escape any fish which is of a kind which is not ordinarily resident in Britain, or is listed in Part I of Schedule 9 to the Wildlife and Countryside Act 1981 (s.14(1) Wildlife and Countryside Act 1981; see [8.07] above). In addition, the introduction of fish of a genetically different character to wild stocks may have a detrimental effect upon fisheries, either through ecological competition or by adverse genetic effects upon native stocks. Where this can be shown to cause damage to fisheries in the locality of the escape it is, in principle at least, capable of giving rise to civil liability.

14.07   *The Salmon Act 1986*

Another respect in which fishery conservation legislation impinges upon the activity of fish farming concerns the incidental effect upon salmon farming of recent provisions under the Salmon Act 1986. The purpose of this Act was to reform the law on administration of salmon fisheries in Scotland, but significant provisions were incorporated into the Act to curb the unlawful taking of wild salmon in England, Wales and Scotland. Although the illegitimate taking of salmon was comprehensively provided for, under the Salmon and Freshwater Fisheries Act 1975 in England and Wales and the Salmon and Freshwater Fisheries (Protection) (Scotland) Act 1951 in Scotland and various other enactments, the problem of poaching persisted. The legislative response to the problem was the imposition of new controls upon sales and possession of dead salmon and sea-trout. Although principally intended to make unlawfully taken wild fish more difficult to dispose of, these controls will also have important implications for some salmon farmers.

Under the 1986 Act new offences concerning the sale and possession of salmon are provided for in England and Wales and Scotland. In relation to England and Wales enabling provision is made for a dealer licensing scheme in respect of those selling salmon, (s.31 Salmon Act 1986) whilst in Scotland a similar objective is to be achieved by the exercise of powers to permit licensing and regulation of salmon dealing under the Civic Government (Scotland) Act 1982 (s.20). A new offence of handling salmon in suspicious circumstances is created in England and Wales (s.32; and see Howarth (1987C)), whilst in Scotland the equivalent is an offence of possessing salmon which have been illegally taken, killed or landed (s.22).

A.   Dealer licensing in England and Wales

The idea of a dealer licensing system applicable to those trading in salmon had been suggested on a number of occasions as a means of reducing trade in unlawfully caught fish (Bledisloe (1961) para.306; and Hunter (1965) paras.241 and 242). Due to the escalating amount of wild salmon being taken and disposed of with impunity, however, the need for licensing of salmon dealers came eventually to be accepted, and the version provided for under the 1986 Act will, by a combination of the provisions applying to England and Wales and to Scotland, provide a comprehensive network for licensing. As was stated in the Parliamentary debates, 'the Government are on record as wishing to introduce a licensing scheme that will provide as strong a chain as possible, from the time when the salmon starts to change hands until it reaches the consumer' (471 HL DEB 1986 Col. 1011). As a consequence, 'many people who are now used to buying their salmon perfectly legally – perhaps at the back door of a hotel – will in future have to buy from a licensed dealer. This is necessary if we are to deal with poaching' (93 HC DEB 1986 Col. 283).

In England and Wales the dealer licensing scheme is provided for by authorising the Minister of Agriculture, Fisheries and Food and the Secretary of State for Wales to make, by statutory instrument, an order prohibiting persons from dealing in salmon otherwise than under and in accordance with a licence issued in pursuance of the order, or buying salmon from a person who is not licensed to deal in salmon (s.31(1) Salmon Act 1986). A Ministerial Order made by the exercise of this power may be made subject to a series of permissive provisions stating that an order may:

(a) prescribe the manner and form of an application for a licence to deal in salmon and the sum, or maximum sum, to be paid on the making of such an application;

(b) specify the circumstances in which such an application is to be granted or refused and the conditions that may be incorporated in such a licence;

(c) authorise the amendment, revocation or suspension of such a licence;

(d) create criminal offences consisting in the contravention of, or failure to comply with, licensing provisions;

(e) provide for matters to be determined by a person authorized by any such provision to issue a licence; and

(f) make provision, whether by application of the Salmon and Freshwater Fisheries Act 1975 or otherwise, for the purpose of facilitating the enforcement of any provision made under the Ministerial order (s.31(2)).

Further guidance as to the eventual form of the licensing scheme for salmon dealers is indicated by the definition of 'deal' operative in this context, which includes the selling of salmon, whether by way of business or otherwise, and acting on behalf of a buyer or seller of salmon (s.30(6)). 'Salmon' is stated to mean all migratory fish of the species *Salmo salar* and *Salmo trutta* and commonly known as salmon and sea trout respectively, or any part of any such fish (s.40(1)). Although the details of the salmon dealer licensing scheme have not yet been finalised present indications are that the scheme will have significant implications for some, though not all, salmon farmers.

B. Licensing and regulation of salmon dealing in Scotland

The existence of different legal and administrative frameworks in England and Wales and Scotland has the consequence that the dealer licensing schemes have to be separately provided for under the two legal systems. Nonetheless it is of vital importance that the two schemes operate compatibly to avoid commercial obstruction to cross-border trade in salmon and also to avoid enforcement loopholes. The legal foundation for the Scottish dealer licensing system lies in the provisions of s.44 of the Civic Government (Scotland) Act 1982 giving power to designate activities as subject to licensing and regulation. Section 20 of the Salmon Act 1986 makes explicit provision to the effect that this power may be used to make an order relating to dealing in salmon, defined so as to include acts preparatory to or connected with dealing in salmon and excluding dealing in any class or classes of salmon as are specified in the order (s.20(1)(a) Salmon Act 1986). An order of this kind may provide that an offence arising through doing anything for which a licence is required without having one (under s.7(1) Civic Government (Scotland) Act 1982) is to be punishable on summary conviction by imprisonment for a term not exceeding three months, or a fine not exceeding the statutory maximum, presently £2,000, or both, and on conviction on indictment by imprisonment for a term not exceeding two years, or a fine or both (s.20(1)(b) Salmon Act 1986). Specifically it may be provided that it is to be an offence for any person, other than the holder of a salmon dealer's licence, to buy salmon from or sell salmon to a person not having such a licence (s.20(1)(c)) though this may be subject to such exceptions as may be specified by order (s.20(1)(d)). The order may provide that a licence of this kind is only to be required for such a class or classes of persons dealing in salmon and dealing in such class or classes of salmon as may be specified in the order (s.20(1)(e)). In addition the order may provide for the exercise of powers of entry and search by water bailiffs and persons appointed by the Secretary of State for Scotland under s.10(5) of the Salmon and Freshwater Fisheries (Protection) (Scotland) Act 1951 (s.20(1)(f)), though in no case are powers under the order to be exercised in any dwelling house or associated premises (s.20(1)).

Whilst it may be premature to judge the effectiveness of the dealer licensing schemes for England and Wales and for Scotland in advance of their details being determined, the enabling provisions in the Salmon Act 1986 do seem to indicate a significant advance in providing a means of reducing trade in wild salmon taken by unlawful methods. This improvement will inevitably be won at some cost, however, and it is likely that in the case of those salmon farmers, who do not sell exclusively to licensed dealers, this will mean the inconvenience of an increased amount of administration in order to secure conformity with licensing requirements.

C.   Handling salmon in suspicious circumstances in England and Wales

In addition to providing for the establishment of the salmon dealer licensing system, the Salmon Act 1986 sought to outlaw trade in unlawfully taken salmon by means of a specific offence making the possession of illicit fish a criminal offence. Differences in the legal systems of England and Wales and Scotland mean that the offence had to be separately and differently formulated in the two jurisdictions, but once again the need to harmonise legislation in order to avoid enforcement loopholes means that the substance of what amounts to an offence is broadly the same in both jurisdictions. Viewed against the general body of the criminal law, the new crime is peculiarly and broadly formulated, and for that reason its scope will be of importance to all who have charge, or take possession of, salmon, not least salmon farmers.

In England and Wales, the new offence provided under s.32 of the Salmon Act 1986 is that of handling salmon in suspicious circumstances. Subject to certain qualifications, the offence is committed where a person believes, or it would be reasonable for him to suspect, that a 'relevant offence' has at any time been committed in relation to a salmon, and he receives that fish, or undertakes or assists in its retention, removal or disposal by or for the benefit of another person, or if he arranges to do so (s.32(1)). A 'relevant offence' is stated to mean an offence which is committed either by taking, killing or landing a salmon, in England and Wales or in Scotland, or where the salmon is taken, killed or landed, in England, Wales or Scotland, in the course of commission of the offence (s.32(2)). The underlying idea is that the 'relevant offence' involved is an offence under the law of England and Wales if the fish was taken in England or Wales, or an offence under Scottish law if the fish was taken in Scotland (s.32(7)). The maximum punishment for a person found guilty of the offence of handling salmon in suspicious circumstances is, on summary conviction, imprisonment for a term not exceeding three months or to a fine not exceeding the statutory maximum, presently £2,000, or to both, and on indictment, to imprisonment for a term not exceeding two years or to a fine or both (s.32(5)).

The requirement of showing a belief or reasonable suspicion of a relevant offence having taken place in relation to a salmon is notable in that it need not involve establishing belief or suspicion of a *particular* offence. Hence the accused person will be guilty where it is shown that there was belief or reasonable suspicion that *any* relevant offence had taken place in relation to the salmon in question. Accordingly it is stated that it is immaterial that a person's belief or the grounds for suspicion relate neither specifically to a particular offence that has been committed nor exclusively to a relevant offence or to relevant offences (s.32(3)). Consequently it will be no defence for an accused person to maintain that his belief or suspicion did not relate to any particular relevant offence, nor that the belief or suspicion that he had was of a different relevant offence to that which had actually taken place.

It is apparent that if convictions for handling salmon were to depend on the prosecution showing that salmon had been unlawfully taken then relatively few prosecutions would be secured, because it is almost impossible to distinguish a salmon which has been illegally taken from one which has been lawfully taken. The existence of net marks on a salmon, for example, provide no conclusive evidence as to whether the marked fish has been lawfully or unlawfully netted. In recognition of this problem, the new offence does not require the prosecution to prove that a salmon has actually been the subject of a relevant offence. What is required is that there was belief or suspicion, on the part of the accused, that a salmon has been the subject of a relevant offence rather than *proof* that it has actually been the subject of such an offence.

Whilst recognising the difficulty in proving 'relevant offences' in relation to salmon, it would clearly be unjust if a person were to be convicted of handling salmon in suspicious circumstances if it could be shown that the fish concerned had not in fact been the subject of any relevant offence. To cover this possibility it is provided that it is to be a defence to show that no relevant offence had in fact been committed in relation to the salmon in question (s.32(3)). Hence where it could be shown that, for example, the salmon at issue had been produced by fish farming and recaptured without any relevant offence being committed, no offence of handling salmon in suspicious circumstances would be committed. Another exception to the offence is provided for in respect of anything done in good faith for purposes connected with the prevention or detection of crime or the investigation of disease (s.32(4)). Remarkably, this exception does not extend to matters connected with artificial propagation of fish or scientific purposes.

Another legal peculiarity of the offence of handling salmon in suspicious circumstances concerns the burden of proof involved. The prosecution need show that either the accused believed the salmon in question to have been unlawfully taken, or that a reasonable person in the position of the accused would have suspected that the fish had been the subject of a relevant offence. Other than where the accused admits his belief that the salmon at issue was unlawfully taken, the circumstances are to be viewed objectively and the question posed: would a reasonable person looking at the circumstances from the perspective of the accused have suspected that a relevant offence had been committed? (471 HL DEB 1986 Col. 372)

D. Possessing illegally taken salmon in Scotland

The Scottish counterpart of the offence of handling salmon in suspicious circumstances is the offence of possessing salmon which have been illegally taken, killed or landed, which is created by the insertion of a new s.7A in the Salmon and Freshwater Fisheries (Protection) (Scotland) Act 1951 (s.22(1) Salmon Act 1986). The new section provides that a person who is in possession of salmon and believes, or is in possession of salmon in circumstances in which it would be reasonable for him to suspect, that a relevant offence had at any time been committed in relation to the salmon is guilty of an offence. The penalty for this offence is, on summary conviction, imprisonment for a term not exceeding three months, or to a fine not exceeding the statutory maximum, presently £2,000, or both, or on conviction on indictment, to imprisonment for a term not exceeding two years, or to a fine or both (s.7A(1) Salmon and Freshwater Fisheries (Protection) (Scotland) Act 1951).

The Scottish offence corresponds precisely with the equivalent offence in England and Wales in that a 'relevant offence', in relation to the taking of a salmon, is committed by taking, killing or landing a salmon either in Scotland or in England and Wales, or that salmon is taken, killed or landed, either in Scotland or in England and Wales in the course of the commission of the offence (s.7A(3)). Exceptions arise, however, in that it is a defence to show that no relevant offence had in fact been committed in relation to the salmon concerned (s.7A(2)). In addition, a person is not to be guilty of an offence under the section in respect of conduct which constitutes a relevant offence in relation to any salmon, or in respect of anything done in good faith for purposes connected with the prevention or detection of crime or the investigation or treatment of disease (s.7A(6)).

The Scottish offence contrasts with that in England and Wales in some respects. In Scotland special provision is made for both corporate and individual guilt by stipulation that where the offence is committed by a body corporate and is proved to have been committed with the consent or connivance of an individual both will be guilty. Hence where the offence is attributable to any neglect on the part of any director, manager, secretary, or other similar officer of the body corporate, or any person who was purporting to act in such capacity, he as well as the body corporate will be liable to be proceeded against and punished accordingly (s.7A(7)). Similarly where the affairs of a body corporate are managed by its members the offence will arise in relation to the acts and defaults of a member in connection with his functions of management as if he were a director of the body corporate (s.7A(8)).

The Scottish offence of possession of salmon which have been unlawfully taken, along with its counterpart of possession of salmon in suspicious circumstances in England and Wales, appear to be a powerful buttress to the fishery offences which may be committed in the unlawful taking of salmon but have proved to be so difficult to enforce. At the same time they impose a need for caution upon those such as salmon farmers who legitimately take possession of, or trade in, salmon to avoid unwitting commission of the new offences. The need for caution justifies special emphasis in the case of the possession offences where taking possession of salmon where there is an objective reason for suspicion is, subject to the qualifications which have been discussed, an offence.

Chapter 15

Shellfishery Law

15.01 *The general nature of shellfishery law*

The practical distinction between fish farming and fishing is less clearly drawn in shellfish production than in other branches of aquaculture. The relative immobility of most traditionally cultivated kinds of shellfish means that enclosure in cages or other forms of confinement is unnecessary. In the absence of aquacultural containment it becomes difficult in some instances to distinguish shellfish which are the product of husbandry from wild populations. The difficulty of drawing a clear distinction between 'farming' and 'fishing for' shellfish in practice is reflected in the law by a similar lack of subdivision. Both farming and fishing for shellfish are encompassed by the general law of shellfisheries which is discussed in this chapter. Although some of the matters which are to be considered might be placed outside a strict definition of 'aquaculture', it is hoped that they provide a balanced account of the legal features of the most important aspects of the British shellfish production industry.

Although for most legal purposes 'shellfish' are defined to include *any* kind of crustaceans or molluscs, this chapter reflects the fact that commercial shellfishery activity in Britain is concentrated upon the production of a relatively small number of marine species, though there is increasing interest in the rearing of freshwater crayfish. The combination of aquacultural viability and commercial profitability of producing larger marine molluscs result in the widespread cultivation of oysters and mussels and the legal issues involved in the husbandry of these species occupy a large part of the following discussion. Despite the high commercial value of crustaceans such as lobsters, the scientific difficulties involved in their intensive culture are considerable, and aquacultural activity involving these species presently takes place on an experimental rather than commercial scale. Similarly, in respect of smaller and less highly valued species of shellfish such as cockles and whelks, aquacultural activity is confined to the management of a naturally occurring resource to prevent wasteful over-exploitation. In contexts such as these the main legal emphasis is placed upon conservational measures to ensure the maintenance of sustainable yields from shellfish stocks. This discussion of the law of shellfisheries, therefore, spans the regulation of both more intensive aquacultural forms of shellfish production and the balanced management of naturally occurring shellfish stocks.

The legal issues relating to shellfish considered in this chapter are in a number of respects closely related to general matters of aquaculture law dealt with elsewhere in this work. To gain a more complete picture of the law as it affects shellfisheries, therefore, this chapter needs to be read alongside the discussion of a number of other matters which may be relevant to shellfisheries. Shellfish production facilities may need development consent under planning law, (discussed in Chapter 2) and probably will involve the use of an area of the seabed for which a shellfishery lease will normally be required from the Crown Estate Commissioners (discussed in Chapter 3). Shellfishery ventures may be the subject of government or European financial assistance (discussed previously in [5.04] to [5.06]) but will be required to be registered with the appropriate Minister for disease control purposes (discussed previously in [6.02] to [6.03]). Shellfish farms share certain legal features with other forms of aquacultural activity in relation to the movement of fish (discussed in Chapter 8), disease control measures (discussed in Chapter 7) and the control of predators (discussed in Chapter 12). The sedentary nature of shellfisheries makes them especially vulnerable to shortcomings in water quality causing contamination of stock (discussed in [10.05]) and the possibility of contamination leads into a number of distinct legal provisions requiring the cleansing of shellfish for public health reasons (discussed in [16.03] and [16.04] below). On each of these matters cross reference is necessary to relate shellfish production to matters which have been considered as aspects of the general law of aquaculture.

A distinguishing feature of the law of shellfisheries is the relative antiquity of many of the legal provisions regulating the activity. From ancient times the value of shellfisheries has been appreciated and the rights surrounding them have been the subject of much legislation and litigation (see Nowak (1970) at p. 54; and Yonge (1966) at p. 152). Although past legislation governing shellfish has undergone re-enactment into the collection of statutes which presently regulate shellfisheries, several matters of law concerned with rights of shellfishery and the ownership of shellfish continue to be provided for under the common law. It is significant, however, that the common law of England and Wales has formulated different principles from those which apply in Scotland. For that reason the shellfishery laws of the two jurisdictions are discussed separately in the following account.

A range of Parliamentary enactments govern shellfisheries in Britain and potential difficulties of classification and interrelation of these provisions abound. The principal statute governing molluscan shellfisheries in Britain is the Sea Fisheries (Shellfish) Act 1967, concerned with such matters as private shellfishery rights, shellfish disease powers and seasons for the sale of shellfish. Surrounding this central enactment are a diverse collection of additional statutes with particular purposes and which apply within different jurisdictions. In the following account the various enactments concerning shellfish are presented according to their range of operation. Those enactments applicable to the whole of Britain are considered first, those applicable only to England and Wales second, and, third, those applicable only to Scotland. Finally, certain matters relating to the minimum size limits for particular categories of shellfish are determined as a direct consequence of a European Community Regulation. Following this ordering the enactments to be discussed are:

British shellfishery legislation
The Sea Fisheries (Shellfish) Act 1967 (see [15.04])
The Sea Fish (Conservation) Act 1967 (see [15.05])

The Fisheries Act 1981 (see [15.06])
The Coast Protection Act 1949 (see [15.07])

Shellfishery legislation applicable to England and Wales only
The Sea Fisheries Regulation Act 1966 (see [15.08])

Shellfishery legislation applicable to Scotland only
The Oyster Fisheries (Scotland) Act 1840 (see [15.09])
The Mussel Fisheries (Scotland) Act 1847 (see [15.10])
The Sea Fisheries (Scotland) Amendment Act 1885 (see [15.11])
The Inshore Fishing (Scotland) Act 1984 (see [15.12])

European regulation applicable to the United Kingdom
European Community Regulation 3094/86 (see [15.13])

15.02 Common law rights to shellfish in England and Wales

Although now modified in many respects by statute, the common law of
England and Wales incorporates the right to take shellfish as a part of the
general right of public fishery in the sea and in tidal waters and is enjoyed by
all members of the public (*Royal Fishery of the Banne case* (1610) Dav. Ir. 55; and
Attorney-General for British Columbia v. *Attorney-General for Canada* [1914] AC 153).
This principle is subject to the exceptions that a right of public fishery will not
exist where a person has acquired a private property interest of 'several
fishery' which serves to exclude the public right, or where the public right has
been restricted by Parliamentary enactment (see, for example, s.1 Sea
Fisheries (Shellfish) Act 1967, discussed in [15.04] below). In respect of the
taking of shellfish from the sea, therefore, the basic position is that this is
lawful where the transgression of private rights of shellfishery or breach of
statutory provisions for the conservation of shellfish are not involved (*Bagott*
v. *Orr* (1801) 2 Bos.&P 472; and Hall (1875) at pp. 186 to 217). This common
law right extends landward to the mean high water mark of ordinary tides
(*Lowe* v. *Govett* (1832) 3 B&Ad. 862; and *Attorney-General* v. *Chambers* (1854) 4 De
GM&G 206) and as far up any river as the tide ordinarily flows and reflows
(*Malcomson* v. *O'Dea* (1863) 10 HL Cas. 593). Seaward, the right of shellfishery
extends to the fishery limits of United Kingdom waters (*Loose* v. *Williams*
[1978] 3 All ER 89 and *Loose* v. *Castleton* (1978) 122 Sol.J. 487, affirming *Gann* v.
Free Fishers of Whitstable (1865) 11 HL Cas.192). This 'common of piscary'
encompasses the taking of lobsters, crabs, prawns, shrimps, oysters and
various other shellfish along with floating fish (Hall (1875) at p. 192).

The public right of shellfishery in tidal waters is subject to there being no
private, or 'several', fishery in those waters. As Hale states the position:

> 'The common people of England have regularly a liberty of fishing in the
> sea or creeks or arms thereof, as a public common of piscary, and may not
> without injury to their right be restrained of it, unless in such places or
> creeks or navigable rivers, where either the king or some particular subject
> hath gained a property exclusive of that common liberty.' (Hale (1875) p.
> vii)

Before Magna Carta in 1225 it was possible for the Crown to exclude the public right of fishery in the sea by making it exclusive either for the Crown itself (*Royal Fishery of the Banne case* (1610) Dav. Ir. 55) or some individual subject or corporation (*Neill* v. *Duke of Devonshire* (1882) 8 App Cas.135). Since Magna Carta it has been impermissible to do this except by statute (*Fitzhardinge* v. *Purcell* [1908] 2 Ch. 139). However, a number of private fisheries predating Magna Carta continue to exist in tidal waters. In these exceptional cases exclusive rights of fishing have been recognised as the property of the owner of the soil as a consequence of the existence and enjoyment of the right having been granted prior to Magna Carta (*Attorney-General for British Columbia* v. *Attorney-General for Canada* [1914] AC 153). Such a grant of a private and exclusive right of fishery may exist separately from any ownership of the soil of the seabed, and in circumstances where there is nothing to show that the grant was modern in origin it is reasonably presumed that the grant must have been created before legal memory (*Malcomson* v. *O'Dea* (1863) 10 HL Cas. 593; and *Re Company or Fraternity of Free Fishermen of Faversham* (1887) 36 Ch.D 329). In each case, however, the private right of fishery must be that of a particular individual or corporation, or a person claiming on their behalf. A public claim to take shellfish in a several tidal fishery cannot be maintained on behalf of an uncertain body of persons (*Goodman* v. *Mayor of Saltash* (1882) 7 App. Cas. 633).

The acquisition of property rights over shellfish by persons who have gathered them or expended effort in their cultivation is complicated by the general public right to shellfish under the common law of England and Wales. The basic position at common law is that, as wild creatures classified in law as animals *ferae naturae*, they cannot be stolen or become the subject of property until reduced into possession, or 'appropriated', by a person who then becomes their owner (s.4(4) Theft Act 1968, cited in [14.04] above; and see [17.04] below). Although the position is simplified under statute (see s.7(2) Sea Fisheries (Shellfish) Act 1967, discussed in [15.04] below), the issue of whether shellfish which are left in a bed to grow are appropriated for these purposes, may be a matter of some difficulty at common law. Hence in an early case it was decided that a felony was not committed in stealing oysters from oyster-lays, in an arm of the sea, even though the oysters concerned had not been produced there but had been brought from elsewhere for sale (*R* v. *Walford* (1803) 5 Esp 62). Likewise it has been held to be impermissible for oyster fishers to occupy a part of the foreshore for the storage of oysters, to the exclusion of others, and that they had no property in oysters so deposited (*Truro Corporation* v. *Rowe* (1902) 66 JP 821). By contrast, however, a distinction has been drawn between a private right of oyster fishery and the right of ownership of an oyster bed, termed an 'oyster laying', which is a form of property recognised in law independently of any right of private fishery (*Foster* v. *Warblington U.D.C.* (1906) 70 JP 233, at p. 239; and see [10.05] above). Hence where oysters are taken from their natural beds and thereby 'appropriated' to be placed in an area where there are no natural oysters and where the owner has a right of private property in the sea bed, they remain his property despite the existence of any rights of oyster fishery over the same area (see Coulson and Forbes (1952) at pp. 416 to 420).

The difficulty involved in establishing 'appropriation' of shellfish arose in *R* v. *Howlett* ((1968) 112 SJ 150 considered in Ministry of Agriculture, Fisheries and Food (1968)) where the accused took mussels from a natural bed which had been cultivated by another person who had a private right of shellfishery in the bed, by putting in wire netting to make a bank to prevent the mussels from being washed away by the sea. On appeal it was held that this method of cultivation did not serve to reduce the mussels into the possession of the person cultivating the bed. The mussels remained unowned wild creatures and the conviction for stealing them was quashed. Although there may be situations in which evidence can be produced of an established right to take shellfish amounting to reduction into possession (*R* v. *Downing* (1870) 23 LT 298; and *The Swift* (1901) 85 LT 346, discussed in [15.04H] below) the requirement of showing appropriation by an owner before a prosecution for theft (s.1 Theft Act 1968) will be successful remains a potential difficulty where shellfish are taken without authorisation. (Contrast s.7 Sea Fisheries (Shellfish) Act 1967, discussed in [15.04G] below.)

In circumstances where it cannot be satisfactorily established that shellfish have been reduced into possession by a person who cultivates them, for the purposes of a prosecution for theft, the more specific, though less serious, offence of 'taking or destroying fish', may be committed by the unauthorised taking of shellfish. Taking or destroying fish is committed where a person unlawfully takes or destroys, or attempts to take or destroy, any fish in water which is private property or in which there is any private right of fishery. On summary conviction of this offence a person will be liable to imprisonment for a term not exceeding three months or to a fine not exceeding level 3 on the standard scale, presently £400, or both (Sch.1 para.2(1) Theft Act 1968). Under previous legislation (s.24 Larceny Act 1861) it was established that this offence encompasses the taking of all kinds of fish, including all kinds of shellfish, in tidal or non-tidal waters (*Paley* v. *Birch* (1867) 16 LT 410). Thus in one case a trespasser was found guilty where crayfish were unlawfully taken from a private fishery (*Caygill* v. *Thwaite* (1885) 49 JP 614; following *Maldon* v. *Woolvert* (1840) 12 AD&E 13). In another case where a corporation had a private right of several fishery in a tidal river, an unauthorised person collected winkles from pools left by the receding tide. It was held that these were 'fish' within the offence of taking fish from water where there is a private right of fishery, and that the pools amounted to 'water' for the purposes of the offence (*Leavett* v. *Clark* [1915] 79 JP 296). It may be pointed out, however, that many shellfish are capable of being removed at times of low tide when beds are exposed and they are, arguably, not 'in water', in which case the provision would not apply.

It deserves re-emphasis that neither the offence of theft nor that of taking or destroying fish will be committed where there is a public right of fishery for shellfish. Moreover, there may be situations where prosecutions for neither offence will be successful for the reason that the accused person is able to maintain a *bona fide* claim of right to take shellfish though no *actual* right to do so is established. Where, in a hearing before justices of the peace, it transpires that the defence of the accused is that the taking of shellfish was justified by lawful entitlement, and there is some evidence of that entitlement, then the jurisdiction of the justices to hear the case will be ousted. Hence in one case where the accused was charged with an offence equivalent to that of taking or destroying fish (now Sch.1 para.2(1) Theft Act 1968) it was shown that the river where the offence had taken place was a tidal navigable river, where witnesses said that fishing had taken place during a forty year period without interruption. Despite the fact that the prosecutor was able to show that he owned a private right of fishery in the river through purchase of an adjoining manor, it was held on appeal that the accused's *bona fide* claim of entitlement to fish where there was ostensibly a public right to do so provided a ground on which his conviction by justices would be quashed (*R v. Stimpson* (1863) 27 JP 678).

15.03   *Common law rights to shellfish in Scotland*

The common law of Scotland regarding rights to shellfish is significantly different from that of England and Wales. Scottish common law is complicated by a threefold legal distinction drawn amongst the categories of shellfish. In the first category are placed oysters and mussels, in the second other molluscs such as cockles, limpets and clams, and in the third crustaceans such as lobsters and crabs. The common law rights arising in relation to shellfish in each of these three categories are different, and for that reason they are best considered in turn.

In Scotland, in contrast to England and Wales, oysters and mussels are not within the public right of fishery but are vested in the Crown. Under Scots law the patrimonial rights of the Crown are distinguished by the designations *regalia majora* and *regalia minora* according to their alienability (Gloag and Henderson (1987) s.39.2). Thus, *regalia majora*, such as the Crown's right to hold the seashore in trust for the public, are inalienable and cannot be granted to any other person by the Crown. By contrast, *regalia minora*, such as the right to salmon fishing, can be made the subject of a prerogative grant by the Crown to a particular person (*Gammel* v. *Commissioners of Woods and Forests* (1859) 3 Macq. 419). In accordance with this distinction, the Crown right to oysters and mussels has been held to be amongst the *regalia minora* so that a private right to take oysters and mussels in the sea is effectual where it is expressly granted by the Crown (Bell (1899) s.646). Where a right to oysters or mussels has not been granted, however, the right remains a part of the patrimony of the Crown and may only be exercised by the public where the permission of the Crown is expressly or tacitly given (*Grant* v. *Ross* (1764) Mor.Dict. 12801 and (1769) 6 Pat. App. 779).

The reason why oysters and mussels should be treated differently from other forms of molluscs or whitefish, that is sea fish other than salmon, which form a part of the *regalia majora* and in respect of which there is a public right of fishery, is not altogether clear. One, rather unsatisfactory, explanation which has been suggested is that the seabed, or *solum*, is amongst the *regalia minora* allowing the Crown to prevent persons using the seabed for purposes other than recognised public uses (*Lord Advocate* v. *Clyde Navigation Trustees* (1891) 19 R.174) or to make grants to persons to exploit minerals (*Lord Advocate* v. *Weymiss* [1900] AC 48). Because oysters and mussels attach themselves to the seabed 'with a peculiar tenacity' they are to be thought of as 'accessories of the soil', or *partes soli*, and therefore regarded as a part of the *solum* (*Duchess of Sutherland* v. *Watson* (1868) 6 M 199, at p. 213). Interestingly, in England, a right to take shellfish *shells* was doubted for the same reason (*Bagott* v. *Orr* (1801) 2 B&P 472), but in other cases contrasting views have been expressed (*Goodman* v. *Mayor of Saltash* (1882) 7 App Cas 633).

An alternative explanation which has been given for the classification of oysters and mussels amongst the *regalia minora* lies in the strength of the analogy with rights of salmon fishing which are also classified amongst the *regalia minora*. Salmon, along with oyster and mussels, are distinguished from other shellfish in that they have greater value for human food so that it is important to preserve them from indiscriminate fishing (Rankine *Land Ownership* p. 238, approved in *Parker* v. *Lord Advocate* [1904] AC 364 at p. 373) Hence it has been observed that:

'In a private river, a mussel-scalp belongs to the proprietor of the ground adjacent; in a public river, it belongs, like white fish, to the public, and consequently the use of it is open to every one of the lieges; but as such general use tends to root out every mussel-scalp, expediency, supported by practice, has introduced a prerogative of the Crown of gifting mussel-scalps to individuals, which has the effect to preserve them by the exclusive use given to the grantee.' (*Grant* v. *Ross* (1764) M.12,801; affirmed in *Parker* v. *Lord Advocate* [1904] AC 364, at p. 370)

It is evident, therefore, that the need for conservation of oyster and mussel fishery resources has been recognised from an early date and, on this account, forms a basis for their classification amongst the *regalia minora*.

Whatever the precise rationale for distinguishing oysters and mussels from other kinds of shellfish in Scots common law, their distinct status is unequivocally established. In the leading case of *Parker* v. *Lord Advocate* ([1904] AC 364) a prosecution was brought under s.1 of the Mussel Fisheries (Scotland) Act 1847, making it an offence of theft to take mussels from private beds (see [15.10] below, and also s.7(2) Sea Fisheries (Shellfish) Act 1967 discussed in [15.04G] below) against persons who had taken mussels from certain beds. The beds in question were subject to a sub-lease from the Crown granted in conformity with the Sea Fisheries Regulation (Scotland) Act 1895. (Now see s.1 Sea Fisheries (Shellfish) Act 1967, [15.04] below.) In their defence the accused asserted a right to fish for mussels in the defined area as members of the public and claimed that the fishery was vested in the Crown as trustee for the public and, therefore, could not be the subject of a grant to a private individual. On appeal to the House of Lords, it was conclusively affirmed that mussel beds form part of the *regalia minora*, and as such it was within the capacity of the Crown to convey or lease such beds to a subject. Since this had been lawfully accomplished under the provisions of the 1895 Act, the accused were guilty of the offence of theft of the mussels.

The second category of shellfish arising under Scottish common law is that of 'small shellfish', which includes all molluscs other than oysters and mussels. Hence, cockles, limpets, clams, whelks and other small molluscs apart from oysters and mussels are subject to public right where they are found on the foreshore or beyond it and can be reached by the public in a legal manner. Authority for this proposition is to be found in a passage from Balfour's *Practicks* which was affirmed in *Hall* v. *Whillis*. ((1852) 14 D 324; Balfour (1754); and Bell (1899) s.646). In this case an action was brought to prevent fishermen taking limpets from rocks and it was held that limpets and similar shellfish are open to the public because they are capable of motion and not capable of appropriation. Although it might be argued that at certain stages in their development oysters and mussels are also capable of motion, the greater degree of motion of small shellfish was held to justify their assimilation to the category of white fish, the right to fish for which is a matter of public right within the *regalia majora*.

The third category of shellfish provided for under Scottish common law is that of the larger crustaceans, specifically lobsters and crabs. Because lobsters and crabs occupy an intermediate position between floating fish and sedentary shellfish they can not readily be assimilated to either category. Perhaps for this reason the law on their status is uncertain with no clear authority on the question of whether they are capable of being the subject of a Crown grant to an individual. The only case in which the matter was raised, *Duke of Portland* v. *Gray* ((1832) 11 S.14) was decided on the ground of a lack of possession of the lobsters concerned. It was considered whether a finding of possession would have been sufficient to have established an exclusive right to the fishery, but the issue was never decided. Despite the lack of decisive authority on the point, however, at least one commentator has suggested that lobster fishing is a public right for the reason that, as a matter of practice, the Crown does not make grants of this right (Tait (1928) at p. 336, citing Stewart (1892) at p. 82).

From the preceding discussion it is likely that, with the exception of oysters and mussels which have been the subject of a private grant by the Crown, or are protected by statute (see Oyster Fisheries (Scotland) Act 1840, discussed in [15.09] below; Mussel Fisheries (Scotland) Act 1847, discussed in [15.10] below; and s.7(2) Sea Fisheries Shellfish Act 1967, discussed [15.04G] below) all other shellfish may be taken as a matter of public right within the common law of Scotland. This gives rise to a similar difficulty to that discussed in relation to the common law of England and Wales, concerning the rights of property in shellfish possessed by persons who have collected or cultivated them. In relation to the law of England and Wales it was noted that the basic position was that shellfish were not owned until appropriated by some person, and cannot be stolen until appropriated. Outside the exception of oysters and mussels which have been made the subject of private ownership, the position in Scottish common law is the same.

The principle of *res nullius* in Scottish common law requires that a person can only steal that which belongs to someone else, or that something which has never had an owner cannot be stolen but belongs rightfully to the first taker (Gordon (1978) s.14–40; and see [14.06] above and [17.04] below). Whilst in the sea shellfish, other than oysters and mussels, like white fish have no owner, but once caught in a net or otherwise appropriated into possession they become the property of the taker and can then be stolen from him (*John Huie* (1842) 1 Broun 383). As a matter of common law this principle even applied when the taking of fish was a breach of the rights of the Crown or a landowner with a private right, so that theft was not committed and the wrongful taker even gained ownership of his unlawfully acquired haul (*Scott* v. *Everitt* (1853) 15 D.288). As will be seen, however, this position has been reversed by statute in certain situations by the vesting of ownership of shellfish in the owner of the right of shellfishery in the bed in which they are found (see s.7(3) Sea Fisheries (Shellfish) Act 1967, discussed in [15.04G] below).

BRITISH SHELLFISHERY LEGISLATION

15.04   *Sea Fisheries (Shellfish) Act 1967*

A.   Legislative background and history

It is evident from the preceding discussion that the common law rights of public shellfishery in England and Wales and in Scotland raise a number of issues of difficulty and complexity. Today, however, common law rights to shellfish have to be read subject to far-reaching statutory modifications which extend and clarify property rights over shellfish, and in many respects allow for more effective utilisation of shellfishery resources than provided for under the common law. Most significantly, statutory modifications have had the effect of resolving the difficulties surrounding property rights in certain kinds of cultivated shellfish, discussed previously, by vesting their absolute ownership in the owners of private shellfish beds (although some difficulties remain; see Lort-Phillips, Denman and Edwards (undated)). In general legal terms this is a rare, if not unique, exception to the rule that only 'qualified' rights of property can be held in wild animals, with 'absolute' ownership being usually reserved for domesticated animals alone (Bonyhardy (1987) at p. 264; and Blackstone (1766), discussed in [14.06] above and [17.04] below). In practical terms the effect of this alteration of property rights is to allow those cultivating shellfish a higher degree of protection for their stock than would be provided for under common law.

   In addition to the modification of property rights in shellfish, statutory reforms have introduced a range of conservational measures aimed at the better utilisation of shellfishery resources. These include various powers to prohibit movements of shellfish or to take measures to combat disease or pests of shellfish, and the regulation of seasons for sale and size limits for shellfish. Although a complete picture of the statutory provisions governing shellfish in England and Wales and Scotland involves the scan of a diverse collection of enactments, discussed below, the plan of statutory regulation of shellfisheries is simplified by the consolidation of a number of former enactments in the form of the Sea Fisheries (Shellfish) Act 1967. This Act now constitutes the main basis for molluscan shellfishery regulation in Britain.

   The Sea Fisheries (Shellfish) Act 1967 is primarily a consolidation of provisions from three earlier statutes governing shellfisheries: the Sea Fisheries Act 1868, the Fisheries (Oyster, Crab and Lobster) Act 1877, and the Sea Fish Industry Act 1962 (Law Commission and Scottish Law Commission (1967)). The 1868 Act, which itself largely re-enacted the provisions of the Oyster and Mussel Fisheries Act 1866, sought to halt a decline in the productivity of oyster fisheries due to general failure of oyster spat. This decline had been investigated by the Commissioners on Sea Fisheries who reported in 1866 advocating the creation of exclusive oyster beds in order to improve long-term productivity (Royal Commission on Sea Fisheries (1866) Vol.1 p. cv; and Anon. (1877)). This recommendation was originally adopted by empowering the Board of Trade to make orders for the establishment or improvement, and the maintenance and regulation, of fisheries for oysters and mussels (s.3 Sea Fisheries Act 1866). The power was later extended to fisheries for cockles (s.1 Sea Fisheries Act 1884) and today the corresponding provisions have been further extended to apply to clams and any other molluscs of a kind specified by regulations (s.1(1) Sea Fisheries (Shellfish) Act 1967, as amended by s.15(2) Sea Fisheries Act 1968). The original powers granted to the Board of Trade are now vested in the Minister of Agriculture, Fisheries and Food in respect of fisheries in England, and the respective Secretaries of State in relation to Wales and Scotland.

Of the other enactments that were consolidated in the 1967 Act, the Fisheries (Oyster, Crab and Lobster) Act 1877 provided the Board of Trade with the power to make orders restricting the taking of oysters, crabs and lobsters. The 1877 Act also fixed the close season for oysters and prohibited the sale of crabs in certain conditions, and under-sized crabs and lobsters. The Sea Fish Industry Act 1962 contained provisions having as their object the elimination, or prevention of the spread of diseases and pests affecting shellfish (ss.19 to 26 Sea Fish Industry Act 1962). Amongst other things these provisions allowed for the prohibition of importation of shellfish into certain areas.

Having brought together provisions from the three earlier fishery enactments, therefore, the general coverage of the Sea Fisheries (Shellfish) Act 1967 encompasses three broad areas of regulation. First, Ministerial powers are provided for in respect of the grant of rights of several fishery and of a regulated fishery, along with measures for the protection of property rights in such fisheries and related matters (ss.1 to 11 Sea Fisheries (Shellfish) Act 1967). Second, powers are provided with regard to the general protection of shellfisheries by prohibiting the deposit and importation of shellfish in certain cases and elimination of disease and pests affecting shellfish (ss.12 to 15). Third, offences are created with respect to the sale of oysters at specified times of the year, and the taking and sale of certain crabs and lobsters, along with powers of enforcement relating to these offences (ss.16 to 18). Within these areas the 1967 Act is the principal enactment governing shellfisheries in England and Wales and Scotland.

B.   Ministerial orders as to fisheries for shellfish

Provision for the creation of private rights of shellfishery under the Sea Fisheries (Shellfish) Act 1967 arises by means of the exercise of a power of the appropriate Minister to provide by order for the establishment or improvement, and for the maintenance and regulation, of a fishery for shellfish of specified kinds (s.1 and Sch.1 Sea Fisheries (Shellfish) Act 1967). The 'appropriate Minister' means the Minister of Agriculture, Fisheries and Food in relation to England, and the respective Secretaries of State in relation to Wales and Scotland (s.22(1)). 'Shellfish' in the context of an order of this kind initially included oysters, mussels, cockles, clams (s.1(1), as amended by s.15(2) Sea Fisheries Act 1968). A Ministerial power exists, however, to include any other molluscs of a kind specified in regulations and this has recently been exercised to extend the definition of 'shellfish' to include scallops and queens (Shellfish (Specification of Molluscs) Regulations 1987, SI 1987 No.218; and generally see, Ministry of Agriculture, Fisheries and Food (1980A) and (1980B)).

A Ministerial order establishing an exclusive shellfishery may be made in respect of any portion of the shore and bed of the sea, or of an estuary or tidal river, above or below, or partly above and partly below, low water mark, and within waters adjacent to Great Britain to a distance of six nautical miles measures from the baselines from which the breadth of the territorial sea is measured (s.1(1) Sea Fisheries (Shellfish) Act 1967, as amended by Sch.2 para.15 Fishery Limits Act 1976). The order may, if considered desirable, provide for the constitution of a board or body corporate for the purposes of the order (s.1(1) as amended). An order of this kind may only be made after application to the Minister has been made in an approved form which is prescribed by regulations (Several and Regulated Fisheries (Form of Application) Regulations 1987, SI 1987 No.217).

A Ministerial order may confer, for a maximum period of 60 years, a right of several fishery with respect to the whole of the area of the fishery to which the order relates, or a right of regulating a fishery with respect to the whole of that area, or a right of several fishery with respect to a specified part of that area and a right of regulating a fishery with respect to the remainder (s.1(3) Sea Fisheries (Shellfish) Act 1967). Subsequent clarification of the scope the Ministerial power has provided that the power to make an order conferring a right of regulating a shellfishery is to be construed as including a power to enable the grantees, with the Minister's consent, to impose restrictions upon and make regulations respecting the dredging, fishing for and taking of shellfish of a description specified in the order (s.15(3) Sea Fisheries Act 1968). Further elaboration has provided that where an order imposes tolls or royalties upon persons dredging, fishing for and taking specified descriptions of shellfish within the fishery, this is to be construed as conferring upon the grantees, with the Minister's consent, the power to vary the tolls or royalties (s.15(4) Sea Fisheries Act 1968).

Explicit reservations are made in respect of Ministerial orders as to shellfisheries in certain areas, so that no order is to be made over any portion of the sea shore which belongs to Her Majesty in right of the Crown, or forms part of the possessions of the Duchy of Lancaster or of the Duchy of Cornwall, except with the appropriate consent. The 'appropriate consent' is that of the Crown Estate Commissioners (see Chapter 3) or the Chancellor of the Duchy of Lancaster, the Duke of Cornwall or other persons empowered to dispose of lands of the Duchy of Cornwall (s.1(4) Sea Fisheries (Shellfish) Act 1967). Protection is given for established rights in that no order is to take away or abridge any right of several fishery except with the consent of the person enjoying that right. Also specifically preserved are any right on, to or over any portion of the sea shore, which is enjoyed by any person under any local or special Act of Parliament or any Royal charter, letters patent, prescription, or immemorial usage, except with the consent of that person (s.1(5)). Essentially, therefore, pre-existing common law and statutory rights of shellfishery are preserved, and in some respects, it will be seen, extended by the 1967 Act.

The list of several and regulating shellfishery orders presently in effect is as shown in Table 15.1 below.

C.   Effect of a grant of right of several fishery

Where a Ministerial order confers a right of several fishery, the grantees will have the exclusive right of depositing, propagating, dredging, fishing for and taking shellfish of any description to which the order applies, within the

Table 15.1

List of Several and Regulating Shellfishery Orders

(as at October 1988)

England

Several Orders

Blakeney Harbour Mussel Fishery Order 1966 (Mussels)
Brancaster Staithe Fishery Order 1979 (Oysters, Mussels, Clams)
Calshot Oyster Fishery Order 1982 (Oysters)
Emsworth Channel Fishery Order 1975 (Oysters, Mussels, Cockles)
Falkenham Creek Reach Oyster Fishery Order 1976 (Oysters)
Horsey Island Oyster Fishery Order 1963 (Oysters)
Hunstanton Le Strange Fishery Order 1947 (Oysters, Mussels, Cockles)
Marchwood Clam Fishery Order 1972 (Clams)
Old Hall Farm Creek Fishery Order 1972 (Oysters)
Overy Creek Mussel and Cockle Fishery Order 1969 (Mussels, Cockles)
Portchester Channel Oyster Fishery Order 1986 (Oysters)
River Nene Fishery Order 1986 (Oysters, Mussels, Cockles, Clams)
River Taw Mussel Fishery Order 1962 (Mussels)
Southampton Water (Chilling) Oyster Fishery Order 1984 (Oysters)
Stanswood Bay Oyster Fishery Order 1973 (Oysters)
Tollesbury and Mersea (Blackwater) Fishery Order 1938 (Oysters)
Waddeton Oyster Fishery Order 1972 (Oysters)
Yealm Fishery Order 1914, as extended (Oysters, Mussels)

Several Orders with Power to Grant Sub-leases (Grantees not to exercise rights themselves)

Wells Harbour Shell Fishery Order 1972 (Oysters, Mussels, Cockles, Clams)
Boston Several Fishery Order 1930 (Oysters, Mussels, Cockles)
Lynn Several Fishery Order 1932, as varied (Mussels)

Regulating Orders

Morecambe Bay Mussel Fishery Order 1978 (Mussels)
River Teign Mussel Fishery Order 1966 (Mussels)
Solent Oyster Fishery Order 1980 (Oysters)
Truro Port Fishery Order 1936, as varied (Oysters, Mussels)

Regulating Orders (with powers to Grant Sub-leases) (Grantees not to exercise rights themselves)

Boston Deeps Fishery Order 1930 (Oysters, Mussels)
Lynn Deeps Fishery Order 1932, as varied (Oysters, Mussels)

Regulating Orders with Power to Grant Leases of Several Rights

Poole Fishery Order 1915, as varied and extended (Oysters, Mussels, Cockles, Clams)

Wales

Several Orders with Power to Grant Sub-leases (Grantees not to Exercise rights themselves)

Menai Straits Oyster and Mussel Fishery Order 1962, as amended (Oysters, Mussels)

Menai Straits (West) Oyster Mussel and Clam Fishery Order 1978 (Oysters, Mussels, Clams)

Regulating Orders

Burry Inlet Cockle Fishery Order 1965 (Cockles)
Conwy Mussel Fishery Order 1912, as amended and varied (Mussels)

---

terms of the order, but subject to any restrictions and exceptions to which it is subject. Specifically, this allows the grantees to make and maintain beds for shellfish; to collect shellfish at any season and remove them from place to place and deposit them where the grantees think fit; and to do all other things which the grantees think proper for obtaining, storing and disposing of the product of their fishery (s.2(1) Sea Fisheries (Shellfish) Act 1967). A 'shellfish bed' is defined to mean any bed or ground in which shellfish are usually found or which is used for the propagation or cultivation of shellfish (s.22(2)). Notably in this context and others arising under the 1967 Act, however, references to a 'bed for shellfish' or a 'shellfish bed' or an 'oyster bed' are to include reference to any structure floating on, or standing or suspended in, water for the propagation or cultivation of shellfish or oysters (s.34 Fisheries Act 1981). This extension of the law allows the modern practice of suspending shellfish from floating 'rafts', in order to reduce vulnerability to predation, to be brought within the terms of the 1967 Act.

D. Effect of grant of right of regulating a fishery

As an alternative, or in addition, to the grant of a right of several fishery by Ministerial order, such an order may grant a right of regulating a shellfishery. Normally regulating orders of this kind are made to local sea fisheries committees (Under Sea Fisheries Regulation Act 1966, see [15.08] below) or other public bodies (Cole (1956) at p. 8; and Nowak (1970) at p. 64) who administer the fishery in the best interests of shellfish conservation and efficient utilisation. An order conferring a right of regulating a fishery for any specified description of shellfish may impose restrictions on, or make regulations respecting, the dredging, fishing for and taking of any specified description of shellfish, or impose tolls or royalties upon persons so doing. Where provided for by a Ministerial order, the grantees will be empowered to carry into effect and enforce restrictions and regulations imposed by the order; to levy tolls or royalties provided for by the order; to provide for depositing and propagating shellfish to which the order applies for improving and cultivating the regulated fishery (s.3(1) Sea Fisheries (Shellfish) Act 1967).

Subject to certain licensing powers in respect of regulated fisheries which are discussed below, it is provided that all restrictions, regulations, tolls and royalties relating to the fishery are to apply to all persons equally and to be applied for the general benefit, improvement and cultivation of the fishery (s.3(2)). Any person who dredges, fishes for or takes shellfish of any description to which an order applies, in contravention of a restriction or regulation, or without paying a toll or royalty is guilty of an offence. The punishment for this offence is, on summary conviction, a fine not exceeding level 2 on the standard scale, presently £100. In addition the guilty person is to forfeit all shellfish which have been taken or, if they have been sold, a sum equal to their value, and any shellfish or forfeited sum is to be recoverable in a like manner as a fine (s.3(3)). The court by which any forfeiture is imposed may direct that the shellfish or sum forfeited is to be delivered or paid to the grantees or is to be applied by them for the improvement and cultivation of the regulated fishery (s.3(4)).

E.　Licensing powers over regulated fisheries

Where a Ministerial order confers a right of regulating a shellfishery, certain licensing powers are provided for. Specifically, the order may include restrictions prohibiting persons from dredging, fishing for or taking, shellfish to which the order applies except under the authority of a licence issued by the grantees (s.4(2)). Where an order imposes any such restrictions then licences may be issued under the order authorising the dredging, fishing for or taking of shellfish at a time, in a manner, and to an extent determined by the grantees (s.4(4)). If the issuing of licences is proposed by the grantees, unless it is proposed to issue licences to all applicants, the grantees are to inform the Minister of their intention and he may give directions as to the exercise of the licensing power in this respect (s.4(5)). If the grantees issue or withhold licences without complying with the duty to notify the Minister they are to be taken not to be properly carrying into effect the restrictions imposed by the order. Nonetheless, no licence issued in contravention of this requirement is to be invalid only because it was issued in breach of the grantee's duty to notify the Minister (s.4(6)). A licence may, with the consent of the Minister, be cancelled by the grantees if the person to whom it is issued, having been convicted of an offence of contravening a restriction imposed by the order, is subsequently convicted of another such offence. Otherwise a licence is not to be cancelled before it is due to expire, unless the person to whom the licence was issued dies or surrenders it (s.4(7)).

F.　Cesser of shellfishery rights

Where a right of several fishery or a right of regulating a fishery has been conferred by a Ministerial order, but the Minister is not satisfied that the grantees are properly exercising their rights under the order, he may terminate the right which has been granted. This allows for the elimination of 'dormant fisheries' which occupy good shellfishery areas but put them to bad use by neglect or failure to realise their full fishery potential (Nowak (1970) at p. 84). Hence, where the Minister is not satisfied that the grantees are properly cultivating the ground for shellfish of any description to which the order applies, or properly enforcing any restrictions and regulations contained in the order, and levying any tolls or royalties imposed under it, he may issue a certificate to that effect. The consequence of certification in such circumstances is that the right of several fishery or of regulating the fishery is to be absolutely determined in relation to the area specified in the order (s.5(1) Sea Fisheries (Shellfish) Act 1967).

For the purposes of deciding whether a right of shellfishery is to be determined the Minister may make inquiries and conduct examinations, through an inspector or otherwise, and may require from the grantees such information as he thinks proper. It is for the grantees to afford all facilities for inquiries and examination and to provide the information which is sought (s.5(2)). For these purposes any inspector or other person appointed by the Minister may take evidence and require the attendance of any person, and examine him on oath or otherwise, and may administer an oath or take any affidavit or declaration for the purpose of the inquiry or examination (s.5(3)).

The person authorised by the Minister for the purpose of carrying out an inquiry or examination is also to have the right, at any reasonable time, to enter any land within the limits of the fishery to obtain and take away samples of any shellfish. When the purpose for which the sample was taken has been satisfied, the person by whom it was taken may dispose of it as he may determine (s.5(4)). The right of entry is not to be exercised unless at least 24 hours' notice has been given to the occupier of the land, and also to the grantees if they are not the occupiers of the land. The person exercising the right must, if so requested, produce written evidence of his authority before entering (s.5(5)). As with the duty upon the grantees to afford facilities for inquiries and examinations, discussed above, the grantees are also to afford facilities for the exercise of any right of entry exercisable, after giving notice, for the purpose of obtaining samples of shellfish (s.5(6)).

It is an offence for any person to obstruct an inspector or other person appointed by the Minister in the exercise of any power or right of inquiry, examination or sampling, or to refuse or without reasonable excuse fail to provide any information reasonably required by the inspector or other person. The penalty for this offence is, on summary conviction, a fine not exceeding level 3 on the standard scale, presently £400 (s.5(7)). It was noted with some concern in the Parliamentary debates surrounding this provision that it is capable of making a person guilty of an offence merely for refusing to answer questions, perhaps for fear of incrimination (751 HC DEB 1967 Col. 1512). In response, however, it was thought that refusal to answer questions in such circumstances would amount to a 'reasonable' excuse for these purposes and, therefore, no offence would be committed (751 HC DEB 1967 Col. 1516).

G. Protection of fisheries

By contrast with the difficulties involved in establishing common law property rights to shellfish, explained above, one of the key modifications provided for under the 1967 Act is the vesting of a right of property in shellfish where they are within a several fishery created under the Act. Hence where a Ministerial order creates a right of several fishery all shellfish, of a kind prescribed by the order and within the area of the order, are deemed to be the absolute property of the grantees and in the actual possession of the grantees in all courts and for all purposes. Likewise, where a private oyster bed is owned independently of the 1967 Act, and is sufficiently marked out or sufficiently known as such, all oysters in or on the bed are deemed to be the absolute property, and in actual possession, of the owner (s.7(2) Sea Fisheries (Shellfish) Act 1967). Accordingly, if such shellfish or oysters are removed from a bed, unless they are sold in market overt or disposed of by or under the authority of the grantees or owners, they remain the absolute property of the grantees or owners who retain, for all purposes in all courts, the right to the possession of the shellfish (s.7(3)).

In order to secure the protection of shellfish within the area of a fishery in which a right of several fishery is conferred by Ministerial order, or within the limits of a private oyster bed, it is made a criminal offence to disturb the bed in specified ways. Thus it is an offence for any person other than the grantees or owners, or their agent or employee, knowingly to do any of the following things:

(a) to use any implement of fishing except (i) a line and hook, or (ii) a net adapted solely for catching floating fish and so used as not to disturb or injure in any manner shellfish of the description in question or any bed or fishery therefore;
(b) to dredge for any ballast or other substance except under a lawful authority for improving the navigation;
(c) to deposit any ballast, rubbish or other substance;
(d) to place any implement, apparatus or thing prejudicial or likely to be prejudicial to any such shellfish, bed or fishery except for a lawful purpose of navigation or anchorage;
(e) to disturb or injure in any manner, except for a lawful purpose of navigation or anchorage, any such shellfish, bed or fishery.

A person found guilty of the offence will be liable, on summary conviction, to a fine not exceeding level 3 on the standard scale, presently £400. In addition he will be liable to make full compensation to the grantees or owners for all damage sustained by reason of the unlawful act (s.7(4)). By way of an explicit exception to this offence it is provided that it will not be unlawful for a person to do the things mentioned if, in the case of a several fishery granted by Ministerial order, the limits of the fishery are not sufficiently marked out in a manner prescribed under the order, or if no sufficient notice of the limits of the fishery has been given to the person in a prescribed manner. Similarly, in the case of a private oyster bed, no offence will be committed if the bed is not sufficiently marked out and known as such (s.7(5)).

The potential evidential difficulties involved in establishing that a several fishery granted by a Ministerial order is sufficiently marked out to prevent the preceding defence arising are made less problematic by the application of certain presumptions. Whenever it becomes necessary in any legal proceedings to show that there has been buoying or other sufficient marking of the limits of any fishery for shellfish to which an order applies, or that the publication, posting or distribution of notices of those limits have been complied with, this may be shown by certification. That is, a certificate issued by a senior official of the Minister's department certifying that marking requirements have been complied with, or the appropriate notice has been duly published, will be received as evidence of compliance with those requirements or publication of that notice in any legal proceedings in which this needs to be shown (s.8).

H.   Case law on the protection of fisheries

The operation of the provisions relating to the protection of shellfisheries, and the proof of their delimitation, are well illustrated by the case of *Smith* v. *Cooke* ((1914) 79 JP 245) concerning the application of corresponding provisions under earlier legislation (ss.51 and 53 Sea Fisheries Act 1868). In this case a local statute gave a private and exclusive right of depositing, propagating and fishing for oysters, and stipulated that all oysters should be the absolute property of the lessee and be deemed to be in his possession. Despite the fact that the extent of the fishery was sufficiently marked out by buoys and notices, and the accused knew of the oyster bed, he fished in the area with a trawl net which was found to have disturbed and injured the oysters. On prosecution for the offence of knowingly using an instrument for fishing within the limits of a private oyster bed (s.53 Sea Fisheries Act 1868, now s.7(4)(a) Sea Fisheries (Shellfish) Act 1967) the accused claimed that, as the waters concerned were an arm of the sea, there was a public right of fishery which was not defeated by the existence of the private fishery and, therefore, the jurisdiction of the justices to hear the case was ousted by his claim of right (see [15.02] above on claims of right). It was held that the right claimed by the accused was not capable of existing in law given the terms of creation of the private right of fishery under the legislation. Moreover, the fact of his honest though mistaken belief of a claim of right did not prevent his being guilty of the offence of unlawful fishing within the limits of the fishery.

In *The Swift* ((1901) 85 LT 346), a civil action was brought by the owners of a private oyster bed against the owners of a vessel which had grounded on the bed and caused damage to the bed and the destruction of a large quantity of oysters. (Now see s.7(4)(e) Sea Fisheries (Shellfish) Act 1967, discussed in [15.04G] above.) It was found that the bed had been clearly marked by beacons and that warning was given by a watch-boat of the existence of the bed, and that the captain of the vessel knew, or ought to have known, of the location of the bed. Since the grounding could not be justified as the exercise of an ordinary right of navigation, it was found that this was an act of negligence for which the owners of the vessel were responsible. Because the owners of the bed possessed a property right in the soil of the bed, they were entitled to compensation for the trespass involved in the disturbance to the bed. In addition, the effect of the legislation protecting shellfisheries (s.51 Sea Fisheries Act 1868, now see s.7(2) Sea Fisheries (Shellfish) Act 1967, discussed in [15.04G] above) was to vest ownership of the oysters in them and so they were entitled to compensation for the damage to the oysters.

In contrast to the decision in *The Swift* it is noteworthy that the offence of disturbing or injuring shellfish beds is subject to the exception that this is permitted for a lawful purpose of navigation or anchorage (s.7(4)(e) Sea Fisheries (Shellfish) Act 1967, discussed in [15.04G] above). This is in accordance with the acknowledged common law principle that individual rights of fishery in navigable waters are subject to the right of the public to use the waters for all purposes of navigation (*Anon* (1808) 1 Camp 517n; and

Gann v. *Whitstable Free Fishers* (1865) 11 HL Cas. 192). In particular, this may justify the grounding of a vessel where this is necessary for the convenient passage of a vessel. Where grounding takes place, however, damage to oyster beds is not justified where it would have been possible to have avoided it (*Colchester Corporation* v. *Brooke* (1846) 10 JP 217; and see also *The Octavia Stella* (1887) 52 LT 632; and *Whitstable Free Fishers* v. *Foreman* (1868) 32 JP 596).

I. Grants and loans for the restoration of fisheries

In addition to the Ministerial powers relating to the creation and regulation of several and regulated shellfisheries, the 1967 Act also incorporates a number of conservational provisions concerned with shellfish disease and pest control and the restoration of affected fisheries (generally, see Chapter 7 above on fish disease). The first of these is the power of the Minister of Agriculture, Fisheries and Food in England and the respective Secretaries of State in Wales and Scotland, to make grants and loans for the restoration of shellfish fisheries which have been damaged by disease or pest (see also Chapter 5 above on financial assistance for aquaculture). Thus the appropriate Minister, with the approval of the Treasury, may make grants or loans to any person in respect of any expenses incurred, or to be incurred by him, in the cleansing and reinstating, including restocking, of any shellfish beds which have been infected by any disease or pest. This power is specifically limited to either a shellfish bed within the limits of a fishery in respect of which a Ministerial order under the 1967 Act is presently in force, or any other shellfish bed used for the propagation or cultivation of oysters, mussels or cockles, in respect of which a person has an exclusive right to take oysters, mussels or cockles (s.9 Sea Fisheries (Shellfish) Act 1967).

J. Power to prohibit deposit of shellfish

An important power in relation to the control of shellfish disease allows the Minister of Agriculture, Fisheries and Food in England, and the respective Secretaries of State in Wales and Scotland, to designate, by order, any waters in their areas and to prohibit the deposit of shellfish of any description in those waters (generally, see Chapter 8 above on the movement of fish). The shellfish in relation to which the power arises are shellfish from any bed outside the designated waters or shellfish from any shellfish bed in an area specified in the order (s.12(1) Sea Fisheries (Shellfish) Act 1967). These provisions apply in relation to all tidal waters, whether forming part of the sea or not, within the seaward limits of the territorial waters adjacent to Britain (see [3.02] above). They also apply to all inland waters from which, in the opinion of the appropriate Minister, diseases or pests carried by shellfish deposited in them may be conveyed into the tidal waters to which the prohibition applies (s.12(2) Sea Fisheries (Shellfish) Act 1967). A prohibition order of this kind designating waters may also designate land adjacent to those waters if it is land from which, in the opinion of the appropriate Minister, diseases or pests carried by shellfish deposited on it may be conveyed into those waters. Correspondingly, any prohibition imposed upon depositing shellfish in waters is also to apply to depositing shellfish on adjacent land (s.12(3)). Where the appropriate Minister considers it desirable for the purpose of preventing the spread of diseases or pests carried by shellfish, an order of this kind may also prohibit the taking from any waters or land designated by the order of shellfish of any description, or of shellfish of a description specified in the order (s.12(3A), as inserted by s.6(1) Diseases of Fish Act 1983).

Ministerial orders prohibiting the deposit of shellfish may be made subject to exception if the shellfish concerned are deposited or taken under the authority of a licence granted by the appropriate Minister and that any conditions in the licence are complied with (s.12(4), as amended by s.6(1) Diseases of Fish Act 1983). If a person deposits any shellfish in any waters or on any land in contravention of an order of this kind, and is convicted of an offence in respect of that contravention, then the Minister has the power to remove the shellfish from the waters or land concerned. The Minister may also remove from the water or land any other shellfish which, in his opinion, may have become affected by any disease or pest carried by the shellfish so deposited (s.12(5)). Shellfish removed in this way are to be disposed of, whether by destruction, sale or otherwise, as the Minister may think fit. The Minister is entitled to recover from the person convicted any expenses reasonably incurred in removing the shellfish or disposing of them (s.12(6)).

In accordance with the Ministerial power to prohibit the deposit of shellfish two orders are presently in force. The first is the Molluscan Shellfish (Control of Deposit) Order 1974 (SI 1974 No.1555, as amended by SI 1983 No.159; and, generally, see Ministry of Agriculture, Fisheries and Food (1977)) which designates areas of tidal waters within the seaward limits of the territorial sea adjacent to England and Wales and prohibits the deposit in any area so designated of molluscan shellfish taken from a shellfish bed outside the area. The prohibition is subject to an exception where molluscan shellfish are deposited under the authority of, and in compliance with any conditions specified in, a licence granted by the Minister of Agriculture, Fisheries and Food or the Secretary of State for Wales. The Order also designates certain land, adjacent to the designated waters, on which the deposit of molluscan shellfish is prohibited.

The second instance in which the Ministerial power to prohibit the deposit of shellfish has been exercised is under the the Lobsters (Control of Deposit) Order 1981 (SI 1981 No.994). This Order designates specified areas of tidal water within the seaward limits of the territorial waters adjacent to England and Wales and Scotland, and any area of inland water which is used for treating or storing shellfish from which water is capable of being discharged into any of the specified areas of tidal water. The Order prohibits the deposit in any area so designated of lobsters taken from any shellfish bed outside that area except under the authority of, and in accordance with any conditions specified in, a licence granted by the Minister of Agriculture, Fisheries and Food, or the Secretary of State for Wales or the Secretary of State for Scotland. The Order also designates certain land adjacent and within one mile of the designated waters, on which the deposit of lobsters is prohibited.

K.   Power to prohibit importation of shellfish

Where any waters are for the time being designated by an order prohibiting the deposit of shellfish, the appropriate Minister is empowered to make an order designating any part of the coast or other land adjacent to the waters.

Having so designated an area of land he may prohibit shellfish of any
description specified in the order from being imported into that area, except
at such places as may be specified (s.13(1) Sea Fisheries (Shellfish) Act 1967).
A person contravenes an order of this kind if any shellfish to which the
prohibition applies are imported in contravention of the order, and he is in
possession, or is in any way entitled to the custody or control, of the shellfish
at the time when they are imported (s.13(2)). For these purposes 'imported'
means imported on board any vessel, hovercraft or aircraft, whether from a
place outside Britain or not (s.13(4)).

The Ministerial power to prohibit the importation of shellfish has been
exercised in the Lobsters (Control of Importation) Order 1981 (SI 1981
No.995). This Order designates an area consisting of all land which is within
one mile of any of the areas of tidal or inland water designated by the Order
prohibiting the deposit of lobsters discussed previously (Lobsters (Control of
Deposit) Order 1981, SI 1981 No.994, see [15.04]] above). The prohibition
which is imposed is upon the importation into the designated area of land of
lobsters the deposit of which would be a contravention of the deposit order.
Accordingly, the importation of lobsters into the area designated is not
prohibited if the deposit of the lobsters in the area is authorised by a licence
under the deposit order.

L.   Provisions on deposit or importation of shellfish

Where an order is made prohibiting the deposit or importation of shellfish
under the 1967 Act the Minister is to take such steps as he may consider most
suitable for informing all persons concerned of the effect of the order (s.14(1)
Sea Fisheries (Shellfish) Act 1967). Any person contravening the provisions
of a prohibition order, or a licence granted under such an order, is guilty of an
offence and liable on summary conviction to a fine not exceeding level 4 on
the standard scale, presently £1,000, or to imprisonment for a term not
exceeding three months, or to both (s.14(2)).

An inspector authorised by the Minister has a right of entry, at any
reasonable time, upon any land designated by an order prohibiting the deposit
of shellfish, or land covered by waters. This right of entry may be exercised
where, either the inspector has reasonable grounds for believing that the
prohibition imposed by the order is being contravened, or entry is required
for the purpose of removing any shellfish which the Minister is empowered
to remove. Where an inspector has the right to enter any land or waters in
this way, he also has the right to obtain and take away samples of any shellfish
found there, and dispose of samples as he may determine (s.14(3)). The right
of entry given to an inspector for these purposes is not, however, to be
exercised in respect of any occupied land unless 24 hours' notice of the
intended entry has been given to the occupier, and written evidence of the
inspector's authority is produced on entry if required (s.14(4)). Any person
who obstructs an inspector is guilty of an offence and liable on summary
conviction to a fine not exceeding level 3 on the standard scale, presently
£400 (s.14(5)).

M.   Elimination of disease or pest in public fisheries

The generally sedentary character of shellfish makes them especially vulnerable to certain kinds of diseases and pests, and the need for controls has long been recognised (Cole (1956) at pp. 20 to 23; Yonge (1966) at p. 158; and Ministry of Agriculture, Fisheries and Food (1974) and (1982B)). Hence, as long ago as 1600 it was an offence in Essex not to kill a starfish, a major shellfish predator, on finding it on the shore (Yonge (1966) at p. 154; and Nowak (1970) at p. 67). Modern Ministerial powers of disease and pest control arise under the 1967 Act in relation to waters in which the public have a right to fish other than waters where a right of several fishery or a right of regulating a fishery are conferred under the Act, or waters in respect of which a person has an exclusive right to take shellfish (s.15(1) Sea Fisheries (Shellfish) Act 1967). In public fisheries of this kind the appropriate Minister may take any action which appears to him to be required to destroy any shellfish which are in the waters which appear to him to be affected by a disease or pest, or any action to eliminate from the waters any disease or pest affecting shellfish. Where action of this kind is taken, the Minister may take any action for restocking the waters with shellfish (s.15(2)). The view was expressed soon after the enactment of this provision that it was a measure to be welcomed in empowering the Minister to prevent the spread of such pest species as the slipper limpet, the whelk tingle, tube worms and acorn barnacles (Nowak (1970) at p. 83; and see Cole (1956) at pp. 20 to 23).

N.   Sale of oysters between certain dates

An important mechanism in preventing the decline of shellfish stocks through overfishing is the imposition of a close season during which the sale, or taking, of shellfish is prohibited. The need for close seasons has long been acknowledged and for this reason the dredging for oysters was forbidden between Easter and Lammas by 1577, (Yonge (1966) at p. 152), and traditionally it was said to be a close season for oysters whenever there was not an 'r' in the spelling of the month (751 HC DEB 1967 Col. 1512). Although close seasons for some shellfish may be provided for in particular regions by local sea fisheries committees (Under Sea Fisheries Regulation Act 1966, see [15.08] below), more general close seasons for oysters, crabs and lobsters are provided for under the 1967 Act.

   The 1967 Act imposes seasons for the sale of oysters by making it an offence, subject to specified exceptions, for any person to sell, expose for sale, buy for sale, or consign for the purposes of sale, oysters of any description between 14 May and the following 4 August. The punishment for this offence is, on summary conviction, a fine not exceeding level one on the standard scale, presently £50. In addition, a person found guilty is to forfeit the oysters in respect of which the offence is committed (s.16(1) Sea Fisheries (Shellfish) Act 1967). The offence of selling oysters between the specified dates is made subject to exceptions which arise where the oysters concerned:

(a) were originally taken within the waters of a foreign state, or
(b) were preserved in tins or otherwise cured, or
(c) were intended for the purpose of oyster cultivation within the same district in which the oysters were taken, or
(d) were taken from any place for cultivation with the consent of the appropriate Minister, or
(e) were Pacific or Japanese oysters (*Crassostrea gigas*), Portuguese oysters

(*Crassostrea angulata*) or other members of the genus *Crassostrea* (s.16(2), as amended by s.1 Sea Fisheries (Shellfish) Act 1973).

For the purposes of the exception relating to oysters cultivated within the same district, (c) above, a 'district' is stated to be constituted by the Thames Estuary, bounded by a line drawn from Orford Ness to the North Foreland, and any other area for the time being constituted as a district for these purposes by an order of the appropriate Minister. In addition, where the place at which the oysters are taken is not within any district so specified, so much of the area within ten miles of the place at which the oysters are taken as is not already included in any district is be deemed to be a 'district' for these purposes. This would arise where oysters are sold for the purpose of oyster cultivation within ten miles of the place from which they were taken (s.16(3)). Power also exists for a local fisheries committee for a sea fisheries district to make byelaws constituting within their sea fisheries district, a 'district' of oyster cultivation for the purposes of this exception (s.5(1)(e) Sea Fisheries Regulation Act 1966).

The exception (a), arising in relation to the sale of oysters originally taken within the waters of a foreign state, as provided for under earlier legislation (s.4 Fisheries (Oyster, Crab and Lobster) Act 1877) was considered in *Robertson* v. *Johnson* ([1893] 1 QB 129). In this case the accused had been convicted of selling oysters which had originally been taken in French waters on a day within the period specified in the Act. On appeal it was found that the oysters concerned had been imported in a mature state but laid down for storage in a part of a creek from which they were removed when required for sale during the period during which the general sale of oysters was prohibited under the Act. It transpired that in the months during which the oysters had been stored they had deteriorated in condition and had become unfit for human consumption, but this fact was found to be immaterial to the matter of whether they were oysters which had been taken in the waters of a foreign state. Whilst conceding that the issue was one of fact and degree, the court held that the oysters concerned were taken within the waters of a foreign state and the conviction was quashed.

In addition to the list of exceptions to the offence of selling oysters provided for under the Act, it is also a defence for a person charged with this offence to show, on reasonable grounds, that the shellfish in respect of which the offence is alleged to have been committed were produced by fish farming and have not later been released to the wild (s.33(5) and (6), and Sch.4 para.30 Fisheries Act 1981, discussed in [14.04] above). It follows that this offence will not arise in relation to farmed oysters, though the fine difference between 'farming' oysters and harvesting a natural population may make the practical application of this defence unclear in many situations (see [14.02] above).

O.   Taking and sale of certain crabs and lobsters

Subject to certain qualifications, it is made an offence to take, possess, sell, expose for sale, buy for sale, or consign for the purposes of sale, an edible crab carrying spawn or having recently cast its shell (s.17(1) Sea Fisheries (Shellfish) Act 1967). The offence is, however, subject to the exception that it will not be committed where the crab found in possession, or alleged to have been sold, exposed for sale, bought for sale, or consigned to any person for the purpose of sale were intended for bait for fishing (s.17(2), see discussion of *Jones* v. *Davies* (1967) 111 SJ 980, at [15.08B] below). An analogous offence in relation to the landing, sale, exposure for sale, or possession for sale of lobsters which are carrying spawn, or were carrying spawn at the time when taken, may arise where the appropriate Minister makes an order to that effect (s.17(3)). Formerly close seasons had been imposed to protect lobsters carrying eggs, known as 'berry', which was used as a substitute for caviare and commanded high prices (Anon. (1877) at p. 481; and Nowak (1970) at p. 78). At the present time, however, no Ministerial order has been enacted under this provision and no offence currently exists, though the matter may be provided for under the byelaws of local sea fisheries committees (see [15.08A] below). In respect of either of these offences the punishment, on summary conviction, is a maximum fine of level 3 on the standard scale, presently £400. In addition, the court is empowered to order the forfeiture of all crabs or lobsters found in the possession of the convicted person or all such crabs or lobsters alleged to have been dealt with or possessed in contravention of the prohibitions upon taking and sale (s.17(4) Sea Fisheries (Shellfish) Act 1967).

In respect of the offences relating to the taking and sale of both crabs and lobsters it is a defence to show a reasonable belief that the shellfish in respect of which the offence was alleged to have been committed were produced by fish farming and had not later been released to the wild (s.33(5) and (6), and Sch.4 paras.31 and 32 Fisheries Act 1981, discussed in [14.04] above). Accordingly, these offences will not arise in relation to farmed crabs or lobsters (generally, see [14.02] and [14.04] above). Finally, in relation to crabs and lobsters, it may be noted that certain size limits are prescribed under European Community legislation (considered separately in [15.13] below).

15.05   The Sea Fish (Conservation) Act 1967

An essential element in the strategy for conservation of shellfish is the need to allow a sufficient proportion of stocks to attain maturity and breed to sustain future populations. This object is most simply achieved by the imposition of a minimum size limit for shellfish by law. Accordingly, provisions dating back from 1600 imposed a local requirement that all oysters had to be the size of a half-crown, 1.4 inches, before they were of marketable size (Yonge (1966) at p. 154; and Nowak (1970) at p. 75). The Fisheries (Oyster, Crab and Lobster) Act 1877 imposed more general maximum size limits in stipulating that crabs had to measure at least four and a half inches across the broadest part of the back and lobsters had to be at least eight inches in length (ss.8 and 9 Fisheries (Oyster, Crab and Lobster) Act 1877).

Restrictions upon the landing and commercial use of undersized sea fish, including shellfish, in Britain now arise under the Sea Fish (Conservation) Act 1967. Subject to the exception of authorised taking of fish for the purposes of scientific investigation (s.9(1) Sea Fish (Conservation) Act 1967), no person is to land any sea fish of a smaller size than is prescribed in relation to sea fish of that description by an order of the Ministers (s.1(1)). 'The Ministers' means the Minister of Agriculture, Fisheries and Food acting in conjunction with the Secretaries of State respectively concerned with the sea fishing industry in

Wales and Scotland (s.22(2) and (3)). 'Sea fish' means fish, whether fresh or cured, of any kind found in the sea, including shellfish, and any parts of such fish, and 'shellfish' includes crustaceans and molluscs of any kind, and any spat or spawn of shellfish (s.22(1)).

The prohibition upon landing undersized shellfish in Britain is paralleled by an analogous prohibition relating to their sale. This applies where a person sells, exposes for sale or has in his possession for the purpose of sale, sea fish of a smaller size than prescribed for fish of that description by order of the Ministers (s.1(2)). Likewise, fish of below the minimum prescribed size are not to be carried on a British fishing boat, or a foreign fishing boat in waters adjacent to the United Kingdom within British Fishery limits (s.1(3)). Moreover, the evasion of the prohibition upon sale of undersized fish by processing such fish before sale is made unlawful, since it is also an offence for a person to have possession of such fish for the purpose of processing or otherwise using in the course of any business (s.2(1)). In respect of any of the offences under the Sea Fish (Conservation) Act 1967 in relation to undersized fish a person found guilty is liable, on summary conviction, to a fine not exceeding £1,000, or on conviction on indictment to a fine of an unlimited amount (s.11(1)(b)). In respect of the landing, selling and carrying offences (under s.1(1)), the court before which a person is convicted may order the forfeiture of any fish in respect of which the offence was committed (s.11(2)(a)). Alternatively, on summary conviction, an additional fine may be imposed of an amount not exceeding the value of the fish in respect of which the offence was committed (s.11(3)). In no case, however, is a court to order *both* the additional fine *and* the forfeiture of the fish in respect of which the offence was committed (s.11(4)).

Three of the orders made by the exercise of the Ministerial power to impose restrictions upon the landing, sale and commercial use of undersized sea fish are concerned with undersized shellfish. The first is the Undersized Scallops (West Coast) Order 1984 (SI 1984 No.1522) which prescribes for scallops of the species *Pecten maximus* a minimum size below which the fish may not be landed in certain western parts of Britain, subject to an exception for boats other than British-owned fishing boats. The minimum size prescribed is 110 mm across the broadest part of the flat shell. The second order is the Undersized Crabs Order 1986 (SI 1986 No. 497) which prescribes minimum sizes for edible crabs, *Cancer pagurus*, below which it is an offence to land, sell, expose or offer for sale or possess crabs for the purpose of sale. The offence also extends to the master, owner or charterer of a fishing boat in that it is an offence for these persons to carry edible crabs below the minimum size, subject to an exemption to the landing of crabs from boats other than British-owned fishing boats. Although different minimum sizes are prescribed in relation to different areas and crabs of different sexes in relation to landing, the minimum size prescribed for the sale of edible crabs is 115 mm carapace width, measured across the broadest part of the back. (On size limits for crabs, see also [15.13] below.) The third order is the Undersized Velvet Crabs Order 1989 (SI 1989 No.919) which prescribes a minimum size of 65 mm carapace width for the landing of velvet crabs, *Liocarcinus puber*, and for carriage of this species on British fishing boats.

A person is not to be guilty of an offence relating to landing or carrying undersized sea fish (s.1(1) and (3) Sea Fish (Conservation) Act 1967) by reason of anything done or omitted in the course of fish farming where exemption is conferred by the appropriate Minister, and the act or omission is in accordance with any conditions attached to the exemption (s.33(1) and Sch.4 para.12 Fisheries Act 1981, discussed in [14.02] and [14.03] above). At present, however, the Ministerial power to confer exemption in this respect has not been exercised and so the exception is not yet available. It will, however, be a defence for a person charged with the offence of selling undersized fish (under s.1(2) Sea Fish (Conservation) Act 1967) or possessing undersized fish for the purpose of processing or otherwise using in the course of business (under s.2(1)) to show that he believed on reasonable grounds that the fish concerned were produced by fish farming (s.33(5) and Sch.4 paras.33 and 34 Fisheries Act 1981, discussed in [14.04] above). In respect of shellfish, however, the lack of a clear distinction between harvesting and farming shellfish, commented upon above, may mean that the scope of the fish farming exemption is not always clearly determined.

Another provision of conservational significance in relation to shellfish, arising under the Sea Fish (Conservation) Act 1967, is the Ministerial power to restrict fishing for sea fish. This allows the Ministers to prohibit fishing for all sea fish, or for fish of a specified description, or for fishing by a specified method, in any specified area for either a specified or unlimited period (s.5(1) Sea Fish (Conservation) Act 1967, as amended by s.22(1) Fisheries Act 1981). Amongst the orders introduced by the exercise of this power the Scallops (Irish Sea) (Prohibition of Fishing) Order 1984 (SI 1984 No.1523, as amended by SI 1988 No.988) is specifically concerned with fishing for shellfish and prohibits fishing for scallops, *Pecten maximus*, during a period from 1 July to 31 October, both days inclusive, in a specified area of the Irish Sea.

15.06   The Fisheries Act 1981

The Fisheries Act 1981 introduces a number of measures serving distinct purposes relating to fish farming. Some of these, relating to exemptions from fishery law for fish farming activities, have been considered elsewhere (see [14.01] to [14.04] above). This section deals with two matters of special relevance to shellfisheries arising under the Act – first, the status of the Sea Fish Industry Authority and, second, financial assistance for the sea fish industry (see also Chapter 5 above).

A.   The Sea Fish Industry Authority

The Fisheries Act 1981 provides for the establishment of the Sea Fish Industry Authority, a body with the duty of promoting the efficiency of the sea fish industry, including the shellfish industry, in the United Kingdom. The Act also provides for the payment of financial assistance to the industry. The Authority comprises not more than twelve members appointed by the Minister of Agriculture, Fisheries and Food, and the Secretaries of State concerned with the sea fish industry in Wales, Scotland and Northern Ireland (s.1(2) and 14(1) Fisheries Act 1981). Of the twelve, there is a chairman and deputy chairman who are persons appearing to the Ministers to have no financial or commercial interests likely to affect them in the discharge of their functions as members who are independent of the sea fish industry (s.1(3)).

The other members of the Authority are persons appearing to the Ministers to represent the interests of the sea fish industry or of any part of that industry (s.1(4), details of the composition and constitution of the Authority are provided in Sch.1).

Amongst the duties of the Sea Fish Industry Authority is that of exercising its powers to promote the efficiency of the sea fish industry and to serve the interests of that industry as a whole (s.2(1)). After consultation, the Ministers may give such directions as they think necessary for ensuring that the activities of the Authority are consistent with this (s.2(3)). When exercising its powers the Authority is also to have regard to the interests of consumers of sea fish and sea fish products (s.2(2)). The Ministers may give the Authority such directions as appear to them to be requisite in the public interest and the Authority is bound to give effect to any such directions (s.2(3)).

The powers and duties of the Sea Fish Industry Authority are concerned, in various ways, with 'sea fish'. For these purposes 'sea fish' are defined to mean fish of any kind found in the sea, including shellfish, but not including salmon or migratory trout (s.14(1)). In turn, 'shellfish' is stated to include crustaceans and molluscs of any kind, 'salmon' includes any fish of the salmon species, and 'migratory trout' means any species of trout which migrates to and from the sea (s.44). It follows from these definitions that the Authority has no responsibility with relation to the extensive salmon farming industry which takes place in coastal waters but, most pertinently for present concerns, it does have powers and duties in respect of the cultivation of shellfish.

The principal duty of the Authority in relation to shellfish is to promote the efficiency of the shellfishery industry, as a part of the sea fish industry as a whole, and to do this with regard to the interests of consumers. The powers of the Authority are the following:

(a) to carry out research and development with respect to any matters relating to the sea fish industry;
(b) to give advice on any such matters;
(c) to provide training in such matters or to assist in the provision of such training by making grants or by exercising supervisory or co-ordinating functions;
(d) to promote the marketing and consumption in, and the export from, the United Kingdom of sea fish and sea fish products;
(e) to make loans for assisting persons to meet capital expenditure on constructing, reconditioning or improving fishing vessels or on acquiring, reconditioning or improving plant for making ice or processing sea fish;
(f) to give financial assistance (by way of loan, grant or guarantee) to persons incurring expenditure in forming, carrying on or extending the activities of co-operatives for the sale of sea fish or for the purchase of fishing gear, fuel, stores or other materials requisite for the sea fish industry (s.3(1)).

Although the Authority may charge fees for any services which it provides, and may accept voluntary contributions to its expenses (s.3(2)), the financial provisions of the Act state that, for the purposes of financing its activities, the Authority may impose a levy on persons engaged in the sea fish industry (s.4(1)). A levy of this kind is, however, imposed by regulations made by the

Authority and confirmed by an order of the Ministers (s.4(2)). The levy may be related to either the weight of sea fish or sea fish products landed in the United Kingdom, or trans-shipped within British fishery limits, up to a maximum of 0.8p per kilogram, or related to the value of such fish products, up to a maximum of 1 per cent of that value (s.4(3)). Different rates of payment of the levy may be prescribed for sea fish or sea fish products of different descriptions (s.4(5)) and the levy may be payable by persons engaged in the sea fish industry in such proportions and at such times as are prescribed by regulations (s.4(6), see Sea Fish Industry Authority (Levy) Regulations 1988 Confirmatory Order 1989, SI 1989 No.425). A person is regarded as 'engaged in the sea fish industry' if he carries on the business of operating vessels, registered in the United Kingdom, for catching or processing sea fish or for transporting sea fish or sea fish products. Similarly, 'engaged in the sea fish industry' are persons who carry on, in the United Kingdom, the business of breeding, rearing or cultivating sea fish for human consumption. Likewise engaged are persons selling sea fish or sea fish products by wholesale or retail, importing sea fish or sea fish products, or of processing sea fish, including the business of a fish fryer (s.14(2) Fisheries Act 1981). It is apparent, therefore, that the categories of persons who may be bound to contribute to the levy are broadly formulated, and evident that a person who fishes for, or farms, shellfish would be amongst them.

Regulations imposing a levy upon persons engaged in the sea fish industry to fund the Authority may require such persons to keep and preserve records and to furnish the Authority with such information as is specified in regulations (s.5(1) Fisheries Act 1981). An officer authorised by the Authority may, on producing on demand evidence of his authority, require the production of, and take copies of, any records which a person is required to keep by virtue of the regulations. For the purposes of requiring production of records the officer may at any reasonable time enter any premises occupied for the purposes of a business by a person who is or who may be liable to pay the levy and board any vessel owned by or in the possession of that person (s.5(2)). Failure to comply with regulations requiring the keeping and preservation of records, or the production and copying of records by an authorised officer, without reasonable excuse, will amount to an offence, as will the wilful obstruction of an officer in the exercise of his powers. In either case a person will be liable on summary conviction to a fine not exceeding level 4 on the standard scale, presently £1,000 (s.5(3)). A person who in purported compliance with the requirement to keep and preserve records knowingly makes a record or furnishes any information which is false in a material particular, or knowingly alters a record made in compliance with any such requirements so that it becomes false, commits an offence. In this case the person will be liable, on summary conviction, to a fine not exceeding level 5 on the standard scale, presently £2,000, or to imprisonment for a term not exceeding three months or to both (s.5(4)).

The information provided by those engaged in the sea fish industry is inevitably of a commercially confidential nature and for that reason restrictions are imposed upon its unauthorised disclosure by the Authority. No information with respect to a particular undertaking which has been obtained by or on behalf of the Authority under the 1981 Act is to be disclosed without the consent of the person carrying on the undertaking, otherwise than for the purpose of the discharge of the Authority's functions (s.12(1)). This is not, however, to preclude the disclosure of information by the Authority to the Ministers for the purpose of their functions relating to the sea fish industry and the regulation of sea fishing, or for the purposes of any legal proceedings or of any report of any such proceedings (s.12(2)). Unauthorised disclosure contrary to these requirements is an offence which is punishable, on conviction on indictment, by a fine or to imprisonment for a term not exceeding two years or to both, or on summary conviction, to a fine not exceeding the prescribed sum, presently £2,000, or to imprisonment for a term not exceeding six months or to both (s.12(3)).

The Authority is given substantial borrowing powers for the purpose of financing its activities subject to these powers being exercised in accordance with regulations made by the Ministers and with the approval of the Treasury (s.6). Similarly, provision is made for the loan of large sums of money to the Authority by the Ministers, on such terms as the Treasury may approve, and for purposes approved by the Ministers and the Treasury (s.7). Also the Ministers, with Treasury consent, may make grants to the Authority on such conditions as they think fit in respect of expenses and losses incurred by the Authority in specified circumstances, and the Ministers may guarantee the repayment of money borrowed by the Authority (s.9). It is the duty of the Authority to keep proper accounts and records and to prepare a statement of accounts in respect of each financial year to be audited by persons appointed by the Ministers (s.11).

B.   Financial assistance for the sea fish industry

Also arising under the Fisheries Act 1981 are Ministerial powers to devise a scheme of financial assistance for the sea fish industry which are separate from the direct powers of the Sea Fish Industry Authority, discussed previously, and other provisions relating to financial assistance specifically for fish farming (generally, see Chapter 5 above). The Ministers are empowered, in accordance with a scheme made by them, with the approval of the Treasury, to make grants or loans for the purpose of reorganising, developing or promoting the sea fish industry or for contributing to the expenses of those engaged in it (s.15(1) Fisheries Act 1981). Such a scheme may be limited so as to apply to a specified part or area of the United Kingdom and may authorise the Ministers to make provision for any purpose specified in the scheme (s.15(2)). Although made by the Ministers, a scheme of this kind may be administered by the Sea Fish Industry Authority, and in such circumstances the Authority is empowered to exercise any discretion vested in the Ministers under the scheme (s.16(1)).

In order to prevent fraud in relation to schemes of financial assistance for the sea fish industry a range of criminal offences are created. Hence it is an offence for a person, in furnishing information in purported compliance with a scheme, to make a statement or produce a document which he knows to be false in a material particular, or recklessly to make a statement or produce a document which is false in a material particular, or wilfully to refuse to supply any information or to make a return or produce any document when required to do so by or under any scheme. This offence is punishable on summary conviction by a fine not exceeding level 5 on the standard scale, presently £2,000 (s.17).

The possibilities for Ministerial schemes of financial assistance for the sea fish industry are broadly formulated given that 'sea fish' for these purposes is defined to mean any fish of a kind found in the sea, including shellfish, but excluding salmon and migratory trout (s.18(1)). In addition, the requirement of 'engagement in the sea fish industry' is widely formulated for these purposes (s.18(2), and see discussion of s.14(2) above). Despite the wide potential for provision of financial assistance for the sea fish industry, however, those schemes which have actually been devised since the enactment of the 1981 Act (schemes for financial assistance for fishing vessels created under previous legislation, Sea Fish Industry Act 1970, continue to have effect as if introduced under the 1981 Act, under s.13(2)) have tended to be more directly concerned with the provision of fishing vessels and gear rather than shellfisheries or fish farming. (For example, the Fishing Vessels (Acquisition and Improvement) (Grants) Scheme 1981, SI 1981 No.1765, as amended by SI 1984 No.1879, the Fishing Vessels (Temporary Financial Assistance) Scheme 1982, SI 1982 No.1686, and the Fishing Vessels (Financial Assistance) Scheme 1987, SI 1987 No.1136.) One order of this kind which might be of more direct relevance to shellfisheries is the Fish Producers' Organisations (Formation Grants) Scheme 1982 (SI 1982 No.498, as amended by SI 1985 No.987) which makes provision for payments to be made for the purpose of promoting the sea fish industry, and in particular for grants to recognised fish producers' organisations in respect of administrative expenses incurred on formation and during subsequent operation for a specified period.

15.07   *The Coast Protection Act 1949*

Another statutory provision of potential relevance to the cultivation of shellfish in British coastal waters arises under the Coast Protection Act 1949. This provides that where, in consequence of the carrying out of coast protection work in exercise of their statutory powers (ss.1 to 33 Coast Protection Act 1949) coast protection authorities cause damage to oyster or mussel beds, the owners are entitled to claim compensation (s.19(1)(a)). The right to recover compensation against a coast protection authority is subject to the proviso that a person will not be entitled to compensation unless the act or omission causing the deprecation or disturbance would be actionable if it was done or omitted otherwise than in exercise of statutory powers (s.19(1)). That is, coast protection authorities will enjoy no special immunity if coast protection work causes damage to, amongst other things, shellfish beds.

SHELLFISHERY LEGISLATION APPLICABLE TO ENGLAND AND WALES ONLY

15.08   *The Sea Fisheries Regulation Act 1966*

The Sea Fisheries Regulation Act 1966 is a consolidating measure which re-enacts, with minor amendments, the Sea Fisheries Regulation Acts of 1888 to

1930. Most significantly, in relation to the present discussion, the 1966 Act makes provision for sea fisheries districts and local sea fisheries committees in England and Wales, though not in Scotland which is outside the scope of the Act (s.22(2) Sea Fisheries Regulation Act 1966; on the corresponding provision in Scotland see [15.11] below). Local sea fisheries committees are given a range of powers with respect to the regulation of sea fisheries which may have considerable importance in relation to sea fisheries including shellfisheries and shellfish farming. This section is subdivided to consider, first, the powers of local sea fisheries committees as they arise under the 1966 Act and, second, case law illustrations of the operation of local fisheries byelaws concerning shellfish.

A.   Local fisheries committees

In the first place the Minister of Agriculture, Fisheries and Food in England, or the Secretary of State in Wales, on application of a county council, has the power:

(a)   to create a sea fisheries district comprising any part of the sea within the national or territorial waters of the United Kingdom adjacent to England or Wales, either with or without any part of the adjoining coast, and

(b)   to define the limits of the district, and the area chargeable with any expenses under the Act, and

(c)   to provide for the constitution of a local fisheries committee and for the regulation of the sea fisheries carried on within the district (s.1 Sea Fisheries Regulation Act 1966, as amended).

The composition of a local fisheries committee for a sea fisheries district is to be a number of members to be appointed by the council, or the constituent councils, in such proportions as may be determined. Along with the council appointees there are to be a number of additional members, not exceeding the number of council appointees. These are to include one person appointed by the National Rivers Authority and the remainder are to be persons appointed by the Minister as persons acquainted with the needs and opinions of fishing interests in the district (s.2).

When duly created by Ministerial order, and constituted in accordance with the powers of appointment given to councils, the National Rivers Authority and the Minister, local fisheries committees have significant powers to regulate sea fisheries in their district. Subject to any special regulations made by the Minister for a particular sea fisheries district, a local fisheries committee may make byelaws to be observed within their district for a range of purposes. Amongst these purposes is that of making of byelaws for restricting or prohibiting, either absolutely or subject to any exceptions and regulations, the fishing for or taking of all or any specified kinds of sea fish, and protecting salmon (s.37(1) Salmon Act 1986) during any period of the year (s.5(1)(a) Sea Fisheries Regulation Act 1966). Likewise, byelaws may be made restricting or prohibiting, either absolutely or subject to such regulations as may be provided by the byelaws, any method of fishing for sea fish or the use of any instrument of fishing for sea fish; byelaws may also be made for determining the size of mesh, form and dimensions of any instrument of fishing for sea fish (s.5(1)(b)). More pertinently for the present discussion, byelaws may be made for the regulation, protection and development of fisheries for all or any specified kinds of shellfish, including:

(i)   the fixing of the sizes and condition at which shellfish may not be removed from a fishery, and the mode of determining such sizes;

(ii)   the obligation to re-deposit in specified localities any shellfish the removal or possession of which is prohibited by or in pursuance of any Act;

(iii) the protection of shellfish laid down for breeding purposes;

(iv) the protection of culch and other material for the reception of the spat or young of any kind of shellfish; and

(v)   the obligation to re-deposit such culch and other material in specified localities (s.5(1)(d)).

The making of byelaws by local fisheries committees to operate within their district is subject to a number of specified restrictions. Amongst these is the stipulation that no byelaw will be authorised which prejudicially affects any right of several fishery, or any right on, to or over any portion of the sea shore, where any such right is enjoyed by any person under any local or special Act of Parliament, or any Royal charter, letters patent, prescription, or immemorial usage, except with the consent of that person (s.6(a)). Another restriction upon the exercise of the byelaw-making power is that no byelaw will be authorised which affects any byelaw made by the National Rivers Authority in force within the district of the committee, or restricting the power of the National Rivers Authority to make any byelaw having effect within that district in the future (s.6(b)).

B.   Case law on local fisheries byelaws

The operation of the byelaw-making power of local fisheries committees under the 1966 Act may be illustrated by examples from case law decided under corresponding earlier legislation. In *Thomson* v. *Burns* ((1896) 61 JP 84) a local fisheries committee had exercised its power to make byelaws fixing the size and condition at which shellfish may be removed from a fishery (s.1(1) Sea Fisheries (Shell Fish) Regulation Act 1894, now s.5(1)(d)(i) Sea Fisheries Regulation Act 1966). A byelaw which it had created stipulated that no person was to remove from a fishery any cockle which will pass through a gauge having an oblong opening of three-quarters of an inch in breadth and not less than two inches in length. An additional byelaw required that any person who took a shellfish, the removal of which from the fishery was prohibited, was to deposit it without injury as nearly as possible in the place form which it was taken. On the facts which arose, the accused had collected a large number of undersized cockles which he had intended to remove from the fishery but returned them to the fishery when requested to do so by a bailiff appointed by the local sea fisheries committee. It was held that the offence of removing the undersized cockles from the fishery, contrary to the byelaw, was complete when the cockles had been taken up from the fishery with the intention of eventually carrying them away, notwithstanding that the intervention of the bailiff meant that they were not actually removed from the fishery.

In *Friend* v. *Brehout* ((1914) 79 JP 25) a local fisheries committee had exercised its statutory powers to create a byelaw to restrict or prohibit fishing for specified kinds of sea fish (s.2(1) Sea Fisheries Regulation Act 1888, now s.5(1)(a) Sea Fisheries Regulation Act 1966). Specifically, the committee had prohibited trawling in specified areas, originally for the protection of immature fish, but later to prevent interference with the catching of crabs on a sandbank within the area. When a person was convicted of trawling in the area in contravention of the byelaw he claimed, on appeal, that the byelaw was unreasonable and in excess of the byelaw-creating powers of the committee. It was held that the Act was for the general regulation of sea fisheries and 'sea fish' included crabs, therefore, it was within the objects of the Act to make regulations for the protection of crab fisheries. Moreover the particular byelaw at issue was a reasonable means of achieving the objective of protecting crab fisheries, and the conviction under the byelaw was affirmed.

In *Jones* v. *Davies* ((1967) 111 SJ 980) a local fisheries committee made a byelaw prohibiting the use of edible crab, of any size, for bait (s.1(1)(a) Sea Fisheries (Shell Fish) Regulation Act 1894, now s.5(1)(d)(i) Sea Fisheries Regulation Act 1966). The intention behind the byelaw was that the taking of undersized crab should be prohibited, but difficulties in ascertaining whether any particular crab used as bait was undersized meant that the byelaw had to be formulated to cover both undersized crabs and those of a takeable size. The accused used crab of a takeable size for bait and was convicted of an offence under the byelaw. On appeal the accused maintained that the byelaw was unreasonable and beyond the powers of the local fisheries committee to create. This was for the reason that an explicit proviso in another Act authorised the possession of crabs intended for bait for fishing, and no direction had been given by the committee that this provision should cease to apply (s.2(1)(c) Sea Fisheries Regulation Act 1888, now s.17(2) Sea Fisheries (Shellfish) Act 1967, discussed in [15.04O] above). The proviso authorising the use of crabs for bait arose under s.8 Fisheries (Oyster, Crab and Lobster) Act 1877 (now s.17(2) 1967 Act). It was held that the byelaw prohibiting the use of edible crab for bait was neither unreasonable nor beyond the powers of the committee. Moreover, the byelaw implicitly overrode the provision permitting the use of crab for bait under the other Act, and the court ruled that the case should be remitted to the lower court with a direction to convict.

SHELLFISHERY LEGISLATION APPLICABLE TO SCOTLAND ONLY

15.09   *The Oyster Fisheries (Scotland) Act 1840*

Whilst it has been noted that the principal measure for the protection of property rights in private shellfisheries in Scotland is, as in England and Wales, the Sea Fisheries (Shellfish) Act 1967 (see discussion of s.7(2) Sea Fisheries (Shellfish) Act 1967, in [15.04G] above) the protection of private shellfisheries is also provided for under older legislation. At a relatively early point in the history of shellfishery legislation distinct provision was made for the protection of Oyster Fisheries in Scotland under the Oyster Fisheries

(Scotland) Act 1840 which creates offences of theft in relation to the taking of oysters. The Act provides that the offence of theft is committed where any person wilfully and knowingly takes and carries away any oysters or oyster brood from any oyster bed, laying, or fishery, which is the property of any other person and is sufficiently marked out or known as such (illustrated by *R* v. *Thompson and Mackenzie* (1842) 1 Broun 475). An offender found guilty of theft in these circumstances will be liable to a punishment of imprisonment for a period not exceeding one year (s.1 Oyster Fisheries (Scotland) Act 1840).

The offence of attempted theft is provided for where any person unlawfully and wilfully uses any dredge, net, instrument, or engine, within the limits of an oyster fishery, for the purpose of taking oysters or oyster brood, even though none are actually taken. Similarly, attempted theft is committed if a person allows a net instrument or engine to drag upon the ground or soil of any oyster fishery. A person deemed to have committed attempted theft in these circumstances will be liable to be punished by a fine or imprisonment or both, up to a maximum fine which was originally stated not to exceed £20 and imprisonment not exceeding three calendar months (s.2).

The offences of theft and attempted theft of oysters arising under the Act are made subject to two provisos. The first is that the offences will not prevent persons from catching or fishing for any floating fish within the limits of any oyster fishery with a net, instrument or engine adapted for taking floating fish only (s.3). The second proviso is that nothing in the Act is to prevent any person from exercising any right which may be lawfully exercised within the limits of an oyster fishery (s.4).

An interesting application of the offence of taking oysters contrary to the 1840 Act arose in *R* v. *Garrett and Thomas* ((1866) 5 Irv.259) where the accused had obtained a licence to dredge for oysters from the proprietor of an oyster fishery, granted on the condition that no oysters of less than two and a half inches in diameter were to be removed from the fishery. In contravention of the condition in the licence the accused removed undersized oysters. It was held that, despite the dredging taking place lawfully under the owner's authorisation, an offence under the Act was nonetheless committed by removing the undersized oysters since this was an act not covered by the permission provided by the licence.

15.10 *The Mussel Fisheries (Scotland) Act 1847*

The Mussel Fisheries (Scotland) Act 1847 is similarly formulated to the previous Act to make analogous provision for theft and attempted theft for the protection of mussel fisheries in Scotland (see also s.7(2) Sea Fisheries (Shellfish) Act 1967, discussed in [15.04G] above). Hence, theft of mussels is committed where any person wilfully, knowingly and wrongfully takes and carries away any mussels or mussel brood from any mussel bed, scalp laying, or fishery, which is the property and in the lawful occupation of any other person, and is sufficiently marked out or known as such. Such an offender is liable to be sentenced to imprisonment for a term not exceeding one year (s.1 Mussel Fisheries (Scotland) Act 1847). This offence was found to have been committed in *Parker* v. *Lord Advocate* ([1904] AC 364: see [15.03] above) despite claims by the accused that the private ownership of mussels beds was inconsistent with Crown rights to such beds (see also *Chisholm* v. *Black and Morrison* (1871) 2 Couper 49).

Attempted theft is committed where any person unlawfully uses any dredge, or any net or instrument or engine, or trespasses within the limits of any mussel bed, scalp laying, or fishery which is the property and in the lawful occupation of any other person or persons, and is sufficiently marked out or known as such for the purposes of taking mussels or mussel brood, even though none are actually taken. Likewise, attempted theft will be committed by a person who unlawfully uses a net, instrument, or engine, or by hand or otherwise, to drag or fish upon the ground or soil of a mussel bed, scalp laying or fishery. A person convicted of attempted theft of mussels under these provisions will be liable to be punished by a fine or imprisonment, or both, with a maximum fine originally set at £10, and a period of imprisonment not exceeding three months (s.2 Mussel Fisheries (Scotland) Act 1847).

The offences of theft and attempted theft of mussels arising under the Act are made subject to two provisos. The first is that the offences will not prevent any lawfully entitled person from fishing for or catching any floating fish within the limits of any mussel fishery with a net, instrument or engine adapted for taking floating fish only (s.3). The second proviso is that nothing in the Act is to prevent any person from exercising any right of taking bait, or any other right which may be lawfully exercised within the limits of a mussel fishery (s.4).

15.11   *The Sea Fisheries (Scotland) Amendment Act 1885*

In Scotland, which is not subject to the Sea Fisheries Regulation Act 1966, a power to make byelaws to regulate coastal fishing is vested in the Secretary of State for Scotland under the Sea Fisheries (Scotland) Amendment Act 1885. This provides that when the Secretary of State is satisfied that any mode of fishing in any part of the sea adjoining Scotland is injurious to any kind of sea fishing, he may make byelaws restricting or prohibiting, either entirely or subject to regulations, any method of fishing for sea fish during such time or times as he thinks fit. This power may also be exercised when it appears to the Secretary of State to be desirable to make byelaws to conduct experiments or make observations with a view to ascertaining whether any particular mode of fishing is injurious, or for the purposes of fish culture or experiments in fish culture (s.4 Sea Fisheries (Scotland) Amendment Act 1885). Because the 1885 Act is now to be construed along with the Sea Fisheries Act 1968 (s.1, as amended) the 'fish' in relation to which byelaws may be made include shellfish (s.19(1) Sea Fisheries Act 1968).

The procedure for making byelaws under the 1885 Act prevents the Secretary of State confirming any byelaw until one month's notice of the making of the byelaw has been given by advertisement in one or more newspapers circulating in the county or counties adjoining the part of the sea to which the byelaw is to apply. Before confirmation of the byelaw the Secretary of State must allow persons to make representations objecting to the confirmation, and if such representations are made he may, if he sees fit, allow the parties to be heard thereon. When confirmed, a byelaw is to be published in the *Edinburgh Gazette*, and this is to be evidence in all legal proceedings, unless the contrary is proved, of the due making, confirmation, and existence of the byelaw (s.4 Sea Fisheries (Scotland) Amendment Act 1885).

Any person contravening a byelaw is guilty of an offence and liable on summary conviction to a fine, originally stated not to exceed £100, or in the case of a second or subsequent conviction to imprisonment for a term not exceeding three months or a fine, originally not exceeding £200, or both. In addition the court by which an offender is convicted may order the forfeiture of any net or other fishing gear used in committing the offence (s.4). Where a fine is imposed by a sheriff on the master, owner or charterer or a member of the crew of a fishing boat, the sheriff may issue a warrant for the arrestment and sale of the boat and its gear and catch and any property of the person convicted. Any fishing gear forfeited in this manner may be destroyed or otherwise disposed of as the court may direct. If the boat concerned is a foreign fishing vessel, the sheriff may order it to be detained for a period not exceeding three months from the date of the conviction or until the fine is paid, whichever occurs first (s.4, and s.12(2) Sea Fisheries Act 1968). Jurisdiction to try offences is provided for by a stipulation that an offence under the provisions may for all incidental purposes be treated as having been committed in any place in the United Kingdom (s.4, and s.14 Sea Fisheries Act 1968).

Where an offence under a byelaw made by the Secretary of State under the 1885 Act is committed by a person belonging to a sea-fishing boat, the master of that boat is deemed guilty of the offence. This stipulation of vicarious liability of the master is, however, subject to the proviso that it is a defence for him to prove that he issued proper orders for the observance, and used due diligence to enforce the observance, of the byelaw contravened, and that the offence was actually committed by some other person without his connivance (s.6A, as amended by Sea Fisheries Act 1968).

Another provision arising under the 1885 Act which is of potential importance to shellfishery regulation in Scotland, is the power of the Secretary of State to require statistics in relation to sea fisheries. The Secretary of State is empowered to require all fishermen and other persons belonging to British sea-fishing boats, and all fish curers catching or curing any kind of sea fish in Scotland, or in any part of the sea adjoining Scotland, to make returns, in a prescribed form, of all sea fish which are caught or cured by them respectively. Any person failing to make a full and correct return as required by the Secretary of State will be guilty of an offence and liable on summary conviction to a fine, originally stated not to exceed £50, and the powers of the court in relation to forfeiture of boat and gear and the detention of foreign fishing boats, described previously in relation to byelaw offences, are similarly applicable to the offence of failing to make a return (s.6).

15.12 *The Inshore Fishing (Scotland) Act 1984*

The Inshore Fishing (Scotland) Act 1984 makes certain provision for the regulation of inshore sea fishing in Scotland including fishing for shellfish. In particular the Act empowers the Secretary of State, after consultation with such bodies as he considers appropriate, to make orders regulating fishing for sea fish in any specified sea area within Scottish inshore waters (s.1(1) Inshore Fishing (Scotland) Act 1984). An order of this kind may prohibit, within the specified area, all fishing for sea fish, or for a specified description of sea fish, or fishing by a specified method, or from a specified description of fishing boat. In addition an order may specify the period during which the prohibition is to apply and make exceptions to any prohibition (s.1(2)). The Secretary of State is similarly empowered to make orders prohibiting the carriage, for any purpose, in any British fishing boat, in any specified area within Scottish inshore waters, of a type of net specified in the order (s.2(1)).

The 1984 Act also imposes unqualified prohibition upon persons fishing by means of a trawl, seine or other gear designed for fishing from a moving vessel within half a mile of any fixed salmon net (s.3). Contravention of this provision, or any Ministerial order under the Act, is an offence which is punishable by a fine not exceeding £5,000 on summary conviction, or by a fine of an unspecified amount on conviction on indictment (s.4(2)). In addition to the fine a court may order the forfeiture of any fish in respect of which the offence was committed or, alternatively, impose a fine not exceeding the value of such fish, and order the forfeiture of any net or other fishing gear used in the commission of the offence. Any fish or gear forfeited under a court order of this kind is to be disposed of as the court may direct (s.4(4)).

EUROPEAN REGULATION APPLICABLE TO THE UNITED KINGDOM

15.13   *Shellfish size limits under European Community law*

Alongside the British legislation governing shellfisheries certain matters are provided for directly under European Community legislation, and are most conveniently considered separately. Of greatest relevance amongst these are the provisions made for the size limits provided for certain species of crustacea, including lobsters. Although provision is made for size limits to be imposed upon the landing and commercial use of shellfish under the Sea Fish (Conservation) Act 1967 (ss.1 and 2 Sea Fish (Conservation) Act 1967; and see Undersized Crabs Order 1986, SI 1986 No.497) no provision has been made for minimum sizes for certain crustacea such as lobsters. The reason for this omission is that the size limit for lobsters is now directly provided for under a European Community Regulation.

The European Council Regulation of 1986 laying down certain technical measures for the conservation of fishery resources within the Community (EEC No. 3094/86, replacing 171/83, as amended) is intended to ensure the protection of marine biological resources and the balanced exploitation of fishery resources in the interests of both fishermen and consumers. To that end the Regulation stipulates technical measures for the conservation of fishery resources, specifying, amongst other things, the mesh sizes, by-catch rates, and fish sizes permitted, as well as the limitation of fishing gear within certain areas and periods (Preamble). The Regulation specifies that a crustacean or mollusc is undersized if its size is smaller than measurements stipulated in Annex III to the Regulation, and that if more than one method of measuring the minimum size is permitted, the crustacean or mollusc is undersized if it is smaller than any of the minimum sizes specified (Art.5(1)).

In particular, the Regulation provides details as to how the size of the various crustaceans and molluscs are to be measured and the minimum sizes when so measured. The size of a lobster, *Homarus gammarus*, is to be measured as either the length of the carapace, measured parallel to the mid-line from the back of either eye socket to the distal edge of the carapace, or as the total length, measured from the tip of the rostrum to the rear end of the telson, not including the setae (Art.5(2)(b)). In relation to these measurements the minimum size limit is 85 mm carapace length, or 24 cm overall length (Annex III). Another species specifically provided for is the spinous spider crab, *Masia squinado*, which is to be measured along the mid-line from the edge of the carapace between the rostrums to the posterior edge of the carapace (Art.5(2)(d)). Measured in this manner, the minimum size for the species is 120 mm (Annex III). A third species for which a size limit is provided is the scallop, *Pecten maximus*, which is to be measured across the longest part of the shell (Art.5(2)(e)) and the minimum size for this measurement is to be 100 mm (Annex III). It is stipulated that any undersized crustaceans or molluscs are not to be retained on board a vessel, or be trans-shipped, landed, transported, stored, sold, displayed or offered for sale, but are to be returned immediately to the sea (Art.5(3)). An exception is provided for in that the regulation is not to apply to fishing operations carried out during the course of artificial restocking or transplantation of crustaceans or molluscs, provided that they are not sold directly for human consumption, or held in possession, displayed or offered for sale in contravention of other provisions of the Regulation (Art.12).

The legal mechanism by which the Community Regulation laying down certain technical measures for the conservation of fishery resources is given effect in the United Kingdom is through the provisions of the Fisheries Act 1981 and the Sea Fishing (Enforcement of Community Conservation Measures) Order 1986 (SI 1986 No.2090). The 1981 Act provides that the fisheries Ministers, that is, the Minister of Agriculture, Fisheries and Food and the Secretaries of State for Wales and Scotland, may make such provision as appears to them to be requisite for the enforcement of any enforceable Community restriction or other obligation relating to sea fishing (s.30(2) Fisheries Act 1981). The Community Regulation comes within the meaning of 'enforceable Community restriction', and accordingly the Ministers have exercised their power by making the 1986 Order.

Amongst other respects in which the 1986 Order gives specific effect to the Community Regulation is the stipulation that any person who, in the United Kingdom, lands, transports, stores, sells, displays or offers for sale any fish in contravention of Article 5 of the Council Regulation is guilty of an offence (Art.3(2) Sea Fishing (Enforcement of Community Conservation Measures) Order 1986). It is provided that a person found guilty of this offence is liable, on summary conviction, to a fine not exceeding £2,000, and either to a fine not exceeding the value of the fish in respect of which the offence was committed, or to the forfeiture of the fish in respect of which the offence was committed (Art.4(3)). On conviction on indictment, the corresponding penalties are a fine of unlimited amount and the forfeiture of the fish in respect of which the offence was committed (Art.4(4)). These offences are made subject to powers of enforcement given to officers authorised by any of the Ministers, officers of a market authority, and fishery officers of local sea fisheries committees (Art.6) and additional provision is made for the punishment of persons found guilty of obstructing an officer in the exercise of his powers (Art.7).

Chapter 16

The Sale of Fish

16.01 The general law of sale of goods

This chapter deals with a range of miscellaneous matters arising in relation to the sale of fish (generally, see Shaw and Muir (1987)). To some extent transactions involving the sale of fish can be regarded as being subject to general law relating to sales of goods. In other contexts sale restrictions upon dead fish arise from specific controls upon the sale of unwholesome food and the concomitant need for hygiene requirements. Similarly motivated are specific regulations dealing with sales of shellfish for which especially stringent public health requirements have been found necessary. Finally, the problem of fish nomenclature and the passing off of one kind of fish as another more highly valued species has necessitated special regulations dealing with the labelling of fish at the point of sale.

The final stage of the aquacultural process is the sale of the end product. This may involve transactions between fish farmers dealing in live fish, or the sale of live fish to the owner of waters for restocking (see Chapter 8 above). Alternatively the transaction may involve the sale of dead fish, either directly to the consumer or to an intermediary purchaser for resale to the eventual consumer. Into whichever of these categories the sale falls the contract which is made will be subject to the ordinary law of sale of goods, as provided for under the Sale of Goods Act 1979 which, subject to particular terms of the contract, will govern the rights of the buyer and seller of fish. Amongst other important features of the 1979 Act, conditions are implied into contracts for sale of goods to the effect that goods are of reasonable fitness for their purpose and of merchantable quality (s.14(1) Sale of Goods Act 1979). As against a consumer of the goods these conditions cannot be excluded by any contractual term, and against a person buying goods other than as a consumer, for example for business purposes, the conditions can only be excluded to the extent that it is reasonable to do so (s.6(2) and (3) Unfair Contract Terms Act 1977). In effect, therefore, the sale of fish for consumption is an assurance on the part of the seller that they are fit to be eaten, and a sale of live fish carries the implication that the fish are as free from disease as can reasonably be ascertained.

In addition to basic contractual rights in relation to fish sales, where a fish farmer sells goods which are misdescribed this is capable of giving rise to liability for misrepresentation (Misrepresentation Act 1976), or criminal culpability where the misdescription amounts to a false trade description (Trade Descriptions Act 1968; and see [16.05] below). In addition to these matters an alternative form of liability may now arise in relation to product liability. The Consumer Protection Act 1987 (implementing EC Directive 85/

374) introduces a system of strict liability in relation to personal injuries and damage to property caused through a defect in goods supplied as consumer items. Under the 1987 Act liability arises without the need for fault to be established against the producer of the defective product, or the supplier where the producer is not identified. This form of liability may apply to agricultural produce, including the produce of farming or fisheries, but it is specified that liability will not arise where such produce has not undergone an industrial process (ss.1 and 2 Consumer Protection Act 1987). Although the meaning of 'industrial process' is not specified, it has been suggested that, though sales of fresh fish or shellfish from a farm will be exempt from liability, as soon as any process such as cleansing or packaging has taken place the provisions of the 1987 Act could apply (Robertson, D. (1988) p. 141). The matter, however, has not yet been the subject of any authoritative determination. Nonetheless it is clear that the general law relating to sales of goods provides ample grounds for liability in relation to sales of fish where evidence can be produced to establish a defect in the goods concerned.

16.02   *The Food Act 1984*

The considerable potential for shellfish to become contaminated, by pollution or otherwise, and to be a cause of illness in an eventual consumer has resulted in a section under the Food Act 1984 being devoted to the provision of facilities for the cleansing of shellfish by county councils or local authorities in England and Wales. To this effect it is provided that a county council or a local authority may provide tanks or other apparatus for cleansing shellfish, and may make charges in respect of the use of any tank or other apparatus so provided (s.30(1) Food Act 1984). Similarly, where facilities for the cleaning of shellfish are jointly or indirectly provided, a county council or local authority may contribute towards the expenses incurred by any other council, or any joint committee, or towards expenses incurred by any other person in providing, and making available to the public, means for cleansing shellfish (s.30(2)). It is specifically provided that 'cleansing shellfish' for these purposes includes the subjection of shellfish to any germicidal treatment (s.30(4)). A reservation, to which the power to make available provisions for the cleansing of shellfish is subject, stipulates that this power is not to authorise the establishment of any tank or other apparatus, or the execution of any other work, on, over or under tidal lands below high-water mark of ordinary spring tides, except in accordance with prior permission granted by the Secretary of State for Transport (s.30(5)).

In addition to the permissive powers given to county councils and local authorities to make available facilities for the cleansing of shellfish, Regulations operative under the Food Act 1984 impose positive obligations upon local authorities to take action in relation to possible dangers to health arising from the consumption of shellfish. The basis of these provisions lies in the Ministerial power given to the Minister of Agriculture, Fisheries and Food, the Secretary of State for Social Services, and the Secretary of State for Wales, acting jointly, to make regulations as to food hygiene. In particular, the Ministers are empowered to make such regulations as appear to them to be expedient for securing the observance of sanitary and cleanly conditions and practices in connection with the sale of food for human consumption. Likewise such regulations may deal with the importation, preparation, transport, storage, packaging, wrapping, exposure for sale, service or delivery of food intended for sale or sold for human consumption, or otherwise for the protection of the public health in connection with those matters (s.13(1) Food Act 1984). Moreover, it is specifically stated that regulations may be made for prohibiting or regulating, or enabling local authorities to prohibit or regulate, the sale for human consumption, or the offer, exposure or distribution for sale for human consumption, of shellfish taken from beds or other layings designated by regulations (s.13(2)).

16.03   The Public Health (Shell-Fish) Regulations 1934

Although the Ministerial power to make food hygiene regulations in relation to shellfish now arises under s.13 of the Food Act 1984, a corresponding power existed under previous legislation and this was exercised in the enactment of the Public Health (Shell-Fish) Regulations 1934 SR&O 1934 No.1342, as amended by the Public Health (Shell-Fish) (Amendment) Regulations 1948, SI 1948 No.1120, the Food (Revision of Penalties) Regulations 1982, SI 1982 No.1727, and the Food (Revision of Penalties) Regulations 1985, SI 1985 No.67). These Regulations continue in force as if made under the 1984 Act but apply only to England and Wales.

A key provision under the Public Health (Shell-Fish) Regulations 1934 concerns the action to be taken by a local authority on suspicion of danger to public health from shellfish. If the medical officer of health of a local authority is in possession of information that any person is suffering, or has recently suffered, from infectious or other disease attributable to shellfish, or that the consumption of shellfish exposed within the district is likely to cause danger to public health, the officer is to make such enquiries and take all practicable steps to ascertain the layings from which such shellfish were derived, and is to report thereon to the local authority (Reg.4(1)). In this context 'laying' means a foreshore, bed, pond, pit, ledge, float, or other place where shellfish are deposited (Reg.2(2)). For the purposes of the enquiries to be pursued by a medical officer of health, the local authority may require any fishmonger supplying shellfish in the district to furnish to the officer, within a reasonable time, a list of all the layings, so far as he can with reasonable diligence ascertain them, from which his supply of shellfish has been derived during any period up to six weeks immediately preceding the date of the requisition. In addition, the fishmonger is to supply any information in his possession which will assist the medical officer of health in ascertaining the particular laying or layings from which any suspected shellfish were derived. If the supply of any part of the suspected shellfish was obtained through any other fishmonger the local authority may make a similar requisition upon that fishmonger (Reg.4(2)).

If the laying from which suspected shellfish are found to have been derived is within the district of the local authority the medical officer of health is to make an investigation with regard to the laying and is to report to the local authority thereon furnishing a copy of any bacteriological or other reports obtained by him (Reg.4(3)). If the laying concerned is not within the district of the local authority, the authority is to send to the local authority within whose district the laying is situated a copy of the report of the medical officer of health and any other information in their possession indicating the possible danger to public health from the consumption of shellfish derived from the laying (Reg.4(4)). Upon receipt of such information, the local authority for the district in which the laying is situated is to instruct its medical officer of health to make an investigation with regard to the laying and to report thereon and this report is to be accompanied by copies of any bacteriological or other reports obtained by him (Reg.4(5)).

On receipt of a report of the medical officer of health, it is in the first instance the duty of the authority to take the report into consideration. If the authority is satisfied that the consumption of shellfish taken from the laying is likely to cause danger to public health it may make an order prohibiting the distribution for sale for human consumption of shellfish taken from the laying either absolutely or subject to such exceptions and conditions as it may think proper having regard to the interests of public health (Reg.5(1)). The procedure involved in making an order of this kind requires the local authority to give at least 21 days' notice of the proposal to make the order, stating the grounds on which it is to be made, and affording all interested persons a reasonable opportunity of making representations (Reg.5(2)).

Special provision is made for notification in the case of a proposed local authority shellfish order in respect of a private laying. A 'private laying' means a laying where shellfish are not habitually taken or deposited except by the owner or by a tenant of the laying, and a 'tenant' includes any person authorised by the owner to take or deposit shellfish, or sub-tenants authorised by such persons (Reg.2(2)). In the case of a private laying notice is to be served on every owner and tenant of the laying whose name and address can with reasonable diligence be ascertained. If the laying is a public laying, in which no private right of ownership exists, notice is to be given by the local authority by means of posters affixed in conspicuous places in the vicinity of the laying or in such other manner as the local authority think best calculated to bring the proposal to the attention of persons interested. In either case a copy of the notice is to be sent to the Sea Fisheries Committee (see [15.08] above) in whose district the laying is situated (Reg.5(3) Public Health (Shell-Fish) Regulations 1934). The local authority is to supply a copy of the report of the medical officer of health to any person interested on payment of a reasonable sum (Reg.5(4)).

As soon as practicable after a local authority shellfish order has been made the authority is to publish in one or more local newspapers circulating in the district, and send to the Sea Fisheries Committee in whose district the laying is situated, a notice stating that the order has been made. This notice must either set out the terms of the order or name a place where a copy of the order may be seen at all reasonable hours. If the order relates to a private laying the authority is to serve a notice, either personally or by post, upon every owner and tenant of the laying whose name and address can with reasonable diligence be ascertained (Reg.6(1)). Before an order of this kind comes into operation, or as soon as practicable thereafter, the local authority must, if the laying is a public laying, and may, if the laying is a private laying, cause warning notices containing a copy of the order or a sufficient statement of its terms to be posted in conspicuous places in the vicinity of the laying (Reg.6(2)). In addition the local authority is placed under a duty to inform the Minister of Agriculture, Fisheries and Food, or the Secretary of State for Wales of any action taken as soon as possible (Reg.7). Any person aggrieved by the order may appeal to the appropriate Minister within 14 days after the publication of the notice of the order, or if the appellant has been served with a notice of the order as an owner or tenant of a private laying within 14 days after the receipt of the notice (Reg.9(1)). After considering the appeal the Minister may confirm the order, with or without modification, or he may quash the order as he thinks fit (Reg.9(2)).

The main consequence of a local authority shellfish order having been made is that certain offences arise in relation to shellfish taken from the area covered by the order. Specifically, it is an offence for a person, contrary to the provisions of the order to sell or expose, distribute or offer for sale or have in his possession for the purpose of sale for human consumption any shellfish taken from the laying (Reg.12(1)). A person found guilty of this offence is liable, on summary conviction, to a fine not exceeding £2,000 (amended by SI 1985 No.67) or on conviction on indictment, to a fine or imprisonment for a term not exceeding two years or both (Reg.12(2) Public Health (Shell-Fish) Regulations 1934).

16.04   Health conditions for molluscs and fishery products

The discussion of food hygiene regulations relating to shellfish in the last section leads into an anticipation of imminent changes in the law governing the sale of live bivalve molluscs and fishery products in general. As has previously been mentioned, the need to harmonise trade legislation within the European Community by the end of 1992 has prompted a number of provisional Community Regulations concerning trade in aquacultural products (see [1.04] and [7.04] above). Two such measures which are presently under consideration by the European Commission are most appropriately considered at this point: the provisional Regulation on the health conditions affecting the production and the placing on the market of live bivalve molluscs, and the provisional Regulation on health conditions affecting the production and the placing on the market of fishery products. Although not yet in a final form, both of these measures concern the hygiene conditions relating to the production and sale of aquacultural commodities and will, when they pass into Community law, have significant effects upon fish farming and fish marketing in all Member States of the Community.

The first of the proposed Regulations, on the public health conditions affecting the production and placing on the market of live bivalve molluscs, is intended to facilitate intra-Community trade in molluscs through the imposition of common product standards to safeguard public health. The European Commission proposal entails the formulation of detailed health standards of different kinds which are to be satisfied before molluscs can be marketed for human consumption (contrast provisions discussed in [10.06] above). Amongst other matters provided for, shellfish harvesting areas are to be classified according to a range of public health criteria applicable to the harvested shellfish, and marketing restrictions and cleansing treatments are specified accordingly. One feature of the proposal, therefore, is that shellfish harvesting areas are to be placed into three hygiene categories, which may be termed 'acceptable shellfish areas', 'treatable shellfish areas' and 'unacceptable shellfish areas', depending upon the degree of contamination of shellfish produced. Marketing authorisation and restrictions are to be made dependent upon these classifications. Thus in the highest category of 'acceptable shellfish areas' live bivalve molluscs may be collected direct for human consumption. The hygiene requirements associated with this designation are specified according to satisfactory visual characteristic and detailed contamination specifications relating to faecal coliforms, *E. coli*, salmonella, toxic compounds, radionuclide content, paralytic shellfish poison and diarrhetic shellfish poison. By contrast, shellfish from the second category of 'treatable shellfish areas' may only be marketed after treatment in a purification system, or after relaying by transfer to natural sea areas for purification, or after processing under heat treatment. Shellfish collected from 'unacceptable shellfish areas' may only be marketed after relaying to clean waters for a long period or after relaying combined with purification so that the criteria for shellfish from 'acceptable shellfish areas' are satisfied.

In addition to the classification system to be imposed upon shellfish harvesting areas, the proposed Regulation makes a wide range of provisions for other matters associated with the production, processing and marketing of bivalve molluscs. Thus specifications are formulated for the collection and transportation of molluscs to approved expedition centres or purification plants; the suitability of sea waters for relaying purposes; the approval of establishments for handling and purification; the requirement of a public health control system to verify that health requirements have been complied with; requirements as to wrapping and containers for molluscs; requirements as to storage and transportation; and the requirement that all packages of live molluscs are to carry a health mark. Although all these matters are presently at a discussion stage it is apparent that the measures to be introduced at Community level will have a major effect upon the production and marketing of shellfish in the United Kingdom.

The second of the proposed European Community Regulations under discussion concerns the health conditions affecting the production and the placing on the market of fishery products. The purpose of the Regulation is to remove disparities in national standards by providing at Community level for regulation of the production and marketing of fishery products either fresh, frozen, prepared or processed. In relation to farmed fishery products it is indicated that slaughter is to take place under hygienic conditions, so that the method of killing is not liable to spoil or modify the product, and similarly fish are not to undergo excessive scale loss, bruising or tearing of muscle fibres or become soiled with earth, slime or faeces. Processes such as packaging, preparation and freezing are to take place only in inspected and approved establishments. Farmed fishery products are to have undergone a health check before marketing, and are to be packaged, labelled, stored and transported in accordance with requirements set out in the proposed Regulation. Again, the implications of these harmonised public health measures are of considerable significance to the organisation of aquaculture and fishery product marketing throughout the Community.

16.05   Food labelling and fish

In England and Wales (s.136(2) Food Act 1984; the corresponding provisions for Scotland are considered in [16.06] below) the Food Act 1984 empowers the Minister of Agriculture, Fisheries and Food, the Secretary of State for Social Services, and the Secretary of State for Wales, acting jointly, to make regulations for a range of purposes concerned with food (ss.4, 7 and 132(1)). Such regulations may be made by the Ministers so far as appears to them to be necessary or expedient in the interests of public health, or otherwise for the protection of the public, or to be called for by any European Community obligation. Amongst these purposes regulations may prohibit or regulate the sale, possession for sale, offer or exposure for sale, consignment, or delivery, of food which does not comply with any of the regulations (s.4(1)(c)). In addition, regulations may impose requirements or otherwise regulate the labelling, marking or advertising of food intended for human consumption and the descriptions which may be applied to such food (s.7). These regulations are stated to be without prejudice to the offence which is committed where a person who gives or displays with any food exposed by him for sale, a label which falsely describes the food or is calculated to mislead as to its nature or its substance or its quality (s.6(1); see also Trade Descriptions Act 1968).

By exercise of the Ministerial power to create regulations governing food sales, there have been enacted the Food Labelling Regulations 1984 (SI 1984 No.1305, as amended) which give effect to the European Council Directive on the approximation of the laws of Member States relating to the labelling, presentation and advertising of foodstuffs for sale to the ultimate consumer (EEC 79/112). Whilst these Regulations, which are intended amongst other things to prohibit the misleading presentation of food, are wide-ranging in their effect upon the labelling of food generally, they have quite specific implications for the sale of fish to the consumer. The basic requirement is that where a name is prescribed by law as being required to be used for a particular food, then that name must be used for that food (Reg.7). Accordingly, Schedule 1 to the Regulations lists a range of different species of fish of kinds that are sold for food, and alongside each the common name which is to be used to describe that species of fish is stated. Thus the name to be used for any species of fish specified in column 2 of the table is to be the name specified in the corresponding entry in column 1 of that table. The table of fish names prescribed by law is as shown in Table 16.1.

16.06   The Food and Drugs (Scotland) Act 1956

As has been noted, the provisions of the Food Act 1984 which provide for the introduction of Regulations to govern food labelling apply only to England and Wales. The equivalent powers in Scotland are provided for under the Food and Drugs (Scotland) Act 1956 (ss.4, 7, 26(3) and 56 Food and Drugs (Scotland) Act 1956). In accordance with these powers the Secretary of State for Scotland has introduced separate regulations implementing the European Council Directive on the approximation of the laws of Member States relating to labelling of food (EEC 79/112) in Scotland. The measure

Table 16.1

Food Labelling Regulations 1984: Schedule 1

Names Prescribed by Law: Fish

(1) Subject to sub-paragraph (2) of this paragraph, the name used for any species of fish specified in column 2 of the following Table shall be a name specified for that species in the corresponding entry in column 1 of the said Table.

(2) A customary name may be used for any species of fish which has been subjected to smoking or any similar process, unless the name of the species in column 2 of the following Table is followed by an asterisk. In such cases the name used for the food when the fish is smoked shall be either –

(a) a name specified for that species in column 1 of the said Table preceded by the word 'smoked', or
(b) except in the case of *Salmo salar* L., 'smoked Pacific salmon'.

Table

Column 1 Name	Column 2 Species of Fish
Sea fish	
Anchovy	All species of *Engraulis*
Bass	*Dicentrarchus labrax* (L.)
Brill	*Scophthalmus rhombus* (L.)
Brisling	*Sprattus sprattus* (L.), when canned
Catfish or Rockfish	All species of *Anarhichas*
Cod or Codling	*Gadus morhua* (L.) (including *Gadus morhua callarias* and *Gadus morhua morhua*)
Pacific cod or cod	*Gadus macrocephalus*
Greenland cod or cod	*Gadus ogac*
Coley or Saithe or Coalfish	*Pollachius virens* (L.)
Conger	All species of *Conger*
Dab	*Limanda limanda* (L.)
Dogfish or Flake or Huss or Rigg	All species of *Galeorhinus* All species of *Mustelus* All species of *Scyliorhinus* *Galeus melastomus* Rafin. *Squalus acanthias* (L.).
Dory or John Dory	*Zeus faber* L.
Eel	All species of *Anguilla*
Flounder	*Platichthys flesus* (L.)
Forkbeard	All species of *Phycis* All species of *Urophycis* *Raniceps raninus* (L.).
Garfish	All species of *Belone*
Grey mullet	All species of *Mugil* All species of *Liza* All species of *Chelon*
Gurnard	All genera of Triglidae *Peristedion cataphractum* L.
Haddock	*Melanogrammus aeglefinus* (L.)

Hake or Silver hake	*Merluccius merluccius* (L.)
Cape hake or Hake	{ *Merluccius capensis* (Castelnau) { *Merluccius paradoxus* (Franca)
Atlantic hake or Hake	{ *Merluccius hubbsi* (Marini) { *Merluccius bilinearis* (Mitchell)
Pacific hake or Hake	{ *Merluccius productus* (Ayres) { *Merluccius gayi* (Guich)
Halibut	{ *Hippoglossus hippoglossus* (L). { *Hippoglossus stenolepis*
Black halibut or Greenland halibut	*Reinhardtius hippoglossoides* (Walbaum)
Herring	*Clupea harengus* L.
Lascar	*Pegusa lascaris* (Risso)
Ling	All species of *Molva*
Mackerel	All species of *Scomber*
Megrim	All species of *Lepidorhombus*
Monkfish or Angler	*Lophius piscatorius* L.
Pilchard	*Sardina pilchardus* (Walbaum)
Pacific pilchard	{ *Sardinops sagax caerulea* (Girard) { *Sardinops sagax sagax* (Jenyns) { *Sardinops sagax melanosticta* (Schlegel)
South Atlantic pilchard	*Sardinops sagax ocellata* (Pappe)
Plaice	*Pleuronectes platessa* L.
Pollack or Pollock or Lythe	*Pollachius pollachius* (L.)
Pacific pollack or Pacific pollock or Alaska pollack or Alaska pollock	*Theragra chalcogramma* (Pallas)
Pout or Pouting	*Trisopterus luscus* (L.)
Redfish or Ocean perch or Rose fish	{ All species of *Sebastes* { *Helicolenus maculatus* { *Helicolenus dactylopterus* (De la Roche)
Red mullet	All species of *Mullus*
Roughback	*Hippoglossoides platessoides* (Fabr.)
Sardine	Small *Sardina pilchardus* (Walbaum)
Sardinella	All species of *Sardinella*
Scad	All species of *Trachurus*
Sea bream	All genera of Sparidae
Slid	{ Small *Clupea harengus* L., when canned { Small *Sprattus sprattus* (L.), when canned
Skate or Ray or Roker	All species of *Raja*
Smelt or Sparling	All species of *Osmerus*
Sole or Dover sole	*Solea solea* (L.)
Canary sole	*Solea senegalensis* Kaup.
Lemon sole	*Microstomus kitt* (Walbaum)
Sprat	*Sprattus sprattus* (L.), except when canned
Thickback	*Microchirus variegatus* (Don.)
Tuna or Tunny	{ All species of *Thunnus* except { *Thunnus alalunga* (Bonnaterre) { All species of *Neothunnus*
Albacore tuna	*Thunnus alalunga* (Bonnaterre)
Bonito tuna	All species of *Sarda*
Skipjack tuna	{ All species of *Euthynnus* { *Katsuwonus pelamis* (L.)
Turbot	*Scophthalmus maximus* (L.)
Tusk	*Brosme brosme* (Ascanius)

Whitebait	Small *Clupea harengus* L. (except when canned) Small *Spratuus sprattus* (L.) (except when canned)
Whiting	*Merlangius merlangus* (L.)
Blue whiting	*Micromesistius poutassou* (Risso)
Winter flounder	*Pseudopleuronectes americanus* (Walbaum)
Witch	*Glyptocephalus cynoglossus* (L.)

Salmon and freshwater fish

Salmon	*Salmo salar* L.*
Cherry salmon	*Oncorynchus masou* (Walbaum)*
Chum salmon or Keta salmon	*Oncorhynchus keta* (Walbaum)*
Medium red salmon or Coho Salmon or Silver salmon	*Oncorhynchus kisutch* (Walbaum)*
Pink salmon	*Oncorhynchus gorbuscha* (Walbaum)*
Red salmon or Sockeye salmon	*Oncorhynchus nerka* (Walbaum)*
Spring salmon or King salmon or Chinook salmon	*Oncorhynchus tschwytscha* (Walbaum)*
Brown trout	*Salmo trutta* L. which has spent all its life in fresh water
Sea trout or Salmon trout	*Salmo trutta* L. which has spent part of its life in sea water
Cut-throat trout	*Salmo clarkii* Richardson
Rainbow trout or Steelhand trout	*Salmo gairdneri* Richardson

Shellfish

Abalone or Ormer	All species of *Haliotis*
Clam or Hard shell clam	*Mercenaria mercenaria* L. *Venus verrucosa* L.
Clam or Razor clam	All species of *Ensis* and *Solen*
Cockle	All species of *Cerastoderma*
Crab	All species of the section Brachyura All species of the family Lithodidae
Crawfish or Spiny lobster or Rock lobster	All species of the family Palinuridae
Crayfish	All species of the family Astacidae All species of the family Parastacidae All species of the family Austroastacidae
Lobster	All species of *Homarus*
Slipper lobster	All species of *Scyllaridae*
Squat lobster	All species of the family Galatheidae
Mussel	All species of *Mytilus*
Oyster	All species of *Crassostrea* All species of *Ostrea*
Oyster or Portuguese oyster	*Crassostrea angulata* (Lmk.)
Oyster or Pacific oyster	*Crassostrea gigas* (Thunberg)
Oyster or Native oyster	*Ostrea edulis* L.
Prawn or Shrimp	Whole fish of – all species of *Palaemonidae*, all species of *Penaeidae*, and all species of *Pandalidae*, which are of such a size that, when cooked, they have a count of less than 397 per kg (180 per lb)

	The tails of –
	all species of *Palaemonidae*,
	all species of *Penaiedae*, and
	all species of *Pandalidae*,
	which are of such a size that, when
	peeled and cooked, they have a count
	of less than 1,323 per kg (600 per lb)
Shrimp	Whole fish of –
	all species of *Palaemonidae*,
	all species of *Penaeidae*, and
	all species of *Panadalidae*,
	which are of such a size that, when
	cooked, they have a count of 397 per
	kg (180 per lb) or more
	The tails of –
	all species of *Palaemonidae*,
	all species of *Penaeidae*, and
	all species of *Pandalidae*,
	which are of such a size that, when
	peeled and cooked, they have a count
	of 1,323 per kg (600 per lb) or more
Shrimp or Pink shrimp	*Pandalus montagui* Leach
Shrimp or Brown shrimp	All species of *Crangon*
Scallop	All species of *Pectinidae*
Scallop or Queen scallop or Queen	*Chlamys (Acquipecton) opercularis* (L.)
Scampi or Norway lobster or Dublin Bay prawn	*Nephrops norvegicus* (L.)
Whelk	All species of *Buccinum*
Winkle	All species of *Littorina*

introduced is the Food Labelling (Scotland) Regulations 1984 (SI 1984 No.1519). This provides that if there is a name prescribed by law for a food, that is the particular name required to be used for the food, and that name is to be used as provided for by Schedule 1 to the Regulations (Para.7). Schedule 1 to the Regulations, concerning the names prescribed by law for fish, is identical to that provided for in relation to England and Wales under the Food Labelling Regulations 1984 (SI 1984 No.1305) and cited in the previous section.

16.07   The Fishmongers' Company

Finally, it is pertinent to note the position of the Worshipful Company of the Fishmongers of London, now known as the Fishmongers' Company, in relation to the enforcement of aspects of fishery law relating to the marketing of fish. The Fishmongers' Company was incorporated by charter in 1604 and entrusted with the duty of investigating persons selling salted or fresh sea fish, salmon, stock fish or any other fish whatsoever, within the City of London, to discover whether such fish were wholesome and fit to be sold. For the purpose of exercising this duty to 'search and survey' fish, the Wardens and Commonalty of the Mistery of Fishmongers, as they were referred to, were authorised to enter premises in which fish were present to ascertain their fitness to be sold. In the event of inspected fish being found to be unwholesome, the wardens were empowered to to seize and dispose of it and do, in the words of the 1604 Charter, 'according to our Laws of England and the usages and Customs of the City of London'

The value of the function performed by the Fishmongers' Company in overseeing trade in fish in London has been recognised in recent times (see Bledisloe (1961) para.302) and with the transfer of the main London fish market to New Billingsgate, the City of London (Various Powers) Act 1979 transferred the regulatory powers of the Company to the new market (s.12(5) City of London (Various Powers) Act 1979). Alongside the powers of investigation and seizure provided for under the original Charter of the Company, however, the officials of the Company, referred to as 'fishmeters', are now also possessed of a range of particular powers which are provided under various fishery enactments. For example, the Salmon and Freshwater Fisheries Act 1975 creates an offence of consigning a package containing salmon or trout by any common carrier without the package being conspicuously marked as to its contents (s.24(1) Salmon and Freshwater Fisheries Act 1975). In relation to this offence it is specifically provided that an officer appointed by the Company is empowered to open any package consigned by a carrier and suspected to contain salmon or trout (ss.24(2) and 41(1)(d)), and detain the package until proof is given that the salmon or trout contained are not being dealt with unlawfully (s.24(3)), and any person who obstructs an officer of the Company in exercise of these powers is guilty of an offence (s.24(6)). More generally, the officials of the Company are empowered to seize any salmon, trout or freshwater fish bought, sold or exposed for sale by, or in the possession for sale of, any person in contravention of the 1975 Act (Sch.4 para.7). This authorises the officials of the Company to exercise a supervisory role in relation to the offences under the 1975 Act relating to buying, selling, exposure for sale or possession of unclean or immature fish (s.2(2)(b)); buying, selling, exposure for sale or possession of fish at prohibited times of the year (s.22(1)); and entering for export or exporting fish which are unclean or caught at a time when their sale is prohibited (s.23(3)). Although, as has been noted, none of these offences are committed in relation to fish which are reasonably believed to be the product of fish farming (s.33(5) Fisheries Act 1981, discussed in [14.04] above), the practical problem remains that of determining whether or not a particular fish is reasonably believed to be the product of fish farming. For the resolution of this difficulty the Company have required a certificate of origin before allowing the sale of fish which might come within the terms of the prohibitions. The officials of the Company undertake the administration of this branch of fishery law within the precincts of Billingsgate Market.

Other matters of fishery law over which the officials of the Company exercise a regulatory jurisdiction arise in relation to sea fish and shellfish. Thus under the Sea Fish (Conservation) Act 1967, (s.16(1)(e) Sea Fish (Conservation) Act 1967) and the Sea Fish (Shellfish) Act 1967 (s.18 Sea Fish (Conservation) Act 1967) an authorised officer of the Company may seize any sea fish, lobsters, nephrops and crabs which are sold or exposed or offered for sale by any person in contravention of those Acts or Orders made under them, or possessed in contravention of the Acts or Orders. In addition, the

Minister of Agriculture, Fisheries and Food is empowered (under s.7(2) and (3) Sea Fisheries Act 1968) to appoint officials of the Company to exercise within the Billingsgate Market the powers of a British sea-fishery officer. In the exercise of this power the Minister may authorise the exercise of powers under the Sea Fish (Conservation) Act 1967 (ss.7 and 15(2)(d) Sea Fish (Conservation) Act 1967) in relation to the Salmon and Migratory Trout (Restrictions on Landing) Order 1972 (SI 1972 No.1966, as amended by SI 1975 No.639 and SI 1983 No.58) requiring declarations and enabling the seizure of fish under that Order. Also, the Minister may appoint officials of the Company to exercise powers under the Sea Fishing (Enforcement of Community Conservation Measures) Order 1986 (SI 1986 No.2090, and see [15.13] above) for the purpose of the Order in so far as it applies to undersized fish (Arts.6(5)(a) and 6(6)(a) Sea Fishing (Enforcement of Community Conservation Measures) Order 1986).

Chapter 17

The Prospect of Salmon Ranching

17.01 The future of salmon farming

The main aim of this book has been to provide an account of the law governing the most important commercial forms of aquacultural activity presently undertaken in Britain. This final chapter ventures beyond description of the laws which regulate contemporary fish farming practice to consider legal provisions which constrain certain kinds of future development in the industry. In particular, consideration is given to the legal issues raised by the prospect of the British industry adopting techniques of 'salmon ranching', which have proved to be successful when followed by other fish farming nations (generally, see Thorpe (1980A)). The premise behind this discussion is that, despite the remarkable technical advances which have been achieved in salmon production, it needs to be considered whether the environmental and economic costs of present practice are necessary, and whether the biological potential for the industry is being fully realised. A major impediment to further progress in the industry may not involve a dramatic advance in aquacultural technique, but rather the provision of an appropriate legal structure for a more efficient form of salmon farming. A combination of inappropriate property rights in wild creatures and fishery legislation designed for the exploitation of wild stocks of fish may serve to place the commercial production of salmon upon the wrong footing and need reconsideration in the near future.

17.02 Limitations of cage rearing

The mastery of techniques necessary for the farming of the Atlantic Salmon has been amongst the greatest technical achievements in the history of aquaculture (generally, see Beveridge (1987)). The profitable and expanding industry which those techniques now support is self-evidence of their commercial success. An appreciation of the extent of this achievement must take note of the fact that the salmon is one of a small number of 'anadromous' species of fish to be found in the British Isles. Anadromous species, under natural conditions, are characterised by propagation and early growth taking place in freshwater, followed by migration seaward and marine feeding, and a return to freshwater for spawning. In relation to salmon it was the peculiar requirement of a progression from fresh to saline water which previously constituted a major technical obstacle to the cultivation of the species, and remains the major distinction between salmon farming and the farming of trout or other purely freshwater, or purely saltwater, species. Nonetheless, the problem of simulating the varied conditions required for the artificial rearing of salmon, as an anadromous species, has now been surmounted.

Aquacultural replication of the sea-dwelling stage of the salmon's life cycle has been achieved by using one of two methods. The first method involves pumping sea water into onshore tanks, though this has been found to involve relatively high energy costs and is used in only about 6 per cent of salmon farms (Cobham Resource Consultants (1987) para.2.9). The second, and most common method, is to transfer salmon smolts to sea cages, placed in sheltered coastal water. Containment under these conditions for about a year, with controlled feeding, is normally sufficient for a large proportion of the fish to mature as grilse, whilst the remainder are retained for another year to be marketed as salmon proper (Cobham Resource Consultants (1987) para.2.11).

As with other branches of intensively practised agriculture, high productivity is won at a cost to the environment, and the dramatic expansion of this branch of the industry has inevitably given rise to a range of matters of environmental concern (generally, see Royal Commission on Environmental Pollution (1979)). Notable amongst environmental concerns are matters which have had their legal features presented in previous chapters: the visual disamenity of unplanned development in coastal locations (considered in Chapters 2 to 4) the increased risk of disease transfer (considered in Chapter 7) the problem of escapes of farmed fish with a different genetic make-up from wild populations (considered in Chapter 8) problems of water pollution caused by cage culture (considered in Chapter 11) and the potential misuse of chemicals in fish farming to the detriment of the aquatic environment (considered in Chapter 13). These issues, amongst others, feature in a growing debate on whether the environmental cost of the salmon farming industry is an altogether acceptable one.

In economic terms simulation of the marine life of the salmon by placement in sea cages is a relatively expensive activity, since, as fish become larger containment costs, feeding, and a range of other overheads are considerably greater than during earlier, freshwater, stages of development. Because of the disproportionate costs of cage rearing of salmon to a marketable size, losses at this stage are especially serious. Moreover, the potential for losses is enhanced by the vulnerability of high-density cage culture methods to particular kinds of hazard such as storm damage, predation and disease, to a degree not found in other forms of fish farming.

17.03 Sea ranching of salmon

The natural migratory behaviour of the salmon as an anadromous species, migrating to sea and returning to freshwater to spawn, provides the mechanism for fundamentally different culture techniques from those presently used in Britain. The wastefulness of the salmon's natural history means that the potential for diminishing losses by husbandry through protection of fish from hazards encountered in the wild is considerable. The application of aquacultural techniques of propagation and rearing, in conditions which exclude the principal causes of mortality encountered during the first year of life in the wild, allows production to be increased to levels many times greater than those achievable under natural conditions (Thorpe (1980A) at p. 3). It is this combination of factors which provides the alternative to cage culture: sea ranching.

It has been shown by other fish farming nations that, as a matter of practice, the possession of this homing instinct means that salmon smolts released from a particular point in freshwater return to that point on maturity as fully grown salmon. Accordingly, in the farming of both Pacific and Atlantic species of salmon in the United States, Canada, Japan and other major fish farming nations this faculty has been utilised by releasing hatchery-reared smolts to be recaptured on return after a period of natural feeding and growth at sea. This process of rearing salmon by ranching has considerable environmental and economic advantages over cage culture techniques.

The basic mechanics of salmon ranching involve the release of smolts, usually a year after propagation, from the point to which it is intended they should return. If the point of release is not a hatchery in which they have been reared, acclimatisation to the release waters may be needed to 'imprint' the fish with the unique water character of the home stream, the recognition of which guides salmon back on their return from sea migration by its distinctive 'smell' (Saunders (1977) at p. 18). Release of fish to pasture at sea means, of course, that sea cages and their associated environmental and economic problems are obviated.

In addition to its environmental and economic advantages, ranching has the merit of biological rationality in that released fish forage naturally for their food at sea and have no need to be fed an artificial high-protein diet. The present use of low-quality fish meal to produce pellets for caged salmon results in a overall loss of protein by conversion of a larger amount of low quality fish meal pellets into a lesser amount of high-quality salmon (Bishop (1987)). Moreover, ranching is thought to be a means of increasing total quantities of fish protein without direct competition with other means of harvesting protein from the sea, nor with wild stocks of salmon. Because it is commonly accepted that the Atlantic has previously supported much greater numbers of salmon than at present (generally, see Netboy (1980)) its biological carrying capacity should not be rapidly overloaded by ranching (Berg (1981) at p. 95; and Thorpe (1980B) at p. 153). Another incidental advantage (Edwards (1978) at p. 176) to be gained from this approach is that the food consumed by ranched salmon is likely to consist to a large extent of fish and crustacea which are not already harvested, either because they are species which are unpopular with consumers, or because they are located in areas where harvesting is uneconomic (Thorpe (1980A) at p. 4). Ranching could, therefore, be a genuine means of increasing the production of high-quality protein in Britain by converting salmon from net consumers into net producers of protein.

Having noted the advantages of salmon ranching over present cage culture methods, it must also be noted that the method is not altogether a 'something for nothing' activity. Although hatchery rearing to smolt stage results in lower rates of mortality than in the wild, thereafter, life at sea is no less hazardous for farmed salmon than for wild fish at the same stage of development. It follows that anticipated return rates will be low as a proportion of the number of fish released. This has been found to be the case in ranching experiments and commercial operations in other countries (Nash (1977) at p. 44; and Thorpe (1980A) at p. 161) with the proportion of fish returning invariably amounting to only a small proportion of the number released. This low return rate has, however, to be gauged against the even smaller proportion of fish which need return to make a ranching operation financially viable (Berg (1981) at p. 87). Weighing all factors into the balance, other nations have concluded that, despite low return rates, the economic viability of ranching is, in principle, conclusively established.

Despite the potential for salmon ranching in Britain, certain legal difficulties surround the protection and equitable distribution of the enhanced stocks which would be produced by salmon ranching. In theory, it might be thought that those who make available a greater amount of a resource should also have the first claim to the harvesting of that resource. In the context of harvesting ranched salmon, however, the competing claims of different interest groups are not easily resolved. In particular, the lack of a legal structure to provide a clear resolution of property rights involved in salmon ranching, and the difficulty of reconciling the activity with existing salmon fishery laws, provide a serious obstacle to aquacultural development in Britain. Essentially there are two aspects to the problem of property rights over ranched fish in Britain, the first concerns the rights of ownership over salmon which have been released as a part of the ranching process. The second legal problem concerning ranched fish relates to permitted methods of recapture of ranched fish under fishery law.

17.04   *Legal rights over ranched fish*

For reasons relating to the common law of animal ownership, devised many centuries before the artificial rearing of salmon was envisaged, the legal position with regard to ownership of released fish is a matter of some difficulty for the prospective salmon rancher (generally, see Wildsmith (1982) Chapter 4). The explanation for this lies in the previously considered common law division of the animal kingdom into the two categories of domestic animals, termed *domitae naturae*, and wild animals, termed *ferae naturae*. (Generally, see Williams (1939); North (1972); and discussion in [14.06] above.) As has been noted, the distinction between domesticated and wild animals corresponds to the difference between those animals in which the possessor has an absolute right of ownership and those where the right is merely that of 'qualified' ownership. The consequences of this distinction become apparent if an animal is released, or escapes, from possession. A domestic animal remains the absolute property of its owner despite the escape, whereas the qualified ownership of a wild animal is maintained only for so long as it is retained in the possession of an owner. (See quotation from Blackstone (1766) in [14.06] above.)

Because wild animals are not owned, they cannot be the subject of theft (see s.4(4) Theft Act 1968, cited in [14.06] above) and for that reason special statutory provision has been made in England in Wales for an offence of unlawfully taking or destroying fish in private waters (Sch.1 para.2 Theft Act 1968; and Howarth (1987C)). Similarly in Scotland, it has been made an offence for any person without legal right, or without written permission from a person having such right, to fish for or take salmon in any waters including any part of the sea within one mile of low water mark (s.1 Salmon and Freshwater Fisheries (Protection) (Scotland) Act 1951). Again, because of the wild and unowned character of the fish concerned, a person committing this offence would not normally commit the offence of theft.

The acquisition of a right of ownership in fish requires the complete act of capture of a fish in order that it be 'reduced into possession' (R v. Hundsdon (1781) 2 East PC 611). Acts falling short of successful capture would not serve to reduce fish into possession for these purposes, and until that point is reached the fish might be captured by any other person (Young v Hitchens (1844) 6 QB 606). If after having been captured a fish is released into the wild, so ending the reduction into possession, it is capable of becoming the property of any person who subsequently captures it. In general, therefore, fish, even if reared in captivity become in law wild animals when qualified ownership is relinquished by their release. It is likely that this is the position at common law when a salmon rancher releases fish to migrate to sea, with all right to ownership of such fish being lost upon their release.

A qualification to these general principles relating to the loss of ownership of wild animals arises in the case of wild animals which are said to possess the instinct or intention to return to captivity, termed *animus revertendi* (Wildsmith (1982) at p. 97). It was the authoritative legal commentator Blackstone who observed that

> 'my tame hawk that is pursuing his quarry in my presence, though he is at liberty to go where he pleases, he is nevertheless my property; for he hath *animus revertendi*. So are my pigeons, that are flying a distance from their home ... all which remain still in my possession and I preserve my qualified property in them, but if they stray without my knowledge and do not return in the usual manner, it is lawful for any stranger to take them.' (Blackstone (1766) Vol. 2 p. 392)

Hence, the principle of *animus revertendi* has been held to apply in recent times in *Hamps* v. *Darby* ([1948] 2 KB 311) where racing pigeons were found to possess an instinct to return to captivity after being released in the wild and, therefore, to remain the property of the person releasing them.

As a matter of theory the principle of *animus revertendi* has considerable potential relevance to the enterprise of salmon ranching where it could be argued that the anadromous instinct of salmon to return to their native river to spawn is an indication of this instinct. Unfortunately, though, the analogy between the behaviour of homing pigeons, which head directly homewards, and the salmon, which may spend several years ranging vast areas of the north Atlantic before returning to spawn, is a tenuous one. No common law authority determines the legal position, and a remote possibility that a salmon's homing instinct might amount to *animus revertendi* for the purpose of a salmon rancher's claim to maintain ownership of it looks to be a highly speculative legal basis on which to found what is capable of becoming an intensively capitalised branch of the aquaculture industry.

The probable predicament of the salmon rancher at common law is, therefore, that release of fish to pasture at sea amounts to the relinquishment of ownership over them. Moreover, there is no reason to suppose the position would be any different if a rancher were to identify the released fish by means of a tag (a method of identification used by fish hatcheries in Oregon: see Berg (1981) at p. 83) or other mark (contrast Owen (1978) at p. 290). As a consequence of this, any person with a lawful right to fish for salmon in the sea (see Hale (1875) App.I p. viii; and *Attorney-General for British Columbia* v. *Attorney-General for Canada* [1914] AC 153; and Stair (1832) Book II Title 1 para.5., and Title 3 para.69) may take as great a benefit from the rancher's endeavours as their commercial fishing or angling skill enables them to.

Having summarised the likely legal position of the salmon rancher in relation to released fish it is to be noted that the weakness of this position need not be fatal to the enterprise of salmon ranching. In the United States, for example, though there has been considerable political pressure by ranchers for protection of ranched stocks from exploitation by commercial and recreational fishermen (Berg (1981) at pp. 93 to 94 and pp. 96 to 97), ranchers presently operate under analogous provisions to those which apply in Britain. That is, released fish become the property of the state, as the owner of wild creatures, and so are not the subject of any special protection beyond that of other wild fish. As a consequence, losses to commercial and recreational fishing are seen as an overhead which the ranchers are obliged to bear and with which they have, grudgingly, learned to live. Likewise in Britain, the almost insuperable difficulty of providing special legal protection for ranched fish, which are indistinguishable from their wild counterparts, means that this is an adversity which must be conceded as an unavoidable cost in ranching operations (Thorpe (1980B) at p. 7; contrast Wildsmith (1982) at p. 101).

17.05   *Recapture of ranched fish*

An additional difficulty to that which arises through the loss of ownership of ranched fish on release concerns the need for special legal provision for recapture of returning fish. The difficulty here is that, without specific provision for harvesting a crop of ranched salmon, lawful recapture must be in accordance with the general salmon fishery laws. As has been noted (in [14.01]) these laws have been enacted for the protection of scarce stocks of wild fish requiring conservation and protection from over-exploitation (Howarth (1987A) preface xi). However strong the conservational justification for salmon fishery laws may be in protecting wild fish, these laws also operate to make unlawful any practicable means of exploiting artificially enhanced stocks of ranched salmon at the time when they are most profitably harvested. Conservationally motivated legislation is unnecessary, to the point of perversity, where fish are the product of aquaculture since, if properly conducted, the harvesting of the ranched salmon should pose no threat to wild stocks of fish.

The most appropriate method of recapturing returning ranched salmon would be by means of a net or inscale bar trap placed near the point from which the fish were originally released. This method would ensure near 100 per cent recapture of returning fish with relatively little difficulty or expense. The problem, however, is that the installation of such a device in England and Wales or in Scotland would, without special provision, be an offence under laws relating to the use of 'fixed engines' for taking salmon (Howarth (1986B) at p. 345). In England and Wales, the offence involved in the installation or operation of a fish trap of this kind would be that of placing or use of an unauthorised fixed engine in any inland or tidal waters (s.6(1) Salmon and Freshwater Fisheries Act 1975, as amended by s.33 Salmon Act 1986; and see Part II Salmon and Freshwater Fisheries Act 1975 generally on obstructions to the passage of migratory fish). Although the National Rivers Authority and local sea fisheries committees are empowered to authorise a fish catching device of this kind (s.6(3)(c) Salmon and Freshwater Fisheries Act 1975, as amended by s.33(2) and s.37(2) Salmon Act 1986; and para.21 of Part II Sch.3 Salmon and Freshwater Fisheries Act 1975, as amended by s.33(3) Salmon Act 1986) it is unlikely that they would ever be prepared to do so. The general policy followed for over a century has been that of reducing the number of authorised fixed engines permitted to be used to take salmon, and allowing the use of only those 'privileged engines' which were certified by the Special Commissioners on Salmon Fisheries (appointed under the Salmon Fishery Act 1865) to have been in established use before 1861 (s.39 Salmon Fishery Act 1865).

In Scotland, the recapture of ranched fish would be problematic since it is unlawful to fish for or take salmon in any inland water, except by rod and line, or by net and coble. Net and coble is a method of fishing in which a net is paid out from a rowing boat whilst a rope attached to the end of the net is held on the bank, the net being swept through the water while a person on the bank moves to the other end of the sweep and retrieves the net (*Hay* v. *Magistrates of Perth* (1863) 4 Macq. 535, 551; Hunter (1963) para.35; and Hunter (1965) para.79). The limitation to rod and line and net and coble fishing is subject to the exception that any right of fishing in existence at the commencement of the Salmon and Freshwater Fisheries (Protection) (Scotland) Act 1951 may continue to be exercised as if the Act had not been passed (s.2(1) Salmon and Freshwater Fisheries (Protection) (Scotland) Act 1951; see also s.21 Salmon Act 1986). The likely effect of this proviso is that the only kinds of fixed engine permitted in Scotland are the small number of traps known as 'cruives' that have been in existence since before the Act.

It is notable that the general exclusion of offences under fisheries conservation legislation in relation to fish farming, introduced under s.33 Fisheries Act 1981 (see Chapter 14) would probably not be applicable to the recapture of ranched fish for two reasons. First, although s.33(1) allows for a Ministerial order to exempt acts done in the course of fish farming, no exemption is provided for in respect of the main offences in relation to fixed engines. Second, 'fish farming' is defined in s.33(6) of the 1981 Act to mean the breeding, rearing or cultivating of fish ... whether or not for the purpose of producing food for human consumption, but in relation to defences against certain offences it is stipulated that it 'does not include fish bred, reared or cultivated in captivity which have later been released to the wild'. The import of this appears to be that general exemptions from fishery offences in relation to fish farms would not apply in respect of ranched salmon released to sea.

A more likely possibility, in relation to Scotland at least, is that a recently introduced measure under the Salmon Act 1986 may be applied to salmon ranching contexts. This is the stipulation that a person is not, in respect of any act or omission relating to fishing for or taking salmon, to be guilty of contravention of an enactment prohibiting or regulating that act or omission if it has been exempted by the Secretary of State for Scotland (s.27(1) Salmon Act 1986). The Secretary of State is empowered to exempt an act or omission of this kind only if he is satisfied that consent has been given to the exemption by the proprietor of every affected salmon fishery entered in the valuation role in the salmon fishery district in which the act or omission is to take place and, if there is one, the salmon fishery board for that district (s.27(2)). Further qualifications require that an exemption of this kind may relate only to a person specified in it, and may be subject to such conditions as may be specified. The exemption is to be in writing and is to specify the limits of the waters to which it relates, its duration and the enactment to which it relates (s.27(4)).

The provision allowing the Secretary of State to provide exemption from offences in relation to the taking of salmon appears sufficiently widely formulated to be used to authorise salmon ranching ventures in Scotland, and it has been suggested that this is a purpose for which the provision was intended (93 HC DEB 1986 Col. 239). However, it is capable of use in a wide range of other situations in which it is thought proper to make make lawful the taking of salmon by a means other than those provided for under fishery law (for example, in situations where fish escape from fish farms, discussed in [14.06] above). The discretion of the Secretary of State is circumscribed by no specific indications as to what purpose his powers are intended to accomplish, and it might be thought desirable that an explicit indication would be given that authorisation for salmon ranching was envisaged, and the circumstances in which such a venture would be permitted. It is likely that the recapture of ranched salmon might be permitted under special authorisation by the Secretary of State, but the capacity of Scottish law to provide for this has not been fully tested.

17.06   *Salmon ranching in international law*

Salmon ranching is unlike aquaculture activities which presently operate in Britain in that it would involve the migration of fish far beyond the extent of national waters and would, therefore, be subject to international as well as national law. Fortunately, however, international law is more favourable towards the prospective salmon rancher that the provisions under the domestic laws of England and Wales and Scotland which have been considered. Indeed it is the supportive nature of international provisions which has allowed other nations to embark upon this branch of aquacultural activity.

The key issue of property rights over ranched fish is mirrored on a global scale in the difficulty as to whether a state from which anadromous fish originate is entitled to claim any preferential rights against other states who might seek to take them whilst outside the waters of the state of origin. Helpfully, the international issues which this involves have been largely resolved under the provisions of the United Nations Convention on the Law of the Sea 1982, 'UNCLOS III' (Cmnd.8941; and generally see, Aglen (1980); and Kent (1978)). The general plan of the Convention involves the imposition of responsibilities upon coastal states to conserve, manage and maintain the living marine resources within their 'exclusive economic zone' (Art.56(1)(a)

UNCLOS III). The exclusive economic zone is defined as an area beyond and adjacent to the territorial sea, not extending beyond 200 nautical miles from the low-water baselines from which the breadth of the territorial sea is measured (Art.57). Within this zone a coastal state has important rights and duties in relation to the exploitation of the natural resources of the marine environment. In particular, a state has the right to determine the maximum level of exploitation of a living resource which permits a sustainable yield of the resource to be maintained (Art.61(1)). Beyond this a state is bound to promote optimum utilisation of living resources subject to the constraint of avoiding over-exploitation (Art.62(1)). As a consequence of these provisions it follows that salmon ranching should be provided for in so far as it is a means of achieving the optimal utilisation of fishery resources envisaged under UNCLOS.

Despite the responsibilities of coastal states under UNCLOS, it is apparent from what is known about the life cycle of the salmon that migration of the species takes it considerably further than the bounds of the United Kingdom's 200 mile exclusive economic zone. Indeed, if ranched fish follow natural patterns of migration, it is likely that they will pass through the zones of several different coastal states, and also through international waters which are outside the exclusive economic zone of any particular state. The potential for exploitation brought by these movements raises the question of what is a proper level of exploitation of the resource between different states. This matter is specifically provided for under Art.66 of UNCLOS, concerned with anadromous stocks, which enunciates the basic principle that states in whose rivers anadromous stocks originate are to have primary interest in, and responsibility for, such stocks (Art.66(1)). As a counterpart of this, however, it is for the state of origin to ensure the conservation of anadromous stocks by the establishment of appropriate regulatory measures for fishing in all waters within its exclusive economic zone, and may establish total allowable catches for stocks originating in its rivers (Art.66(2)).

The stipulation that fishing for anadromous species is to take place only within the exclusive economic zone of a state (Art.66(3)(a)) provides a general solution to the problem of salmon being taken whilst in international waters. This prohibition is subject to an exception in circumstances where preventing fishing for anadromous stocks would result in economic dislocation for a state other than the state of origin. In such a case the states concerned are to maintain consultations with a view to achieving agreement on terms and conditions of such fishing, giving due regard to the conservation requirements and the needs of the state of origin. The state of origin of the stocks is to co-operate in minimising economic dislocation in other states fishing the stocks, taking into account the normal catch and the mode of operations of such states and the areas in which such fishing takes place (Art.66(3)(b)). In particular, where a state participates with the state of origin in measures to renew anadromous stocks, particularly by expenditures for that purpose, it is to be given special consideration by the state of origin in the harvesting of stocks originating in its rivers (Art.66(3)(c)). Otherwise, where anadromous stocks migrate into or through waters within the exclusive economic zones of other states there is to be co-operation with the state of origin with regard to the conservation and management of stocks (Art.66(4)). The state of origin of anadromous stocks, and other states fishing the stocks, are to make arrangements for the implementation of these provisions, where appropriate, through regional organisations (Art.66(5)).

The duty imposed under UNCLOS to enter into international agreements for the implementation of the provisions of Art.66 has been given effect through the Convention for the Conservation of Salmon in the North Atlantic Ocean 1982. This Convention applies between states with interests in the conservation of stocks of salmon in the North Atlantic and prohibits fishing for salmon beyond the areas of fisheries jurisdiction, that is, the 200 mile exclusive economic zones of coastal states. Within the areas of fisheries jurisdiction of these states, in most instances, fishing for salmon is prohibited beyond 12 nautical miles from the baselines from which the breadth of the territorial sea is measured (Howarth (1986B) at p. 347). Further conservation, restoration, enhancement and rational management of salmon stocks is to be brought about through consultation and co-operation under the guidance of an international organisation known as the North Atlantic Salmon Conservation Organisation.

The effect of Art.66 of UNCLOS, and the Convention for the Conservation of Salmon in the North Atlantic Ocean, with respect to potential salmon ranching operations in Britain is highly favourable. The possibility of international 'poaching' of ranched fish are resolved by restrictions upon marine fisheries for anadromous stocks, generally limiting the taking of such fish to the territorial waters of the North Atlantic states. Whilst this may not amount to complete protection of ranched fish in waters outside the United Kingdom's exclusive economic zone it provides sufficient protection to make the threat to ranching operations relatively small in comparison with natural hazards facing salmon at sea.

Despite the generally favourable disposition of international law towards salmon ranching operations, a cautious approach might be needed in the more distant future if projects of this kind were ever to exceed the scale envisaged under Art.66 of UNCLOS. The main motive behind the Article is the *conservation* of anadromous stocks, with management of such stocks arising as a secondary and ancillary consideration. The conservational motivation indicates that wild fish were the first concern in the drafting of the Article, since it is inappropriate to talk of 'conservation' of plentiful supplies of farmed fish. Ranching has the potential to become a highly efficient means of harvesting an increased amount of protein from the sea and, moreover, from the sea's international waters beyond the limits of exclusive economic zones of coastal states (Smith and Marshall (1974) at pp. 329 to 336). This potential is hinted at in the observation that 'ranching substitutes predatory fish for ships: the growing free-ranging salmon obtains its own protein by foraging, packages this in a form highly acceptable for human consumption, and returns to deliver itself to the harvester with only minimal use of boats in the whole production process' (Thorpe (1980A) at p. 4). Given this potential it is conceivable that future use of ranching techniques might in some respects amount to an effective alternative to conventional methods of commercial fishing (Joyner (1975) at p. 5). On that scale it might be thought improper that a conservationally intended provision should be used to justify disproportionate harvesting of living marine resources by those states relying upon it (Kent (1978); and Gulland (1979)). In such circumstances the equitability of ocean use as an international fishery resource between ranching and non-ranching states would need to be reconsidered (Nash (1977) at p. 45). For the present, however, that potential difficulty lies some way in the future and presents no obstruction to the *commencement* of ranching programs.

17.07   *Conclusion*

This chapter has covered the general legal principles relating to the activity of salmon ranching whilst avoiding the legal detail which would be required to ensure that particular ranching operations were properly managed. Naturally, the environmental features of any proposed operation would need to be investigated in depth before approval is given. Safeguards would be needed to ensure minimal interference with natural stocks of fish before any particular venture of this kind could be embarked upon. It might be appropriate to restrict ranching operations to locations in which competition with natural populations, and genetic problems caused by interbreeding (see Wilkins (undated)), would be minimal. Alternatively, restrictions might properly be imposed to prohibit a rancher taking any fish other than those identifiably marked to show that they had been released as a part of the ranching program, to prevent any damage to wild stocks. An appropriate legal mechanism to achieve objectives of these kinds might be that of a licensing system to ensure that each operator in the new industry adhered to the requirements of a central licensing authority in respect of a wide range of operational matters.

Matters of detail apart, however, all the indications are that the enterprise of salmon ranching has a lot to offer as an advance in aquacultural technique. Regrettably, a significant part of difficulties which obstruct the realisation of this potential appear to be legal in character. There is good reason to suppose that substantial environmental and economic improvements upon present practice would be secured if an appropriate legal mechanism were available to facilitate the commencement of salmon ranching operations in Britain.

Bibliography

Anon., 'The Lobster, Crab and Oyster Fisheries', (1877) 288 *Quarterly Review* p.475.

Anon., 'Section 17 Determination', (1949) *Journal of Planning and Environment Law* p.421.

Anon., 'Proposed Amendments to the General Development Order' [1984] *Journal of Planning and Environment Law* 219.

Anon., 'Fish Farming and the Medicines Act', (1987A) *Fish Farmer* September p.42.

Anon., 'Cage Pollution Equals Sewage', (1987B) *Fish Farmer* March p.24.

Anon., 'Last-Minute Judgement', (1987C) *Fish Farmer* March p.3.

Anon., 'Norwegian Aquaculture: Controlling the Antibiotic Explosion', (1988A) 166 *Animal Pharmacy* 4 November p.8.

Anon., 'Fjords provide shelter from toxic algae . . .', (1988B) *New Scientist* 9 June 1988 p.36.

Anon., 'Algal blooms blamed on acid rain', (1988C) *New Scientist* 23rd June 1988 p.27.

Anon., 'Cyprinus carpio – an ornamental?', (1988D) *Fish* April 1988 p.3.

Aglen, A.J., 'International Law and the United Nations Law of the Sea Conference in relation to Atlantic Salmon' p.30 in Went, A.E.J., *Atlantic Salmon: Its Future*, (1980) Fishing News Books Ltd.

Alabaster, J.S., and Lloyd, R., *Water Quality Criteria for Freshwater Fish*, (1980) Butterworths.

Alabaster, J.S., *Report of European Inland Fisheries Advisory Commission Workshop on Fish Farm Effluents*, (1982) EIFAC Technical Paper 41.

Alderman, D., 'Fish Medicines: A Dictionary', (1988) 5 *Trout News* p.11.

Anderson, J.I.W., 'Salmon Farming in Scotland', (1973) paper delivered at Salmon and Trout Association London Conference 20 November 1973.

Association of River Authorities/National Water Council, *Salmon Propagation in England and Wales*, (1978) National Water Council.

Balfour, Sir J., *Prackticks: or a System of the more Ancient Law of Scotland* (1754) and Stair Society 1962–3.

Bathers, D., 'Fishery Prosecution – Practice, Policy and Procedure', Ch.10 in *Poaching and Protection: The Proceedings of a Joint Welsh Salmon and Trout Angling Association/Water Authorities Association Symposium*, (1986) Welsh Water Authority.

Beck, L., 'Setting Fish Farm Standards', (1988) paper delivered to Institution of Chemical Engineers (Aquaculture Branch) 2 November 1988.

Bell, G.J., *Principles of the Law of Scotland* (10th ed. 1899) T. and T. Clark.

Berg, E.R., 'Private Ocean Ranching of Pacific Salmon and Fishery Management: A Problem of Federalism', (1981) 12 *Environmental Law* 81.

Beveridge, M.C., *Cage Aquaculture*, (1987) Fishing News Books Ltd.

Bishop, G.M., *The Impact of an Expansion of the Scottish Fin Fish Aquaculture Industry on Wild Fish Stocks Used to Supply Fishmeal Components of Feedstuffs*, (1987) Report to World Wildlife Fund cited by Scottish Wildlife and Countryside Link, *Marine Fishfarming in Scotland*, (1988) at para 12.2.

Blake, B.F., *The Environmental Impact of Fish Farming in Scotland*, (1983) CST Report No.473 Nature Conservacy Council.

Blackstone, Sir W., *Commentaries on the Law of England*, (1766) (18th ed. by Lee, J. 1829) S. Sweet, R. Pheney, A. Maxwell and Stevens and Sons.

Bledisloe, Viscount, *Report of the Committee on Salmon and Freshwater Fisheries*, (1961) Cmnd.1350.

Bonyhardy, T., *The Law of the Countryside*, (1987) Professional Books.

Bowden, G., *Coastal Aquaculture Law and Policy*, (1981) Westview Press.

British Field Sports Society, *Predatory Birds of Game and Fish* (1985) Working Party on Avian Predators, British Field Sports Society.

Brown, J.R., Gowen, R.J., and McLusky, D.S., 'The Effect of Salmon Farming on the Benthos of a Scottish Sea Loch', (1987) 109 *Journal of Experimental Marine Biology and Ecology* 39.

Bryant, P., Jauncy, K., and Atack, T., *Backyard Fish Farming*, (1980) Prism Press.

Cobham Resource Consultants, *An Environmental Assessment of Fish Farms*, (1987) Report to Countryside Commission for Scotland, Crown Estate Commissioners, Highlands and Islands Development Board, and Scottish Salmon Growers' Association.

Cole, H.A., *Oyster Cultivation in Britain* (1956) Ministry of Agriculture, Fisheries and Food.

Cooper, M.E., *An Introduction to Animal Law*, (1987) Academic Press.

Coulson, H.J.W. and Forbes, U.A., *Coulson and Forbes on the Law of Waters* (6th ed. 1952) by Hobday, S.R., Sweet and Maxwell Ltd.

Crown Estate, *Marine Fish Farms*, pamplet A not dated.

Crown Estate, *Marine Fish Farms Application for Lease*, pamplet B not dated.

Crown Estate, *Consultative Procedures on Applications to the Crown Estate for Leases for Fish Farm Developments in Scottish Coastal Waters*, (1986) Crown Estate.

Crown Estate, *Fish Farming – Guidelines on Siting and Design of Marine Fish Farms in Scotland*, (1987) Crown Estate.

Crown Estate, *Environmental Assessment of Marine Salmon Farms*, (1988) Crown Estate.

Dale, J.R. and Appelbe, G.E., *Pharmacy Law and Ethics*, (1989) Pharmaceutical Press.

Davies, I.M., Bailey, S.K. and Moore, D.C., 'Tributyltin in Scottish Sea Lochs, as Indicated by Degree of Imposex in the Dogwhelk, *Nucella lapillus* (L.)', (1987) 18 *Marine Pollution Bulletin* 7 p.400.

Davies, I.M. and McKie, J.E., 'Accumulation of Total Tin and Tributyltin in Muscle Tissues of Farmed Atlantic Salmon', (1987) 18 *Marine Pollution Bulletin* p.405.

Deans, M.E., 'The Crown Estate Commissioners: Their role and Responsibilities in Respect of the Foreshore and Seabed around Scotland', (1986) *Journal of Energy and Natural Resources Law* p.166.

Department of Agriculture and Fisheries for Scotland, *Proposed Regulations for the Passage of Salmon: Consultation Paper* (1988).

Department of Agriculture and Fisheries for Scotland, *Diseases of Fish Act 1937*

(As Amended) Notifiable Diseases in Fish Farms in Scotland A CODE OF PRACTICE (Undated).

Department of the Environment, Circular 17/84, *Water and the Environment,* (1984).

Department of the Environment, Circular 36/85, *Discharges to the Water Environment: Public Registers,* (1985).

Department of the Environment, Circular 3/86, *Changes to the General Development Order,* (1986A).

Department of the Environment, Pollution Paper No.23, *Public Access to Environmental Information,* (1986B).

Department of the Environment, Circular 19/87, *Control of Pollution (Anti-fouling Paints and Treatments) Regulations,* (1987).

Department of the Environment, Circular 15/88, *Town and Country Planning (Assessment of Environmental Effects) Regulations,* (1988).

Edwards, B., 'Financial Assistance for Aquaculture', (1987) 3 *Trout News* p.3.

Edwards, B., 'Financial Assistance for Aquaculture', (1988) 5 *Trout News* p.2.

Edwards, B., 'Beyond 1992: Controls in the EC Without Internal trade Barriers', (1989) paper delivered at Institute of Fisheries Management Workshop on the Dangers Associated with the Importation of Ornamental Fish, 13 April 1989.

Edwards, D.J., *Salmon and Trout Farming in Norway,* (1978) Fishing News Books Ltd.

European Inland Fisheries Advisory Commission, *Report of the Working Party on Withdrawal Period for Drugs,* (1988).

Ferguson, J., *The Law of Water and Water Rights in Scotland,* (1907) Green and Sons.

Freeman, L., 'Change in Law for Fish Farms?', (1984) *Water Bulletin* 3 February p.6.

Garner, J.F., *Control of Pollution Act 1974,* (1975) Butterworths.

Gloag, W.M. and Henderson, R.C., *Introduction to the Law of Scotland* (9th ed. 1987) by Wilkinson, A.B. and Wilson W.A., W.Green and Son Ltd.

Gordon, G.H., *The Criminal Law of Scotland* (2nd ed. 1978) W. Green and Son Ltd.

Golding, J., 'A Fishy Business' (1987) *Taxation,* 25 September p.549.

Gowen, R.J., and Bradbury, N.B., 'The Ecological Impact of Salmon Farming in Coastal Waters', (1987) 25 *Oceanographic Marine Biology Annual Review* p.563.

Gulland, J., 'Developing Countries and the New Law of the Sea', (1979) 22 *Oceanus* p.36.

Haigh, N., *EEC Environmental Policy and Britain,* (2nd ed. 1987) Longman.

Hailsham, Lord, *Halsbury's Laws of England* (4th ed.) Vol.18 *Fisheries* (1977) Ed. Sturt, R.H.B., Butterworths.

Hall, R.G., *Hall's Essay on the Rights of the Crown and the Privileges of the Subject in the Sea Shores of the Realm* (2nd ed. 1875) by Loveland, R.L., Stevens and Haynes.

Hale, Lord Chief-Justice, *De Jure Maris et Brachiorum Ejusdem,* (undated) reprinted as Appendix I to Hall, R.G., *Hall's Essay on the Rights of the Crown and the Privileges of the Subject in the Sea Shores of the Realm* (2nd ed. 1875) by Loveland, R.L., Stevens and Haynes.

Howarth, W., 'Reservoir Safety Reforms', (1986A) *Journal of Planning and Environment Law* p.583.

Howarth, W., 'The Regulation of Commercial Fishing for Salmon in England

and Wales: the Changing Law on Fixed Engines', (1986B) *International Journal of Estuarine and Coastal Law*, p.345.

Howarth, W., *Freshwater Fishery Law*, (1987A) Financial Training Publications/ Blackstone Press.

Howarth, W., 'The Legal Status of Fish Farming', (1987B) *Journal of Planning and Environment Law* p.484.

Howarth, W., 'Handling Stolen Goods and Handling Salmon', (1987C) *Criminal Law Review* p.460.

Howarth, W., 'Fish Farming and Agriculture: Some Legal Contrasts', (1987D) 67 *Journal of the Agricultural Society (UCW)* p.114.

Howarth, W., *Water Pollution Law*, (1988A) Shaw and Sons.

Howarth, W., 'A Norse Saga: The Salmon, the Crown Estate and the Udal Law', (1988B) *Juridical Review* p.91.

Howarth, W., 'Aquacultural Possibilities and Legal Obstructions: Salmon Ranching in the United Kingdom', (1989A) *International Journal of Estuarine and Coastal Law* p.1.

Howarth, W., 'Water Pollution: Improving the Legal Controls' (1989B) 1 *Environmental Law* p.25.

Howarth, W., 'Present Controls upon the Movement of Fish', (1989C) paper delivered at Institute of Fisheries Management Workshop on the Dangers Associated with the Importation of Ornamental Fish, 13 April 1989.

Howarth, W,. 'The Single Market: the Case of Fish Disease', (1989D) paper delivered at W.G. Hart Legal Workshop on *The Single European Market and the Development of European Law*, Institute of Advanced Legal Studies 4 July.

Huet, M., (revised by Timmermans, J.) *Textbook of Fish Culture*, (2nd ed. 1986) Fishing News Books Ltd.

Hunter, Lord, *Report on Scottish Salmon and Trout Fisheries*, (1963) First Report, Cmnd. 2096.

Hunter, Lord, *Report on Scottish Salmon and Trout Fisheries*, (1965) Second Report, Cmnd. 2691.

Inland Revenue, *Capital Allowances on Agricultural or Forestry Buildings and Works*, (1980) Leaflet CA3.

Institute of Fisheries Management, *Water Quality and Pollution*, Training Course Part I Section 5 (1981).

Joyner, T., 'Towards a Planetary Aquaculture – the Seas as Range and Cropland', (1975) 37 *Marine Fisheries Review* p.5.

Kane, T.E., *Aquaculture and the Law*, (1970) University of Miama Sea Grant Program, Sea Grant Technical Bulletin No.2.

Kent, G., 'Fisheries and the Law of the Sea: A Common Heritage Approach', (1978) 4 *Ocean Management* p.1.

Kirk, R., *A History of Marine Fish Culture in Europe and North America*, (1987) Fishing News Books Ltd.

Landless, P., 'Pollution and the Law', (1984A) *Fish Farmer* January p.7.

Landless, P., 'Are You Prepared ?', (1984B) *Fish Farmer* March p.10.

Laird, L., and Needham, T., *Salmon and Trout Farming*, (1988) John Wiley and Sons Ltd.

Law Commission and Scottish Law Commission, *Sea Fisheries (Shellfish) Bill*, (1967) Cmnd. 3267.

Lightowlers, P., 'British scientists link seal deaths to cattle pest', (1988) *New Scientist* 22 October 1988 p.28.

Lort-Phillips, D., Denman, D.R., and Edwards, E., *Farming Foreshores and Inland Waters* (undated) Shellfish Association of Great Britain.

Lucas, S., 'That fish may safely pass', (1988) *Water Bulletin* 5 August p.8.

McAnuff, J.W., 'Towards a Strategy for Fish Farming in the UK', (1979) *Food Policy* August 1979.

Marston, G., *The Marginal Seabed*, (1981) Clarendon Press.

Markson, H.E., 'Derating Doubtfully Defined: A Tale of Two Fish Farms; or, As You Like It', (1976) *Journal of Planning and Environment Law* p.487.

Mills, D.H., 'The Impact of the British Gas Corporation Pipeline Project on Fisheries: Precautions and Claims', (1976) 7 *Fisheries Management* p.78.

Mills, D.H., 'Some Thoughts on Insurance Claims', (1979) paper delivered at Fish Farming conference in Oban.

Milne, P.H., *Fish and Shellfish Farming in Coastal Waters*, (1979) Fishing News Books Ltd.

Ministry of Agriculture, Fisheries and Food, *Legal Position of Shellfisheries*, (1968) Press Notice, 4 March.

Ministry of Agriculture, Fisheries and Food, *Oyster Pests*, (1974) Laboratory Leaflet (New Series) No.19, by Hancock, D.A., Fisheries Laboratory.

Ministry of Agriculture, Fisheries and Food, *Deposit of Molluscan Shellfish* (1977) Laboratory Leaflet No.34, by Key, D., Directorate of Fisheries Research.

Ministry of Agriculture, Fisheries and Food, Fisheries Notice No.59, *Disinfectants in Fish Farming*, (1978) Directorate of Fisheries Research.

Ministry of Agriculture, Fisheries and Food, *Coho Salmon in North-west Europe* (1979) Laboratory Leaflet No.49, by Solomon, D.J., Directorate of Fisheries Research.

Ministry of Agriculture, Fisheries and Food, *Mussel Cultivation in England and Wales* (1980A) Laboratory Leaflet No.50, by Dare, P.J., Directorate of Fisheries Research.

Ministry of Agriculture, Fisheries and Food, *The Scallop and its Fishery in England and Wales* (1980B) Laboratory Leaflet No.51, by Franklin, F., Pickett, G.D., and Connor, P.M., Directorate of Fisheries Research.

Ministry of Agriculture, Fisheries and Food, *Review of Inland and Coastal Fisheries in England and Wales*, (1981).

Ministry of Agriculture, Fisheries and Food, *Malachite Green: A Code of Practice for its Use in Fish Farming* (1982A) Fisheries Notice No.72, by Alderman, D.J., Directorate of Fisheries Research.

Ministry of Agriculture, Fisheries and Food, *Bonamia, a New Threat to the Native Oyster Fishery* (1982B) Fisheries Notice No.71, by Bannister, R.C.A. and Key, D., Directorate of Fisheries Research.

Ministry of Agriculture, Fisheries and Food, *Guidelines for the Use of Herbicides on Weeds in or near Watercourses and Lakes* (1985A) Booklet B2078.

Ministry of Agriculture, Fisheries and Food, *Iodophor Disinfectants: A Code of Practice for their Use in Fish Farming* (1985B) Fisheries Notice No.74, by Alderman, D.J., Directorate of Fisheries Research.

Ministry of Agriculture, Fisheries and Food, *Multi-annual Guidance Programme*, (1987A).

Ministry of Agriculture, Fisheries and Food, *Report of the Director of Fisheries Research 1985–86*, (1987B) Directorate of Fisheries Research.

Ministry of Agriculture, Fisheries and Food, *Multi-annual Guidance Programme*, (1988 progress report) (1989).

Montgomery, Sir D., *Report of the Committee of Inquiry into the Functions and Powers of the Islands Councils of Scotland* (1984) Cmnd. 9216.

Nash, 'Ocean Ranching: The Achievements, the Problems and the Possibilities', (1977) *Fish Farming International* September p.42.

National Farmers' Union, *NFU Code of Good Husbandry for Fish Farmers Rearing fish for the Table and Restocking Markets* (1984A).

National Farmers' Union, *Guidelines for the Safe Use of Chemicals on Fish Farms* (1984B).

National Office of Animal Health, *Compendium of Data Sheets for Veterinary Products 1988–89*, (1988) Datapharm Publications Ltd.

Netboy, A., *Salmon the World's Most Harassed Fish*, (1980) Andre Deutsch.

Newbold, C., Hambrey, J.B., and Smith, I.R., *Nature Conservation and Freshwater Fish Farming*, (1986) Nature Conservancy Council.

Newsom, G., and Sherratt, J.G., *Water Pollution*, (1972) John Sherratt and Son Ltd.

North, P.M., *The Modern Law of Animals*, (1972) Butterworths.

Nowak, W.S.W., *The Marketing of Shellfish*, (1970) Fishing News Books Ltd.

Owen, S., 'The Response of the Legal System to Technological Innovation in Aquaculture: A Comparative Study of Mariculture Legislation in California, Florida and Maine', (1978) 4 *Coastal Zone Management Journal* p.269.

Pain, S., 'Are British Shellfish Safe to Eat?', (1986) *New Scientist* August p.29.

Phillips, M.J., Beveridge, M.C.M. and Ross, L.G., 'The Environmental Impact of Salmonid Cage Culture on Inland Fisheries: Present Status and Future Trends', (1985) 27 *Journal of Fish Biology* p.123.

Phillips, M.J. and Beveridge, M., 'Cages and the Effect on Water Condition', (1986) *Fish Farmer* May p.17.

Rankine, Sir J., *Law of Land Ownership in Scotland* (3rd ed. 1884) Blackwood and Sons.

Roberts, R.J., and Shepherd, C.J., *Handbook of Trout and Salmon Diseases*, (2nd ed. 1986) Fishing News Books Ltd.

Robertson, D., 'Legal Aspects of Fish Farming' in Sea Fish Industry Authority Report No.335M, *Scottish Marine Farming Strategic Study, Part I*, (1988).

Robertson, J.P., 'Allowances – Are You Getting Enough ?', (1988) *Fish Farmer* January p.52.

Ross, A., *Controlling Nature's Predators on Fish Farms*, (1988) Marine Conservation Society.

Ross, A. and Horsman, P.V., *The Use of Nuvan 500EC in the Salmon Farming Industry*, (1988) Marine Conservation Society.

Royal Commission on Environmental Pollution, Seventh Report, *Agriculture and Pollution*, (1979) Cmnd. 7644.

Royal Commission on Environmental Pollution, Tenth Report, *Tackling Pollution – Experience and Prospects*, (1984) Cmnd. 9149.

Royal Commission on Sea Fisheries of the United Kingdom, Fourth Report, *Report on the Sea Fisheries of the United Kingdom*, (1866) [3596] XVII.

Royal Commission on Sewage Disposal, Fourth Report, *Pollution of Tidal Waters with special reference to Contamination of Shell-Fish*, (1904) Cd.1883.

Sandys-Winsch, G., *Animal Law* (1984) Shaw and Sons.

Saunders, R.L., 'Sea ranching: A Promising Way to Enhance Populations of Atlantic Salmon for Angling and Commercial Fisheries', (1977) *International Atlantic Salmon Foundation Special Publications Series 7*, p.17.

Saunders-Davies, C.G., 'A Fish Farmer Replies', (1984) *Water Bulletin* 30th March p.6.

Scrase, A.J., 'Agriculture – 1980s Industry and 1947 Definition' (1988) *Journal of Planning and Environment Law* p.447.

Schwind, P., *Practical Shellfish Farming*, (1977) International Marine Publishing Co.

Scottish Development Department, *Environmental Assessment: Implementation of the EC Directive*, (1988) Circular 13/1988.

Scottish Wildlife and Countryside Link, *Marine Fishfarming in Scotland*, (1988).

Seagrave, C.P., *Aquatic Weed Control*, (1988) Fishing News Books Ltd.

Sedgwick, S.D., *Salmon Farming Handbook*, (1988) Fishing News Books Ltd.

Sedgwick, S.D., *Trout Farming Handbook* (4th ed. 1985) Fishing News Books Ltd.

Shaw, S. and Muir, J.F., *Salmon: Economics and Marketing*, (1987) Croom Helm Ltd.

Shaw, S., 'Fish farming's place in a closer European Community', (1988) *Fish Farming International* July p.22.

Shepherd, J., and Bromage, N., (Eds.) *Intensive Fish Farming*, (1988) Professional Books.

Simes, E., and Scholefield, C.E., *Lumley's Public Health Law: the Public Health Acts Annotated*, (12th ed. Vol.V 1954) Butterworths Ltd.

Smith, J.O. and Marshall, D.L., 'Mariculture: A New Ocean Use', (1974) 4 *Georgia Journal of International and Comparative Law* p.307.

Smith, P., 'Use of Medicines on Fish Farms', (1988) 5 *Trout News* p.10.

Solbe, J., *Water Quality for Salmon and Trout*, (1988) Atlantic Salmon Trust.

Solbe, J., 'Water Quality', Ch.3 in Laird, L., and Needham, T., *Salmon and Trout Farming*, (1987) John Wiley and Sons Ltd.

Stair, Viscout, *The Institutions of the Law of Scotland*, Ed. by J.S. More (1832) Bell and Bradfute.

Stevenson, J.P., *Trout Farming Manual*, (2nd ed. 1987) Fishing News Books Ltd.

Stewart, C.S., *A Treatise on the Law of Scotland relating to Rights of Fishing*, 2nd ed. by Shairp, J.C., (1892) T and T Clark.

Street, H., *The Law of Torts* (8th ed. 1988) by Brazier, M., Butterworths.

Swift, R.S., *Aquaculture Training Manual*, (1985) Fishing News Books Ltd.

Tait, J.H., *A Treatise on the Law of Scotland as applied to The Game Laws and Trout and Salmon Fishing*, 2nd ed. by Taylor, J.O., (1928) Green and Son Ltd.

Taylor, J.O., *The Law Affecting River Pollution*, (1928) Green and Son Ltd.

Tervert, D.J., 'The Impact of Fish Farming on Water Quality', (1981) *Water Pollution Control* p.571.

Thorpe, J.E., *Salmon Ranching*, (1980A) Academic Press.

Thorpe, J.E., 'Ocean Ranching – General Considerations', p.152 in Went, A.E.J., *Atlantic Salmon: Its Future* (1980B) Fishing News Books Ltd.

Thorpe, J.E., 'Some Biological Problems in Ranching Salmonids' (1986) *Institute of Freshwater Research Drottningholm* Lund (Sweden).

Tromans, S.R., 'Riparian Rights and Water Authority Negligence', [1987] *Conveyancer and Property Lawyer* p.368.

Warham, A., 'The Seashore', (1974) *Journal of Planning and Environment Law* p.705.

Water Authorities Association, Fish Farm Working Party, *Consent Conditions for Fish Farms* (1984).

Water Authorities Association, *Water Pollution from Farm Waste 1988 England and*

Wales, (1989).

Wathern, P., Young, S.N., Brown, I.W., and Roberts, D.A., 'UK Interpretation and Implementation of the EEC Shellfish Directive', (1987) 11 *Environmental Management* p.7.

Wildsmith, B.H., *Aquaculture: The Legal Framework*, (1982) Emond-Montgomery Ltd.

Wilkins, N.P., *Salmon Stocks: a Genetic Perspective* (Undated) Atlantic Salmon Trust.

Williams, G.L., *Liability for Animals*, (1939) Cambridge.

Wisdom, A.S., *The Law of Rivers and Watercourses*, (4th ed. 1979) Shaw and Sons Ltd.

Wood, E., *Organotin Anti-Fouling Paints, an Environmental Problem?*, (1986) Marine Conservation Society.

Yonge, C.M., *Oysters* (1966) Collins.

Index

References are to section numbers.